EXPLORATIONS
IN SOCIAL THEORY

EXPLORATIONS
IN SOCIAL THEORY

William J. Goode

NEW YORK · OXFORD UNIVERSITY PRESS
London 1973 Toronto

Chapters 7 and 8 "Religious and Economic Action" and "Religious and Political Action" are reprinted by permission of The Macmillan Company from *Religion Among the Primitives* by William J. Goode. Copyright © 1951 by William J. Goode.

Apart from the Introduction, Chapter 14 "The Theoretical Limits of Professionalism" is reprinted by permission of The Macmillan Company from *The Semi-professions and Their Organization*, edited by Amitai Etzioni. Copyright © 1969 by The Free Press, a Division of The Macmillan Company.

Preface

When an author binds some of his essays into a book, he comes under some suspicion of narcissism, and he therefore writes a Preface to defend himself against that allegation, however likely the charge may seem. I can do no less.

For most of my life as a sociologist, I have been theorizing about three great social institutions: Family, Work, and Religion. That is, I have been developing sets of more or less integrated or linked empirical propositions about social behavior in these areas. To do this, a mastery of "grand theory" is not enough. I early learned that between the formulations of grand theory and their application to specific institutional areas a considerable theoretical and empirical gap often yawned. The broad formulations had to be transformed even to be tested by real data.

Moreover, it was clear that much "theory" is not theory in my sense at all, but is metatheory, theory about theory, or "What sociology would be like if there were a sociology." That is, much broad theory contains few empirical propositions. As George C. Homans remarks in a somewhat different context, it is a dictionary of a language that contains no sentences. Finally, of course, as all researchers know, confronting hypotheses with real data often discloses relationships that are new, surprising, or even illuminating, an event that occurs much less frequently if one remains at the level of grand theory.

Because our field is still at the primitive scientific stage where "theory" is viewed as a separate kind of activity, and I have written few analyses under the title, "Theory of . . . ," most of this theoretical work often appears to the unwary reader as mere description of social patterns. It occurs in a highly empirical context, and many will not perceive that the exposition is the gradual development of linked propositions. It may be useful, then, to draw some attention to this aspect of the work.

In addition, I have for many years taught a course in theory that to a considerable extent focused on what theorists (again, in my sense) were actually doing when they developed an inquiry from a vague hunch, through the stage of making hypotheses, to an elaborate set of integrated propositions. Sometimes, instead, my analysis tried to locate the generating ideas that underlay the more specific hypotheses. It seemed worthwhile to make such commentaries or glosses on some of my own writings.

Even if those aims could be accomplished, I thought it also important to make a selection that could form a genuine book, and not a mere collection of miscellaneous research reports. In order to do this, I have written several essays especially for this publication, in addition to the commentaries.

Nevertheless, I should never have embarked upon this task if it had not been urged upon me by my close friend, Cynthia Fuchs Epstein. A talented sociologist who has carried out imaginative researches, she has contributed theoretically and editorially to my thinking and writing over the past decade, to a far greater degree than she can guess, while also encouraging me to complete this particular work. She has graced our years together with her gifts of wit, laughter, and joy. If I have not fully achieved in either this work or my life all that she has hoped, I have learned much from the attempt to meet her high standards, and I trust that she will perhaps consider it worthy of being communicated to others.

William J. Goode

New York, New York
July, 1972

Acknowledgments and Sources

I wish to thank the following people, not all of whom have actually seen the unpublished sections of this book, but who have nevertheless helped me through various dialogues I have enjoyed with them: James S. Coleman, Mary Ellen Curran, Cynthia Fuchs Epstein, George C. Homans, Alex Inkeles, Talcott Parsons, Stanley Raffel, Peter H. Rossi, Arthur Stinchcombe, Joel Telles, Melvin Tumin, and Lenore J. Weitzman. At various phases of its development, this manuscript has been helped by an NSF Grant (G.S. 2180); I am also grateful to NIMH for the gift of time, a Senior Scientist Career Award.

I extend my thanks to the editors and publishers of the journals listed below for permission to reprint the following papers:

"A Theory of Role Strain," *American Sociological Review*, 25 (August, 1960), pp. 483-96. Completed under National Institute of Mental Health Grant No. 2526-S. I am indebted to several of my colleagues for criticism of this and related papers, and especially to Amitai Etzioni, Johan Galtung, Robert K. Merton, Charles H. Page, Morris Zelditch, and Hans L. Zetterberg.

"The Protection of the Inept," *American Sociological Review*, 32 (February, 1967), pp. 5-19. The 1965 MacIver Award lecture, delivered at the annual meetings of the Pacific Sociological Association, April, 1966, in Vancouver. For aid in preparing this paper the author is indebted to Gresham Sykes, Florence Kluckhohn, Melville Dalton, Amitai Etzioni, Alvin W. Gouldner, Peter McHugh, Robert K. Merton, Walter Goldfrank, Seymour M. Lipset, Yehudi Cohen, Nicholas Tavuchis and Marshall Childs. This paper was prepared with the support of NIMH Grant No. NH 11389-01.

"Violence Among Intimates," in: *Crimes of Violence:* A Staff Report to the National Commission on the Causes and Prevention of Violence prepared by Donald J. Mulvihill and Melvin M. Tumin with Lynn A. Curtis. Washington: U.S. Government Printing Office, 1969, Vol. 13, pp. 941-77.

"The Theoretical Importance of Love," *American Sociological Review*, 24 (February, 1959), pp. 38-47. This paper was completed under a grant (No. M-2526-S) by the National Institute of Mental Health.

"Illegitimacy, Anomie, and Cultural Penetration," *American Sociological Review*, 26 (December, 1961), pp. 910-25. For aid in preparing this paper the author expresses his thanks to Nicholas Tavuchis.

"Mobility, Family, and Revolutionary Potential." An earlier version of this paper was printed in German in: *Kölner Zeitschrift für Soziologie und Sozialpsychologie*, Jg. 18, 1966, Heft 2, pp. 227-52. This paper was prepared with the aid of NIMH Grant No. MH11389-01. I have had the benefit of advice from several people to whom I here wish to express my thanks: Jessie Bernard, Walter Goldfrank, Edward W. Gude, S. Lehman, and Ralph Swisher.

"Incentive Factors in a Low Morale Plant," *American Sociological Review*, 14 (1949), pp. 618-24. This article was written in collaboration with Irving Fowler. Paper read at the annual meeting of the American Sociological Society held in Chicago, December 28-30, 1948. For aid in clarifying the present discussion, the authors are particularly indebted to Nelson Foote of Cornell University, Melvin Tumin of Princeton University, and Irving Rosow of Harvard University.

"Work Incentives in a Self-Determined Group," *American Sociological Review*, 16 (1951), pp. 679-87. This article was written in collaboration with Nicholas Babchuk.

Contents

I. ISSUES IN CONTEMPORARY SOCIOLOGY

1. *The Social Topography of the Field*

INTELLECTUAL DISCIPLINES ARE ALWAYS MADE UP OF A DOMINANT MAINSTREAM, DYING REMNANTS OF OLD ISSUES AND THEORIES, AND new fads and foibles. Only a few of the new developments (sometimes indistinguishable from their predecessors) contribute to the mainstream of thought. Current doctrine contains unquestioned assumptions and banalities that cannot withstand skeptical examination, as well as a continuing, growing body of more adequate explanations and descriptions whose meaning and validity will later be accepted but refined.

Like all his contemporaries, the talented scientist is caught in the mental ruts of his own generation, but he will achieve a better score than the less talented in distinguishing among these bits and pieces. However, all scholars must make their own gambles. No man can know exactly which elements of his field he can safely ignore, and which will instead burgeon into the seminal ideas of the future. Over time, it is likely that the work of giants in the field will be regarded with diminishing awe. As a student, Marion J. Levy once remarked of a famous economist that one ought to be as surprised to hear his outdated ideas as if one were to see a dinosaur stalk across Harvard Yard; but (putting aside Levy's optimism about progress in economics) those ideas did once reign, as in the Mesozoic Era dinosaurs did stalk across what later became Harvard Yard.

On the other hand, at some points in intellectual history the wisest course would have been to continue to follow in the footsteps of the dominant figure of that epoch; for example, the generation after Newton did so. At still other times, the lucky scholar might have achieved great success by exploiting the discoveries made by a little-known scientist, such as Mendel. Still, many interesting ideas of little-known thinkers also turn out to be as unproductive as those published by men of high renown. At any time, only the miraculously prescient scientists can be sure which new or old "discoveries" will contain the seeds of future discoveries.

Almost every theoretical exposition argues at least implicitly for the wisdom of choosing one orientation rather than another, one set of variables rather than another. Nevertheless, what seems to be wisdom now may prove to be foolishness a decade hence, and indeed many polemics in sociology are less a set of arguments about "the facts" than a debate about the definition of an ideal sociology in the future, that is, what it ought to become.

An *assessment* of the field, weighing the fruitfulness of validity of its various parts, is worthwhile, but it is different from a description, and among various possible descriptions a summary of the findings in the field is different from a social topography. This chapter attempts the last of these: it is not so much concerned with the personnel of sociology, the social relations of the sociologists in various specialties, as with the broad intellectual conceptions that make up the definitions and orientations of sociology, together with related aspects of its social organization. Such a mapping is inevitably crude in its details, and focuses far more on the dominant areas and groups, while neglecting to some extent the rebellious backlands. Some of these dissident intellectual forces will be analyzed in greater detail in later chapters, but brief descriptions will suffice here for simple mapping. I believe that the current attacks on sociology, by outsiders and insiders, will not soon diminish in intensity, and some of these will be noted, but at present they are only part of the whole sociological enterprise.

Sociology as a Nomothetic Science. Until the middle of the nineteenth century, most precursors of sociology were primarily philosophers, and were therefore occupied with the foundations of knowledge and the ultimate reality that may lie behind that knowledge.

Although their epistemological and ontological theories varied greatly, perhaps no major figure in philosophy took the position that it was possible to develop laws of human behavior, like those about the heavenly bodies, based on man's sense perceptions. Consider, for example, Plato's central conception, that the philosopher must pierce through the buzzing confusion of the apparent world (men's biases, sense perceptions, and so forth) to the Forms that are unchanging reality, from which one could deduce powerful truths about man's nature. That description of the fallibility of man's senses obviously affirms the impossibility of general social propositions based on sense data.

The medieval theological synthesis aimed at expounding eternal beliefs and obligations, and continued the faith of all major civilizations in an underlying order of all things, but it avoided the difficulties of discovering general laws to explain real human behavior. Indeed, like most theories about sin, Christianity required a belief in man's free will, his power of free choice; if in spiritual and intellectual matters man's acts are as determined as the movements of physical objects, he should not be punished for behaving as he does.

That God revealed His design in the physical universe was a nearly universal assumption in Western intellectual history; and to discover it remained a conscious goal of natural philosophers until perhaps the nineteenth century.[1] But though the existence of that design was not doubted, scholars did not believe their knowledge about it was based on sense observation. Moreover, critical philosophers continued their scrutiny of the weaknesses in the foundations of science (sense data, time, causality, and so forth). And whatever were the august regularities observable in the sidereal bodies, it is perhaps safe to say that no epistemologically sophisticated philosopher argued that parallel laws could be discovered in man's behavior by using sense data. In that comparison, man's social behavior seemed hopelessly chaotic, whimsical, free, internally willed; and in any event no observer could look at it without bias, preconception, and error. It was possible to speculate on the *meaning* of man's behavior, to contemplate with wonder man's unique rise from darkness (or descent from innocence) in history, to describe the chronology of human events, or the particularities of a human being such as Caesar, but real laws of human behavior seemed unattainable.

Late in the history of philosophy, Kant's generous concession—surely one of the first formal uses of the argument: whatever is, is possible—that valid knowledge must be possible in *physical* science (for it does exist) merely accentuated the inherent barriers of the human spirit against such rigorous formulations: things of the spirit by contrast were not to be captured or explained within the bounds of time, space, and causality.

Whatever criticisms the great philosophers directed against the foundations of knowledge, almost all succumbed to the temptation of offering some generalizations about man and his behavior. As for physical scientists, as the security of their findings grew during the late seventeenth and early eighteenth centuries their interest in such grand epistemological problems waned. As for social scientists, whose findings never became very secure, this polemic about the possibility of a *science* of man remained of great concern until well into the twentieth century. The skepticism did not stop inquiry, however, and from the time of Adam Smith onward an increasing number of social philosophers became social scientists, aggressively pursuing the dream of discovering valid laws of social behavior.

The French heirs of Comte firmly reiterated this ideal, which in Durkheim's writings was presented as a reality: universal social laws are possible, and here are some of them. Although anthropologists have been a bit more hesitant, especially after they witnessed the downfall of their grand theories of social evolution at the end of the century, and political scientists have lagged still more in their allegiance, by and large the official doctrine of sociologists in all disciplines—social anthropology, political sicence, social psychology, and sociology proper—has not retreated from this general position: they aspire to general laws of social behavior. That is, sociology should be nomothetic, not idiographic.

True enough, humanists and philosophers continue to form a substantial part of the recruitment pool from which sociologists come, and they are likely to set themselves against such an allegiance. They are less likely to believe that "laws" of human behavior are possible, or that such an aspiration is the true task of sociology. However, the conflict between the historicist or humanistic orientation (which aims at understanding man in his splendid uniqueness) and the scientistic position, which seeks general laws, is not a conflict between "old-fashioned" sociology and the new. It is a perennial conflict, because the study of social phenomena continues to attract scholars from both of these different orientations.

Needless to say, this conflict also arises from differences in temperament, and again is not merely a historical phase. In any field, but especially in sociology, where both nomothetic and idiographic works are applauded, some investigators typically seek the most universal laws and quickly move to generalizations from a few cases or many, while others really enjoy examining the particularities of an individual case. Some social analysts may be more concerned with the human significance and even poetic meaning of a particular incident, community, or set of relationships. The historicity of an event, with its ramified and unique qualities, will always attract some social analysts far more than the angular, spare, austere, and necessarily somewhat more remote and abstract set of "forces and relationships" toward which the man who seeks universal laws will work. In short, both an ancient epistemological tradition and differences in temperament and taste will justify either a nomothetic or an idiographic stance.

In any event, a correct mapping of sociology today will show that the dominant orientation is nomothetic: sociologists do, by and large, accept as a major task of sociology the search for "social laws" at some level of abstraction and generalization—whether comparing whole nations or studying small groups—rather than merely interpreting the particularities of specific times and places. It is (that is, ought to be) not a historical discipline, but a scientific one.[2] Some sociologists are dismayed that the field has not produced, in their opinion, a single valid universal law, and some believe that this search is inherently chimerical, but most proceed with considerable certainty that the proper task of sociology is to uncover such general relationships.

METHODOLOGICAL BARRIERS

Whether sociology can achieve general laws of social behavior, or should instead focus on an exact description and interpretation of particulars, is a question that overlaps substantially with other fundamental epistemological questions, and specifically with the issue of inherent barriers against achieving a valid or objective description of social patterns (whether or not they can be described as "laws"). This question, as has already been noted, has been debated for over two thousand years. By and large, the more common philosophical position has urged that the biases of human observers, the intrinsic nature of human thinking and behavior, or the impossibility of an experiment, will always prevent any security about the conclusions the sociologist reaches if they are based on observation.

Here it is sufficient merely to note that as an outcome of the last century of debate, most sociologists now concern themselves very little with this question, except for a token or ritualistic claim that no inherent methodological barriers exist that would prevent sociologists from achieving valid scientific descriptions and analyses. Their general position is that there are no fundamental methodological or epistemological problems that cannot be solved in principle. Put differently, the epistemological assumptions and canons of science in other fields are thought to be completely applicable to the study of social behavior, with appropriate translations to adjust to the obvious concrete facts of the case: for example, rocks don't talk and human beings do; while human beings can lie and rocks cannot, and the like.

That the general canons of science apply to social research does not mean that sociologists believe the specific technical problems of research have been solved. It is conceded that since human beings know they are participating in an experiment or form part of a field study, they may not act as they normally do. Observation typically changes people's behavior somewhat. Neither molecules nor bacteria ordinarily resent the intrusion of the experimenter, and do not care at all whether he is of the appropriate class, ethnic or racial group, sex, or political philosophy; but individuals and groups may hide, distort, or refuse to cooperate in other ways because the investigator displeases them.[3] Nevertheless, such problems can be solved in part, and where bias or error seem likely, other tests and checks can be introduced to ensure the acquisition of accurate knowledge.

Since the end of the Renaissance, philosophers have expressed far more objections to the achievement of scientific objectivity than have working scientists themselves, and once a given field has begun to uncover a considerable number of regularities, the men in it typically become bored with epistemological questions. Standard introductory textbooks in sociology still argue the issue of validity in sociology, while introductory texts in physics or chemistry need not bother. Physicists may indeed discuss such questions on a lofty plane when writing popular books about the larger human significance of indeterminacy, chance and statistics, the reversibility of time, or causality, but these problems not only fail to bar them from seeking physical order and regularity—they hardly enter into their formulations of day-to-day research problems. Without so spectacular an achievement on which to base their stance, most working sociologists have also moved steadily in that direction.

Again, many minority positions are not only expressed vigorously, but perhaps all sociologists entertain recurring doubts about the correctness of such a positivistic orientation. These doubts are fed by obvious discrepancies among what people really want, what they say they want, and what they actually do; by each individual's recognition of his own vagaries and obscure motivations; by theoretical debates about the reality of social systems and the many variables that sociologists invoke in order to explain phenomena whose measurement seems beyond attainment; or by the frequent experience of reading highly variant interpretations of even so massive an event as the French or English Revolution (that is, what *did* happen?).[4] Always, too, both humanistically inclined and politically dissident students in the field may scornfully reject the notion that the now dominant descriptions and interpretations represent anything but an expression of each individual's prejudices, biases, and mental ruts, either in the service of the individual's peculiar personality or that of the government.

If we assume, as sociologists have done by and large, that there are no fundamental epistemological or methodological barriers to achieving objectivity and validity in the analysis of social behavior, then it must be viewed as salutary that the energy once poured into larger epistemological problems has been diverted instead to what are now called "methodological" problems, that is, the elaboration and testing of particular techniques of research and statistical analysis. Bypassing the question of *whether* objective scientific sociology is possible, the working sociologist focuses rather on how to do it. On the other hand, historically this has not been a true diversion of energy, since those who have been most occupied with larger epistemological questions are not the same people who are interested in the technical problems of questionnaire construction, observation, formulations of experiments, new techniques of statistical analysis, and the like.

That is, those whose temperaments attracted them to grand problems of causality and truth in the social sciences were not the intellectual ancestors of those whose energies have been devoted to the development of new statistical techniques, observational procedures, questionnaire construction, or scaling, nor have men in mid-career usually shifted their talents from the former to the latter. Nevertheless, we can speak of a historical diversion of ability, since at present fewer social scientists expend their work on grand philosophical questions than formerly, and more feel pressed to carry out empirical investigations.

Needless to say, from a philosophical point of view it cannot be proved that such barriers do not exist, which would prevent an adequately scientific description of social reality, or for that matter any other reality. There are no techniques by which we can get outside the limitations of our minds, to test whether the "underlying reality" is indeed what we are describing. The very tools and instruments that one would have to use for such a test, whether laboratory techniques or the human mind, are those that were used to produce the observations in the first place.

Some ethnomethodologists follow the generations-old tradition of critical philosophy in challenging the sociologists' assumption of "correspondence with reality," but they too are hoist with their own petard. Their careful microobservations are forced to rest on the same faith, that what we observe, see, sense, or measure does correspond to what is "out there"; if not, then both their criticisms and the observations that are to be a new answer to the criticism are open to the charge (once again) that we have no way of knowing how *they* correspond with reality.[5]

If we really cannot surmount this limitation, sociologists have been correct in adopting (along with their scientific forebears) the pragmatic position that since they are indeed developing analyses and descriptions which do seem to correspond with the reality they perceive, the problems cannot be overwhelming. That is, if the limitations cannot be surmounted, the issue cannot be of much importance in scientific research: we shall never in any event observe any contradictions between the "apparent" reality and the "real" reality. Meanwhile, most sociologists have come to feel that empirical research is intellectually more exciting than reasoning about the ultimate nature of social reality and its epistemological connections with observation.

THEORY CANNOT BE CONTRASTED WITH "FACT"

If there was ever a time when a genuine polemic existed between theorists who worried not at all about the facts, and fact-grubbers who cared little about the significance of their descriptions, it was at worst a historical phase in which such conflicts stimulated sociologists not to be content with book reading and armchair speculation, but rather to go into the field and actually observe human behavior. Needless to say, it would be difficult to find a sociological theorist who ever proudly proclaimed interest only in the larger theoretical significance of things, and not in the facts; just as it would be difficult to find one passionately interested in uncovering facts, but cared not at all about their larger bearing. Both sides of this "theory vs. fact" argument always attacked a position that was not really defended.

Whatever the historical phases, however, sociologists now accept with little question the notion that any scientist worthy of his salt will try to seek descriptions and facts that will be relevant for or bear on somewhat important hypotheses, and that any theory is by definition a *structure* of empirical propositions about phenomena. In the ideal case, they are linked in logically neat ways, but any approximation to a theory must contain sets of propositions about the real world, linked in as logical a fashion as can be achieved.

Thus, the dominant sociological position asserts there is not only no quarrel between theory and fact; they are inextricably linked and indeed at some level are images of one another. Game theorists, social experimenters, ethnomethodologists, and possibly demographers are perhaps the subgroups in sociology that especially perceive little distinction between their theories and the facts that are integrated into those theories.

On another level, of course, this tension between a concern for descriptive facts and a concern for broad theories remains, since it is a fundamental element in the dialectic of science, and it expresses strong differences in taste and temperament. There are indeed some who feel (Thomas Henry Huxley so accused Herbert Spencer) that a tragedy is a pretty theory brutally destroyed by a fact. Darwin once remarked, by contrast with Spencer's supposed view, that theories and hypotheses come and go, but a first-rate description would remain unassailable, unlikely to be pushed aside, and against it new hypotheses and theories would have to be tested.[6]

Others would emphasize instead the notion that laboratory accidents happen to the prepared mind; or that there is a literal infinitude of observations to be made, but without theory to guide those observations we are only by remote chance likely to focus upon the most useful observations. People with the latter bent also note how often in the past the laboratory measurements and observations were not quite accurate, enough so indeed that if the theory maker had merely held tightly to *those* "facts," he would never have located the theory that ultimately pointed to more precise relationships, and that required and forced the replacement of those rough measurements with finer ones.[7]

This division of temperament and also of labor is to be found in every field, not alone sociology, and is expressed in both serious attacks and joshing. These divergences do not typically erupt in public debates, since in every developed field it is well understood that fact and theory have no quarrel with one another and are rather interwoven; each is dependent upon the other. Nevertheless, each side has its pejorative vocabulary for the other, and—without presuming to make a sociological "law"—we would predict that a century from now these same divergences will be observable and will continue to spice the conversations of scientists in every field.

THE ACCEPTANCE OF QUANTIFICATION

Sociologists who accept quantification are also likely to have a taste for facts, but the debate about the merit of quantification is not the same as the "fact vs. theory" debate. For the most part the debate about quantification has ended. Few sociologists would seriously debate the utility and necessity of quantification, although many would argue that *specific* variables (social cohesion, anomie, alienation, and so on) may be very difficult to quantify. Even sociologists who remain somewhat skeptical about quantification would hardly wish to organize a public attack on it. In some countries, of course, one may still encounter sociologists who wish to argue against quantification, sometimes quaintly labeled "the statistical approach," but almost anyone who has done research feels in that situation that he is being asked to debate against the ghosts of his ancestors.

Whether the field is guilty of "quantophrenia," to use a jibe made by P. A. Sorokin (one of the most indefatigable of recanted quantifiers)[8] continues to be debated, but only in informal complaints exchanged among colleagues, or in accusations published by humanists. Some sociologists do feel that young sociologists, trained in the use of computers, often seize upon numbers as a substitute for rigorous analysis and conceptualizations. Humanists claim that sociologists all too quickly suppose that if they can find a number they need no longer concern themselves with the deeper significance of human relations. In any event, sociologists generally believe that their aim is not quantification per se, but valid sociology, and that hypotheses can be much more precisely tested to the extent that measurements and indicators are transformed into some numerical form. Doubtless this stance grew from both the practical necessity of statistics for summarizing and interpreting a greater quantity of empirical observations, and the simple faith that if one uses statistics the resulting work automatically will become "more scientific."

An additional impetus, however, has come from the funding agencies, whose grant committees (made up mostly of the more successful sociologists) have been more generous to proposals that plan statistical analysis, and which appear to be more like the hard sciences. Thus, one study of the styles of presenting data in sociological journals reveals that the percentage of all articles reporting statistical findings rose from 9 per cent in 1895-1904 to 55 per cent in 1955-64, and of all empirical articles from 33 per cent to 76 per cent.[9] More to the point is the finding that during 1955-64, in thirteen of the fifteen major substantive areas the grant-supported articles were "much more likely to report statistics than the unsupported articles."[10] Of course, over the past generation the use of more sophisticated statistics has also sharply increased (for example, for Chi-square and other nonparametric statistics, from 2 per cent in 1935-44 to 28 per cent in 1955-64).

Yet not all sociologists enjoy numerical calculations, or even the secular trend toward quantification. Many sociologists simply feel uncomfortable with numbers, since they come from a liberal arts tradition in which the numerical measurement of a social force is looked upon with some suspicion, and because their own technical training did not emphasize quantification. Even so, most sociologists without sophisticated training in statistical analysis now take for granted this major element in the topography of modern sociology.

VALUE JUDGMENTS VS. EMPIRICAL PROPOSITIONS

From the welter of debate extending over centuries as to what science can or cannot do, most sociologists have come to accept the propositions that science or objective observation and rational analysis cannot demonstrate the rightness of values, the correctness of political action, the existence of the gods, or the aesthetic rank of an artistic work. It can prove only empirical assertions, not value judgments. Evaluations add nothing to the truth value of any proposition. Linked with this belief, and with the increasingly empirical bias of modern sociology, research articles and monographs in the field express far fewer value judgments now than thirty years ago. At a minimum, sociologists are much more alert to the distinction between empirical propositions and value judgments.

Few sociologists would reject the position that (a) the distinction can be made and (b) the goal of sociology is to make empirical propositions. Because of the peculiar form in which some arguments about this matter are expressed, however, contemporary debate is often emotional and confused. Most who take a dissident stance, however, will concede in the course of the argument that there is, nevertheless, a distinction between the two kinds of assertions, and that science itself cannot prove a value assertion.[11] In the renewed concern with the political stance of sociology as a whole, and as a rhetorical mode for attacking mainstream sociology, many dissidents have argued that avoiding value judgments is but a coverup for actually making them in a more surreptitious way, and that sociologists have rather an obligation not merely to take value stands but to utilize their empirical tools to support radical ideological positions.

Even such dissidents, however, are not willing to accept the ultimately nihilistic or solipsistic position, that because of one's value commitments, class interests, and emotionally distorted lenses, *none* of us can achieve a defensible empirical proposition. Rather, only one's *enemy* is so affected. This, of course, is the dilemma that the sociology of knowledge was not ultimately able to solve, either. The debate has been especially confused because many dissidents, both radical and humanistic, have attacked a straw horse, the notion that sociology can or ought to be "value-free." It is nearly impossible to find sociologists who would argue that sociology can be value-free, even if it should be so. Even without a systematic statement, sociologists have recognized for decades that science is after all an activity, and especially a social activity, and to that extent it is interwoven with many evaluations.[12]

At every phase of research, from the first choice of a topic or hypothesis through the selection of research designs, modes of analysis, and type of presentation; in the appraisal of scientific work by others; in the motivations to science as a human activity—at all these points, sociologists make evaluations. They may evaluate the elegance or the incompetence of the man's work. They may scorn the choice of a topic, as being motivated by personal interest or parochial commitments. Values themselves are data and thus enter our analyses. Sociology can be used in the service of values and of course it is so used. Increasingly in recent years there have been serious debates about the ethics of various forms of research, such as participant observation, unobtrusive measures for watching and surveillance, the use of human subjects in research.[13] Evaluation enters constantly at these points, too.

These relations can be spelled out, and in the following chapter we propose to discuss them at greater length, but it is at least obvious that no serious sociologist can maintain, or has maintained, that evaluations are not intrinsically interwoven in sociological research. Such a position does not, however, affect at all the possibility of distinguishing between a statement that asserts or describes an empirical relationship, and one that evaluates that relationship.

At the same time we should note as sociologists that social analysts who *have* taken strong value positions, or those who have attempted to achieve adequate analyses while also expounding an ideological position, have had far wider audiences both among laymen and among the men in the field. Those who have written with passion, without neglecting the canons of proof, have evoked a much warmer response among their readers. Because of the historical fact that sociologists are generally to be found left of the political center, and thus have identified themselves consistently with proposals and programs for bettering the human condition, their works have especially been read by the young, the rebels, the disadvantaged, and of course by their ideologically more cautious colleagues. On the other hand, even those who find this intrusion of evaluative comments in an otherwise analytic work somewhat offensive, must concede (if sometimes with difficulty) that such statements need not undermine or vitiate the empirical content of such an analysis.

METHODS AND THEORY ARE "FIELDS"

It is an index of the scientific immaturity of sociology that at present there are specific subfields called methods and theory. This is contrary to the pattern in the developed sciences. There, from the very beginning of instruction, the student learns his techniques of research as part of an ongoing pedagogical process in which the techniques are simply used to test again the theoretical findings that are to be found in textbooks. Thus, in chemistry and physics there are indeed separate laboratory periods in which technical skills are learned, but these in turn are simply ways of demonstrating the truth of theoretical formulations that have been learned in the classroom. Since, as noted before, theory is by definition a structure or architectonic of empirical propositions, it is not viewed as a separate subdiscipline within the field; it is the field *itself*. One learns the theory of the field while learning the technical skills, and the skill learning constantly refers back to the structure of empirical propositions.

Of course, as already noted, in all fields some practitioners simply enjoy fact-gathering, instrumentation, and experimental testing far more than creating integrations of facts into new theoretical formulations. In the hard sciences, moreover, advanced seminars are sometimes offered in "the theory of. . . ." However, most of the factual knowledge in the physical sciences is expressed in hypotheses, laws, principles, or theories, and it is not presented as a differentiated or separate body of "data." Seminars on "the theory of . . ." actually deal with new or as yet unsettled problems on the frontiers of a subfield, and aim at developing ideas that will interpret more adequately the known facts. Theories published before World War I are analyzed in the rare courses on the history of science, and are mostly relevant as precursors not (in contrast to sociology) as a source of today's interpretations of data.

The mapping of contemporary sociology requires us to note that many courses are devoted to specific technical skills of research, in which relatively little attention is paid to theoretical propositions. And, however we may deplore it, courses in theory (not merely the history of theory) make only occasional and passing references to the problems of research techniques. Occasionally it may be noted that advances in research technique embody and draw upon theoretical notions and that advances in theory are likely to be generated by problems that have been solved or at least tackled by specific research techniques. But for the most part these are not merely viewed as separate activities, but as subfields—indexed most strikingly by the existence of specific suborganizations devoted to these two "specialties" within the American Sociological Association. The situation is not fundamentally different in other countries.

Naturally, there are sociologists who are likely to be attracted more by instrumentation, measurement, observation, and so on, just as there are physicists who have always felt uncomfortable in manning the machines and who devote most of their energy to manipulating symbols. Few men in any field are masters of both techniques and theoretical exploration. Similarly, there are periods or phases in all sciences during which technical skills move forward rapidly, followed by theoretical work, which in turn ultimately challenges existing measurements in a continuing dialectic. Within the physical sciences, especially at the growing edge of instrumentation, even mature scientists may take short courses devoted to technical skills. When a new instrument is invented, old skills may have to be sharpened or transformed. However, this does not constitute a separate field of activity. It is simply part of the ongoing research development.

Although one can argue that in the physical sciences this distinction between methods and theory is not characteristic, sociology cannot automatically and mechanically move forward by simply stating that these should be overlapping complementary activities not to be separated, or that we should all be both technical and theoretical experts. We are in one phase of scientific development in which our empirical mastery is somewhat precarious, and our armamentarium of techniques small and under much criticism. There is little integration in sociology between its technical skills and its theoretical structure, and the latter is very loose.[14]

Since hypotheses are not rigorously formulated, they cannot easily be demonstrated within a few minutes or hours within a laboratory, as can many propositions in elementary chemistry. Our flights of theory go far beyond any existing instrumentation. Thus it is easy to predict that this distinction, this specific labeling and separation of the two fields from one another, will doubtless continue far into the future in sociology, and will not be erased until there is a rigorous body of theory, many of whose propositions can be quickly tested by some technique that the beginning student needs to learn as part of his understanding of that theory.

COMMON THEORETICAL ORIENTATION

At any given time, those who keep abreast of the latest work perceive the field as hopelessly split into warring factions. By contrast, except for periods in which really new theoretical orientations emerge, historians of science who look back, or outsiders who merely observe (like members of one ethnic group looking at one another) see the field as relatively homogeneous in its conceptual orientation. It is difficult to prove that a discipline is, say, "fifty per cent in agreement on its theoretical structure." It is even more difficult, if not illusory, to make such a statement in the face of the likely counterchallenge: can one state succinctly what its theoretical structure is? Those who feel especially antagonistic toward the leaders of the field are likely to exaggerate their disagreement, while cooler heads might urge that those who attack and those who defend do not really seem so far apart. I would argue that most sociologists in all subfields now follow a very similar theoretical orientation and for the most part use a common conceptual apparatus.

This may be nicely indexed, if not demonstrated, by the fact that although many sociologists do attack mainstream sociology, most of them do not typically offer or use an alternative conceptual or theoretical orientation in their own empirical analyses.[15] Not many exceptions to this statement can be located, although a few will be noted just below. It is difficult to locate within the field more than a few minor "schools." For some decades American sociology has not been characterized by distinct schools, possibly not since the emergence of the "Harvard tradition" as against the "Chicago tradition." Even this difference was a fairly minor one. Within recent years, a distinct Marxist grouping has emerged, which almost certainly will become more prominent. Empirically oriented, it challenges much of contemporary sociology, but both the latter and the former will be improved, because some of the changes now taking place in mainstream sociology converge on problems and orientations that once were mainly cultivated by Marxists outside the university.

This is not the place to attempt a careful exposition of this dominant theoretical structure, but it has been polemically identified with the numerous works of Talcott Parsons.[16] Many contemporary sociologists proclaim themselves to be anti-Parsonian, but this stance always has special meanings, largely political. The main body of the field is a synthesis of theoretical formulations that attained some explicitness in the work of Weber and Durkheim, was expounded with success in the Park and Burgess textbook of the 1920's, and was propounded in various forms by the so-called "functionalist" social anthropologists in that decade and the 1930's.[17] With a considerable impetus from the attempts by Parsons to analyze the methodological and theoretical underpinnings of this mainstream orientation, most textbooks in sociology have not so much deviated from it or developed a new one, as rather worked out its fuller implications. In this sense, the contemporary political dissidents in the field are correct in asserting that the theory of mainstream sociology is relatively monolithic, in spite of the polemics that enliven any issue of the sociological journals.

As will be noted in a moment, this does not mean at all that every sociologist works on the same problems, or with exactly the same variables. For example, both demographers and ecologists have been occupied far more with the flow of people and activities in space and time, than they have with the value systems or social forces that create those movements and changes. Demographers have utilized modern sociological theory to only a modest extent, but on the other hand they have not repudiated it or offered any alternatives.

The "culturology" of Leslie A. White and his followers claims to be alternative theory but in fact it merely suggests that a greater weight should be given to cultural (rather than social) variables. It may well be that the "structuralism" of Lévi-Strauss is a somewhat different theoretical orientation, since it seems to look for underlying organizing principles ("cooked vs. raw vs. rotted; elaborated vs. unelaborated, and so forth) that may not be known to even the members of a society.[18] As yet, its importance is to be found mainly in social anthropology, and its methods of proof and interpretation seem more whimsical and idiosyncratic than Freud's, with which they share more than a passing resemblance.

The "social interactionist" school can hardly be called more than a minor variant on the main theoretical orientation of the present generation, although its members have proclaimed their independence for decades.[19] Their main tenets are hardly disputed by most sociologists. In any event they stem from a well-entrenched body of notions to be found in the work of George Herbert Mead and his followers.

Perhaps the "school" of ethnomethodology comes the closest to a potential alternative theoretical orientation, since (as expounded by some of its adherents) it offers a thoroughgoing attack on many of the current basic assumptions about even the kinds of evidence that might be relevant. It also asserts a fundamental skepticism about the mainstream findings that have been accepted up to this point.[20] Whether ethnomethodologists can move from their extreme focus on the microelements in social behavior, to analyze from the larger structural problems that are central to sociology, remains to be seen. Certainly the empirical research of ethnomethodology has so far mainly uncovered new relationships that traditional sociology has mainly ignored, but those empirical findings are easily incorporated into mainstream sociology.[21] The theoretical skepticism expressed in ethnomethodology has not as yet generated, either, an alternative theoretical orientation that can adequately analyze the larger problems of traditional sociology.

But though I am asserting a widespread if vague agreement on a common theoretical orientation, there is *no intellectual center* in contemporary sociology. There is no sociologist of stature who is not strongly attacked (if only informally and privately) by a goodly minority of the field. Although a handful of departments of sociology are conceded to be most prestigious[22] they are not viewed as the source of new, creative sociology. Instead, they are an agglomeration of talented sociologists. Some of these men may create, but they are in a given department only by chance, and their being together creates no social or intellectual center at all.[23] Within special subfields (mathematical sociology, the sociology of science, and so on) there are, of course, particular men whose work forms a "center," but no group could be viewed seriously as a center of contemporary sociology.

Whether that is to be viewed as progress (no one group is now "dominant") or as regression (we have no leadership, and *no* group is moving forward) is an open question. In any event, it is certainly in part a result of the widespread diffusion of research funds and facilities. It is no longer true that a talented young man in Madison, Austin, Chapel Hill, Ann Arbor, Seattle, or even Los Angeles need feel that his scope and horizons will be limited if he does not accept an invitation to join the department at Columbia, Berkeley, Harvard, or Chicago, where the "great men," research organizations, and funds are available.

He can obtain the latter two where he is. And if the mature sociologists in those first-ranking departments are somewhat more prestigious, or even possibly more able, he can easily talk with them at conferences, by telephone, through visiting seminars, and the like. More important, those *particular* men may not even *be* the leaders in his own specialty.[24]

Thus, the general acceptance of a common theoretical orientation, together with the availability of intellectual facilities of all kinds in a wide range of universities, has created a very different market structure for ambitious young sociologists, as compared with that in the past. Not only is the demand for their abilities much greater, but they can now obtain adequate material and intellectual support in far more departments than in the past. Although this dispersion of talent and work is not the prime element that underlies the lack of a recognized creative center in sociology, it does support it to some extent. The prime element remains the great dissidence (to be analyzed further in the next chapter) against mainstream sociology without as yet an adequately seminal theoretical alternative.

THE BURGEONING OF SPECIALTIES

In the expanding economy of all industrial nations, sociology has grown spectacularly, as measured by the amount of money devoted to research, the numbers of people dedicated to scientific work, and its readership among people outside the field. As the field has grown, more and more subareas of human action are analyzed, and a division of labor inevitably arises. Some of these subfields are generated by the application of new observational techniques, such as computer methods of reading and abstracting, and the measurement of social interaction in a laboratory. Others are stimulated because new funds have become available, for example, industrial sociology or market research.[25] Since honor in science typically goes to those who explore new fields or expound new hypotheses, younger people quickly flow into the new specialties.

However, one must not suppose that these new subfields are mere fads which rapidly rise and disappear. They may arise with rapidity, and for a brief time the more talented young men are attracted to the latest thing, but the new specialties do not then disappear.[26] The old specialties, such as the sociology of the family, social stratification, political sociology, and so on, remain also. Although "small groups research" no longer possesses the intellectual chic of its heyday in the early 1950's, the total amount of research in this area has not diminished. Within the past few years the sociology of science has moved forward rapidly, and there is no reason to suppose it will fail to attract in the future a substantial number of dedicated workers. Medical sociology was a quickly burgeoning specialty, beginning in the mid-1950's (of course, it should be kept in mind that almost all of these "new" specialties had precursors quite early in the history of contemporary sociology). But though I believe medical sociology is no longer a fast-growing subfield (it was the *fastest* growing field in 1963) it has continued to grow and to occupy a secure place among the specialties. It would be difficult to locate more than a few specialties that have become popular suddenly, and then have simply died out.

MATHEMATICS, FORMALIZATION AND AXIOMATIZATION

The main body of sociological work is relatively unmathematical, even if quantified. Few sociologists enter the field with any substantial mathematical training, as Sibley noted in 1963.[27] Most sociologists who actually use tables in their reports know no more than elementary statistics, and a decade after receiving their doctorates most sociologists are mathematically no more advanced than to about the level of high school algebra.

However, contributions to mathematical sociology will yield a faster career mobility than almost any other type of achievement. Consequently, this sub-branch of the discipline has burgeoned substantially over the past two decades. Among the men who have contributed to this work are Herbert Simon, Howard Raiffa, Duncan Luce, James S. Coleman, Leo Goodman, N. Rashevsky, Paul F. Lazarsfeld, Anatol Rapoport, Louis Guttman, Herbert M. Blalock, and Frederick Mosteller. Most sociologists have a definite, if sometimes incorrect, conception of what "hard science" is like, and they suppose that the physical sciences achieved their great discoveries by the power of mathematics. Consequently, some sociologists have for decades cherished the dream that through the mathematization of sociology a giant step could be made in the field. In physics at least it is evident that mathematical manipulations have generated vast numbers of discoveries. Perhaps this might also be true for sociology. We might thus bypass the arduous, tedious work of fact-gathering over many generations, and at once leap to the heart of the forces that shape the social patterns we actually observe.

This is almost certainly a chimerical view, since this pattern is evidenced (with minor exceptions) only in physics. Chemistry did not make its great advances through mathematics. Biology has never developed an overarching mathematical structure. Some branches of economics have done so, but this was made possible primarily by paying relatively little attention to observable behavior. In sociology as well, the contributions of mathematical sociologists have not as yet generated important new insights about social behavior.

On the other hand, the problems posed by social phenomena have challenged mathematicians and statisticians to develop *their* own subfields, and to make a substantial number of mathematical "discoveries," that may be important in time, just as mathematical achievements in other fields have often been utilized generations after their first appearance. That is, sociology has up to this point been far more useful in stimulating mathematical discoveries than the latter have been useful in the development of sociological theories.

As mathematical sociologists have explored social processes, they have moved from the simple assumptions of a generation ago, that restating an empirical generalization in a simple equation, or in some kind of algebraic form, would by itself generate new ideas. They have at least begun to locate the types of mathematical techniques— Poisson Series, Markov chains, lattices, path analysis—that might better fit the realities of social interaction.

At the same time, the gap between their work and that of most sociologists is probably even greater than a generation ago, because more sociologists now know some higher level mathematics, and more know *some* mathematics, but the great majority know no more than did their intellectual forefathers forty years ago. Thus, the gap is greater. Computer programs save most working sociologists from having to calculate even ordinary statistical measures. They neither read nor seek translations of contributions by mathematical sociologists. That the two groups will begin to talk with one another intellectually over the next decade seems doubtful.

Although axiomatization is not necessarily mathematical, it is linked socially with the task of developing sociology mathematically, since many specialists in either of these tasks are likely to be interested in the other as well. Both can read mathematics and both share the ideal of attempting to locate crucial variables, specify possible formal manipulations, and develop new propositions that can be tested in the field or laboratory. The mathematician is much more likely to start from prior mathematical formulations, while sociologists who work with either formalizations or more fully developed axiomatizations are more likely to base their work on formal logic, and a wide body of empirical findings. From them, the key propositions and propositional linkages are extracted, so as to maximize the chance of there being some common theory or set of hypotheses that could explain this body of findings. Once the central variables have been extracted they are reduced to the smallest possible number that might generate the findings with which the researcher began. If these propositions are to be generated, along with new ones, formal logic requires that certain primitive elementary assumptions and definitions have to be made, and some specification of what logical operations are to be carried out. The "language" in which both the original and the new propositions are stated may be that of symbolic logic or mathematics.[28]

Those who carry out such axiomatizations are more likely than mathematical sociologists to test various of their subhypotheses through a series of laboratory experiments, which hopefully will capture those variables in social reality that are at issue. By contrast, the mathematical sociologist can rely far more on the logical validity of his deductions.

Neglected Sources of Data. Any description of contemporary sociology must note that the past generation has neglected some important sources of data. The major ones are historical materials, cross-cultural or comparative studies, and field observation.

For nearly half a century, sociologists have paid little attention to historical data, although prior to World War I it was taken for granted that any social scientist would at least include many historical references in his works. At the present time, sociologists have become increasingly concerned with testing sociological generalizations by historical research.[29] Still others have at least drawn upon historical data using the writings of historians as their main sources.[30]

Nevertheless, the past two decades have actually witnessed an increase in the number of *and* percentage of papers that utilize data from one time point only.[31]

Given the high need over the past half-century for developing rigorous techniques of research in order to move beyond the armchair speculations of prior generations, it cannot be surprising that sociology did emphasize *contemporary* social behavior: at least, one's respondents were still alive to respond, so that sociological hypotheses could be tested. In addition, until World War II, historians themselves had moved only gradually toward a fuller appreciation and use of the detailed archival data that deal with ordinary social behavior, that is, the main data of sociologists, rather than those of monarchs and nobles. Far more historical studies are now stimulated by socio-logical theory, so that their findings seem more relevant to the mod-ern sociologist.

However, few sociology students develop any enthusiasm for the tedious archival research that is necessary for the serious use of his-torical data in testing sociological hypotheses. Moreover, most are interested in social problems which are drawn from only one point in time: now. Consequently, the main emphasis of sociology even in the future is likely to be on data drawn from only the present.

Another source of data that has been neglected until recently is cross-cultural materials, especially those on "primitive" societies. Until World War I, of course, most sociologists drew heavily upon anthropological monographs, indeed utilizing such data in the devel-opment of broad evolutionary schemes, rather than observing con-temporary life in their own cities and towns. The decline in compara-tive sociology was gradual but clear until the last ten years. Now, with a renewed interest in social change, modernization, and revolu-tion, a growing segment of younger men have been focusing on at least the emerging nations. They are once again proclaiming Durk-heim's dictum that sociology *is* (that is, should be) *comparative.* In addition, systems of information retrieval in the form of computer archives make comparisons possible that once would have been beyond the capacity of a lone sociologist.[32]

Doubtless sociologists will continue to emphasize contemporary data from the social world closest to them, that is, other industrial nations as well as their own nation. However, for many major soci-ological hypotheses dealing with power systems, changes in class systems, conflict, and modernization, it will be necessary to draw upon data from other, less industrialized countries, too.

Interviews and questionnaires were developed as research tools because they yielded contemporary data and were, therefore, testable in part against ordinary experience, but the data source that has been least developed over the past half-century is also contemporary: field observation. As with historical and comparative techniques, sociolo-gists have recently begun to take a renewed interest in this source of information.[33] But though more sociologists are both developing and applying this technique than two decades ago, even if one includes with it the observation of groups in a laboratory the larger secular trend in the field runs in an opposite direction: still *more* research in sociology is based on interviews and questionnaires than in the past. Specifically, the percentage of empirical studies drawn from this source nearly doubled from 1940-41 to 1965-66, from 25 to 48 per cent. If one includes studies that are *based* on secondary data whose *primary* source was interviews and questionnaires, the total is closer to 64 per cent.[34] That is to say, a major portion of sociological research in the U.S. (and this would not be different in most countries) mainly analyze data about "attitudes, feelings and opinions rather than . . . factual accounts of past behavior interactions."[35]

Those who criticize the modern sociological enterprise because of its heavy reliance on the questionnaire have thus a rather strong case. The contrast and discrepancy between the findings from such data and those from other types of data-gathering requires serious study. We do know that surveys can yield immense quantities of valid information, but they are often only approximations, and in certain crucial encounters (for example, how parents socialize children, black-white interaction, how bosses control their subordinates, and so on) they may simply be incorrect.

NEGLECTED PROBLEMS

Critics in sociology have charged the field with neglecting many important problem areas. So stated, the charge seems trivial; to the extent that a body of knowledge exists at all, it fails to deal with *some* important problems. Indeed, the significant discoveries of one generation are likely to grow from the investigation of puzzles that earlier were neglected.

However, the charge is not trivial, and it is by and large correct. It states laconically a central issue about which there is now much bitter and sometimes confused polemic. Part of the debate will be discussed in more detail in the succeeding chapter. Here, let us do no more than to outline the disagreement.

First, let us simply list a few of the problem areas that have been somewhat neglected in sociology over the past generation. Without any claim to completeness, they include: the pervasive place of force in all societies, the importance of self-interest in social behavior, revolution, war and peace, social change, possible utopias, the social

conditions for creativity, personal fulfillment, and democratic participation, and the social mechanisms by which dominant classes maintain their position in society.

Clearly, these are not like the anomalies and puzzles at the growing
edge of a physical science, which are neglected because their importance has not yet been perceived by many researchers. Sociologists
have long recognized these as of fundamental significance, and indeed
it could be argued that sociologists dealt with them before World War
I more than in the generation afterward. Both conservatives and
radicals agree they are worth investigating. Their subject matter is
the powerful social forces that affect all our lives. Not only are they
theoretically important; they are also "social problems," that is,
many people view them as calling for some kind of a practical
solution.

Dissident sociologists charge that these great broad problems have
been neglected because:

> to investigate them is to challenge the status quo, but main-
> stream sociologists are paid to defend it instead;

> the power structure of the society will not permit such studies;

> mainstream sociological theory cannot deal with such problems
> anyway.

Needless to say, few mainstream sociologists would simply plead
guilty to these charges. Their defenses are more often stated in informal discussions among friends than in publications, and can be
summarized briefly:

> in fact, sociologists have made many studies that at least
> helped to illuminate these topics by furnishing many descrip-
> tive data about them;

> research in sociology has exposed many of the evils in our
> society (for instance, the social forces that generate juvenile
> delinquency, racism, class discrimination, white collar crimi-
> nality, and the like); and most criticism of the status quo
> draws upon such data;

> some of these problems were considered to be the task of other
> fields (social psychology, political science);

most of these problems have not been dealt with adequately, simply because the technical and theoretical difficulties loom large (for example, social change).

Stated so flatly, both the charges and defenses lose much of the passion with which they are currently pervaded. As in all such polemics, it is not possible to weigh the merits and demerits of each side fully, and to determine thereby who is "right." In any event, these issues will be discussed at greater length in the two succeeding chapters. Here, we wish only to note the fact that contemporary sociology is the site of a considerable debate about the appropriate content of the field, its failures in the past, and what political principles it should espouse.

TEAM RESEARCH

Since large-scale studies have become much more common, team research has come to characterize a large part of contemporary sociology in the United States, and this is hardly less true for other West European nations. Large grants have encouraged this change, and the emergence of social research organizations has facilitated it technically. The "lone researcher" of the past remains common, but far more socially prominent are the research groups.

These groups cannot, however, be simply equated with the team research to be found in the physical sciences, with respect to either organization or results. Sociological research is far less often the work of a genuine team, if by that we mean a group of peers who are working on a related problem. Since a very large part of empirical research in sociology is some type of survey, the social research unit is much more likely to be hierarchical, and the "team" is really made up of one senior person or sometimes two, who direct subordinates at less advanced levels of skills. Frequently, when a monograph is authored by several people, it is again likely that the work is not that of a genuine team. Instead, two or more directors and subdirectors have really worked on separate parts of the larger topic but have published together. Sometimes, a duo is made up of a "theorist" and a "methodologist."

The intellectual structure of the problem is also different in that the survey may be likened to a large pie. If the pie is sufficiently large and rich, a goodly number of independent researchers may slice from it their own independent monograph or article, often as graduate students engaged in writing their dissertation.

In the biological and physical sciences, by contrast, it is much more common that the investigation is a broad, theoretically linked set of problems, split into many subproblems as the inquiry proceeds. The solution of one of these at an early stage may well lead to the abandonment of some previously formulated notions, and to an entirely different direction of research. Success in one series of experiments may generate several other sets of studies. Collaboration is closer, and social rank more dependent on intellectual contribution among students and colleagues. There is likely to be joint authorship simply because everyone has contributed to all the sets of solutions. And, most notably, over a period of a year or so there may be literally dozens of such sets of experiments, while the typical survey research represents a single dip into social reality at one point in time, with several years devoted afterwards to its elaboration and even comprehension.

THE SELF-CONCEPTION OF SOCIOLOGISTS

Since this chapter has been concerned not only with the intellectual structure of contemporary sociology, but also with many social relations within it, a final note may be in order with respect to the conceptions that sociologists hold of themselves and their own work. Sociologists attack one another's preconceptions, assumptions, techniques, and theories, but in spite of widespread political dissidence only few publish strong attacks on the field itself. Perhaps some refrain because the researcher who rejects vehemently all the major work of his time arouses an expectation in his readers. Those who proclaim the incompetence of the men now occupying the field are implicitly asserting that they can substitute far richer and more precise findings than are now available. Ultimately, that must become their responsibility. Not many readers and still fewer writers will accept the notion that destructive criticism is as constructive as an alternative theory.

Much more fundamental, however, and also not to be found typically in publications, is the characteristic lack of ease that sociologists feel about themselves and their own work. Part of this, of course, is the feeling of ambitious men generally, that they have not quite achieved the heights to which they had once aspired. Much deeper, however, is the feeling that their findings and theoretical insights should have been more fundamental, should have opened far wider horizons, should have yielded better answers. Not only do sociologists contrast their failures with the successes of physical scientists but they also sense that physical scientists feel a much greater security about what they are doing, about the worth of their own contributions.

This self-deprecation may derive in part from the very looseness of theoretical work in sociology. Specifically, even a modest chemist may be able to locate and solve problems within his or her capacities, and can gain some satisfaction from this research even if he or she knows a first-rate chemist could solve them more easily. A field that is theoretically more advanced recognizes a wide range of problems as worth doing, even though they require only modest creativity. Thus the hard-working but less talented physical scientist can feel he or she has made his or her own contribution.[36] It is now *done*, and he or she did it. Of course, in the engineering fields, this sense is increased by the knowledge that the professional can also do something to *help*.

By contrast, the sociologist is sure that the data he or she has derived from a given survey or observational study are relatively accidental, in the sense that he or she would not expect another study to reproduce exactly those numerical relationships (though presumably some general correlations might still hold).

The sociologist cannot be sure, having "done" a given piece of research, that it will not be largely irrelevant to other investigators, and especially to succeeding ones. A chemist would not, ten years later, feel the need to do over again a research study already completed adequately unless, of course, he saw a possible flaw in the techniques. The sociologist does not believe what he or she does is strictly speaking an "intellectual brick" to be fitted into a great wall or cathedral that is under construction. He or she is more likely to be secretly pleased that he or she has written with elegance (if he or she so believes) than to be secure in having propounded a new hypothesis and demonstrated its truth.

They may avoid confronting their own self-deprecation as they go about their daily work, but sociologists when relaxing among themselves are likely to confess such feelings of unease, or to express some self-denigration, not even primarily directed against themselves or an absent sociologist. It is really a complaint against the field and its task. It is possible that they are correct in their general assessment, but wrong in their historical perspective. At this point in the history of sociology, perhaps it is not yet possible to create the sociology they seek in their dreams. Each science takes off in its own time—chemistry did not until late in the eighteenth century, and even the cleverest physical scientists at the beginning of the nineteenth century could not decipher the puzzle of organic compounds. The most brilliant biologists of the nineteenth century could not puzzle out pneumonia.

Unfortunately, no one can know for a certainty that his or her field is not ready for such a development. Perhaps, instead, the time has come. Meanwhile, even the best people in the field suffer from the nagging anxiety (or are rosily suffused with hope) that the secret, the breakthrough, the elegant, creative formulation is just lurking in the corner of their minds, only needing to be surprised and captured. Without that certainty that a great breakthrough in sociology is not possible now, it is difficult for most contemporary sociologists to achieve any serenity about the achievements of either the field or their own work.

2. *The Place of*
Values in Social Analysis

THE CURRENT BITTER POLEMIC ABOUT THE PLACE OF VALUES IN SOCI-
OLOGY ILLUSTRATES NEATLY THE MAJOR WEAKNESS OF HEGEL'S PECUL-
iarly dramatic view of the historical process as a sequence of thesis,
antithesis, and synthesis. For though Marxists have seized on this
notion as a scientific "tool" for extracting truth from confusion, often
in fact there are several theses, and perhaps no true antithesis or synthesis at all. History often discloses neither climax nor denouement
as in a well-constructed play, but rather a luxuriant, disorderly, organic growth that takes many forms and directions, not all of them
either in harmony or in direct conflict with one another.

Social movements often succeed because their supporters are
younger and outlive the dominant group, rather than because they
have bested it in evidence or argument. Few participants are con-
verted. Looking back, later generations often take the "new view,"
now an old one, so much for granted that they cannot understand
why people once fought about it.

The contemporary debate about the relations between value positions and research is bitter because most partisans believe their opponents are guilty of moral or ethical faults. It is confused not only
because there are many sides and positions but also because the two
main sets of opponents misperceive and misstate the others' philosophical positions. We shall attempt in this chapter to clarify the
issues, and to suggest some solutions.

The dominant voices in sociology, as noted before, have for decades asserted that their aim was scientific truth and accurate empirical descriptions, not moral or aesthetic preachments. Following the lead of their elders in the developed sciences, they have affirmed that scientific sociology could tell us what is, not what should be; or, in more cautious terms: value judgments add no truth value to an empirical proposition, for they are cognitively irrelevant to scientific descriptions.

Many political philosophers, amateur social analysts, and sociologists of some standing have not, however, accepted this limitation on social inquiry. In measured tones or snarling invective, they have strongly challenged the position they believe is dominant in sociology. It is especially the younger, politically involved sociologists who have attacked the reigning doctrine, but others have also joined this battle. The following small sampling of the published literature is but a pale index of the intense political passions now being expressed. These excerpts will serve only to remind readers of more vigorous conversations and confrontations that they have themselves perhaps experienced.

The sociology of the underdog is justified because, and to the extent, that his suffering is less likely to be known and because—by the very reason of his being underdog—the extent and character of his suffering are likely to contain much that is avoidable.[1]

. . . much of liberalism today is the well-financed ideology of a loosely organized but coherent establishment. It is the dominant ideology of a powerful group that sprawls across the academic community . . . in its meaner moments it is an intellectual Mafia . . . like any other member of an establishment, the sociologist who is a political liberal is expected to lie along with his fellow members of the Establishment, to feel the rightness of their cause and a responsibility for its success.[2]

As Tom Lehrer puts it with bitter humor, the politically noncommitted scientist, having no significant human group loyalties, is motivated by expedience only, and can therefore be expected to choose the side of the highest bidder, regardless of the nature of the job requirements. . . .

. . . the so-called a-political scientist is likely to be a cad or a coward; and . . . we sociologists are, at least theoretically, particularly well qualified to point the way to a good society. . . .[3]

The sociologist as a researcher in the employ of his employers is precisely a kind of spy. . . .

The honored sociologist, the big-status sociologist, the book-a-year sociologist, the sociologist who always wears the livery, suit and tie, of his masters—this is the kind of sociologist who sets the tone and the ethic of his profession . . . who is nothing more nor less than a house servant in the corporate establishment—a white intellectual Uncle Tom. . . .[4]

Sociology is not now and never has been any kind of objective seeking out of social truth or reality. Historically, the profession is an outgrowth of nineteenth century European traditionalism and conservatism, wedded to twentieth century American corporation liberalism.[5]

. . . If technical competence provides no norm for making value judgments, then what does?

One latent meaning of the image of a value-free society emerges: "Thou shalt not commit a critical or negative value judgment—especially of one's own society."[6]

There is no position from which sociological research can be done that is not biased in one or another way. . . .[7]

These quotations seem to hurl a direct challenge to the mainstream position on values, but the real issue is not yet presented. For a more careful reading of the literature uncovers two surprising facts about this contemporary swirl of acerb debate, and also illustrates the problem, noted above, of locating the correct antitheses:

1. A goodly number of dissident sociologists have denounced mainstream sociologists for proclaiming that sociology must be "value free" but no sociologist of stature has argued that sociology is or ever could be "value neutral" in all its activities. After all, it is a form of social action and it is, therefore, pervaded with evaluations.

2. A large number of mainstream sociologists are convinced that politically dissident sociologists deny the possibility of objective analyses, as the above quotations suggest, or even of making the distinction between value judgments and scientific propositions, but in fact no serious sociologist (including those cited above) has taken such a position.[8]

Even to bring to both sides the news that what each believes it is fighting against is not what the other is fighting for, should be useful in clarifying the debate. On the other hand, this major agreement between and among obviously warring factions (surely startling to both) forces us to look elsewhere for the core of conflict.

What Are the Real Issues?

If enemies attack one another for their heresies, but neither believes the doctrine the other supposes he or she believes, and indeed both accept similar doctrines, we know as sociologists that merely bringing this news to both will not transform either into friends. The antagonism must originate elsewhere. We know the conflict is nevertheless real, and they disclose its nature in other ways than their rhetorical style in print. After all, in any doctrinal dispute antagonists use whatever rhetoric is common in their generation, even if it does not quite fit the issues. Puritans talked in the rhetoric of theology even when they were arguing about political power, Southern whites have used the rhetoric of race when they felt their economic domination was threatened, and sociologists may well argue about values in sociological research when they are really in conflict about what kind of sociology or society we should try to create.

We also know as participants in this era that neither side is the main source of antagonism; it is endemic to our times, and encountered in every major country where dissent is permitted, as well as some where dissent encounters official repression. Thus, whatever sin the various conflicting groups of sociologists have in fact committed, none can be held fully responsible for causing the *intensity* of the others' response. None is even the major cause, which is to be found in the fundamental, puzzling value changes that are taking place in contemporary world society. Each group is simply a partial representative of some of the opposing forces that are generating new definitions of a future society. If all sociologists were to cease their debate, that conflict would remain, and accusations with this style and content would still be encountered in other groups.

Parallel battles, each with its own rhetoric, are to be found within all the social science disciplines. The attacks are probably less bitter in sociology than in anthropology where, granted, passions do run a bit higher than sociology. They are perhaps somewhat less acerb than either in political science, where the style is generally less acrimonious than in sociology. In the physical sciences, the debate does not, of course, focus on whether the scientific work has been distorted by a conservative political bias, since their faith in their intellectual achievement is hardly to be shaken, but they do engage in vigorous battles about which political stands the academic association should proclaim. While anthropologists must witness the denigration of honored men of the past, as having been supporters of colonialism and imperialism (and sociologists may be somewhat comforted by perceiving the rancor elsewhere), sociologists do perceive correctly that in certain ways they are a major center of the polemic, and the peculiarities of the field create this conflict about values.

The physical sciences are at one end of this range of political and philosophical dissent, for their intellectual work is closely directed by a sense of what is relevant for a rigorous body of theory. At the other end are the literary fields where the traditional intellectual tasks are guided by neither a body of rigorous theory nor by explicit political concerns. In the middle are the social sciences where conflict is greatest: the guidance of intellectual work by traditional theory is important but not great; and it is understood that new political and philosophical values are highly relevant to the choice of problems. It is the very subject matter of sociology with which the larger conflict outside sociology is concerned: whether various types of revolutions are possible or desirable; whether the vast trend toward a more pervasive bureaucratization, higher political control, and an ever increasing Gross National Product can be reversed; whether the exploited and downtrodden segments of the society can gain adequate power and economic rewards; in short, with the quality of social, political, and economic life. As in all such attacks on traditional views, the most active leaders are the newer men in the field, although they also enjoy the support of some established sociologists who welcome these emerging forces.

It is, then, the very content of sociology that is at issue in these skirmishes about values. In addition, its content in the past has in fact generated some part of the radical politics of our time. Almost all detailed social research creates dismay or anger among both attackers and defenders of the status quo. Objective descriptions of nearly every institution, organization, or group uncover deplorable conditions: lack of doctrinal commitment among churchgoers, theft, sabotage, and shirking among employees, police brutality and authoritarianism, parental abuse of children, discrimination by and against perhaps every group, the deprivation of civil rights, the tax advantages of the rich, governmental espionage against its citizens, and so on.

Over a hundred years ago, Marx illustrated the destructive power of social investigations when he used dozens of officials' reports in his analysis of the English capitalist system. Correspondingly, every competent critic of modern society must draw upon sociological research in order to buttress his accusations. Rarely if ever does even a careful study of a social institution or organization disclose a state of affairs that seems worthy of admiration. Sociology is a center of controversy, in part because its very findings are an attack on the social order.

In yet another way sociology generates some part of the political dissidence that is now turned against it. As both Weber and Durkheim understood at the turn of the century, the very objectivity and rationality of the sociological view undermines that moral commitment, legitimacy, and credence without which most social and institutional patterns would dissolve, their foundations washed away by a lack of faith. By looking at ongoing social life as one would view any other interesting customs in a distant tribe, the sociological stance creates an attitude of perhaps not disbelief but at best desacrilization and detachment from tradition.

At the same time, while encouraging dissident modes of thought and research in its students and practitioners, the sociology of the past half-century has discouraged a wholehearted program of major, not to say radical, transformation of political and social structures. For it has emphasized the slow growth of custom, the massive resistance of people to great change, their attachment to existing rituals and social patterns (even to some that seem destructive or profitless), and the difficulty of altering things by new laws.

Students and young practitioners in sociology hear or read how outrageous conditions really are, but are in effect told they cannot be changed, or changed very much. They learn how various social mechanisms maintain the status quo, but they perceive that analysis may be biased, simply a defense of the existing system, or it is too lacking in theoretical imagination to offer any real steps of improvement. In sum, sociology is a major center of value controversy because of its subject matter, and because it has itself created some part of that controversy.

Moreover, both young and old dissident sociologists can more safely throw themselves into this conflict because established professors enjoy less control over them than in the past. The dissidents are not so dependent as in the past upon the goodwill and approval of the more conservative sociologists who hold dominant positions in the field. Many are talented, and thus can obtain jobs in spite of their dissident beliefs. There is much cultural support for not seeking jobs at the most prestigious universities (where the sponsorship of senior professors might be more crucial), or for that matter for not taking a job at all. In addition, there is a growing market for social criticism outside the university. In short, a growing minority of sociologists who challenge the reigning view about the place of values in the field can afford to be less respectful than in the past.

But in saying all this, however true, we must not run the risk of lumping together the conflict about values in sociology with the world-wide conflict about the political direction of future society. Their roots are the same, but their specific patterns are different in sociology.

In so doing, I run the risk of all who attempt intuitive generalizations in the absence of adequate attitude studies, and anyone can rejoin that his *or* her opinions are very different. However, if I make such errors others can correct them with better data. Needless to say, I shall not rely only on public manifestoes or articles, where the norms of propriety or good manners impose limits on what may be expressed.

I shall also focus on the attacks rather than the counterattacks, for the attacks presage the future, and in any event the only vindication of established sociology must be its work, while its defenses are likely to be ignored now or forgotten later. Even so, their defenses are of some interest, as casting light on the issues in the conflict. Some of them will be repeated in the succeeding chapter on functionalism, for reasons to be noted there, but their relevance here is also unquestionable.

Here, then, is a summary of the main indictments made by sociologists who challenge the value position of the dominant sociology of our time. These are the charges, but underlying them are the *real* issues, which will be presented afterwards. In any event, these indictments do express the issues as they are now stated in public and private arguments.

CHARGES AGAINST MAINSTREAM SOCIOLOGY

Hypocrisy

Mainstream sociologists (indeed, an overwhelming majority of *all* sociologists voting a few years ago) have voted against the American Sociological Association taking strong political positions, on the grounds that they are scientists and that the Association is a learned, not a political organization; and they have avoided taking personal political positions when speaking "as sociologists," not because they are trying to describe social behavior and structure as they are rather than as they should be, but actually in order to avoid political repercussions. They hide behind the mask of "ethical neutrality" in order to escape political counterattacks.

Pretentiousness

For decades, mainstream sociologists have claimed to be following in the footsteps of their predecessors in other sciences, making discoveries, exploring new paths and frontiers, formulating powerful and interesting propositions, and building a body of cumulative knowledge. In fact, they have not moved our knowledge forward by much. They have instead published tiny descriptions of relatively unimportant behaviors, while proclaiming them to be "important findings." They have picked problems because project money was available, or because easy research techniques could be applied. They have made no discoveries. "Theory" is hollow verbiage; as Homans remarked in a criticism of one major theorist, it is a dictionary of a language that has no sentences. As Mazur remarks with respect to all these pretensions, "An empirical, theoretically-connected body of knowledge is science only *when the people who know the theories know more about the real world than the people who don't know the theories.* Is sociology a science? No."[9]

Heartlessness

Mainstream sociologists are guilty of having no compassion for their less fortunate fellow men. They are engaged in a false attempt to build a grand science, while people are suffering. In short, they are fiddling while Rome burns. Of what avail is science if people are everywhere exploited, starved, and repressed? By not attacking a system they know is wrong, they are supporting it.

Irrelevance

The charge of irrelevance is made not only in its catchword sense, but in a deeper meaning: what sociologists have seized upon are essentially trivial variables, of no great consequence in ordinary behavior, so that their findings have little relevance for understanding the actual condition of men and the forces that move them, which are more likely to be force and violence, domination of economic resources, corporations, war, and class politics. For example, they describe the problems of the poor, but avoid tackling the problem of why the poor are kept in that position. In short, for lack of moral or intellectual nerve, they avoid the "big problems."

Venality

Because the rewards of supporting the status quo are substantial, and because a successful sociologist can live reasonably well, mainstream sociologists have essentially sold out. They write monographs and articles that basically defend the system as it exists, knowing that as a consequence they will be rewarded by the class that dominates and exploits the society.

As Churchill once commented with reference to the attacks made against those in power, the young fail to anticipate fully both the cunning and the staying of the old. However, even when they are able to hang on to their jobs and income, the old are much less secure in their possession of prestige, more vulnerable to denigration. If the dominant sociologists lose the respect of the rising generation, from whom any future footnote citations must come, they will enjoy but little their tenure and steady salaries. They are therefore hurt, bewildered, and angry at the foregoing accusations, while suffering from a nagging sense that their opponents are partly justified.

But though such charges sting, a close reading shows that three of them nevertheless affirm the worth of science and the possibility of objective research. Thus, the charge of venality suggests that scientific achievement is possible, but that sociologists have chosen instead another value, worldly success. The charge of irrelevance asserts that a good scientist should and can locate the key variables. The charge

of pretentiousness claims that one of the norms of scientific work has
been violated: a researcher should not make exaggerated claims when
his work is trivial. By implication, that indictment also argues that if
sociologists did not give so much praise to unimportant work, inflat-
ing their claims to achievement, they might go on to more worthwhile investigations.

The other charges are really variations on a central theme, that
sociologists as scientists should *in their work* take value positions,
should be politically active, should use their science to help political
causes. They should not permit any concern about their political
safety or economic security to swerve them from science in the
service of political action.

So much agreement between dissident and establishment on the
importance and the possibility of objective science should not, however, surprise us (that is, now that we know it). Anyone who makes
a serious attack on sociology *must* believe that objective social science
is possible; that value judgments are not scientific descriptions; and
that in spite of differing value positions, scientific analysis of social
behavior can be achieved. After all, we need not give credence to any
charges made by anyone who cannot accept such a dictum: if he denies the possibility of objective descriptions, then his own charges are
also destroyed by that denial. If objective analyses cannot be distinguished from personal wishes, political philosophies, or moral norms,
then we need not listen to anyone's accusations: if they have no truth
value, why waste time on them? If "truth" is only a set of value judgments or political assertions made by people who espouse a special
political position, then we need not support or believe in that "truth"
unless of course we happen to share those values.[10]

Plainly, the only way to ascertain whether the "science-oriented"
sociologists have been hypocrites, dissemblers who do not believe
scientists should avoid political strife but who instead are afraid of it,
is to ask them in secret interviews whether that is so, perhaps after
strapping them in a lie-detecting machine. I believe most would come
through that examination unscathed; they really do believe that scientific findings give no warrant for taking political positions; they do
believe that science cannot prove any value assertions; they were not
merely trying to avoid political trouble.

With respect to the usefulness of avoiding value judgments, one critic of the dominant doctrine of sociologists (knowing surely that his own statement is false), comments about Max Weber, "his myth was that science should and could be value free."[11] He goes on to claim that this position has served sociologists well, because thereby they could obtain many economic rewards and social advantages. As he puts it, "it is somehow useful to those who believe in it."[12]

Of course, that a belief is useful because the outside society will be pleased with believers, does not prove that (1) the belief is wrong or (2) believers come to that conclusion because they would be rewarded because they believed. In any event, the history of science as of religion is replete with both types of cases, believers who were persecuted for deviant or new causes, and those who were instead rewarded.

In Weber's time, for example, it was almost certainly "more useful" for a German professor or docent to express his values or political positions in class if his beliefs were sufficiently conservative—and without question most were. Weber was taking an *un*popular view. More fundamentally, the doctrine that science does not demonstrate the "truth" of value positions has weighty epistemological support. Sociologists may have come gradually to separate preaching from scientific research simply because the difference between the two became clearer over the decades, and scientific work seemed more worthwhile.

Recently, United States sociologists have gained by claiming that they are scientists and not propagandists. They have acquired thereby some of the prestige of science. Politically, they have gained little, since they were and are (correctly) identified as left of center. Laymen have looked askance at sociology because its findings seem to be subversive of the moral order and to constitute an exposure of social problems that should be kept hidden.

The charges that sociologists were making inflated claims about their high achievements, and did not attack any important problems, are cruel, but they expose the accuser to an early counterchallenge: can the accuser do better? If not, the indictment is weakened. It is even possible the task is a difficult one.

Certainly, most sociologists have "wrestled with the big problems," for, after all, the great figures in sociology—Marx, Weber, Durkheim—did just that, and everyone begins his career by studying their analyses. However, not being great figures, most sociologists have not created new grand solutions, and most suspect that few other sociologists, young or old, and of whatever political persuasion, will soon create any, either.

If sociologists have nevertheless encouraged each other by praising researches that are less than earthshaking, we should be touched by their kindness rather than offended by their pretensions. If (in any field) we paid respect only to those who achieved magnificently, almost all of us would lose courage.

Perhaps the "purely scientistic" sociologist is hurt more by the charge that his work is trivial and boring than that he is heartless, but most sociologists would also reject the latter accusation. Most of the eminent sociologists have a rather persuasive record of both public and private political action, including participation in radical movements.

What such sociologists have done, however, is to expend more energy and thought in analyzing society than in changing it fundamentally. This was a value decision, and the coming generation is not likely to alter it greatly, however strongly they attack it. Whether that relative emphasis is to be deplored or encouraged depends on one's values and one's guesses about the chances of success in either.

Nevertheless, we cannot prove heartlessness by the dictum, "if we don't attack the system we are supporting it." Granted, inaction is of course a form of action, too, but that fact does not specify *which* act the inaction is. Any person with discriminating taste will daily encounter dozens of situations, people, and scenes that are somewhat offensive or outrageous, from TV programs to thoughtless bureaucrats, racism, indifferent cooks, imperialism, or trash in the streets, but not stopping to correct all of these is not the same as applauding them, either logically or psychologically. The personal problems of living cannot be simplified into a dichotomy in which every action or inaction of the day is either for or against the status quo. To many people, a large part of all United States radio programs and governmental actions are offensive, but such people do not vote for them merely because they fail to denounce each one publicly.

Those who attack sociologists as venal, protecting the status quo because they are paid well, fail to understand the goals and evaluations of researchers of both the past and the present generations.

Their prime goal is and was to gain prestige among their colleagues. Needless to say, they also expect to receive raises and promotions for good work, but these are thought to be by-products of the respect that colleagues pay to one's work. Sociologists who devote their energies to making money, like those who work hard at university politics, have a lesser chance of achieving this central goal. Those who wish to gain prestige among their colleagues can do so only by propounding and testing hypotheses that seem to describe and explain social behavior better than did their predecessors.

There are hollow men in this as in other fields, some who gain temporary esteem for their eloquence or style, for their success in obtaining grants or in conference entrepreneurship, or for accepting advisory posts with the federal government. Some achieve temporary prestige because their intellectual leads seem promising for a while though empty later. Nevertheless, sociology tends to reward those who improve the explanatory power of their theoretical formulations, or develop new research techniques for doing so. Certainly no sociologist in the past half-century has been applauded or become prestigious among his colleagues merely because he vigorously defended the United States society or government, the capitalist or any other economic system, any war against any group or nation, any corporation or corporations generally, the police system, the university system, or even American family patterns. Neither in public awards nor in private gossip have sociologists praised their peers because they published analyses that supported the status quo.

No sociologist of any merit would ever so misconceive the reward pattern as to suppose he could obtain honor by such a defense. *Other publics* might praise a sociologist for that support—university administrators, government agencies and officials, or possibly little-known "front" foundations devoted to political action—but even now, when many dissidents are eager to locate and denounce venal men who have gained honor by defending the status quo, few can be found. No sociologist who has taken that road enjoys more than a modest prestige in the field itself. Perhaps more cruelly phrased, it would be hard to find any sociologist who has really "sold out," because few or none of those who do so have had the option of becoming first-rate in their field.

Still more broadly, both warring parties partly misconceive the choices the other faces. Those who denounce contemporary sociology for its political failure perceive the sociologist as choosing between the worldly success that political venality enjoys, and the worldly failure that courage brings, but these are both false choices.[13] As a literary critic remarked long ago, financial failure does not demonstrate artistic achievement; or, as Lynd noted long ago in his review of Mills's book, *The Power Elite*, "those who write denunciations of 'the system' are likely to be rewarded with much material success and public acclaim"—and the comment applies to Lynd as well. Gouldner has noted with respect to some of the researchers who analyze society from the viewpoint of the underdog:

> But while an underdog standpoint thus has its risks, it may also bring higher and quicker returns than the adoption of an overdog standpoint which, being common, tends to glut the market and to depress the price paid for individual contribution. An underdog perspective may, then, be thought of as a career strategy more appealing to high variance bettors, who, in turn, are more likely to be found among the ambitious young.[14]

Doubtless, more sociologists and more people in general would choose venality or political cowardliness if it assured success, but it does not.

However, Lynd (along with many disgruntled conservatives) by implication suggests a partly incorrect observation, for denunciation may not bring success, either. It requires no great analytic powers or sociological talent to express one's outrage at the iniquities of this and every other government known to man—after all, one needs only to read the newspapers to obtain enough factual materials. But in sociology the risk of being a bore is greater than the risk of being fired. Mills's writings were successful not primarily because they expressed courage, or contained new scientific revelations about how modern society works, but because they were exciting. Most political diatribes, alas, are tedious both as art and as science.

Unfortunately, therefore, most sociologists do not have the choices that are expressed in the rhetoric of either antagonist. Almost no one has the luxury of giving up a brilliant sociological discovery in order to devote his time to preaching against the ways by which the political, economic, and social systems exploit the common man; and almost no one turns away from writing a powerful condemnation of our social failure in order to move beyond the current frontiers of social science. Most sociologists face the alternative of contributing a small bit to political and social action, and hopefully a small bit to science. If they must decide between these two, the choice may be difficult because the improvement in either is likely to appear marginal.

Charges and defenses, countercharges and answers, in family squabbles as a doctrinal conflict about heresy, can never be fully balanced out, and even when they are they do not lead necessarily to wisdom or "the" truth. Consequently, I do not think it is worthwhile to assign praise or blame to one side or the other.

I have already taken the risk of intuiting without systematic data the main accusations against the science-oriented mainstream of sociology and now I wish to clarify further these issues by asserting that the sometimes confusing character of both agreement and opposition is expressed by their differing answers to three major value questions. Each researcher answers them by decisions he makes in the course of any investigation:

1. When one poses a research question or plans an analysis, is it more worthwhile to aim at moving science forward, or one's political program?

2. When writing a report, should one freely express one's moral indignation at the state of affairs described, or should one simply present the data?

3. How large a part of one's time and energy should one allocate to political and social action?

As is obvious, these are not dichotomous or contrary choices, although some adversaries transform them into either-or decisions. For few on either side reject the importance of science *or* of helping mankind. These are value decisions about the *relative* weight or emphasis to be given one or the other at any given time.

On the other hand, because the evaluations overlap greatly, each side seems to the other to be guilty of inconsistency, of claiming to carry out scientific research while really engaging in propaganda. Each side angers the other, precisely because each partly believes in the other's doctrines, but believes the other's actions belie his words.

The distinction can be seen by trying to locate questions, findings, or relationships that (a) can be used politically now, but do not add much to our sociological understanding; and (b) seem to be scientifically fruitful, but which could not be put to immediate political advantage as easily. The reader may dispute each example, but I believe that even trying to think of candidates for both categories helps us to understand what the conflict is.[15]

The following research findings, I suggest, can be put to immediate political use, but add little to our grasp of sociological principles:

> The police use more violence on people in lower social classes than on people in higher classes even when they have apparently committed the same crime.

> Merchants in ghetto areas use the law to take advantage of the poor.

> University boards of trustees enjoy higher incomes and are politically more conservative, than the average of even the alumni of their respective universities.

> Mental institutions, reformatories, prisons, schools, and the defense forces deprive their inmates or members of some basic constitutional rights.

The attempt to categorize findings and relationships into these two categories helps us to know where we ourselves are on the continuum from "scientific" to "political," and challenges us to state our criteria for "importance" or "triviality." It also forces us to recognize that it is much more difficult to think of findings that are scientifically fruitful than of relationships which could be put to political use. For much of even our "scientific" work simply ascertains more surely what we have believed or suspected all along. At best it settles an argument about "the facts" by proving that laymen's guesses (and sometimes ours) have been wrong—for example, that Southern officers in World War II, because they "understood" blacks would make better leaders of black troops; that Northern blacks would be more discontented in Southern-based camps; that military police contingents, with low promotion rates, would feel less optimistic about the chances of promotion in the army, that divorce rates are higher toward the higher social strata, and so on. It was worthwhile to refute these "facts," but only by dint of good theoretical work could any of them be made to yield any scientific insights. If it is more difficult to think of scientifically fruitful findings than either politically useful findings, or simply interesting journalistic descriptions, perhaps that is a fundamental fact about sociology to which this generation must adjust.

With, then, some anticipation of scorn from either side for these illustrations, here are some findings or relationships that seem to yield scientific understanding of how social forces work, but cannot be easily put to immediate political use:

> Regions in which partible inheritance was practiced experienced a higher population growth and less industrial development than those with single-heir inheritance.

> People are more likely to feel friendly toward the individual who is high in prestige but low in leadership duties, than toward those who are high on both, low on both, or low in prestige but high in leadership duties.

> In non-Communist countries, there is a substantial correlation between the use of coercion and overt political unrest; in Communist countries, this correlation is not to be observed.

> The more the members of a group like one another, the more likely they are to conform to group norms.

> If under mild pressure, people are somewhat unwillingly persuaded to do harm to others, they are likely to change their opinions of their victims or the experience, for example, by deprecating their victims or minimizing their victims' suffering.

Sociologists who are more science-oriented will prefer the second list because they will be able to make more fruitful scientific inferences from it than from the first. At the same time, I have deliberately included more political relationships in the second list to emphasize a hidden point, that almost any proposition of any power might eventually be useful to actionists as well, for instance, in drawing up plans for the reorganization of society.

The contrast between the two lists remains, however, for they express agreement between the two sides: both sets of findings are interesting to students of society, and both should be of some help to anyone who wishes to improve the quality of living; as well as disagreement: the first list could be much more easily put to immediate political use as the basis of an attack on the status quo.

It is not enough, however, to clarify the areas of conflict, and I stated earlier that I wish to suggest steps for reducing its intensity. To understand better the utility of those steps, it seems worthwhile to review briefly both what a value judgment is, and the junctures or phases of social inquiry where they *necessarily* enter which affect the final report.

Philosophers have argued for at least two millennia as to whether value assertions can be proved. The question bristles with technical difficulties, notably the metaphysical impossibility of ultimately *proving* that even physical science actually proves its propositions. Philosophers and scientists generally hold that it is possible to work out designs of proof for empirical judgments. By contrast, few recent philosophers have held that proofs of value judgments are logically equivalent.

In sociological terms, this has meant that researchers may agree on sets of procedures for proving that certain events actually happened. For example, a pointer moves two millimeters over a measured time period; the mercury in a thermometer rises a certain distance; an object has moved in space from point X to point Y; a sample of respondents have expressed certain opinions; and so on.

By contrast, few philosophers or scientists argue that procedures exist by which it is possible to prove that "God is good"; "human beings are inherently evil"; or that "Mozart is a greater musician than Vivaldi." Of course, this is only a persuasive negative argument, not a compelling one.

On the other hand, philosophers and scientists believe that statements of that type are not really descriptions of events "out there" in space and time, not equivalent to the reporting of a conversation, or the description of divorce rates over time. Instead, they are expressions of the speaker's *values*. These expressions simply report preferences, attitudes, norms, or wishes. That is to say, value judgments are statements that do not even require empirical proof, because they are self-evident (a person reporting his own feelings doubtless knows what they are). If instead we suppose that they can be derived from other, firmer conclusions, and we try to elicit them by asking why, the answer turns out to be still another value principle. (For example, we should teach our children not to kill, because human life is sacred.) If we stubbornly persist in this kind of questioning, we shall not find an empirical proposition as the ultimate root of the original value judgment. The ultimate response must be, "because it is right, or good, or evil, or beautiful."

Since so much of social science has been charged with lack of objectivity, its practitioners have been at great pains to work out procedures for empirically demonstrating its conclusion. Thus, they have felt it necessary to clarify the distinction between value judgments (for instance, nazism is bad; democracy is good; the elite should be allowed to rule, and so forth); and the findings drawn from empirical procedures about which honest observers could agree, that is, with respect to which procedures should be used, and whether they justify the summary results (for example, there is a general inverse correlation between class position and divorce rate; people who have not made up their minds about a political contest are less likely to listen to political propaganda than are partisans of either side; plays that have been denounced by New York City critics have a lower chance of a long Broadway run than plays that have been praised by those critics).

The distinction is not, of course, between "correct" conclusions and wrong ones. Sociologists believed until recently that divorce was more common among the upper social strata, but this proposition was simply incorrect for the twentieth century, not a value judgment.

The distinction can perhaps be elucidated by noting how one can "transform" a value judgment into an empirical one, by specifying research operations for approximating a test of the (transformed) value judgment. In each case, however, the content is also changed, thus indicating once more that the distinction is grounded in reality, not in our prejudices.

For example, the value judgment, "Mozart is a greater composer than Vivaldi," could be tested by using the consensus among music critics as an operational index of "greatness." Thus, if most music critics agree that Mozart is the greater composer, the value assertion is proved. Unfortunately, most of those critics would also assert that the original statement actually means something else. So it does, but that fact only emphasizes the distinction once more.

We can similarly transform the assertion that psychotherapy is "better" than prison for heroin addicts, by defining "better" to mean a lower rate of return to addiction. If that rate is lower when addicts receive psychotherapy than when they are merely confined in a federal prison, we can "prove" our value assertion. Nevertheless, without some such transformation into an agreed upon procedure, the assertion that something is "better" is merely an expression of our preferences.

Similarly, we could transform the statement, "it is less sinful to lie than to steal; to steal than to kill," by weighing the amount of public disapproval that each act evokes, or its consequences, or its economic costs to society. But in the transformation, the notion of sinfulness is lost—again, an indication of how real is the distinction between the value assertion and the empirical proposition.

The idea that it is "better" to consult with underlings before making decisions, or to permit subordinates to help make decisions may also be changed by comparing the observable results of decision-making both with and without consultation. Again, only if we *like* the consequences of participation can we say it is "better." By contrast, the consequences themselves are empirically observable.

It is obvious that even if we can agree on these transformations, and on the data that flow from them, we might still disagree honestly with others who dislike those consequences. Transforming a value judgment does not erase the epistemological distinction between it and an empirical description, since the translation also changes its meaning. If we object to that loss, the translation does not help.

Because sociologists after the turn of the century aimed increasingly at creating a science, and establishing a claim to objectivity, they expressed far fewer value judgments in their technical monographs and reports. A comparison of articles or books written fifty years ago with those of today shows that value judgments do not now appear as often in the descriptions and analyses published in standard journals. The researcher simply presents the relationships he has found, typically without expressing his attitudes about them.

Moreover, sociologists are now much quicker to recognize expressions of such preference in the work of others. These are likely to be viewed as a gratuitous intrusion; they lie outside the realm of what can be agreed upon by observers. Thus, everyone is entitled to his or her own evaluation.

Nevertheless, insistence on the distinction is far removed from the notion of value neutrality in sociology. We must avoid any confusion between (a) insisting that the distinction can and should be made and (b) supposing that science of any kind *is* free from evaluations or value judgments. The question is not so much whether one can make science without evaluations (for one cannot) as it is how to recognize when and where they are *inevitably* made, and how to prevent them from undermining the objectivity of scientific findings at those points. If these evaluations cause us to avoid important problems, to omit or change crucial data to fit our hopes, or to ignore logically valid empirical conclusions which arise from our data, then we must be able to recognize them immediately. Nevertheless, such an awareness need not be confused with the literally impossible "ideal" (defended by no one) that there be no evaluations in science.

Perhaps the best way to locate those points is to take note of the many aspects or areas of scientific work where evaluations are unavoidable. They are many, because making science or engaging in scientific research is a *social* activity, and it is therefore shot through with evaluations at every phase. In noting those areas, we are only restating facts that seem obvious upon examination but are often overlooked in the current debate. The participants sometimes appear to believe that Max Weber asserted that sociology should be or could be "value-free"; to the contrary, he himself spelled out over half a century ago many of the ways by which these evaluations do in fact enter the activity of social analysis.[16]

We can begin with a set of assumptions that cannot be technically called "value judgments," although they *are* nonempirical judgments. They form the epistemological and ontological assumptions upon which all science must be based. These have been the subject of endless discussions among philosophers ever since men began to wonder whether it is even possible to achieve valid empirical knowledge—perhaps ever since people first sat around a fire hundreds of thousands of years ago, and wondered aloud which of several divergent stories by their kinsmen they should believe. Each of them has been questioned by numerous philosophers on good grounds, and though the average man takes them all for granted, they cannot be proved by any procedure that critical judgment could accept.

Most fundamental is the belief that the world of objective reality actually exists. Equally important is the belief that somehow we can come to know this world. One might agree that it does exist, but assert that there is no way by which we can know it. In theological arguments, of course, this distinction looms large: we might well suppose the existence of supernatural or divine worlds, which we cannot know in this life.

Another basic assumption is that we can know this world through our *senses*. It is not enough to try to deduce it, to intuit it, or to interpret divine texts, as a way of understanding it. Scientists do assume that there are no ways of knowing this world except through the senses or through their extensions, the sensing instruments that we invent. Scientists also assume some order or regularity in this outside world. Moreover, these phenomena will occur in a space-time framework, and they are related causally.[17]

Still more complex assumptions could be adduced about the empirical status of deduction, and the type of real world that will be found by science (for example, most scientists believe that when valid relationships are discovered, they are likely to be esthetically "elegant" as well as correct) but here we are not attempting to summarize all of these beliefs. We are asserting that anyone engaging in scientific work must begin with a great number of unprovable assumptions. Whether one would wish to call them "value judgments" because they do in fact express preferences, or instead call them ontological guesses, is a technical matter that need not detain us here.

Scientific work interacts with evaluations at the most fundamental level, through the impact of the culture itself upon the development of science. Most value systems in the great historic cultures have given only modest support to rigorous empirical investigation. Post-Reformation Western society is a rare example of one whose values have firmly endorsed some type of objective inquiry into empirical phenomena.

Even within that general support, however, cultural patterns or values give higher priority to some areas than to others. Until the late nineteenth century, Western society supported research in chemistry and physics far more enthusiastically than in the biological sciences. It has not as yet given as much support to social science, though the tradition of social science is as old as that of physical science.

To the extent that general values of the society support scientific research, individuals growing up within the culture accept those values and will come to be motivated to engage in it. Thus scientists come to share that commitment to the general value of science and, of course, to enjoy the social prestige as well as self-satisfaction that they derive from participating in that enterprise.

Consequently, a wide array of goals can be achieved by dedication to science which might otherwise be satisfied by other occupations. That is, they are able to enjoy their work and at the same time satisfy *other* value preferences (friendship, prestige, travel, new experiences).

Although in an advanced scientific field important problems are usually generated by ambiguities or problems in previous research, people may engage in science for a wide range of other motivations. A sociologist may study juvenile delinquency because of the adventures of his own adolescence, or because he wishes to understand his own life history better. Or he may enjoy the titillation that is to be found in doing research on sexual behavior. These evaluations *may or may not* affect the validity of his findings. That question is separate from the ways his motivations or value preferences have affected his choice of problem.

It is equally evident that not only may the values of the larger society guide the selection of a problem, just as those of the individual may direct research, but that specific evaluations may also be a *source of hypotheses*. For example, given the generally liberal value preferences of social scientists, it is not surprising that their research has emphasized the effects of social environment (rather than heredity) on the creation and support of criminality; that they have looked carefully for evidence that a "democratic" type of work or social structure is not only more pleasant to live in but is also more productive; that they have documented in great detail the oppression of blacks in the United States; but because they object to its use have by and large ignored the possible efficacy of force in human relations.

Such a liberal bias in the framing of hypotheses may or may not have weakened the design of proof used by these social scientists for many decades. By and large, we suppose that the answer is no. Since most of their conclusions (however correct) seemed to fly in the face of common sense, and since they typically encountered an unbelieving lay audience, they were forced to develop better technical procedures for proving their liberal hypotheses.

Thus far, we have commented only on how evaluations support science and shape the choice of problems within it. This does not, however, exhaust the points at which value judgments necessarily enter and affect scientific work. Far less obvious, but perhaps equally pervasive, is a set of ethical judgments that might together be called the "ethic of science."

Essentially scientists believe it is good to know, or better to know than not to know. It is embodied in many normative judgments of scientists about one another's work, and is passed on to the younger generation of scientists during their training. It is expressed as scorn or praise for other scientists. It includes an organized skepticism toward not only the work of others, but one's own work, and a moral imperative to change one's conclusions if new facts arise to disprove them.

Under the pitiless publicity of repeated studies—far more common in the physical sciences—few men succumb to the temptation of faking or fudging data. The norm is a strong one. Scientists who hide their data or who do not publish it are viewed askance, and indeed most scientists have not been willing to work on projects that forbid publication unless they are rewarded for contributing to a national cause. Scientists feel violated when they are not permitted to publish data, or when a political regime distorts their findings.

Similarly, scientists generally feel that they are under a moral imperative to protest against political policies that destroy or prevent the development of scientific inquiry. In this last case, of course, the norm is congruent with their personal stake in the enterprise, but it is also an ethical belief as well.

With the growth of social science, human ingenuity in devising studies and experiments has created a new set of moral problems, where new codes of ethics are required. The ethical imperative to find out sometimes conflicts with the need to respect the integrity or even the health of experimental subjects. Under conditions of extreme psychological stress, subjects may have temporary breakdowns. Scientists may probe into private matters, and create anxieties in their subjects or even may expose them to reprisals. Unobtrusive means of surveillance and observation—spying of various kinds —now used routinely by government agencies, are also available to social scientists.[18] Social scientists may be tempted to violate the privacy of their human subjects. Social scientists have gone far in such violations of privacy, personal integrity, and health over the past two decades, and within recent years the fields of psychology, anthropology, and sociology have all developed codes of ethics in an effort to lay down rules controlling those violations.

Perhaps value judgments affect scientific work most obviously in the preferences expressed for one kind of inquiry over another. Such comments are routine in informal discussions. They are less often stated in publications. Some types of problems are considered chic or important. For example, studies of "power" are rated more important than studies of leisure activities.

Some types of results are preferred to others: for example, solutions in the form of equations or formulas, or at least as coefficients or correlation. Elegance of writing is preferred to clearly expressed analyses without grace. Some research designs are thought of as neat while others are viewed as crude or inexcusably sloppy.[19] The constant ranking of scientists by each other is based on these and other value preferences.

Science and values interact in yet another way: scientific findings can be used as tools to implement values; that is to say, to the extent that valid conclusions are reached, they may be used in the service of policies. Society does demand solutions to certain kinds of problems, and salaries are paid to men who claim to have adequate solutions. For example, a sociologist might attempt to analyze the foundations of white racism and suggest empirical means for reducing it. Social psychologists have devoted hundreds of studies to the question of how to teach disadvantaged children more adequately.

Without question, those who wield the greatest power and influence in society are best able to use any scientific findings, and typically are better able to use them in the service of their own values.[20] They can give more rewards to social scientists who offer adequate solutions to *their* problems. On the other hand, not only do they rarely do so (except in industry and business), but findings that are useful only for so narrow a set of preferences ordinarily arouse far more criticism from other social scientists and far less prestige than findings that can be applied more widely. Nevertheless, given this link between science as an instrument and the evaluations of the powerful men who support science, it cannot be surprising that political critics may denounce some work as "research for hire," rather than "pure science."

Finally, scientists can study evaluations themselves. Indeed a good part of social psychology, market research, political sociology—and as noted earlier, a large part of all questionnaire research—has been devoted to the analysis of evaluations. It must be emphasized that the conclusions are not value judgments; they are rather empirical judgments *about* value judgments. That is to say, they describe as objectively as possible what these values are, not what they ought to be.

The study of evaluations can go further, because it can locate and describe the value tensions between groups that try to achieve different goals. It may also point out (as Weber noted) the contradictions among different values. For example, the major theme of Myrdal's *An American Dilemma* is precisely the contradiction between the egalitarian values of white people in American society and their prejudice against blacks.

The relationships between value judgments and science have been well known to social scientists for many years. The conclusions of scientific work must aim at empirical descriptions and analyses which should be irrelevant to what scientists want or prefer. Indeed, if a supposedly scientific inquiry can be adequately attacked by the charge that the sociologist is using it simply to support his values, then we must conclude that the work itself was poorly designed and inadequate as science.

To insist, however, that the distinction between value judgment and empirical judgment is a valid one, but to sketch out the many points at which evaluations are an inherent part of day-to-day scientific work, leaves us with a further step in elucidation. The question is how we can prevent the inevitable evaluations in sociology from distorting our results. The problem can be phrased in a still more pragmatic way: which types of value judgments are most likely to shape our findings in ways that are not easy to discern? It is to this problem that we must apply our critical acumen in the next decade of debate about these issues.

Let us consider it by noting again some of the phases of research where we know values shape our decisions. Often we may be attracted to study a problem area because money is available, a senior professor asks for help, we wish to contribute to social welfare, or for many other reasons. It is not likely, however, that our values create much political or scientific bias at the outset; we have not yet narrowed our research to a set of hypotheses.

At some point, we begin to consider various sites, specific places where we plan to look for our data. We can study class relations in a bordello, criminality in a machine shop, or family behavior in a Greek neighborhood. But, although the chances of bias increase, they are not likely to be great, and in any event they are likely to be visible.

Biases of evaluation can also enter at the later phases of research design, technique, and analysis, but in these areas social critics are sharp and not easily fooled, whatever their political stance. If a researcher wants to know whether old people would like an increase in government payments to the aged, but he samples (as one did) only the elderly with adequate incomes, his critics will be quick to laugh or scorn. If he asks leading public opinion questions, such as "Don't you believe that . . . ?" we label him amateurish. If he refers to "big differences," but his subjects are too few to tolerate any test of significance, we do not take his findings seriously. If he asserts a strong causal link but his coefficient of correlation is only 0.1 to 0.2, we view that as a triumph of optimism over technical weakness.

In short, it is especially in a researcher's design of proof, sampling, data-gathering, and later statistical analysis that we see less likelihood of values or wishes dominating objective description, because that part of the social science structure is open to inspection and critics can easily perceive its weaknesses. If unconscious deviations from objectivity occur they are quickly uncovered. It would be foolish to favor a particular political position at these phases of research, since the biases will be highly visible, and the researcher would earn the contempt of his colleagues.

It is at the stage of framing the basic research questions that political bias most easily enters, and is most difficult to detect. It is especially difficult to detect because many questions with implicit bias are also legitimate empirical problems whose answers are not yet certain. Yet these questions may seem (to at least part of the socio-

logical audience) to be generated by a wish to find a politically motivated answer. The following are examples of such questions:

> Do blacks have genetically an average I.Q. lower than that
> of whites?

> Do military leaders of coups modernize more rapidly and
> effectively than civilian ones do?

> Do dissident student leaders (or, in an earlier decade, Com-
> munists) have more personality or psychological problems
> than nondissidents?

> Do children whose mothers work grow up with more person-
> ality problems than children whose mothers do not work, and
> is there more family conflict in such homes?

> Are members of the lower classes less in favor of civil liberties
> than members of the middle classes?

> What are the best techniques of counterinsurgency?

> Which are the traits or qualities of the lower classes that pre-
> vent them from coping adequately with problems they con-
> front daily?

It must be emphasized that such investigations need not be biased
at all, and if well designed, their findings could help us to understand social behavior better. Moreover, mainstream sociologists
would argue correctly that if the work is adequately done, and the
findings are fruitful, they do not in themselves become either "conservative" or "radical." There is no such thing as "valid leftist science" any more than there is "leftist genetics" or "rightist physics"
—although some totalitarian governments have so claimed. Marx
himself, as we know, drew heavily on bourgeois social science data
and theories in his work. Moreover, his predictions may in fact have
been put to use by *conservative* regimes. One can argue that some of the
liberal legislation pushed through by Bismarck was in part supported by the fears aroused by Marxist analyses.

Nevertheless, such an answer is not sufficient, so long as sociology
so often fails to consider research whose findings could be used by
the poor or the downtrodden, as a knowledge base for gaining advan-

tages in the system, just as managers use the findings of industrial sociologists. Little research has been devoted in the last two decades to understanding how white racism might be diminished, how the upper strata or elite manipulate the system in their own favor, which elements in the power structure are most vulnerable to attack and change, what the consequences of a different distribution of privilege and income might be, and so on. Such questions might be of more help to the disadvantaged, and would more clearly disclose how the social system does in fact operate.

Suggested Steps for Minimizing Biases. Because it is technically difficult to prove such biases and distortions, whether on the Right or Left, perhaps it would be wise to work out ways of minimizing them. A first step would be to recognize that (1) all research and analysis is affected at various points by the evaluations of the men who produce it, whether or not their values agree with our own and (2) even when we object to the implicit value position of any researcher, we must recognize that he has the right to take a value position diverging from our own. He may not have sold out at all.

All sides however must also recognize that the distinction between an evaluation and an empirical description is valid and that confusion between the two only leads to muddled thinking. Even if we disagree with a researcher's findings our concern should not be that they violate some wishes of ours; our grounds for attack must rather be that his findings are invalid, or that they are of no consequence. That is, the first question to be asked about a reported finding or relationship is, Is it correct? and the second is, Is it important? It is intellectually lazy merely to ask whether we like his politics or value preferences.

It should also be recognized, especially by more conservative sociologists, that a researcher may express his indignation without at all undermining his empirical findings. If he feels so moved, he has the right, and many would argue the duty as well, to announce his outrage at the processes and data he discovers. He does not distort his findings by doing so or even by making policy suggestions for change.

To the extent that both sides accept the fundamental distinction between these two kinds of activities, there will be much less confusion. Sociologists should become much more conscious of their own evaluations, at every phase of research. As we encounter the pervasive effect of evaluations in every aspect of scientific activity, we must engage in a process of self-discovery, to ascertain what our values are, and how they affect the decisions we are making. Since many of these decisions are made by a team of researchers, it should be possible to record them, making explicit their evaluational bases. Presumably we would thereby at least become aware of the points at which the ultimate report has been shaped by values whose effect might otherwise be undiscovered.

However, self-criticism is like self-psychotherapy: it is a noble calling to which most of us should aspire but at which only few can succeed. *Our* values are so "true and right" that we are often not conscious of them at all. They are simply part of the natural order of things. Thus we are often not aware that we have indeed expressed our evaluations in the course of a research project.

On the other hand, as sociologists we know that people are more likely to improve their choice of problems and of research designs if they are praised for their good research and dispraised for the bad. Indeed, that effect is already visible in contemporary sociological research, as a response to the strong attacks on the work of the past two decades. Radical student and colleague criticism on both particular projects and the general thrust of sociological inquiry have altered substantially the kinds of investigation now approved among sociologists. It is not merely that universities and individuals have moved away from classified or military projects. They have also responded to pressures to engage in far more studies of conflict, power, police behavior, riots, exploitation of the poor, and revolution. In addition, far more are engaging in policy research designed to implement some of the range of proposals offered by the politics of the Left.

Thus it might be wise to inaugurate a policy of requiring that reviews and critiques of research comment routinely on the implicit evaluations made in the course of the research, from first formulation to final conclusions. Perhaps authors should also be asked to include such an analysis of their values and evaluations in their reports, as an aid to understanding what they have been doing, just as we expect descriptions of their research procedures. We should not conceal these judgments any more than we hide the analytic techniques we have used to order and understand our statistical tables.

Whether we must all accept in addition the moral responsibility of being preachers and reformers, as well as scientists, I believe should be left to each man's choice. In any event, I know of few sociologists who have not accepted that responsibility at times and that responsibility belongs to every citizen, no matter what his occupation.

However, the two kinds of action are different, and require different skills. One can be a great preacher and political leader without much talent at social research, just as some good social scientists can write popular books while others cannot. It would be wasteful of skill and manpower to drop any of our scientific inquiry in order to devote most of our energies to reform or revolution.

It is not clear that either reform or revolution would be speeded up substantially if all sociologists were to bend most of their energies to those tasks. If the population and its leaders have listened so little to their critical findings in the past, they are not likely to be persuaded more easily if sociologists become prophets and preachers. It is even possible that the work of prophecy and sermonizing, or reform or radical change, would be furthered as much by excellent empirical sociology as by such a diversion of energies.

In any event, sociological research is valuable in its own right— and this, too, is a value judgment. Since I also believe that many of the great social problems of our time can at best be ameliorated, not eliminated; that we do not yet have the scientific knowledge to solve any of them in more than a very modest degree; and since my own values rank sociological inquiry very high, I would urge that sociologists continue to help solve these problems—but I would urge that most of us (not being talented as reform leaders) can best use our intellectual resources by pushing beyond our present horizons of social science.

3. *Functionalism: The Empty Castle*

PERHAPS THE MOST ASTONISHING INTELLECTUAL PHENOMENON IN CONTEMPORARY SOCIOLOGY IS THE CONTINUING, PERHAPS INCREASING, attack on functionalism. Two decades after Merton published the most widely read analysis of functionalism, much of it both an attack on the weaknesses of Malinowski's and Radcliffe-Brown's versions and an exposure of the false issues in the debate about functionalism, and the rest devoted to an exposition of the important questions *any* sociologist must raise in an adequate scientific analysis, antifunctionalists still attack him as the *defender* of precisely the version he assaulted. A decade after Davis effectively argued that functionalism in any version accepted by contemporary sociologists is indistinguishable from sociology itself, the polemic continues unabated or even more bitter.[1]

All this might be viewed simply as the normally slow adjustment of a field to correction. This issue was acidly debated in the 1920's and 1930's. Perhaps another generation is needed to erase all interest in the issue. Much more astonishing, however, is that the attacks continue without rejoinder. Here is a polemic, a debate, without any response from those attacked. Surely it is a prime indicator of a false issue that no one defends functionalism. Is there no one inside the castle against which these engines of war are mounted?

One might also ask, why does a "theory" that is so patently erroneous, to judge by the attacks on it, survive so long? Both of these ways of stating the problem, it is clear, turn away from the question of what is fruitful or not in functionalism, and suggest the sociological question—pejoratively it might be called *ad hominem*—as to what are the social characteristics of the attackers and presumed defenders who create this curious spectacle.

The bitterest attacks are mounted by politically dissident sociologists, old or young, for reasons already noted in Chapters 1 and 2. However, whatever their political stance, their main arguments are intellectual, and should be answered in those terms. Some critics are philosophers of science, like Carl G. Hempel, Ernest Nagel, and Dorothy Emmet, who have simply not read enough in the field to understand the issues.[2] On the other hand, some critics are not politically dissident, but continue the debate because they believe it contains problems of theory that remain obscure. Most sociologists, by contrast, do not concern themselves with the problem from one day to the next, because they are trying to solve real problems in sociological analysis. Confronted with problems posed by their data, they correctly perceive that whether they should be classed as "functionalists" is of no consequence.

With respect to all of these groups, since our aim is not *ad hominem* comments, however they may be disguised as the sociology of knowledge, but the fashioning of better theoretical tools, it seems more productive to lay bare the intellectual issues in this debate. Perhaps we can thereby alter both the intensity and the direction of the polemic.

First, if we accept Merton's useful distinction between a sociological orientation and theory proper, there is no separate body of hypotheses within sociology that could be called *functional theory*. That some writers once labeled themselves "functional theorists" and others believed that they espoused that theory, is merely folk categorization and does not prove that functional theory exists as a distinctive enterprise. As a sociological orientation, functionalism has had considerable impact, for it did indicate the "types of variables which are somehow to be taken into account," but it has not specified "determinate relationships between particular variables."[3]

Functionalism has offered a "context of inquiry," an approach, a way of looking at social realities, but it was never a specific structure of empirical propositions. Indeed, it is that very looseness that makes it an easy target for all manner of diverse and even contradictory attacks, and correspondingly it cannot be overthrown by a simple, contrary empirical finding.

Similarly, such a general orientation is difficult to state precisely; there is likely to be great disagreement as to what it "really" is. Objective analysis of functionalism will continue to be rare if both sides point to a different set of ideas. For example, if one group attacks all those who believe that every social trait is functional, that is, contributes to the continuation of society as it is, but no one defends the principle being attacked; or if one side sneers at those who assert that any society is a harmonious whole and who deny conflict, and no one comes forward to defend such an assertion, we are bound to concede that either the attacks are ritual exercises in the service of social solidarity among an undefined network, or at best that some analysts are being mislabeled.

Clarity might be served by sketching some of the history of functionalism as it gradually took shape after the turn of the century. Perhaps then we might discover, if not what functionalism *really* is, at least what people are attacking.

Like all intellectual movements in the social sciences—and even specific theories in the physical sciences, as Merton has so cogently demonstrated—functionalism was not the product of a single mind, nor did it appear on a certain date.[4] Often, it is only later that we can see that a mode of thought was emerging from a diffuse range of writings on a certain problem. For this reason the question, what is *real* functionalism? must be translated into such questions as: What did people called functionalists say they were doing? What were they really doing? (Malinowski's analyses, for example, are very different from his statements of what functionalism is.) And to whom was the label *then applied* and how has that changed?

Two decades ago, in considering the question: who was the first functionalist? I answered that he "was very likely the first man who ever thought systematically and somewhat objectively about human society."[5] That statement was based upon the view that functionalism was most fundamentally a mode of thought which studied the links or interconnections among various areas or forces of social action. The work in which that statement appeared exemplified this approach by showing how action in such institutional areas as political power, economic production and allocation, and the family were tied with religious behavior: it represented at least a *minimal* statement of what functionalists have been *doing* from the time of World War I, whatever they said they were doing. In going on to assert that "almost all good current sociology is functionalist," I was following not only my own view of the core mode of thinking in the functionalist orientation, but also that of the much wiser Robert Lowie, who asserted that functionalism ". . . studies several aspects of culture closely intertwined and influencing one another," and also asserts that "probably everywhere scholars have followed this practice intuitively."[6]

Lowie's gentle comment does not reflect the bitterness of the debate in the 1920's and 1930's between those who labeled themselves functionalists and others. A brilliant polemicist like Malinowski could assert that functionalism represented a new departure, a move forward from old-fashioned anthropology, but men like Boas, Kroeber, and Lowie took a position which is almost standard with reference to the appearance of any relatively new mode of thought: whatever is good in it is what excellent analysts have always done and its more extreme statements were simply wrong.

However, behind that period of a generation ago lies a perhaps equally important phase of intellectual history that sets the stage for both the contemporary polemic and that of the recent past: the rise of evolutionism and the reappearance of organicism. Of course, if my answer to the question of who was the first functionalist is even remotely correct, the most fundamental origin of functionalism is the insight, which some unnamed campfire philosopher reached thousands of years ago, that a human society is something like an animal, an organism: it lives in an environment, it must battle the elements and ward off its enemies; it can be destroyed; its various parts have profound impact upon one another; it must be fed and it must produce offspring; and so forth. Even Spencer, who phrased this analogy a century ago, recognized that it contains many dangers and errors. For example, strictly speaking, there is no brain in the society; it is not a single organism, and parts of the society may break off to form a wholly self-subsistent new one; and so on. Nevertheless, the analogy has been fruitful for sociological thought and perhaps is usually fruitful before its dangers become serious. Needless to say, this insight is constantly rediscovered (for example, as in communications theory and cybernetics).

Its reappearance in the writings of the early 1920's based mainly on field work analysis in the previous decade,[7] was structured by the spectacular importance of evolutionist theory during the nineteenth century for most schools of sociological thought. Let us consider the intellectual situation at the turn of the century when men like Radcliffe-Brown and Malinowski grew to maturity.

The publication of *The Origin of Species* in 1859 nicely illustrates the notion that nothing is so powerful as an idea whose time has come. Not only was the first printing of this tedious book quickly sold out, but it immediately became the center of a raging controversy. There is hardly a work in the general field of sociology during the succeeding half-century that was not shaped to some extent by evolutionism.

The intellectual ground had been prepared for this work by nearly a century of speculation and hard scientific work on evolution. Among the many topics which that restless poet-scientist Goethe thought about was evolution, and he even offered several interpretations of changes in structure and function, such as the gradual evolution of a flower from leaves or the development of the brain from spinal nerves. Darwin's grandfather, Erasmus Darwin, himself published a small work on evolution. Philosopher-sociologists like Saint-Simon and Comte presented with great eloquence their versions of societal and human evolution. Even Darwin's specific ideas were independently discovered by Wallace, thus precipitating Darwin into publication.

Evolutionary thought in social science was reinforced by the much more adequate development of paleontology, which in the work of men like Lyell and Cuvier, or even for that matter Louis Agassiz, slowly built a body of knowledge about the succession of life forms on the planet.

A decade after the publication of *The Origin of Species*, Tylor also presented a "technique" for tracing the origins of social patterns, that of survivals. That is, if we find a social trait that seems not to be of much use, or to be somewhat ambiguous in its meaning, we can treat it as if it were a fossil from a prior age, and thus retrace the history of man. For example, if we find that when a bride's relatives make a ritual show of resistance when her future husband's relatives come to her hut to "take her away," we might infer that once upon a time these people actually engaged in wife capture.[8] This pseudo-solution to the problem of discovering the past was widely accepted for decades.

For our purposes it is not necessary to outline the evolutionist ideas of the last half of the nineteenth century, since what evolved is now fairly well known.[9] With some disagreement in detail, social seers postulated a unilinear evolutionary series of societal types. This was viewed by many as the gradual unfolding of rationality and thus, as Durkheim described the intellectual movement at the end of the century, the disappearance of magic and religion together with an increase in human happiness. The social patterns of contemporary Europe were viewed as the culmination of man's rise from the primordial slime. Stone Age men, when found here and there on the earth's surface, were supposed to have evolved little, so that one could learn about Paleolithic man from studying these modern but primitive remnants. There arose, in short, a powerful set of ideas which could be used to order and interpret almost all of the range of human behavior as it was then reported. These ideas could explain not only the variations in social patterns, but also the changes of the past and present. Moreover, they found, at least apparently, confirmation of their hypotheses in good biological data.

For reasons that (as far as I know) have not been traced, this grand unilinear evolutionary scheme suffered a catastrophic debacle at the turn of the century. It is not so much that a new group of leaders arose who destroyed it by presenting irrefutable data, as that with the growing body of information about contemporary nations and contemporary tribes, the theory as a whole seemed to be hollow and insubstantial.

The results of this disillusionment for social thought were profound. In official anthropology, as a consequence, two major schools developed which self-consciously avoided large-scale theorizing. Both remained historical in emphasis, as anthropology had always been, and both expended much energy on the development of specific fact-gathering procedures. One of these was American ethnography, which in any event had always been characterized by a strong emphasis on meticulous fieldwork techniques, as exemplified in the publications of the Bureau of American Ethnography. Leaders such as Boas and later Kroeber, Lowie, Goldenweiser, and others discouraged grand theories, but set higher standards for technical skills and for tracing the history of a society. It was perhaps in this school that the settled conviction first grew that no one could be called a real anthropologist who had not lived among the natives.

Although the culture-diffusion or *Kulturkreis* school of Germany (and to a lesser extent, of England) was often charged with making grand speculations, the major emphasis of their work was on the exact, detailed, objective descriptions of the movement of social and cultural traits from one geographical area to another.[10] There was relatively little emphasis upon the inner emotional or social meaning of a given trait. The analytic work typically was done in the museum on large-scale collections of material objects (masks, shields, war clubs) or social traits, and interpretation could be based upon common sense or general rationality. It did not require seeing the world through native eyes.

Functionalism became a third reaction to the demise of evolutionism. Its leaders did engage in theorizing. However, they also emphasized extremely detailed field work, in which the analyst lived as much as possible with the tribe, and did not accept the reports of travelers, hunters, explorers, missionaries, and district commissioners as adequate descriptions of real social life. It also self-consciously avoided speculative reconstructions of the distant past.

By the time of World War I the field work had been completed on the first two classics of functionalism, which were published after the war was over. Malinowski and Radcliffe-Brown both had sharp words for one another later, since each viewed himself as the proper spokesman for functionalism, but their work initiated a new style of social analysis in anthropology. More important, that style of orientation was also developed in other fields of thought. At this early stage, functionalists did not draw any of their ideas from biology, and specifically not from the new developments in physiology at the end of the century. Their closest intellectual relatives were the classical scholars who were analyzing the place of religion in society, such as William Robertson Smith, and with the Durkheim group associated with *L'Année Sociologique*. On the other hand, they drew not at all (as far as I am able to ascertain) from Max Weber's writings.

I believe that the problem of tracing the transmission of ideas from one man to another is much more difficult than has commonly been supposed, and especially so when they overlap somewhat in time.[11] It is worth noting, however, that it is during this period, about the time of World War I, that Parsons claims a convergence of thought occurred in the ideas of Vilfredo Pareto, Emile Durkheim, and Max Weber, which he labels "voluntarism," and whose main structural elements would in fact have been accepted by the early functionalists.

Sociologists have increasingly relegated Malinowski's "theoretical" writings to the dust, and justly so. His programmatic statements about functionalism during the 1920's and 1930's aroused great ire and are not now viewed as important theoretical analyses. However his field reports have always been viewed as excellent and sociologists continue to read them. Malinowski's work is a salutary warning to those who believe they have understood a man's "theory" when they have read what the man says about his own theory. If theory is a structure of empirical propositions, then we must find out what it is by reading the man's analyses, not his general assertions about theory and theorizing. The latter are likely to be "metasociology," or "what I think sociology would be like if there were sociology." In any event, a man is no more to be trusted when analyzing theoretically his own empirical work than a composer is when analyzing the musical structure of his own compositions. In both cases, we should check his statements by studying what he actually created.

I believe that considerable confusion in the contemporary debate about functionalism grows from precisely an overly great reliance upon "theoretical" statements by Radcliffe-Brown and Malinowski, and a footnote count in the writings of especially the antifunctionalists over the last twenty years would, I suspect, show a disproportionate percentage of references to the metatheories of these two men, rather than the wide range of the empirical work by these and other functionalists.[12] If we examine carefully the empirical work that was being done, that is, the analyses of field observations, I believe that the work of the self-labeled functionalists would exhibit (as conservative opponents like Lowie claimed) no great development of new theories that were different from the best work of other men. It does, however, contain certain new emphases of approach or orientation which distinguish the "new" work of thirty years ago from the old.

Readers can check this difference in emphasis by comparing the reports in the Bureau of American Ethnology series, or the work of Boas on the Kwakiutl, Lowie on the Crow, Benedict on the Zuñi folktales, Kroeber on various California tribes, with Radcliffe-Brown on the Andaman Islanders, Malinowski on the Trobrianders, W. Lloyd Warner on the Murngin, the work of Hogbin, of Evans-Pritchard, and so on. I believe that these contrasts in style and approach can be summarized, though with the iteration that the differences are those of emphasis not radical divergence.[13]

1. Functional theory has paid less attention to the history of a given society, or to social change than did traditional anthropology and sociology. Explanations of social behavior were less often sought in "how it came to be" than in what is going on now."

2. In general, functionalist descriptions contained a higher ratio of social interaction as compared with descriptions of technology, artifacts or external descriptions of rituals, than did traditional social analysts.

3. Thus, functionalists reported more informal social behavior, including courtship, play, jokes, and the like, as well as nonrational behavior.

4. Functionalists were more likely to analyze the meaning of rituals, symbols, dances, objects, and so on from the viewpoint of the believer rather than that of the European observer. The social behavior was interpreted through the feelings and values of the persons observed, not the external observer.

5. They also emphasized individual differences more strongly, and even deviations from the supposed "standard way." It should be kept in mind that this was not a radical departure from earlier work.

6. Functionalists emphasized far more the unity of the entire social structure, and especially the interrelations among

subgroups of the society or subareas of social interaction (power and property, religion and power, kinship and property, and the like).

7. Funtionalists attempted, more than traditional social analysts, to locate the interconnections among parts of the social structure of which the members of that society are somewhat less aware: for example, the classical interpretation by Malinowski of the Trobriand use of magic in open sea fishing, which is contingent and dangerous, but not in lagoon fishing; thus, the fishermen will feel more secure and be more competent in open sea fishing than they would otherwise be, although their conscious explanation is, of course, a belief in the reality of magic. That is, Malinowski tries to connect two kinds of fishing with magic and contingency, a relationship the Trobrianders did not perceive.

With the exception of certain special subfields, such as ecology, demography, or the "culturology" of Leslie A. White, functionalist emphases have come to pervade much of modern sociology. It is also evident that in the early part of the century such emphases began to appear in a wide range of investigations such as the economic history of Beard, the sociological economics of Thorstein Veblen, the reconstructions of the ancient world by Gilbert Murray, Jane Ellen Harrison, and Francis Cornford, the muckraking of Lincoln Steffens, or (not typically labeled "functionalist") the field studies done later by the Chicago School (*The Jackroller, The Professional Thief, The Gang*, and so forth).

In their actual analyses of social behavior, the functionalists (along with many other social scientists) were the first to exhibit these differences in emphasis. It is clear, however, that modern sociologists who now think of themselves as antifunctionalists also utilize this same theoretical orientation and indeed in their empirical work are simply not distinguishable in their theoretical stance from their presumed functionalist opponents.[14] Consequently, we face once more the problem of labeling: what is "real" functionalism?

The issue can be clarified somewhat by listing the main traits of functionalist theory as given by *anti*functionalists. The contrast with the above list is striking. Functionalists, we are told, believe that:

1. Society is a functional unity, internally consistent and harmonious, so that its culturally supported activities contribute to the existence of the whole society (as well as to the people living in it).

2. "All standardized social or cultural forms have positive functions."[15]

3. All the social patterns and customs, the cultural forms and material objects are *indispensable*, all are needed for the functioning of the society.

4. The social system is a self-regulating organization that resists change (like a utopia) and, therefore, we need not investigate conflict, disharmony, alteration, or revolution.

5. Teleological reasoning is acceptable in functional analysis: the end is the "cause" of the steps toward it. For example, not only do people create incest rules "in order to" prevent family role conflicts (for instance, father's role would conflict with that of lover in father-daughter incest), but the "social need" for such incest rules actually generates a force which creates such incest rules. Perhaps a comparable statement in evolutionary theory would be: vultures were created by Nature in order to get rid of corpses.

6. We have explained both the origin and the continuation of a social pattern if we can show it "contributes to the continued existence of the society."

The second list clears up one mystery, why the functionalists (if there is a group so labeling themselves) do not defend themselves against antifunctionalist attacks. It would be difficult to locate any sizable group of social scientists—they must constitute a reasonable number if they are to be called a "school"—who would accept those principles. To find anyone who espouses the first three, one would have to go back a generation to catch Malinowski or Radcliffe-Brown in a careless bit of writing. Even then, however, as Merton has shown, most such statements are followed or preceded by some qualification or redefinition.

The fourth doctrine is a cliché, ever-renewed, that although societies do remain similar from one generation to the next, they are always in flux. That few sociologists made historical investigations (as noted in Chapter 1) from World War I until recently, or examined carefully the problems of long-term social change,[16] cannot be used as proof that they denied social systems change. Not a single sociologist of any eminence has argued against the importance or the reality of social change.

As to teleological reasoning, social analysts have often engaged in it somewhat, because even the wisest of men may be guilty of empirical error or poor logic, but certainly no contemporary social analyst would accept teleological reasoning as valid, unless it is precisely limited to the cybernetic model of feedback in which an approach toward a given goal does in fact shape the further steps toward that goal.[17] An example of such teleological reasoning is exposed in George C. Homans's and David M. Schneider's *Marriage, Authority and Final Causes*, in which they attack Lévi-Strauss's analysis of prescriptive mate choice in primitive societies. However, few people would concede, and certainly not the author being attacked, that Lévi-Strauss could therefore be categorized as a "functionalist."

Finally, for at least half a century, social scientists have accepted the general notion that to show the utility of any social pattern does not fully explain either how it originated or why it continues. By now everyone would concede that in order to explain how a social pattern continues we have to gather a great number of descriptive facts, among them who now benefits from the social pattern, the prior patterns of socialization, the contemporary resistances to it, and so on.

It might be difficult to test my own description of functionalism as it first appeared in the few actual analyses of men labeled "functionalists" a generation ago, but it would be comparatively easy to test the second list of supposed functionalist doctrines by footnote references in antifunctionalist literature: do they in fact cite specific pages in the works of contemporary sociologists who espouse such theoretical principles? The answer is no. It would also be easy to ascertain by simple mailed questionnaires whether any sizable number of sociologists would concede those principles. Any adequate investigation will show that the functionalism that it attacked by antifunctionalists has no defenders simply because no one accepts such a theoretical position.

The intellectual issues in this polemic are dead. The antifunctionalists have won: no one defends what they attack. However, they have also been outflanked: both they and their presumed opponents utilize the same theoretical orientation when they search for *empirical* links between real variables. Clearly, I am urging that the people historically called "functionalist" did not present any specific body of theories or hypotheses by which they could be set off from other sociologists, but did adopt a certain theoretical orientation that has become characteristic of most present day sociologists when they carry out empirical studies—whether they now call themselves functionalists or antifunctionalists. Their primary task—as Davis wrote with some exasperation, given the subject matter, the least they could do—is to relate the parts, elements, forces, or people of the society to the whole, and to one another. This is simply what any science does when it investigates its topic. No other task, problem, or theoretical stance, as it is visible or observable in actual empirical reports, can be found to characterize sociologists, and no other can be found to which people calling themselves "functionalists" would be willing to claim allegiance. They neither espouse nor defend the theoretical stances that antifunctionalists assert are their doctrines. Either the antifunctionalists have won or perhaps "functionalism" in that sense never existed.

Nevertheless, I do not believe this crucial test, that is, whether any group exists whose members accept such "functionalist" doctrines, is sufficient to convince antifunctionalists that there is no one in the castle, or to reduce the present intensity of feeling about this issue. Two further steps are needed, (1) to look at some of the political and intellectual issues that may underlie the present attacks on functionalism and (2) to suggest some concrete procedures for reducing the importance of the problem. Davis argued that attacks on functionalism were actually attacks on sociological analysis itself,[18] but apparently he thought they were based mainly on an intellectual preference for reductionist theoretical orientations (psychologism, technologism, economism, and the like), or on simple-minded empiricism, that is, a taste for "the facts." His suggestion can be improved, however, since it is now clear that sociological analysis, as a *theoretical* view, whether called "functionalist" or not, is not the target, for antifunctionalists do not differ much in their theoretical views: the target is the content of mainstream sociology. If that is so, and if (as I believe) some of their charges are correct, the future will be more cheerful, since presumably their own researches will correct the deficiencies of the past, and attacks against the empty castle will diminish.

If this transformation of the debate is correct, that it is not the theoretical orientation of "functionalism" or sociology itself that offends many, but (as suggested in Chapters 1 and 2) the very content of sociology over the past generation, our analytic task in this section is also easier. We are no longer puzzled by arguments against a theoretical position held by no one, since those arguments merely utilize the easy rhetoric of the day to mount attacks against the field as a whole. Moreover, and more important, it is not difficult to state what these deficiencies, errors, and failures in the content of sociology are. Finally, the answer to such attacks is not a defense of the field, but the creation of better sociology, and to this both the new critics and the older sociologists can make a contribution.

These criticisms are to a considerable extent politically motivated, expressing objections to the "conservatism" of sociological works, but their content is mainly intellectual: most dissident sociologists allege—correctly in my view—that sociological research viewed as social science is wanting in various ways. Often, they "explain" these deficiencies by charging that sociologists have failed because they have sold out, lacked intellectual or moral nerve, or were insufficiently radical. I believe that these explanations are false, but even if I am correct, their attacks on the intellectual worth of sociological findings still remain to be considered.

Let us consider the main charges. They can be noted briefly, since they contain a core of truth, and since a defense is not in order. The appropriate intellectual answer is not debate, but improvement in sociological research. In any event, since all are *partly* correct, the objective analyst could at best reply, "guilty, but with an explanation."

Let us first consider the central political accusation before looking at the main body of intellectual charges. Viewed against the present efflorescence of political radicalism, the content of sociology has been, on balance, conservative. Against that concession, it must however be granted (as I noted in Chapter 2) that sociologists have not gained any prestige from their colleagues by defending the status quo, by offering rationalizations for war, by expressing support for the capitalist economic system, or by showing that the elite rule us wisely and well. Indeed, no sociologists of any standing have taken such stances. Moreover, as even a cursory glance at a wide variety of subfields in sociology will show, sociologists have consistently attacked racism, have sympathetically described the deprivations of the poor, have shown how prisons generate more criminality, have exposed white-collar crime, and have analyzed the pathologies of bureaucracy: they have demonstrated that a great many social forces help to generate the very problems that the society officially claims it wishes to solve.

At a deeper level, moreover, as Berger and others have argued, sociology is a liberating discipline and is "subversive of established patterns of thought."[19] Its research reports inherently are exposés of dismaying situations and conditions, simply because almost any close-grained analysis of how things operate necessarily discloses circumstances and relationships that we deplore. By analyzing truly and rationally many of the values, norms, ideologies, and institutions of a society, sociology also undermines the faith and commitment that support those institutions.

Nevertheless, the charge of conservation is by and large correct, because "sociology is conservative in its implications for the institutional order."[20] Indeed, as suggested earlier, it may be that this very tension between its conservatism and its attacks on the status quo creates some part of the frustration and anger that is felt by many sociologists who now attack the field. On the one hand, sociology presents a vast array of descriptive data and relationships that call for reform or radical change, but on the other hand, its analyses suggest that only a modest amount of improvement is likely.

Sociology is conservative in content, in that it has long asserted that communities demand a considerable amount of order, and will not for long tolerate radical programs of change. A considerable amount of historical and contemporary evidence supports that general conclusion. Second, sociology has also emphasized how much people want some continuity in their lives, how much they demand tradition, rituals, and even respect for what they have believed and done earlier in their lives; simply put, they do not change easily or willingly. Third, sociologists must continue to note, by their emphasis upon individuals, individual decisions, and the importance of small groupings in a larger society, that most people are not willing to live on a high plane of grand issues and philosophies. That is what Berger calls "the imperative of triviality."[21] As he puts it, triviality is "one of the fundamental requirements of social life."

There are many other ways of phrasing these assertions, but all of them point to the conclusion that much of sociological analysis is conservative. It is not so much that sociologists themselves have been conservative (except by contrast with avowed radicals), but the field itself sees social forces and institutions as not easily moved or as vast and slow moving. Moreover, it seems very likely that if sociologists turn their attention more and more to the problems of revolutions, or even to the engineering of revolutions, they will still come to a similar conclusion in the future.

With reference to the more purely intellectual charges made against the field of sociology, let us consider one that is not frequently expressed in print, but often emerges from heated exchanges: dissidents allege the findings of sociology, after nearly a half-century of increasingly rigorous technical improvement, are skimpy, thin gruel indeed. In contrast, the propositions in the physical sciences are powerful; in a wide range of settings, they still hold true. They also go far beyond the insights or guesses of ordinary wise men who rely upon their own experience.[22] Our sociological findings are neither precise enough to give concrete guidance in specific problem situations, nor powerful enough to apply across a broad spectrum of circumstances. Of course, it is granted that we have not only accumulated a vast quantity of descriptive information, but have offered tens of thousands of propositions expressed as correlations,[23] and doubtless most of these are "correct." Nevertheless, they do not possess the sweep and power of propositions in chemistry and physics.

It is no refutation to argue that sociological analyses by radicals are also wrong, as they sometimes are; or weak and loose in their methods of adducing or organizing evidence, as they often are, or that they are not intellectually exciting. Most sociologists have read many radical investigations of one sort or another, and typically find that they do not open any important doors to understanding and present no new and powerful scientific laws or theories. Like most mainstream sociological researches, studies by radicals present one or two traditional themes, with some new agglomerations of facts, but not the new and powerful ideas for which we hunger.[24]

Such a counteraccusation only diverts the issue, for sociology has had at least a half-century in which to develop such scientific laws, and it has not done so. The more challenging question is whether it *can* do so. In answer I have suggested elsewhere[25] that we may find, a half-century from now, that sociology is destined for a long time to be much like biology in the scope and grasp of its findings. From the late eighteenth century until very recently, biology not only possessed no grand overarching theory, but most of its findings were small-scale, confined to the description and elucidation of tiny subsystems, whether ecological or physiological. Its results were not powerful, and few propositions could be called "laws." Perhaps that suggestion is too pessimistic but time may yet prove it to be correct.

Another charge is that traditional sociology has given far too much prominence to how much people are moved by their norms and how little they are moved by their rationally calculated interests, the seeking of profit or simple selfishness. The field has only in the last decade or so begun to reassess this emphasis.[26] It has also overly emphasized the extent to which people in a community or group are bound together and act together because of a consensus, a set of shared norms. In a similar vein, it has taken note far more of the extent to which change does not occur, and the status quo is maintained, while neglecting chaos, conflict, and anomie.

A main contribution of sociology, as contrasted with the emphases of both political science and economics, has been to bring to our intellectual awareness the extent to which people are moved by norms and values that do not bring them profit, make sacrifices for the group rather than for personal or private interests, and maintain the continuity of their traditions, I believe that this overemphasis does not represent an intellectual failure. Indeed, the exploration of such relationships will remain as a lasting contribution. Nevertheless, it is high time that we began to reintegrate the ancient common sense notions about rational calculation, personal profits, and the stakes and interests of groups, organizations, and individuals.

Similarly, sociologists have largely neglected the importance of force and its threat in maintaining any social system, of violence in pressing people toward conformity and even in shaping their attitudes and norms. Thus they have neglected the extent to which people may act to maintain the status quo, while objecting to it or not being committed to it in various ways. Since I have myself been working on this problem many years, I can affirm that the problem is much more difficult than many critics believe.[27] It is especially subtle and complex, since most force and its threat are not observable: people behave in conformity with the *possible* pressures of force and violence. Thus it is not easy to ascertain whether and to what degree those factors shape their behavior. The problem is not simple even in a concentration camp, as Bettelheim's analysis demonstrates.[28] In a civil society, the problem is methodologically and technically murky. Nevertheless, sociology has for too long left this problem to the political scientists, who have dealt with it almost not at all, except with reference to war between nations.

A further charge of considerable intellectual weight, and one that is especially dismaying because it emerges so naturally from any view of society as a coherent structure, is that sociologists have busied themselves with small-scale relationships and correlations, showing how men's actions are determined by a wide array of social forces, but have typically ignored the extent to which the larger social system of opportunities, alternatives, and choices has prevented people from acting very differently. It is as though we were to describe in great detail how shopkeepers and customers argue about prices, without describing the larger set of market forces that determine how narrowly their choices are limited. As long as people in the society are pressed to focus their attention on the immediate and concrete bargains they can make, and are diverted from the larger structure of force, propaganda, economic power, and other structural variables that determine the larger system of alternatives, they are not likely to seek many opportunities for improving the society.

Without regard to this task of political engineering, however, it is quite clear that an adequate sociological analysis of the larger *systemic* forces that structure the daily choices of individuals is still lacking in our field. I wish to emphasize here that I am not speaking of some grand political exposé that would disclose "how the elite exploit us." After all, that has been done, whether satisfactorily or not, hundreds of times. More fundamentally, we do not know whether any of these exposés are correct, because sociology as a field has failed to tackle large-scale system problems adequately.

Finally, the charge has been made many times that "functionalism" (that is, mainstream traditional sociology) cannot deal adequately with social change. Some sociologists have written monographs on social change, as noted earlier, but a basic core of truth remains. The field has not in general seized upon the intellectual and scientific potentialities of social change as a site, a place to study. The interaction of important social forces must be investigated under a wide variety of conditions, not just relatively static ones. It is a cliché that one can view societies as either changing relatively little, or changing continually. Both statements are partly correct. Nevertheless, sociologists have found it intellectually easier to deal with society, any society, at a given point in time, rather than over a longer period of time, and they have been far more struck by the extent to which social structures change little, rather than by how much they change. As noted in Chapter 1, an increasing number of younger sociologists are investigating problems of social change and revolution in many countries, especially in the emerging nations. It is to be hoped that their reports will over time gradually repair this deficiency, but at present the accusation is a correct one.

It should be noted, that with reference to most of these intellectual charges, the new but more fundamental question must become *quantitative.* That is to say, societies and social systems do remain to some degree in equilibrium, and they also are often in some degree of disequilibrium. Doubtless, a social group cannot be maintained over any period of time without a substantial amount of consensus, of shared norms, but since people do contribute to such groups while partly disagreeing with their fellow members, we must once again ask what degree of consensus is necessary? And how much commitment to the group's norms is required? People are moved by their norms and values, but they are also moved by force and by the anticipation of economic profit. Again, the question must not be transformed into a simple overemphasis on factors that have been to some degree neglected. We must at least attempt to obtain some answers that measure the impact of these various forces, whether they have been neglected or overemphasized in the past.

Before leaving this subject, at least one challenge should be issued. Without doubt, the men who developed and shaped sociology since World War I were aiming primarily at understanding how social forces operate, and the system of rewards was so organized that men were granted prestige for enlightening others. They certainly tried to achieve that goal. If they failed in many respects, it now remains to be seen whether their successors will easily remedy those deficiencies.

It may well be that the problems themselves are difficult. The fault, in any event, certainly does not lie with some vague entity called "functionalism." It may lie in the social forces that structured the development of sociology during that period. On the other hand, it may well turn out in the future that the problems they did not solve easily are recalcitrant, and will not yield easily to the next generation, either. By openly facing the fact that criticizing functionalism is beating a dead horse and by accepting the interpretation that the attacks upon it are really attacks upon the content of sociology as it has historically emerged over the past generation, some clarity in the current debate ought to result. Let us now take a further step toward diminishing the intensity of the polemic now raging about these issues, by suggesting some concrete procedures for eliminating the term entirely from our analyses and discussions.

First the language of sociological analysis must be clarified. For the antifunctionalists have correctly sensed what they have not yet articulated clearly; that is, whenever anyone uses the term, "function" or "functional," *something is likely to be wrong with the analysis.* I am now convinced, from repeated tests, that both words can be deleted from our discourse with no loss in meaning but a gain in precision. Usually, the analyst who uses either term has fallen back on an outworn, empty word rather than describing clearly the social relations that are presumably under examination. Whenever we encounter either term, we should be on the alert for imprecision and looseness in thinking. In the succeeding paragraphs we shall examine some cases but the reader can collect his own illustrations and test further the case of deleting these terms.

One of the more obvious cases that has always aroused the ire of antifunctionalists is the kind of analysis that begins with: "The functional requisites of a social system are the following. . . ."[29] Two main criticisms are to be made against such a listing. The first is that if the items listed are truly requisite, necessary if the society is to exist at all, then clearly the adjective "functional" is entirely unnecessary. It adds no meaning at all to the phrase. Consequently, it can be deleted with some gain in precision. We do not then have to concern ourselves with what conceivable additional criteria might have to be brought in to prove that a given trait is, let us say, requisite but not functional, functional but not requisite, and so forth.

Second, although this type of listing has frequently annoyed anti-functionalists, it has played a very minor role in real sociological analysis. More important, such a listing constitutes no more than a primitive way of defining a social system or a society. Many such lists have been made, and almost any student can make up his own without much effort. Whether it includes concrete activities such as producing and distributing food, protecting individuals from each other and from predators, engaging in religious rituals, and so on; or whether it includes more abstract variables such as the forces that maintain social boundaries among subgroups of the society or between members of the society and other societies, the implantation and maintenance of values, the integration of individuals with one another in order to accomplish their goals, and the like, such a list typically states no more than: this is what a society or social system is. Almost no theoretical propositions of any merit can be deduced from such a list.

As a rhetorical challenge, in fact, Homans has argued that we ought to be able to reason from such lists to a prediction about the disappearance of specific societies. For example, did the tribes of the Tierra del Fuego die out because they failed to meet some of these functional requisites?[30] I believe that Homans is incorrect in supposing that we know that "these societies met all the social prerequisites on the list." They may well have failed to maintain an adaptive response to the new challenges of the social environment, for example. He urges that they were actually "undone by gunfire, firewater, disease, or some combination of the three."

Again, Homans has failed his own test of logic, since the postulation of such a list of prerequisites or requisites does not deny that a society might be destroyed by *other* forces than a failure to fulfill such needs. On the other hand, he is essentially correct in arguing that: (a) survival is an extremely unclear concept, as is evidenced by the question of whether the Roman Empire has "survived" in Italy; (b) we ought to be able to predict the survival or disappearance of some kinds of real societies if the list is of any theoretical relevance; and (c) we ought to be able to measure the *degree* of success in meeting such needs or measuring the dependent variable of survival and success.

It should also be added that a listing of requisites has not been fruitful in biological reasoning, either. It is possible to argue that mammals require mechanisms for extracting oxygen from air, transporting it to areas in the body where it is needed, maintaining a "proper" calcium level, maintaining a narrow range of temperature variations, distributing digested food to cells where it is to be burned, and so on. But such "requisites for life" largely figure in popular or philosophical commentaries on biological processes. In their day-to-day work, physiologists have rather attempted to link together a specific set of mechanisms by which, for example, the consequences of low or high calcium levels are traced out and measured with precision, the processes by which that variation is kept in narrow limits, the disease processes that may interfere with such processes, and so on. Let us, then, eliminate such listings; at a minimum, let us delete the term "functional" from the discussion.

I believe that the language of functionalism entered at a period when social scientists were still embarrassed (in their new focus on rigor) to use the term "cause." They felt that in the infancy of a new mode of thought, it would temporarily be safer (as it was) to use a term that would suggest some relationship without specifying it adequately. Consequently any proposition in which the term "function" is used as a verb can now be more adequately translated into *causal language*.[31] If it cannot, it should be discarded at once. This translation will once more reduce the use of a murky term.

Let us consider some instances in which "function" can be phrased in causal language.

The proposition, "The potlatch functions to reduce aggression and tension among the Kwakiutl" must mean a description and prediction: that is, if we measure the interpersonal tension and physical aggression before and after a potlatch, it will have caused a reduction. Similarly: "A wedding fiesta functions to announce that a couple has entered the community as adults."

The statement, "criminal punishment functions to affirm the virtuous in their value commitment," must mean, if it is to mean anything, that such an affirmation is one of the *consequences* of punishing criminals. Unfortunately, this phrasing may suggest that we need not consider other consequences. Nevertheless, the proposition as it stands must signify a prediction and it describes a causal relation. Once we recognize that this is the content of the proposition, and there is no added meaning beyond that, we are then also forced to attempt real measurement. The most demanding terms, "cause" and "consequence," also press us to ask whether indeed we can prove our assertion.

Let us consider other cases where we can translate functional language into simpler terms, with a gain in precision and no loss in meaning.[32] The descriptive statement, "The functional importance of a wedding fiesta is to announce that a couple has entered the community as adults and have the support of the two sets of relatives" can be translated most simply by leaving out the term "functional importance" entirely and rephrasing the description as: the wedding fiesta announces that . . ." "Almost every such descriptive statement that begins with the phrase, The functional importance of X is . . ." can be so translated with no loss of meaning at all.

In a similar way, the statement that exogamy or incest rules "function" (a) to link up members of the society with one another who might otherwise be kept within a small, encysted familial grouping, (b) to spread whatever knowledge may have accumulated within a single family, and (c) to expose members of the next generation to other social influences from members of other families so that no single family line may become set apart in its peculiar values, and so on can only mean that exogamy or incest rules *have such consequences*. If so, they should be measurable or testable. If not, the proposition is not falsifiable, and should be forthwith dropped. In either case, the term "functions" in that description can be usefully eliminated.

Let us consider still another example of such translation for the purpose of eliminating this dead issue from contemporary sociology. Such examples are no longer frequent, but perhaps mentioning the type may hasten its total disappearance. An example or two may suffice for the whole category: the Ph.D. orals examination is functional; war is functional; religion is functional. Here perhaps the elimination of the term "functional" would, of course, create a grammatical gap but a healthful one, for then the author would be required to specify what (if anything) he does mean.

If one examines the discussion that follows such a statement, it is quite clear that in almost every case the statement means only: (a) here are some consequences of this social pattern and (b) those consequences are viewed by some members of the society as good. Perhaps typically a generation ago, and occasionally now, the statement also meant the author also likes the consequences.

Usually, however, an examination of the context will show that the author is simply describing some of the consequences of a given behavioral pattern. If he had used a causal language instead of the term "functional," he would have been forced to specify a wider *range* of consequences, but in any event the statement never contains any additional meanings that need be taken seriously for sociological analysis. We are, after all, concerned with the empirical relations among social variables. To illustrate, one might be able to demonstrate that (1) holding Ph.D. orals examinations does in fact raise the anxiety level of students so that they study more; (2) a student who passes an examination feels that he has done something important; (3) professors are able to make the acquaintance of students on this occasion; (4) it permits the professors to judge the capacities of their student; (5) it creates substantial hostility in students against their professor and against the whole system of training; (6) it narrows the range of study so that the student is engaged in trying to anticipate the questions of professors rather than to master the field; and so on. It is at least clear that if we eliminate the term "functional" from such descriptions, we are more likely to ask about any and all important consequences of a given social pattern.

It should be added, in view of the current confusion in the debate, that I have deliberately omitted any reference to the phrase, "contributes to the continued existence of the society," since almost no contemporary sociologist concerns himself with that special relationship, and any reading of actual research reports will show that this kind of "function" or "consequence" has almost disappeared. Certainly the person who says that orals examinations are "functional" does not really mean that they contribute to the continued existence of the society. If he is especially loose and murky in his thinking he may indeed mean that the Ph.D. orals contributes to the continued existence of the Ph.D. system but since that *is* part of the system, such a statement is almost meaningless. Functionalism as a mode of thought cannot be blamed for all individual incompetence. In any event, in general, the term "functional" refers less and less to any such distant and nearly untraceable consequences. If functions exist, they are *consequences* and should be traced and measured.

Since the preceding paragraphs illustrated the salutary elimination of the terms "functional" and "function" and their translation into much more sensible language, it is almost superfluous to note that the term can be profitably deleted from such phrases as "functional importance," "functional meaning," "functional imperative," or "functional explanation." In each of these consequences the elimination of the term also eliminates the feeling of security that some social analysts gain from using this once magical incantation. The use of such a term implies, as I suggested earlier, that something is wrong with the analysis, that is, that the author has not specified adequately the relationship he wishes to describe. If it is not a consequence or cause and we cannot state what the relationship is, then perhaps we ought to start our analysis all over again.

Thus, the phrase "X functions to do the following . . ." means only "X does the following. . . ." "The function of X" must mean "X has the following consequence." If the proposition cannot be so translated, then it is inexcusably murky or imprecise.

If I urge those who still use functionalist language to engage in this self-denying ordinance, and to eliminate this range of terms entirely, perhaps I may also be permitted to urge upon antifunctionalists that they drop the assault, and turn to the real analysis of real social relations. If there are causal relations, or correlations with some predictive power, then perhaps we should turn to those, and examine with more care the links between social variables that look especially fruitful.

As a further by-product of this elimination, we should then be able to eliminate as well the so-called "problem of functional proof." With the term eliminated, we simply have the ordinary problems of proving any kind of correlation between social variables. These range from the easy to the nearly impossible, but they are not changed in quality or character by calling them "functional." Some of them are simply matters of near *definition*. For example, the "consequences" (formerly "functions") of exogamy noted earlier follow almost by definition of the term. That is to say, if individuals must marry outside of a certain limited family group, then obviously some of the consequences listed above would indeed occur.

Other functions may be demonstrated on the basis of fairly well-established sciences. Thus, the people of a community or society may enjoy a morning swim in an ocean lagoon (the Polynesian Tikopians studied by Raymond Firth). We could then say that this social pattern contributes to their health. Here, one is simply utilizing a reasonably well-established relationship between cleanliness and health. On the other hand, it is equally clear that there is no need to use the term "functions" or "functional." It is clearer and more precise simply to refer to the presumed causal relationship.

There remain, of course, some relationships that are difficult to prove, but not because of any special character of *function*. If they have any meaning at all, they state a causal relationship, but like many presumed causal relationships in social science, it is difficult to sketch a logic of proof that would be adequate. Often, of course, they are difficult to prove because we are unable to specify any quantitative relationship, and the correlation or causal relation remains a common sense assertion. Many of these examples can be found in the sociology of religion, where for generations it has been asserted that religious rituals "affirm the unity of the tribal group or social system," "impress upon individuals the validity and believability of both religious beliefs and moral values," "give meaning and significance to the individual human life," and so on.

Such assertions are not necessarily false, but demonstration has lagged far behind assertion. The difficulty lies not in "proving a function" but demonstrating any kind of consequence when controlled experiment is lacking. That is, we cannot compare societies with and without certain types of religious rituals, to ascertain whether consequences such as the above are a result of the rituals.[33] We could, presumably, ask people how they feel after participating in religious rituals, and we might predict that participants will report they commonly experience such effects.

Such reports may not be fully adequate, but statements requiring that we measure consequences which seem to be intuitively observable but for which we have no "social thermometer," will doubtless remain difficult to demonstrate for some time in the future. Nevertheless, if we treat them as simple causal relations, which in fact require the ordinary apparatus of scientific demonstration, they are no longer protected from criticism by the lesser logical and empirical demands of the functional language.

The elimination of functional language in favor of a causal language would also have two worthwhile by-products: our analyses are less likely to be open to the charge of conservatism, and we can stop proliferating new terms based on function. Since Merton's masterly demonstration twenty-five years ago that one may employ a "functional" orientation (if Marx did, why can't we?) in the service of either a radical or conservative political position,[34] it should be clear that even a theoretical analysis which focuses on how a social group maintains itself is not an argument *in favor* of maintenance. One may show the social mechanisms that sustain a Wehrmacht combat group under stress, a criminal gang, or the anti-Semitism of a W.A.S.P. private club, without espousing the aims or principles of such groups. If we express such findings in causal language, as analysts now do for the most part, the specific effects of particular variables are more likely to be our focus, and both destructive and maintaining processes will, therefore, be less likely to escape examination. Such a focus reduces the temptation to overemphasize the conservative elements in social life.

This cleansing of vague language from our theoretical discourse will also eliminate the variety of new concepts based on "function," for example, eufunctions and dysfunctions. Since all functions are simply consequences of some kind, we are bound to locate and measure them along with their causes, but we need not then invent an array of new labels for these causal factors.

From the fall of evolutionism until only recently, social science has neglected (as noted in Chapter 1) the topic of social change. In part, this neglect was a salutary move from vague speculation to a determined wrestling with the technical problems of research and, therefore, with the kinds of data that are most immediately observable and testable, that is, contemporary social life. However, in recent years social change has come to attract an increasing number of sociologists, perhaps to some degree because of a growing confidence that the growth in theoretical rigor and technical precision now permits us to cope with those difficult questions. Doubtless, this renewed interest comes from many larger social factors, such as concern with rapid change in the world, a protest against things as they are, and a determination that we must adjust to change and perhaps engineer it.

We have dealt elsewhere with the theoretical and technical problems in this new orientation[35] and space permits no repetition here, but we must take note of the frequent charge that functionalism has been an obstacle to an adequate theoretical analysis of change.

Of course, if a given theoretical orientation is a poor tool for investigating problems in social change, the social analyst need only propose a better alternative schema. If the new one is fruitful, and leads to increased understanding, it is almost certain that others who have been confused about this topic will take the new proposal seriously. If the new hypotheses or theories explain the facts better, the supposed theoretical obstacles in an older framework are not likely to remain as barriers. The framework will simply be dropped.

It is, in any event, unlikely that a theoretical approach that supposedly concentrated on the problem of how a group, social system, or social pattern is maintained could also neglect the factors that undermine stability and thus promote change. A theoretical orientation that emphasizes maintenance also postulates implicitly a world that requires a large input of energy and attention if it is to survive: that is, it is potentially unstable. Indeed, that approach is embodied in every organismic analogy, whether biological or social. Its core and essence suggests that any system is threatened with dissolution. Any biological analogy must emphasize both the death of the individual animal and the disappearance of given species and, perforce, the death of any society.

A theory of social change is either (1) a set of empirical correlations that describe social patterns over a lengthy period of time or (2) a set of hypotheses about determinate sequences. In either case the substitution of causal language for functional terms will again be salutary.

If we look for the causal relations among any set of variables, the causal formulation presses us much more strongly to measure the

specific factors that caused small-scale changes, or those that alter
fundamentally the larger structure of a social system. The attempt
to specify the particular effects of definite social variables on either
change or maintenance would turn our attention from the empty
question of whether a functionalist orientation might block the study
of social change, to the real and difficult problems of *how* one measures either the changes of the past or the alterations that we are now
able to observe.

After so lengthy a plea to dispose of the imprecise language of
some functionalist discourse, and the analysis of why this is essentially a dead issue, it may seem inappropriate to suggest that there
may well be one type of theoretical analysis to which we can some
day apply the term again, though here again I would hope that we
might eliminate it for a generation or so before doing so.

Specifically, Stinchcombe[36] proposes that we reserve the term
"functional causal imagery" for a causal structure in which some
type of behavior (S) affects a homeostatic variable (H) which is the
end or consequence to be maintained, while there are various "upsetting tensions" (T) that tend to prevent that maintenance. As the tensions increase, H moves from the desired value, and this in turn
affects the original structure or variable, S. This is commonly observable in social life, where people want to maintain desired patterns:
family affection or harmony, social cohesion in battle, profit levels,
or politeness at a cocktail party. As various kinds of upsetting tensions
develop, a wide range of equilibrating forces are set in motion to re-
establish the desired level of affection, cohesion, profit, and so on.

Descriptions and analyses of this form resemble at least some
functional accounts, but Stinchcombe's proposed causal structures
would be fundamentally different. They would describe precisely
which variables are modifying which, thus (1) isolating at least conceptually the specific internally linked mechanism; (2) locating and
measuring the internal or external elements that vary; and (3) noting the circumstances under which there is some failure in the feedback process and a breakdown in the system. Of course, these would
also be causal analyses, and would come close to a physiological
analysis of a feedback, or looped, mechanism, for example, the chemi-
cal transformations that occur in the rods of the retina under the
impact of wide variations in light intensity, or those that force us

finally to gasp for breath when we try to hold our breath for a long time.

In this chapter I have not been trying to force an olive branch on contending parties by persuading them that there is no need for battle. In scientific work, confrontation and the intense focusing of issues are preferable. Since, however, what is being attacked has no defenders, the contemporary attacks on functionalism are no confrontation but a waste of intellectual energy. The "historical" functionalism, the theoretical orientation that appeared at the turn of the century with the demise of evolutionism, did exhibit certain characteristics of intellectual style, but these have become widespread among all sociologists, including those who are antifunctionalist. No one now proclaims and I am convinced no one ever believed, the doctrines that antifunctionalists ascribe to functionalists. Functionalism in that sense is dead, if it ever lived.

Consequently, I have argued that the present-day attacks on functionalism are really directed against the content of recent sociology: specifically, not its theoretical orientation, but its various deficiencies and failures, which certainly could and doubtless will be remedied by future work, generated by a very similar general theoretical stance. These accusations are that the sociology of the past generation has been conservative in its thrust; skimpy and weak in its theoretical attainments; little occupied with social change, violence, force, and revolution; giving too much emphasis to norms and values, consensus, and equilibrium; and failing to see the larger, systematic structuring forces that shape the basis of the individual's actions or decisions, which form the bulk of analysis in most sociological monographs.

I have conceded that there is a core of justification in these attacks. In so doing, I have also hinted that it may be much more difficult to remedy these defects than to describe them. No one in the past generation ignored a solution to any of them, simply because he or she lacked the necessary intellectual or moral nerve to aim so high. Anyone in the present generation who can develop theories to substitute for these past failures will earn high honor from his peers.

I have also proposed, to hasten the turn from an empty polemic toward serious intellectual work, that all the variant forms of the label "functional" be eliminated from our discourse: "functionalist," "functionalism," "function," and so on. The antifunctionalists are fundamentally correct in being suspicious when anyone uses any of these terms: they nearly always herald some imprecision, looseness, or murkiness in the theoretical analysis. We should instead use a causal language, for this demands from us that we specify exactly which kind of relationship we intend to demonstrate. The use of functional language invites intellectual laziness, if not indeed mysticism.

To aid this forward step, I have shown how we can delete all of these functionalist terms from all sociological propositions, with no loss of meaning, and a considerable gain in rigor. For those who still believe that such terms convey some meaning, I have shown how to translate such propositions into causal language and to cast out the totally unnecessary functionalist terms. The real scientific problems of sociological analysis are difficult enough without cluttering them up with debris from a controversy that is both hollow and out of date. To paraphrase an important comic strip philosopher of our time, we have now stormed the castle and have encountered the enemy: we ourselves were that enemy all along.

II. ROLE AND EXCHANGE THEORY

4. A Theory
of Role Strain

INTRODUCTION

IT NOW SEEMS LIKELY THAT THE DEVELOPMENT OF ROLE AND EX-
CHANGE THEORY HAS GRADUALLY TAKEN A FORM THAT AFFECTS THE
theoretical stance and perspective of traditional sociology. Before
World War I, sociology had carved out a set of distinct intellectual
tasks and findings by focusing on the shared or group values and
norms that molded human decisions and actions, in contrast with the
focus of economics, and indeed much of social science, on individual
seeking of profit, based on rational calculation. That break from the
older, rationalistic, often positivistic and utilitarian social theory was
fruitful, even if it caused sociologists to overlook some of the truth in
those quite ancient insights.

Modern traditional sociology uncovered numerous regularities of
considerable power. It emphasized groups and social systems rather
than the individual; the influence of the nonrational (including
religion) rather than the rational; the power of group norms and
values rather than self-seeking and profit; the commitment to norms
and rules and thus the willingness to conform, rather than coercion
by force or economic threat; consensus among group members rather
than their disagreements; the stability of groups and social systems,
rather than their changes. Such emphases were justified by the empirical researches between World War I and the period just after
World War II, which reported many social patterns that could not

have been predicted by the social science of the nineteenth century.

But though such emphases were fruitful, containing as they did an overlooked part of the truth, they have come under increasingly heavy attack, often in the guise of assaults on a largely mythical functionalism. Having exploited the insights that grew from these exaggerations, and having established for itself a set of important tasks and theoretical orientations, sociology can afford now to turn back to assess once more the importance of factors and problems that it had neglected for a while. Some of these have already been discussed in earlier chapters, and some have just been noted. In theoretical terms we now need to explore the importance of force in human society; rational and self-seeking calculation; the extent to which people do not accept the values of their groups; and how order and stability occur even when people are not committed deeply to shared norms. These alterations in theoretical stance are now under way, and are already enriching our understanding of social processes.

Since many would even now deny that this development is occurring, it is safe to say that those who contributed to role and exchange theory did not plan this change. Nevertheless some of its conceptual clarifications and substantive analyses moved away from the traditional ones, without any frontal attack, and offered alternative modes of perceiving social reality.

The following article may be viewed as one contribution to that change. As published, it was separated from its long introduction, which focused on a conceptual clarification of role and status, and which explained why a new or more fruitful view of those concepts was emerging.*

Specifically but briefly, I suggested that the widely accepted Lintonian definitions of these terms contained fundamental confusions not generally perceived; that the distinction between role and status had not been exploited in separate theoretical lines of inquiry; that many sociologists had been trying to clarify matters by inventing new definitions, none of them receiving acclaim as the solution; and that nevertheless the term "role" was gradually supplanting that of "status"; and that the *usage* of the two terms (which is after all the real definition) was gradually crystallizing into a simpler form, for

* "Norm Commitment and Conformity to Role-Status Obligations," *American Journal of Sociology*, 66 (November, 1960), pp. 246-58.

example, the term "status" was increasingly being used to refer to the more institutionalized roles.

In focusing on role, analysts were more likely to emphasize the other person or persons in the relationship, the tensions or conflicts among them, and the contingencies in all social interaction. They were also more likely to take note of the "third parties" whose support or rejection of the Person-Other dyadic relations are so crucial. By emphasizing both the complexity of the role relationship and the extent of possible disagreement among Ego, Alter, and third parties, social analysis keeps in view the importance of norms and values, but reaffirms the importance of individual calculation and even self-seeking. Thereby, the theoretical view is better fitted to real social interaction in a complex modern society, where so much social conformity occurs without any deep moral commitment.

The present article builds on some of the theoretical propositions that were articulated in the conceptual introduction, published separately. It is one version of the many "exchange theories" that have been developed of late. Its fruitfulness may be measured by the number of propositions it generates in this context; in a goodly number of analyses since that time I have exploited it further.*

It is not worthwhile to argue in favor of its theoretical usefulness, however, since it speaks for itself in that connection (or fails to do so). Let me instead note its distinctiveness as a view of social action.

Unlike Homans's version, it is not a psychological theory, based on a particular version of learning theory. It does not state that if the animal is rewarded for its behavior it will be more likely to behave that way again (although that statement is correct).† It rather states that human beings carry with them into the social situation not only their knowledge of what has rewarded them before, and their emotional predispositions to prefer what has done so, but also an immense baggage of norms, values, and social philosophy which can be linked only speculatively with "previous rewards." In social analysis it is simpler to ascertain what they are independently, rather than guess their origins.

---

* Some appear in this book; the most elaborate will be encountered in my continued explorations of prestige and force-threat as control systems. A forthcoming work will be entitled, *The Celebration of Heroes: Prestige as a Control System.*
† I am ignoring as irrelevant the many technical attacks on this and other versions of current learning theory.

In addition, instead of supposing that people are involuntarily pressed by their previous rewards to go on doing the same thing, this version states that they do in fact evaluate and calculate, dimly or wisely, their probable outcomes in *this* situation. Rather than supposing that social systems and action follow a Law of Momentum, it argues that they exemplify the Second Law of Thermodynamics, that is, that previous social and individual patterns are constantly under threat of falling apart, without a recurring input of energy and thought that maintains order.

This version is, like those of both Blau and Homans, a primitive type of "economic" theory, although it clearly enunciates some of the ways traditional economics does not apply to some of our phenomena. All such versions assume a scarcity of resources and the necessity of allocating them for the maximum of gain, whether that gain is in the realm of beauty, morals, friendship, social approval, the command of force, or money. However, this version emphasizes more than others that much of the outcome of the immediate situation is determined by third parties as well as by the social and value assumptions "ego" and "alter" bring into it. That is "the outside social structure" determines much of the role bargaining in the immediate situation. Indeed, it argues in effect that a central set of pressures toward decisions and actions is not so much the maximization of still more "gains" as it is the diminution of role strain.

The present analysis specifies some types of decisions in this process, under two large categories, the mechanisms that determine whether ego will enter a set of role transactions, and those that shape the terms of exchange within that set.

Finally, this view also exploits the theoretical fruitfulness of roles when viewed as elements of any social institution. Thereby, the micro-transactions are linked constantly with the larger social structure, and the inputs and outputs of each are not ignored. This is especially important for the notion put forward here, that it is the strains in social processes that hold the social system in some equilibrium. To use a physical figure of speech, society is more like a suspension bridge or one of Buckminster Fuller's geodesic domes, each part held in place by the tensions each puts on the other, than like a mountain in stable equilibrium. Its degree of consensus may be less important than the myriad pressures and counterpressures encountered in daily social transactions. Of course this view is not a "theory," but a "theoretical orientation," and is simply one more expression of social life as contingency, of continual inputs, of constant rebuilding, and of potentiality for change.

The present paper is based on the general view that institutions are made up of role relationships, and approaches both social action and social structure through the notion of "role strain," the felt difficulty in fulfilling role obligations. Role relations are seen as a sequence of "role bargains," and as a continuing process of selection among alternative role behaviors, in which each individual seeks to reduce his role strain. These choices determine the allocations of role performances to all institutions of the society. Within the limited compass of this paper, only a few of the possible implications of role strain as a theoretical approach can be explored.

The widespread notion that institutions are made up of roles is fruitful because it links a somewhat more easily observable phenomenon, social behavior, to an important but less easily observable abstraction, social structure. In functionalist terms, this notion also links the observed acts and inferred values of the individual with the institutional imperatives or requisites of the society. At the same time, by focusing on the elements in the individual's action decision, it avoids the pitfall of supposing that people carry out their obligations because these are "functional" for the society.

Approaching role interaction in terms of role strain offers the possibility of buttressing more adequately the empirical weakness of the most widely accepted theoretical view of society,[1] according to which the continuity of social roles, and thus the maintenance of the society, is mainly a function of two major variables: the normative, consensual commitment of the individuals of the society; and the integration among the norms held by those individuals. Although this view is superior to earlier ones,[2] it fails to explain how a complex urban society keeps going[3] because it does not account for the following awkward empirical facts:[4]

1. Some individuals do not accept even supposedly central values of the society.

2. Individuals vary in their emotional commitment to both important and less important values.

3. This value commitment varies by class strata, and by other characteristics of social position, for example, age, sex, occupation, geographic region, and religion.

4. Even when individuals accept a given value, some of them also have a strong or weak "latent commitment" to very different or contradictory values.[5]

5. Conformity with normative prescriptions is not a simple function of value commitment; there may be value commitment without conformity or conformity without commitment.

6. When individuals' social positions change, they may change both their behavior and their value orientations.

7. The values, ideals, and role obligations of every individual are at times in conflict.

Under the current conception of roles as units of social structures, presumably we should observe the role decisions of individuals in order to see how the society continues. On first view, as can be seen from the above list of points, the basis of social stability or integration seems precarious, and the decisions of the individual puzzling. For even when "the norms of the society" are fully accepted by the individual, they are not adequate guides for individual action. Order cannot be imposed by any *general* solution for all role decisions, since the total set of role obligations is probably unique for every individual. On the other hand, the individual may face different types of role demands and conflicts, which he feels as "role strains" when he wishes to carry out specific obligations.

In the immediately following sections, the major sources and types of role strain are specified, and thereafter the two main sets of mechanisms which the individual may use to reduce role strain are specified; thereafter, the two main sets of mechanisms which the individual may use to reduce role strain are analyzed.

TYPES OF ROLE STRAIN

It is an axiom, rarely expressed, of social theory that the individuals who face common role obligations *can* generally fulfill them. Indeed, most theories of stratification and criminality require such an assumption, and common opinion uses it as a basis for its moral demands on the individual. We may suppose, as a corollary, that there are theoretical limits to the specific demands which societies may make of men. In addition, the "theorem of institutional integration"[6] is roughly correct as an orienting idea: people generally *want* to do what they are supposed to do, and this is what the society needs to have done in order to continue.

Yet, with respect to any given norm or role obligation, there are always some persons who cannot conform, by reason of individuality or situation: they do not have sufficient resources, energy, and so on. A wider view of all such obligations discloses the following types or sources of role strain:

First, even when role demands are not onerous, difficult, or displeasing, they are required at particular times and places. Consequently, virtually no role demand is such a spontaneous pleasure that conformity with it is always automatic.

Second, all individuals take part in many *different* role relationships, for each of which there will be somewhat different obligations.[7] Among these, there may be either contradictory performances required (the bigamous husband; the infantry lieutenant who must order his close friend to risk his life in battle) or conflicts of time, place, or resources. These are conflicts of allocation (civic as against home obligations).

Third, each role relationship typically demands *several* activities or responses. Again, there may be inconsistencies (what the husband does to balance his family budget may impair his emotional relations with the members of his household). There may be different but not quite contradictory norms which may be applied to the various behavioral demands of the same role (the clergyman as the emotionally neutral counselor, but as a praising or condemnatory spiritual guide). Perhaps most jobs fall into this category, in that their various demands create some strain as between the norms of quantity and quality, technical excellence and human relations skills, and universalism and particularism.

Finally, many role relationships are "role sets," that is, the individual engages, by virtue of *one* of his positions, in several role relationships with different individuals.[8]

The individual is thus likely to face a wide, distracting, and sometimes conflicting array of role obligations. If he conforms fully or adequately in one direction, fulfillment will be difficult in another. Even if he feels lonely, and would like to engage in additional role relationships, it is likely that he cannot fully discharge all the obligations he already faces. He cannot meet all these demands to the satisfaction of all the persons who are part of his total role network. Role strain—difficulty in meeting given role demands—is therefore normal. In general, *the individual's total role obligations are overdemanding.*

Consequently, although the theorem of institutional integration, or the assumption of norm commitment, offers an explanation for the fulfillment of the duties imposed by a single norm, it does not account for the integration of an individual's total role system, or the integration among the role systems of various individuals, which presumably make up the social structure. The individual's problem is how to make his whole role system manageable, that is, how to allocate his energies and skills so as to reduce role strain to some bearable proportions. For the larger social structure, the problem is one of integrating such role systems—by allocating the flow of role performances so that various institutional activities are accomplished.

THE REDUCTION OF ROLE STRAIN: EGO'S CHOICE

A sensitizing or orienting notion in functionalist as well as system theory—perhaps more properly called one element in the definition of a "system"—is that a strain is likely to be associated with some mechanisms for reducing it.[9] The individual can utilize two main sets of techniques for reducing his role strain: those which determine whether or when he will enter or leave a role relationship; and those which have to do with the actual role bargain which the individual makes or carries out with another.

Ego's Manipulation of His Role Structure. Ego has at his disposal several ways of determining whether or when he will accept a role relationship.

1. *Compartmentalization:* This may be defined on the psychological level as the ability to ignore the problem of consistency. Socially,

role relations tend toward compartmentalization because the individual makes his demands on another and feels them to be legitimate, in specific situations where he can avoid taking much account of the claims on that person. There seems to be no overall set of societal values which explicitly requires consistency or integration from the individual. The process of compartmentalization works mainly by (a) location and context and (b) situational urgency or crisis. The latter process permits the individual to meet the crisis on its own terms, setting aside for the moment the role demands which he was meeting prior to the crisis.

2. *Delegation:* This may be seen, at least in part, as one way of achieving compartmentalization. If, for example, secular counseling is inconsistent with the clergyman's moral leadership role, he may be able to delegate it. If secular manipulation by a church is inconsistent with its sacredness, it may delegate some secular acts to lay leaders or to specialized religious orders. A wife may delegate housekeeping, and some of the socialization and nursing of the child. Note, however, that the societal hierarchy of values is indicated by what may *not* be delegated: for example, the professor may not hire a ghost writer to produce his monographs, and the student may not delegate examinations.

3. *Elimination of role relationships:*[10] Curtailment may be difficult, since many of our role obligations flow from our status positions, such as those in the job or family, which are not easily eliminated. Of course, we can stop associating with a kinsman because of the demands he makes on us, and if our work-group sets norms which are too high for us to meet we can seek another job. Aside from social and even legal limits on role curtailment, however, some continuing role interaction is necessary to maintain the individual's self-image and possibly his personality structure: for example, many people feel "lost" upon retirement—their social existence is no longer validated.

4. *Extension:* The individual may expand his role relations in order to plead these commitments as an excuse for not fulfilling certain obligations. A departmental chairman, for example, may become active in university affairs so that he can meet his colleague's demands for time with the plea that other duties (known to his colleagues) are pressing. In addition, the individual may expand his role system so as to *facilitate* other role demands, for instance, joining an

exclusive club so as to meet people to whom he can sell stocks and bonds.

5. *Obstacles against the indefinite expansion of ego's role system:* Although the individual may reduce his felt strain by expanding his role system and thereby diminishing the level of required performance for any one of his obligations, this process is also limited: After a possible initial reduction, *Role strain begins to increase more rapidly with a larger number of roles than do the corresponding role rewards or counter-payments from alter.* This differential is based on the limited role resources at individual's commands. The rewards cannot increase at the same rate as the expansion even if at first he increases his skill in role manipulation, because eventually he must begin to fail in some of his obligations, as he adds more relationships; consequently, his alters will not carry out the counter-performances which are expected for that role relationship. Consequently, he cannot indefinitely expand his role system.

6. *Barriers against intrusion:* The individual may use several techniques for preventing others from initiating, or even continuing, role relationships—the executive hires a secretary through whom appointments must be made, the professor goes on a sabbatical leave. The administrator uses such devices consciously, and one of the most common complaints of high level professionals and executives is that they have no time. This feeling is closely connected with the fact that they *do* have time, that is, they may dispose of their time as they see fit. Precisely because such men face and accept a wider array of role opportunities, demands, and even temptations than do others, they must make more choices and feel greater role strain. At the same time, being in demand offers some satisfaction, as does the freedom to choose. At lower occupational ranks, as well as in less open social systems where duties are more narrowly prescribed, fewer choices can or need be made.

Settling or Carrying Out the Terms of the Role Relationship. The total role structure functions so as to reduce role strain. The techniques outlined above determine whether an individual will have a role relationship with another, but they do not specify what performances the individual will carry out for another. A common decision process underlies the individual's sequence of role performance as well as their total pattern.

1. *The role relationship viewed as a transaction or "bargain":* In his personal role system, the individual faces the same problem he faces in his economic life: he has limited resources to be allocated among alternative ends. The larger social system, too, is like the economic system, for the problem in both is one of integration, of motivating people to stop doing X and start doing Y, whether this is economic production or religious behavior.

Because economic structures are also social structures, and economic decisions are also role decisions, it might be argued that economic propositions are simply "special cases" of sociological propositions.[11] In a more rigorous methodological sense, however, this claim may be viewed skeptically, since at present the former body of propositions cannot be deduced from the latter.[12] Rather, economic theory may be a fruitful source of sociological ideas, because its theoretical structure is more advanced than that of sociology. Since the precise relation between economic and sociological propositions is not yet fully ascertained, economic vocabulary and ideas are mainly used in the succeeding analysis for clarity of presentation, and the correctness of propositions which are developed here is independent of their possible homologs in economics.[13] In this view, economic performance is one type of role performance, a restricted case in which economists attempt to express role performance, reward, and punishment in monetary terms.[14] In both, the individual must respond to legitimate demands made on him (role expectations, services, goods, or demands for money) by carrying out his role obligations (performances, goods, or money payments). Through the perception of alternative role strains or goods-services-money costs, the individual adjusts the various demands made upon him, by moving from one role action to another. Both types of transactions, of course, express *evaluations* of goods, performances, and money.

In his role decisions, as in his economic decisions, the individual seeks to keep his felt strain, role cost, or monetary and performance cost at a minimum, and may even apply some rationality to the problem. At the same time, a variety of pressures will force him to accept some solutions which are not pleasant. His decisions are also frequently habitual rather than calculated, and even when calculated may not achieve his goal. Rather, they are the most promising, or the best choice he sees. Since the analysis of such behavior would focus on the act and its accompanying or preceding decision, the research approach of "decision analysis" seems appropriate to ascertain the course of events which led to the act.[15]

In role behavior, we begin to experience strain, worry, anxiety, or the pressures of others if we devote more time and attention to one role obligation than we feel we should, or than others feel we should. This strain may be felt because, given a finite sum of role resources, too much has already been expended; or because the individual feels that relative to a given value the cost is too high. The relative strength of such pressures from different obligations determines, then, the individual's role allocation pattern within his total role system. This system is the resultant of all such strains. Analysis of role allocation requires, of course, that we know the individual's *internal* demands, that is, the demands which he makes on himself, and which thus contribute to his willingness to perform well or not.[16]

The process of strain allocation is facilitated somewhat, as noted above, by ego's ability to manipulate his role structure. On the other hand, the structure is kept in existence by, and is based on, the process of allocation. For example, with reference to the norms of adequate role performance, to be considered later, the White child in the South may gradually learn that his parents will disapprove a close friendship with a Negro boy, but (especially in rural regions) may not disapprove a casual friendship. The "caste" role definitions state that in the former relationship he is over-performing, that is, "paying too much." Such social pressures, expressed in both individual and social mechanisms, are homologous to those in the economic market, where commodities also have a "going price," based on accepted relative evaluations. Correspondingly, the individual expresses moral disapproval when his role partner performs much less well than usual, or demands far more than usual.

In all societies, the child is taught the "value of things," whether they are material objects or role performances, by impressing upon him *that* he must allocate his role performances, and *how* he should allocate them.[17] These structural elements are considered in a later section.

2. *Setting the role price in the role bargain:* The level of role performance which the individual finally decides upon, the "role price," is the resultant of the interaction between three supply-demand fac-

tors: (a) his pre-existing or autonomous norm commitment—his desire to carry out the performance; (b) his judgment as to how much his role partner will punish or reward him for his performance; and (c) the esteem or disesteem with which the peripheral social networks or important reference groups ("third parties") will respond to *both* ego's performance and to alter's attempts to make ego perform adequately.

The individual will perform well ("pay high") if he *wants* very much to carry out this role obligation as against others. He will devote much more time and energy to his job if he really enjoys his work, or is deeply committed normatively to its aims. The individual's willingness to carry out the role performance varies, being a function of the intrinsic gratifications in the activity, the prospective gain from having carried out the activity, and the internal self-reward or self-punishment from conscience pangs or shame or a sense of virtue, or the like.

With reference to what ego expects alter to do in turn, he is more likely to over-perform, or perform well if alter can and will (relative to others) reward ego well or pay him well for a good or poor execution of his role obligations. Thus, my predictions as to what will make my beloved smile or frown will affect my performance greatly; but if she loves me while I love her only little, then the same smiles or frowns will have less effect on my role performances for her.[18] Similarly, as will be noted below in more detail, alter's power, esteem, and resources affect ego's performance because they allow alter to punish or reward ego more fully. The individual perceives these consequences cognitively and responds to them emotionally. If, then, the individual aspires to be accepted by a higher ranking individual or group, he may have to perform more adequately than for one of his own rank. This last proposition requires a further distinction. Alter may be able, because of his position, to reward ego more than alter rewards others in a similar status, but this additional reward may be no more than a socially accepted premium for extra performance. On the other hand, the additional reward may sometimes be viewed by those others as beyond the appropriate amount. Or the individual may over-perform in one activity of his role relationship to compensate for a poor performance in another—say, the poor breadwinner who tries to be a good companion to his children. Such further consequences of higher performance and higher reward may at times be taken into account by both role partners in making their role bargain.

If alter asks that ego perform consistently better than he is able or willing to do, then he may ease his allocation strain by severing his relationship with that individual or group and by seeking new role relationships in which the allocation strain is less.[19]

3. *Limitations on a "free role bargain":* The third component in ego's decision to perform his role bargain is the network of role relationships—"the third party" or parties—with which ego and alter are in interaction. If either individual is able to exploit the other by driving an especially hard role bargain, such third parties may try to influence either or both to change the relationship back toward the "going role price." Not only do they feel this to be their duty, but they have an interest in the matter as well, since (a) the exploiting individual may begin to demand that much, or pay that little, in his role relations with them; and (b) because the exploited individual may thereby perform less well in his role relations with them. These pressures from third parties include the demand that either ego or alter punish or reward the other for his performances or failures.[20]

It is not theoretically or empirically clear whether such third parties must always be a limited reference group, or can at times be the entire society. Many of the norms of reference groups appear to be special definitions or applications of similar norms of the larger society. Certain groups, such as criminal gangs or power cliques in a revolutionary political party, may give radical twists of meaning to the norms of the larger society. Under such circumstances, the interaction of pressures on ego and alter from various third parties can be complex. We suppose that *which* third party is most important in a given role transaction between ego and alter is a function of the degree of concern felt by various third parties and of the amount of pressure that any of them can bring to bear on either ego or alter.

STRUCTURAL LIMITS AND DETERMINANTS

Strain-Reducing Mechanisms. The individual can thus reduce his role strain somewhat: first, by selecting a set of roles which are singly less onerous, as mutually supportive as he can manage, and minimally conflicting; and, second, by obtaining as gratifying or value-productive a bargain as he can with each alter in his total role pattern.

As the existence of third parties attests, however, both sets of ego's techniques are limited and determined by a larger structural context within which such decisions are made. Not all such structural elements reduce ego's role strain; indeed, they may increase it, since they may enforce actions which are required for the society rather than the individual. Essentially, whether they increase or reduce the individual's role strain, they determine which of the first set of mechanisms ego may use, and on what terms. Similarly, they determine whether ego and alter may or must bargain freely, to either's disadvantage, or to what extent either can or must remain in an advantageous or costly bargaining position. The most important of such elements are perhaps the following:

1. *Hierarchy of evaluations:* Social evaluations are the source of the individual's evaluations, but even if only the frequently occurring types of choices are considered, such evaluations reveal complex patterns.[21] Some sort of overall value hierarchy seems to be accepted in every society, but aside from individual idiosyncrasies, both situational and role characteristics may change the evaluation of given acts. Indeed, all individuals may accept contradictory values in some areas of action, which are expressed under different circumstances. Here, the most important of these qualifying factors are: (a) the social position of ego (one should pay some respect to elders, but if one is, say, 30 years of age, one may pay less); (b) the social position of alter (the power, prestige, or resources of alter may affect ego's decision); (c) the content of the performance by ego or alter (mother-nurse obligations are more important than housekeeper-laundress duties); and (d) situational urgency or crisis. When ego gives the excuse of an urgent situation, alter usually retaliates less severely. However, when several crises occur simultaneously, the allocation of role performances is likely to be decided instead by reference to more general ranking of value.[22]

These illustrations suggest how structural factors help to determine ego's willingness to perform or his performance, in an existing role relationship (Type 1b), and though they reduce his uncertainty as to what he should or must do, they also may increase his obligations. At the same time, these same factors also determine in part whether or when ego will include the relationship at all (Type 1a) in his total role system (for example, a noted physicist should engage in a technical correspondence with a fellow physicist, but may refuse to appear on a popular television show; even a passing stranger is expected to give needed aid in a rescue operation).

This set of interacting factors is complex, but gives some guidance in role interaction. Since there is a loose, society-wide hierarchy of evaluations, and both individuals and their reference groups or "third parties" may be committed to a somewhat different hierarchy of values, at least the following combinations of evaluations may occur:

Evaluations of:

Evaluations by:	Task Content	Rank of Alter	Situational Urgency
Society			
Reference Groups or Third Parties			
Alter			
Ego			

2. *Third parties:* Though third parties figure most prominently in the bargaining within an existing role relationship, especially those which are more fully institutionalized (statuses), they also take part in ego's manipulation of his role structure, since they may be concerned with his total social position. For example, families are criticized by kinsmen, neighbors, and friends if they do not press their children in the direction of assuming a wider range of roles and more demanding roles as they grow older.

3. *Norms of adequacy:* These define what is an acceptable role performance.[23] Norms of adequacy are observable even in jobs which set nearly limitless ideals of performance, such as the higher levels of art and science, for they are gauged to the experience, age, rank, and esteem of the individual. For example, a young instructor need not perform as well as a full professor; but to achieve that rank he must perform as well as his seniors believe they performed at his rank. Such norms also apply to the total system of roles assumed by the individual. The individual may criticize another not only when the latter's specific performance fails to meet such criteria, but also when

the latter's range of roles is too narrow (the wife complains, "We never go out and meet people") or too wide (the husband complains, "You take care of everything in the community except me").

The individual must assume more roles in an urban society than in primitive or peasant society, and the norm of functional specificity applies to a higher proportion of them. This norm permits individuals to bargain within a narrower range, but also, by limiting the mutual obligations of individuals (and thus tending to reduce role strain), it permits them to assume a larger number of roles than would otherwise be possible. This, then, is a role system basis for the generally observed phenomenon of *Gesellschaft* or secondary relations in urban society.

4. *Linkage or dissociation of role obligations in different institutional orders:* The fulfillment of role obligations in one institutional order either rests on or requires a performance in another.[24] Thus, to carry out the obligations of father requires the fulfillment of job obligations. Such doubled obligations are among the strongest in the society, in the sense that ego may insist on rather advantageous terms if he is asked to neglect them in favor of some other obligation. Linking two institutional orders in this fashion limits ego's freedom to manipulate his role system.

At the same time, there are barriers against combining various roles, even when the individual might find such a linkage congenial. (For example: a military rule against officers fraternizing intimately with enlisted men; a regulation forbidding one to be both a lawyer and a partner of a certified public accountant.) In an open society, some role combinations are permitted which would be viewed as incongruous or prohibited in a feudal or caste society.

Such pressures are expressed in part by the punishments which the individual may have to face if he insists on entering disapproved combinations of roles. The barriers against some combinations also apply to a special case of role expansion: entrance into certain very demanding statuses, those which require nearly continuous performance, are subject to frequent crises or urgencies, and are highly evaluated.[25] Even in our own society there are not many such statuses. The combination of two or more sets of potential crises and responsibilities would make for considerable role strain, so that few individuals would care to enter them; but in addition organizational rules sometimes, and common social attitudes usually, oppose such combinations.—The priest may not be a mother; the head of a hospital may not be a high political leader.

5. *Ascriptive statuses:* All statuses, but especially ascriptive statuses, limit somewhat ego's ability to bargain, since social pressures to conform to their norms are stronger than for less institutionalized roles. Some of these require exchanges of performances between specific individuals (I cannot search for the mother who will serve my needs best, as she cannot look for a more filial child) while others (female, black, "native American") embody expectations between status segments of the population. The former are more restrictive than the latter, but both types narrow considerably the area in which individuals can work out a set of performances based on their own desires and bargaining power. Because individuals do not usually leave most ascriptive statuses, some may have to pay a higher role price than they would in an entirely free role market, or may be able (if their ascription status is high in prestige and power) to exact from others a higher role performance.[26] The psychological dimensions of these limitations are not relevant for our discussion. It should be noted, however, that at least one important element in the persistence of personality patterns is to be found in these limitations: the role structure remains fairly stable because the individual cannot make many free role bargains and thus change his role system or the demands made on him, and consequently the individual personality structure is also maintained by the same structural elements.[27]

6. *Lack of profit in mutual role deviation:* Since two role partners depend in part on each other's mutual performance for their own continuing interaction with other persons, mutual role deviation will only rarely reduce their role strain. It might be advantageous to me if my superior permits me to loaf on the job, but only infrequently can he also profit from my loafing. Consequently, both ego and alter have a smaller range of choices, and the demands of the institutional order or organization are more likely to be met. When, moreover, in spite of these interlocking controls, ego and alter do find a mode of deviation which is mutually profitable—the bribed policeman and the professional criminal, the smothering mother and the son who wants to be dependent—concerned outsiders, third parties, or even a larger segment of the society are likely to disapprove and retaliate more strongly than when either ego or alter deviates one-sidedly.

On the other hand, there is the special case in which ego and alter share the same status—as colleagues or adolescent peers, for example. They are then under similar pressures from others, and may seek similar deviant solutions; they may gang together and profit collectively in certain ways from their deviation.[28]

Less Desirable Statuses: Efforts to Change the Role Bargain. The preceding analysis of how ego and alter decide whether, when, or how well they will carry out their role obligations permits the deduction of the proposition that when an individual's norm commitment or desire to perform is *low* with respect to a given status—in our society, many women, blacks, and adolescents reject one or more of the obligations imposed on them; perhaps slaves in all societies do— then alter must bring greater pressure to bear on him in order to ensure what alter judges to be an adequate performance. If the individual does under-perform, he is less likely to have strong feelings of self-failure or disesteem; he may feel no more than some recognition of, and perhaps anxiety about, possible sanctions from alter.

Individuals are especially conscious that they are "training" others in both child and adult socialization, if those others are suspected of being weakly committed to their role obligations. Thus, most whites in the South have for generations held that all whites have an obligation to remind the black by punishment and reward that he "should keep in his place," and that punishment of the black is especially called for when he shows evidence that he does not accept that place. It is the heretic, not the sinner, who is the more dangerous. It is particularly when the members of a subordinate status begin to deny normatively their usual obligations that third parties become aroused and more sensitive to evidence of deviation in either performance or norm commitment. On the other hand, individuals in a formerly subordinate status may, over time, acquire further bargaining power, while those in a superior status may gradually come to feel less committed to the maintenance of the former role pattern.

THE FAMILY AS A ROLE BUDGET CENTER

For adult or child, the family is the main center of role allocation, and thus assumes a key position in solutions of role strain. Most individuals must account to their families for what they spend in time, energy, and money outside the family. And ascriptive status obligations of high evaluation or primacy are found in the family. More important, however, is the fact that family members are often the only persons who are likely to know how an individual is allocating his *total* role energies, managing his whole role system; or that he is spending "too much" time in one role obligation and retiring from others. Consequently, family relations form the most immediate and persistent set of interactions which are of importance in social control. Formal withdrawal from these relationships is difficult, and informal withdrawal arouses both individual guilt feelings and pressures from others.

Moreover, since the family is a role allocation center, where one's alters know about one's total role obligations and fulfillments, it also becomes a vantage point from which to view one's total role system in perspective. Because it is a set of status obligations which change little from day to day and from which escape is difficult, role alternatives can be evaluated against a fairly stable background. Consequently, other family members can and do give advice as to how to allocate energies from a "secure center." Thus it is from this center that one learns the basic procedures of balancing role strains.

Finally, family roles are "old shoe" roles in which expectations and performances have become well meshed so that individuals can relax in them. In Western society, it is mainly the occupational statuses which are graded by fine levels of prestige, just as achievement within occupations is rewarded by fine degrees of esteem. It is not that within jobs one is held to standards, while within families one is not.[29] It is rather that, first, socialization on the basis of status ascription within the family fits individual expectations to habitual performances and, second, rankings of family performances are made in only very rough categories of esteem. The intense sentiments within the family cushion individual strain by inducing each person to make concessions, to give sympathy, to the others. Of course, greater strain is experienced when they do not. These status rights and obligations become, then, "role retreats" or "role escapes," with demands which are felt to be less stringent, or in which somewhat more acceptable private bargains have been made among the various members of the group. One's performance is not graded by the whole society, and one's family compares one's family performance to only a limited extent with that of other people in other families.

The existence of unranked or grossly ranked performance statuses or roles may permit the individual to give a higher proportion of his energy to the ranked performance statuses. The institutions which contain such statuses vary. For example, in contemporary Western society, the layman's religious performances, like his familial performances, are ranked only roughly, but at one time evaluation of the former was more differentiated. However, familial performance apparently is never ranked in fine gradation in any society.[30] Here, an implicit structural proposition may be made explicit: the greater the degree of achievement orientation in a system of roles, the finer the gradation of prestige rankings within that system or organization.[31]

ROLE STRAIN AND THE LARGER SOCIAL STRUCTURE

Social structures are made up of role relationships, which in turn are made up of role transactions. Ego's efforts to reduce his role strain determine the allocation of his energies to various role obligations, and thus determine the flow of performances to the institutions of the society. Consequently, the sum of role decisions determines what *degree* of integration exists among various elements of the social structure. While these role performances accomplish whatever is done to meet the needs of the society, nevertheless the latter may not be adequately served. It is quite possible that what gets done is not enough, or that it will be ineffectively done. As already noted, the role demands made by one institutional order often conflict with those made by another—at a minimum, because the "ideal" fulfillment in each is not qualified by other institutional demands and would require much of any person's available resources. Many such conflicting strains frequently result in changes in the social structure. Within smaller sub-systems, such as churches, corporations, schools, and political parties, the total flow of available personal resources may be so disintegrative or ineffective that the system fails to survive. In addition, the total role performances in some societies have failed to maintain the social structure as a whole.

Thus, though the sum of role performances ordinarily maintains a society, it may also change the society or fail to keep it going. There is no necessary harmony among all role performances, even though these are based ultimately on the values of the society which are at least to some extent harmonious with one another. Role theory does not, even in the general form propounded here, explain why some activities are ranked higher than others, why some activities which help to maintain the society are ranked higher, or why there is some "fit" between the role decisions of individuals and what a society needs for survival.

The total efforts of individuals to reduce their role strain within structural limitations directly determines the profile, structure, or pattern of the social system. But whether the resulting societal pattern is "harmonious" or integrated, or whether it is even effective in maintaining that society, are separate empirical questions.

SUMMARY AND CONCLUSIONS

The present paper attempts to develop role theory by exploiting the well-known notion that societal structures are made up of roles. The analysis takes as its point of departure the manifest empirical inadequacies, noted in the first section, of a widely current view of social stability, namely, that the continuity of a social system is mainly a function of two major variables: (a) the normative, consensual commitment of the individuals of the society; and (b) the integration among the norms held by those individuals. Accepting dissensus, nonconformity, and conflicts among norms and roles as the usual state of affairs, the paper develops the idea that the total role system of the individual is unique and over-demanding. The individual cannot satisfy fully all demands, and must move through a continuous sequence of role decisions and bargains, by which he attempts to adjust these demands. These choices and the execution of the decisions are made somewhat easier by the existence of mechanisms which the individual may use to organize his role system, or to obtain a better bargain in a given role. In addition, the social structure determines how much freedom in manipulation he possesses.

The individual utilizes such mechanisms and carries out his sequences of role behaviors through an underlying decision process, in which he seeks to reduce his role strain, his felt difficulty in carrying out his obligations. The form or pattern of his process may be compared to that of the economic decision: the allocation of scarce resources—role energies, time, emotions, goods—among alternative ends, which are the role obligations owed by the individual. The role performances which the individual can exact from others are what he gets in exchange.

It is to the individual's interest in attempting to reduce his role strain to demand as much as he can and perform as little, but since this is also true for others, there are limits on how advantageous a role bargain he can make. He requires some role performance from particular people. His own social rank or the importance of the task he is to perform may put him in a disadvantageous position from which to make a bargain. Beyond the immediate role relationship of two role partners stands a network of roles with which one or both are in interaction, and these third parties have both a direct and an indirect interest in their role transactions. The more institutionalized roles are statuses, which are backed more strongly by third parties. The latter sanction ego and alter when these two have made a free role bargain which is far from the going role price. The demands of the third parties may include the requirement that ego or alter punish the other for his failure to perform adequately.

Under this conception of role interaction, the bargains which some individuals make will be consistently disadvantageous to them: the best role price which they can make will be a poor one, even by their own standards. However, no one can ever escape the role market. The continuity of the individual's total role pattern, then, may be great even when he does not have a strong normative commitment to some of his less desirable roles. Like any structure or organized pattern, the role pattern is held in place by both internal and external forces—in this case, the role pressures from other individuals. Therefore, not only is role strain a normal experience for the individual, but since the individual processes of reducing role strain determine the total allocation of role performances to the social institutions, the total balances and imbalances of role strains create whatever stability the social structure possesses. On the other hand, precisely because each individual is under some strain and would prefer to be under less, and in particular would prefer to get more for his role performances than he now receives, various changes external to his own role system may alter the kind of role bargains he can and will make. Each individual system is partly held in place by the systems of other people, their demands, and their counter-performances—which ego needs as a basis for his own activities. Consequently, in a society such as ours, where each individual has a very complex role system and in which numerous individuals have a relatively low intensity of norm commitment to many of their role obligations, changes in these external demands and performances may permit considerable change in the individual's system.

The cumulative pattern of all such role bargains determines the flow of performances to all social institutions and thus to the needs of the society for survival. Nevertheless, the factors here considered may not in fact insure the survival of a society, or of an organization within it. The quantity or quality of individual performances may undermine or fail to maintain the system. These larger consequences of individual role bargains can be traced out, but they figure only rarely in the individual role decision.

With respect to its utility in empirical research, this conception permits a more adequate delineation of social structures by focussing on their more observable elements, the role transactions. This permits such questions as: Would you increase the time and energy you now give to role relationship X? Or, granted that these are the ideal obligations of this relationship, how little can you get away with performing? Or, by probing the decision, it is possible to ascertain why the individual has moved from one role transaction to another, or from one role organization to another. Finally, this conception is especially useful in tracing out the articulation between one institution or organization and another, by following the sequence of an individual's role performance and their effects on the role performances of other individuals with relation to different institutional orders.

5. The Protection
of the Inept

INTRODUCTION

THOSE ON THE POLITICAL LEFT ARE GENERALLY COMPASSIONATE ABOUT THE SULLENNESS, SABOTAGE, LAZINESS, AND INCOMPETENCE of people in the lower classes because they perceive that the society did not encourage the lower strata by suitable rewards. By only apparent contrast, the political conservative is likely to be more patient with the mediocre performance of the higher orders; if the General is foolish, he is nevertheless gallant and radiates authority; if the duke is foppish and bankrupts his ancestral lands, he comes from an illustrious family and upholds their tradition of lavishness; if the governor or president does little to solve the problems of the state or nation, it is because little can be done.

Both sets of apologies may have a core of truth to them, but the succeeding analysis asserts that all genuine groups must work out what they perceive as an inacceptable balance between two tensions, goals, or needs, that is, protection of their inept members, and protection of the group from the potential catastrophes the inept may cause. The wisdom of human beings is limited, and this balance may be erroneous. They may protect their inept so well that they fall victim to ineptitude. The military leader may push forward to disaster, as did Sir Douglas Haig in World War I; the President may be overly indulgent with his cronies, as was Harding. Or, by contrast, the less able may be so mercilessly exposed that each member is out for his own ends, as may happen when a new corporation president "cleans house," and few will help the organization. Both extremes are costly, but the mean is sometimes not the wisest solution either, for the environmental problems that the organization or group faces.

This set of relations is also the focus of another pair of tensions or strains not dealt with (but nevertheless assumed) in this analysis. Those outside any given group do not feel it is in their interests that groups protect the inept, and they try as they can to eliminate the mechanisms for protection. For centuries, guildsmen, employees, businessmen, and professionals have fought in subtle or crude ways against the efforts of clients, consumers, or managers to raise performance standards by eliminating the least competent. Each group wants to protect itself, but opposes the efforts of other groups to do the same. Again, we cannot suppose that these tensions have been wisely resolved in any society.

These patterns also point out a significant conception in any theory of social action: that it is false to counterpose "interests vs. values" or "profit vs. norms," because in real decisions we are choosing among various interests, all supported by one or more values, and among many values and norms, which are weighty enough to be perceived as our real interests. Thus we are in favor of efficiency and competence, but also in favor of group integration and protection; we believe that the most competent ought to be rewarded more, but we are less fervent in that belief if we ourselves are not the most competent—whereupon we invoke other values such as seniority, need, friendship, family ties, experience, and so on. Social patterns, whether ideal or real, are rarely *only* ascriptive or achievement-oriented, particularistic or universalistic.

We also see that although the generalizations reported in this analysis would appear to be valid for any society, the structural context in which groups operate within the same society vary, so that the amount of protection of ineptitude also will vary. Clearly, an estate or class society gives more such protection to its higher level groups especially, but special groups in our own society (for example, the building trades' unions and physicians) achieve considerable protection as well. Professional sports teams, as athletes complain frequently these days, cast out the less competent most ruthlessly of all, but there we see that (1) performance is easier to measure than it is in other fields and (2) the high skill of an individual performer actually contributes to the total income of his teammates, since the team that wins earns more. When the demand for a high performance is low, the pressures toward weeding out the less able are lower. When there is high demand for the services of group members, they can more easily ignore outsiders' efforts to eliminate the less competent.

On a broader level, this analysis suggests a theme that has been almost unexplored in traditional sociology: How much organization, how much norm consensus and commitment, how much efficiency must a social system achieve in order to function? I have suggested here and elsewhere that societies can operate with a fairly high degree of anomie, nonorganization, or normative indifference, but we must ascertain what are the conditions under which a social system can continue to exist when it seems to be measurably low in the qualities and traits that sociology has asserted to be necessary.

Finally, the analysis presents a theoretical conjecture that seems valid on its face, but demands more intensive scrutiny: that modern industrial systems achieve a higher productivity than earlier productive organizations, not because they allocate jobs on the basis of competence alone (we know they do not), but because they have solved better the problem of how to get an adequate performance from the less able. Both machines and bureaucracies create tasks that almost anyone can perform reasonably well with only modest training and motivation. They also limit substantially the range of possible error and catastrophe. When these systems work well, even men at the top are limited in the range of their possible foolishness. However, when by mischance or political machination such a vast organization is controlled by men of little wisdom or much evil, the destructive impact is probably still greater than in most nonindustrial systems. Nevertheless, the intellectual question deserves further investigation, as to whether this mode of utilizing the less able is more effective, as I have claimed. The query is even more pertinent today than when this analysis was written, since many social philosophers now argue that in a more humane society we would reduce the competitiveness that so harries our lives.

The dissident have throughout history voiced a suspicion that the highly placed have not earned their mace, orb, and scepter. Plato designed a city in which the ablest would rule, but this was accomplished only in his imagination. Leaders in the Wat Tyler Rebellion expressed their doubts that lords were of finer quality than the peasants they ruled. Against the grandiloquent assertion of kings that they were divinely appointed, both court jesters and the masses have sometimes laughed, and asked, where were their virtue and wisdom? In more recent times, this skepticism about their merit has culminated in the dethronement or weakening of practically every ascriptive ruler in the world.

Nor has the end of kings by birth stifled this doubt that the elite are indeed the ablest, that the inept may be protected in high position. Jefferson spoke of a "natural aristocracy," but he did not suppose the members of the ruling class necessarily belonged to it. In our less heroic epoch, we are assured that we live in an achievement-oriented society, and the norm is to place individuals in their occupations by merit. Nevertheless, the inquiries of sociologists and psychologists demonstrate that as the child passes through the successive gateways to higher position, the cumulative effect of class, race, sex, and other readily ascribed traits grows rather than lessens. For example, lower class or black children who could perform well by comparison with their more advantaged peers in the first few grades drop farther and farther behind. The gap between them widens.[1]

Of course, not all talent at any class level would be transmuted into skill, even in the best of *possible* worlds. However the privileged (at all levels of privilege) do try systematically to prevent the talent of the less privileged from being recognized or developed. And though analysts of stratification assume that social mobility is an index of open competition, ample if unsystematic evidence suggests that both the able and the inept may move into high position.

These comments should not be interpreted as the jaundiced complaints of the misanthrope, or as a call for destruction of the stratification system. Such common observations from Ecclesiastes (". . . the race is not to the swift . . .") and Plato onward describe arrangements which every social system exhibits, and which cope with a universal *system problem:* How to utilize the services of the less able?

The social responses to this problem are the resultant of two sets of factors in tension: protection *of* the inept; and protection of the group *from* the inept. In almost all collectivities, for reasons to be explored later, the arrangements for protecting the less able seem to be more pervasive, common, and effective than those for protecting the group from ineptitude. Industrial society is highly effective at production not so much because it allows the most able to assume positions of high leadership, but because it has developed two great techniques (bureaucracy and machinery) for both using the inept and limiting the range of their potential destructiveness.[2]

Adequate proof of this rather laconic theoretical statement, and a full exposition of its implications, is not possible within the brief compass of a single paper. In subsequent sections we shall consider these issues:

1. Does the evidence suggest there is a widespread pattern of protecting the less competent?
2. In supposedly achievement-oriented societies, is this protection merely an evasion of widely accepted achievement norms, i.e., is it "real," as contrasted with "ideal," behavior, or do people in fact accept many norms contrary to achievement?
3. What are the specific or general processes and patterns protecting the less able?
4. Presumably, different social structures handle the problem of ineptitude differently.
What consequences flow from these differences?

One can at least imagine, even if one will never find, a society in which the division of labor in every type of group allots tasks and rewards entirely on the basis of achievement, or one in which those allotments are made without regard for achievement. All societies fall between these two extremes. Leaders within industrial societies assert, in part as a defense of the system they lead, that the lowly able will rise, and that the highly placed deserve their rank. Even if such statements are classified as exhortations or hopes, evidence can be adduced to show that on the average the successful are more talented or skilled than the less successful, e.g., the research productivity of Nobel Prize winners *vs.* that of nonwinners.[3]

Yet such averages are, after all, derived from *distributions.* These distributions always reveal that *some* of the less successful seem equal or superior to the more successful. Far more important for our present inquiry, all such individuals live and work in *groups*, so that the relevant comparison is not with all other individuals in the same aggregate, such as all full professors, but with other members of the same group, such as the *department*. The protection of the inept is a *group* phenomenon, an aspect of a collectivity.

Let us, then, consider briefly some of the wide array of evidence that groups do not typically expose or expel their members for lesser achievement or talent. The following findings are only a reminder of how widespread our research has shown such social arrangements to be.

Almost every inquiry into the productivity of workers has shown that the informal work group protects its members by setting a standard which everyone can meet, and they develop techniques for preventing a supervisor from measuring accurately the output of each man.[4] Higher level management has for the most part evaded such scrutiny, but industrial sociologists have reported comparable behavior there, too.[5] The protection of one another by lower-level workers might be due to less commitment; the fact that higher-level men do the same suggests the need for a more general explanation.

All professions, while claiming to be the sole competent judges of their members' skills, and the guardians of their clients' welfare, refuse to divulge information about how competent any of them are, and under most circumstances their rules assert it is unethical to criticize the work of fellow members to laymen.[6] Wall Street law firms try to find good positions in other firms for those employees they decide are not partnership material.[7] When a new profession is organized, grandfather clauses permit older practitioners with less training to continue in practice without being tested. When hospitals begin to demand a higher performance standard from those who enjoy staff privileges, inevitably rejecting some, both patients and physicians object.[8] One study of a group of physicians showed that there was little relationship between an M.D.'s income and the quality of medical care he gave to his patients.[9]

Wherever unions are strong, foremen know that promotion by merit rather than by seniority is unwise, and in any event unusual.[10] Many corporations do not fire their managers; they find or create

other posts for them.[11] Employees are close students of promotion behavior, and are "notoriously suspicious and cynical" about management claims that promotion is through merit.[12] Many are not convinced the best men are at the top.[13] More generally, members of
what Goffman calls "teams" (army officers, parents, policemen, managers, nurses, and so forth) protect each other from any exposure of
their errors.[14]

In all societies—if present psychological testing may be extrapo-
lated—there are more talented, in absolute numbers, born into the
lower social strata than into the upper; every detailed study of a class
system describes how the upper strata prevent the lower from acquiring the skills appropriate for higher level jobs. This effort alone
is a good indicator that the upper strata include many who are less
talented. For example, the Southerner as well as the Northerner
would not even *need* to discriminate against the black child or
man, if in fact he were always untalented; performance alone would
demonstrate his inferiority. The same proposition holds for the poor
generally, for Jews (as in banking or heavy industry), for women,
and (in some circles) for Catholics.[15]

Few are fired for incompetence, especially if they last long enough
to become members of their work group. One consequence is that, in
craft or white collar jobs, higher standards are set for obtaining a job
than for performance. The result is that a high level of formal education is often necessary for jobs that any average eighth-grader
could learn to perform rather quickly. Once the person enters his
work group, however, the social arrangements do not permit much
overt discrimination between the less able and the rest. Thus we observe the irony in our generation that the middle classes, with their
greater access to education, continue to have the advantage in getting jobs, though the standards, i.e., formal education, are ostensibly
universalistic and achievement-based.

As Galbraith has pointed out, the greatest source of insecurity for
both individuals and companies has been competition; business men
"have addressed themselves to the elimination or mitigation of this
source of insecurity."[16] Cartels, price and production agreements, tar-
iffs, price fixing by law, and quiet understandings are among the
techniques used to prevent the less able from being pushed to the
wall. The "development of the modern business enterprise can be

understood only as a comprehensive effort to reduce risk . . . (and) in no other terms."[17]

Analysts have reported such behavior most often from work groups, but similar patterns are observable if we look instead at the operation of any type of collectivity. All groups are creating *some* type of output, whether the socialization of a child or sheer entertainment. On the other hand, as we shall note later, the *degree* of protection may vary from one type of activity to another.

In examining the protection of ineptitude, we are considering the division of labor from a different perspective. For our limited purposes, the inept are made up of two classes of people in any collectivity: (1) with reference to one or more tasks, some are likely to be less skilled than others who do not enjoy the rewards of membership in that group; (2) in addition, some in that collectivity will be considerably less skilled than others. Clearly the group does not typically expel these less competent members. Instead, in each collectivity there are structures or processes which protect them.

ACHIEVEMENT NORMS VS. BEHAVIOR

Even so brief a selection from the evidence confirms the impression from daily experience that some social behavior protects the less able from open competition. Is this, however, simply one more instance of action counter to a norm? Perhaps all these cases are only violations of the well-accepted norm of achievement. Let us, then, examine the possibility that people are only partially committed to the criterion of achievement as the basis for reward, and also accept other opposing norms.

The current sociological tradition, following Linton and Parsons, views industrial society as achievement-based, i.e., stratified by achievement criteria, in contrast to most other social systems, in which statuses are mostly ascribed.[18] However, we may question such descriptions, and assert instead that people in our own type of society feel committed to many criteria of ranking that run counter to achievement, and that in the so-called ascriptive societies the principle of placement by birth is in turn qualified a good deal by achievement norms. That is, let us consider whether *both* behavior and norms in all societies prevent the exposure of the less competent and productive.

I have not been able to locate an adequate empirical study of even the American population—the one most studied by sociologists—concerning its commitment to the notion of ranking by achievement, but I shall venture several armchair descriptions of some value patterns that I believe are now observable.

In the so-called achievement societies—the most conspicuous being traditional China and the industrial West—the norm of free competition has been accepted for other people's sons, but most parents have believed their own sons deserved somewhat better than that. On the other hand, I doubt that even a majority of people in ascriptive societies (Western or not) have believed it was right for those *above* them to have been placed there by birth, although of course a majority might have affirmed their right by birth to be above *others*.[19]

Even in relatively "ascriptive" societies, the norm is that those who inherit their place should also validate it by both training and later adequate performance, e.g., knighthood. Almost never is there a norm denying any importance to achievement. Similarly, myths and legends recount with approval the ascent of the lowly to high position through merit.

In our presumably achievement-based society, few whites will fail to sense a twinge of the injustice of it all, when a superior Negro is made their boss. Few men believe that a woman should be promoted over them, even if by the criterion of merit she has earned it. Men with seniority believe it should count for more than achievement; and so on. Note, I am not stating merely that they are resentful, but that their value affirmations are in favor of other norms than performance when by those other norms they can lay claim to preferment.

Similarly, not only do the analyses of class membership, kinship, or friendship ties show the advantages or disadvantages of these non-achievement factors, but most individuals will, if pressed, admit they believe these factors should be used as norms, too. At a minimum, for example, if kinship or friendship is rejected in favor of merit as a norm, most will feel they are obliged either to give an additional justification of such a decision (thus demonstrating their lack of strong belief in the norm of achievement itself), or perhaps to help their role partner in some other way.

In an ongoing work group, both supervisors and members affirm a wide variety of other norms than achievement—seniority, the man's need, loyalty—to justify the retention of all but the most flagrantly inept and non-contributing members.

In all industrial countries, and perhaps especially in the Communist countries, whether industrial or industrializing, the *rhetoric* of placement by achievement is insistent. It has a strong political appeal. It is like a handful of other such normative positions as hard work, opposition to sin, or an open mind: people do not publicly deny their worth, but they do believe they are much better used to measure the worth of the other fellow.

The appeal of this rhetoric is illustrated well by the vociferous objection in the 1870's and 1880's to the introduction of merit placement in the United States Civil Service. People did not, after all, argue much against merit itself. On the other hand, they did introduce different standards, e.g., humanistic and anti-intellectual ones,[20] so as to avoid asserting that jobs should be given to the less able. In short, even in a society which is widely described as adhering to the rule of placement by achievement, not only does this norm not determine action consistently, but the commitment itself is highly qualified or weakened by belief in a wide range of other criteria as bases for rewards. Doubtless, one may argue nevertheless that members of an industrial society are somewhat more committed to this norm than are members of most other societies, but the contrast does not seem so great as contemporary sociology has asserted.

So persistent a phenomenon, even in a society whose rhetoric is permeated by achievement norms, cannot be interpreted as simply the usual failure of any society to implement its own values fully; in fact, people are committed to competing values as well.

The social arrangements (both behavioral and normative) that I have labeled "the protection of the inept" comprise a range of answers to a universal resource problem, which grows from the tension between the challenges of the external environment and the internal resources of the social system. Specifically, these arrangements comprise a partial answer to the question of what to do with that inevitable segment of a group that is relatively less productive or competent. How can the group utilize them, how gain from them that smaller, but measurable, amount of marginal productivity the group believes their efforts can contribute?

More generally, given the existence of the relatively inept in nearly all groups, what are the patterns or processes which will on the one hand protect them from the rigors of untrammeled competition (and thus gain their support and contribution), and on the other hand protect the group from the potentially destructive consequences of their ineptitude? Needless to say, there is no evidence that the social arrangements now observable are the most productive possible, whether of material goods or human satisfaction.

Having broadly reviewed some of the widespread evidence that such protective patterns exist, and that the norms in favor of reward by achievement are not unchallenged, let us now examine more closely the factors that create or support such patterns.[21]

FACTORS THAT INCREASE OR
DECREASE THE PROTECTION OF INEPTITUDE

These factors can be classified by whether they are *mainly* generated in the outside environment, as high or low demands are made on the collectivity for its output; or whether they largely originate in connection with internal social processes of the collectivity.

External Factors. 1. Perhaps the simplest formulation is that when there is a very high demand for a given type of group output or performance, the pressures on the group to fire, expel, or downgrade a member will be low. That is, the collectivity prospers in such an environment without demanding a higher performance from its members, or without recruiting more effective members. This principle is perhaps most clearly illustrated by the extraordinary current expansion of the college and university system in this and several other countries, and particularly by the expansion of graduate education. We do not create high-level men merely by announcing that a department will henceforth grant graduate degrees. Similarly, the increasing contemporary demand in business and government for expertise in a wide range of subjects offers new and increased rewards, and will doubtless eventually produce more skilled men. However, at present the expansion of opportunities occurs faster than that of skills, with the consequent protection of ineptitude in many places.[22]

2. We may also derive from this relation a secondary formulation, that when the supply of services, outputs, or candidates is relatively

low, a similar result is produced: a higher tolerance of ineptitude.[23] The best illustrations can be found at the lower job levels, where few people actively *want* that kind of work. However, at such levels those who hire cannot easily find substitutes, such as machines, or a new source of labor. This type of work is ranked as socially necessary but not important. Thus, though the demand may not be high, it will not drop to meet a low supply. The typical result in most societies seems to be the same: people decide they would rather pay little and tolerate ineptitude than pay good wages and thus be able to demand a high level of performance.

This formulation applies to most slave labor, to domestic work in almost all countries past or present, to nearly all dirty, unskilled tasks, to K.P. in the armed services, and of course by and large to the performance of family role obligations.

By a structural peculiarity of the recruitment process this principle may be observed in the academic world—though instances in other spheres are doubtless to be uncovered. Here the administrative jobs pay relatively well, but the most desirable recruits are likely to be professors who rank that type of job as somewhat of a comedown. Thus, there is a relatively low supply of the highly competent, with the same result, a greater protection of ineptitude than would otherwise occur. This type of recruitment may also be observed in the selection of administrative personnel in foundations.

3. Demand may be *deliberately* kept low by the sociopolitical structure. Here again there is little pressure on the group or collectivity to expose or punish the less productive. It is especially in government that one may locate such sub-units, although perhaps they are common in all organizations large enough to confront the whole society on many fronts, e.g., General Motors or the Catholic Church.

In the recent past, examples have included such agencies as the Office of Civil Defense, numerous antidiscrimination units, vice squads and gambling squads, agencies to reduce or prevent water and air pollution, or to beautify and develop parks and highways, and so on. Safety research in the automobile industry is another such instance. A high level of performance by this type of sub-unit would produce strong political opposition. As a consequence, a fairly low, often ritual, level of output is tolerated, and thus there are few pressures to evaluate the personnel by reference to the supposed target performance.

In general, of course, where clients do not demand high quality in performance, whether in Civil Defense or American cooking, the inept are relatively better protected than in other types of situations.

4. A variant formulation of the basic supply-demand relation is that there will be less or more protection of ineptitude, depending on its consequences for the power or prestige of the person who heads the collectivity. For example, if the subordinate's ineptitude reduces the chief's power, the latter is unlikely to tolerate low competence. This type of case may occur when the subordinate's action is highly visible, or has a public dimension, e.g., the messenger boys of the House of Representatives. An employee whose function it is to move between social systems or sub-systems will be under greater pressure to perform well, if a poor performance would reduce the authority of his chief.

Internal Processes. Of course, such environmental factors can operate only through group processes, but the collectivity also generates protective measures because of its own internal needs as well. Among these, the following may be noted. The first is that the inept create a "floor," a lowest permissible level of competence. To fire them is to raise that level, so that those who are now comfortably above it might be threatened. To some degree, the mediocre "need" the really inept. The Southern white, in this sense, has needed the black. Consequently, in perhaps most collectivities the thoroughgoing application of achievement criteria would be viewed as a threat.

Second, even the less competent have powers of bargaining, resources, pelf, contracts to give. Or they can make their fellow members feel guilty of inhumane conduct, thus invoking an alternate set of standards. In any given set of performance measurements, the costs of firing or downgrading the less able, or replacing them by better men, are weighted against the costs of permitting them to remain in the collectivity. This is simply another application of the general theory of role bargaining.[24]

Third, collectivities also assent to patterned exemptions from role obligations,[25] by which inevitable dips in performance are tolerated. These dips may be of short duration or not. Some permit the relaxing of standards because of another role obligation of high urgency or priority, e.g., the child of a working mother is ill, accidents, death in the family, and so on. Others express the tolerance of the group for individual fluctuations in personal integration, e.g., a man is going through a difficult marital crisis, has a work block, or becomes a heavy drinker for a while.

Another rule recognizes with compassion that the individual has entered on the normal declining curve in productivity with advancing age. What that age is will depend on the kind of activity the man performs. It is low among physical scientists, perhaps highest in politics and the law. In the occupational world, various structural solutions for this problem have been found, such as transferring a man to an essentially honorary or symbolic position, giving him easy physical work in a factory, handing over tasks of an essentially "human relations" type, or making him a representative of the organization in dealing with outside groups. More often, no formal changes are made, but less production is expected of him.[26]

A fourth internal factor is the complex problem of evaluation. That shrewd contemporary social analyst, Peter Ustinov, has noted that if the Secretary of State were to pass himself off as a comic, the observer would know within a few minutes that this is not his *métier*, but if a comic were to become Secretary of State, we would not at once discern any failure. The performance of the university president is especially difficult to measure, because of the complex relations between what the president does and the responses of his professors. Rewards are paid to the effective professor himself, but the prestige of professors may also be used as a measure of the president's achievement (at the levels where presidents are evaluated) even if in fact he has hindered their work. That is, the professor is motivated to work hard for himself, but his achievement may be viewed as proof of the president's competence. By contrast, the president of a municipal university may be given a lower evaluation because he fails to attract creative professors, when it is the low achievement of the tenured men which makes the university unattractive to potential recruits.

In any event, the less able are protected more in those types of performances that are difficult to evaluate. Parenthood, religious behavior, and administration are conspicuous examples. When war included hand-to-hand combat, performance could of course be evaluated much more easily than it is today. Similarly, sports offer an especially clear set of standards by which to evaluate performance, though here too some protection of weaker members by their teams can be observed. To some degree, the adversary system in Anglo-Saxon law tests competence in a public way. The higher levels of basic research constitute another area in which the less able are more likely to be exposed, and their lower performance made known.

These instances are notable because they *do* permit ready evaluation of performance. Granted that measurement is difficult, the interesting sociological question remains: Why do people (who after all constantly measure each other as individuals) not create group techniques for evaluating and making known the individual's performance level? Throughout this analysis, I am, of course suggesting that, in spite of some achievement rhetoric, people do not really want such a measurement system built into the social structure. We can, however, take note of several main *types* of answers to the measurement problem.

Perhaps the most difficult performances to measure are those of interpersonal skills or personal interaction. It is especially in such activities and occupations that the less able have a greater chance of avoiding exposure and—as social commentators have reminded us for centuries—consequently of obtaining a desired post. Of course, people do weigh one another with respect to these skills. However, the individual who can create a friendly atmosphere about himself may be able to escape any exposure of his inability to elicit a high performance from his subordinates, or to execute a bureaucratic task skillfully. He may make friends, but contribute little to the main task or target performance.

In such tasks, one common pattern of avoiding open competition is to assume that the problem of measurement can be skirted by refusing the position to people in low-ranking statuses, such as blacks, Jews, and women, even when these traits are not important for the task, and some available candidates with those characteristics might conceivably manage the job well.

This pattern of "insulation" protects the less able by preventing competition with all but a limited number of pre-selected people. Essentially, then, the group selects an *irrelevant* trait, which can be a status or a performance that makes little or no contribution to the main task. The collectivity may alternatively focus instead on only *part* of the target performance. For example, a man may elicit loyalty among his crew, but cannot persuade them to work hard; the group ranks him by the loyalty of his crew.

A focus on the irrelevant status may combine with insulation to produce a lower skill level among those whose competition might otherwise be feared. If the group or stratum can command the *gateways* to training, insulating their own sons from open competition, then the *ultimate* result is that their own sons can indeed outperform those who were kept from acquiring those skills. The protection of ineptitude, then, begins much earlier, so that at the end point those who receive the training may well be superior. This complex process may be observed among the lower social strata, blacks, Mexican-Americans, women, and so on.

This pattern is most strikingly illustrated in music. The less able can be less easily protected when a conspicuously inborn talent makes a difference, i.e., when measurement is easier. Thus, a goodly number of blacks have achieved great success in popular music, though they were nearly autodidacts. By contrast, concert performance of standard music requires both high talent and a long and costly training. It is notable, but to be expected, that blacks are rare in the latter field.[27]

These "answers" to the problem of measurement—focusing on an irrelevant trait, seizing on an irrelevant performance, insulating members from outside competition, barring the gateways to training —protect the less talented or less skillful. That evaluation of performance may be difficult goes without saying, but it is equally noteworthy that collectivities make few sustained moves toward solving the problem in the direction of rewarding on the basis of achievement. The work of a clergyman is especially hard to measure, in part because there has been little agreement on what the performance ought to achieve. However, both his superiors and clients are more likely to measure his work by, say, an increase in church attendance rather than by the parishioners' increased rejection of sin.

CONSEQUENCES OF PROTECTING THE LESS ABLE

Although we have by implication considered some of the consequences of these forms of protection, let us now examine them directly. One question must be faced at the outset. Does the protection of the less productive result in much inefficiency, so that the sub-system or collectivity (family, church, sports team) might fall or be destroyed?

Three important theoretical principles bear on this question. First, if I am correct in arguing that nearly all groups have social arrangements for protecting their inept, then that fact alone would not neces-sarily handicap any particular group. The soldier or sailor, observing the general disorganization, unwise recruitment, and misapplication of personnel resources during a war, may suppose that his side is bound to lose. However, since the opposing forces are similarly crippled, it is likely that other factors than the protection of the inept will decide the war. In blunt terms, most organizations and individ-uals do not have to perform at peak capacity in order to survive, because the competition is not doing so either.

At a somewhat broader level of generality, as I have elsewhere argued, social systems can operate with considerable anomie and incompetence.[28] This is especially true for societies. Except in the case of war, which measures only one kind of performance, the threat of the environment is almost never so great as to destroy the ad-vantages of human intelligence and organization.[29] Nearly always there is a sufficient surplus of manpower and resources to absorb almost any attack from the environment.

A second principle to be considered in weighing the costs of pro-tecting the less able, is that in fact some collectivities probably do go under because they protect their members too well. Organizations and sub-units compete primarily with others performing the same type of task, rather than with other social units in general. Upper-class families, for example, face their harshest competition for the available power, pelf, and prestige from other families in their own stratum, not from families at lower social ranks. For several genera-tions their margin of safety may be great, but eventually they may fail. Other upper-class families are a more direct political threat. They are eligible for all the lucrative posts any given elite family possesses. Until the advent of the mass army, the elite fought each other in war.

The irony of the universal family pattern of protecting the less able children from open competition is that to the very extent that they succeed in this effort, they risk the diminution of their own family rank, because the next generation will be unable to survive the *intra*-elite contest—or even, possibly, the threat from men who rise from still lower ranks. Moreover, there is some evidence that the chances of revolution increase when a set of elite families succeeds too well in excluding the able who seek to rise.

CONSEQUENCES OF NOT PROTECTING THE LESS ABLE

At a still deeper level of theoretical analysis, even for maximum efficiency the system-needs of any social unit *require* some protection of the inept, no matter what the goals of the group are, from the socialization of the child to the manufacture of transistor radios. The rigorous application of the norm of performance to the actions of all members of a collectivity would under most circumstances destroy both its social structure and its productivity.

It is, however, rare that any measurement of this kind has been carried out. Two of my first inquiries in the sociology of work ascertained: (a) that when sales performance was measured by individual success with the customer, salesmen engaged in several kinds of behavior that lowered *group* totals—holding customers who might have been waited on by others, refusing to replenish stock, and so on; and (b) that when management could prevent the formation of a genuine group, workers might have low morale but high individual productivity.[30] Also Blau outlined the consequences of the objective appraisal of performance in a clerical agency, some of which included falsifying records, undermining of the supervisor's authority, inconveniencing clients, and so on.[31] More recently, people doing industrial research have questioned the general assumption that an objective appraisal process would increase individual production.[32]

The sociological view is that placement, or punishment and reward, on the basis of performance alone, would essentially create a Hobbesian jungle, the undermining of group structure, the loss of the usual benefits of organization and cooperation, and the dissolution of group loyalties. Gouldner expresses this theoretical position effectively in his analysis of the contest system in Athenian society.[33] That system, he argues, "disposes individuals to make decisions that are often at variance with the needs and interests of the group." The type of open competition represented by the Greek contest system leads to bitterness, lowers the individual's commitment to group co-operation, creates strains in interpersonal relations, reduces con-formity to established morality, and undermines the stability of the *polis*. The failure to protect the inept would also, then, lower the out-put of the group.

Needless to say, I am omitting from this sketch the primarily psychodynamic consequences of appraisal by merit. These may in-clude feelings of being threatened, responses of distrust and hostility toward those doing the appraising, aversion of superiors to communi-cate those appraisals to their subordinates, resistance mechanisms of individuals who receive low appraisals, lowering of the individual's performance because of his diminished esteem after receiving a low appraisal, and so on.[34]

Structures With Less Protection of Ineptitude. The laconic asser-tion that not protecting the inept would lower group output needs further analysis, since clearly there are types of activities and groups in which a close approximation of appraisal and reward by merit occurs, without a destructive outcome. Perhaps the closest approxima-tions, as noted earlier, are sports and the basic scientific research in a university department or corporation. The cases may be instructive.

The relevant relationships can be sketched briefly. On a sports team, when an individual does very well, the system of measurement makes this known, but the rewards of the less able are *increased*, while their work load is decreased. This is also true of the basic research team, though less so. In the university department engaged in scien-tific research, this relationship is somewhat weaker—because what one individual first discovers, another cannot. Nevertheless: (a) if the more able do reduce their work output, this will not raise the rela-tive standing of the less able, since performance is measured by reference to achievement in the field as a whole; (b) in addition, men in the same department usually work on different problems; and (c) if all reduce their production in order to protect the less able, all individuals lose somewhat because the prestige of their department drops,[35] and work becomes less fun for the participants.

Cooperation and Output. These relationships do not hold in most work situations, although the more skilled corporation managers try to achieve such a structure where possible. If an individual does his best, knowing that achievement criteria alone will determine his advancement, the less able will drop relatively in the esteem of their supervisors, and possibly the level of required production from each member will rise. The less able members may, in fact, be squeezed out because they do not meet the new standard. Moreover, if each individual is rewarded only for his own performance, then in effect the group has given him nothing; whether his achievement level is high or low, he will feel no loyalty to the group.

If, as is now generally true of work systems, production does in fact partly depend on the efficiency of group organization and cooperation, the end result is likely to be less output, not more. By contrast, if the individual knows that when he needs it he will be protected somewhat by the group, he enjoys his personal relations with its members more, feels more securely identified with them, protects himself less from them, and is willing for the sake of the group to cooperate even when it will not raise his individual standing on the achievement scale.

Of course the professions, for all their emphasis on the rhetoric of individualism and achievement, illustrate the structural pattern common to most work situations, especially those with a strong union: the loss to all members would be greater, if the organizational structure failed, than would be the gain to a few highly able individuals if unrestricted public measurement of skill and effectiveness were permitted.[36]

Even the actual combat situation in war illustrates once more the dependence of organizational effectiveness on some protection of the inept. Without it, the competent will be killed along with the incompetent, for the former need the firepower and the loyalty of the latter. Such loyalty would not be so freely given if the inept could not count on being protected themselves. As implied earlier, the treatment of the demoted in management is an index of the judgment that the less able must be protected, to increase the effectiveness of the larger group.[37]

UTILIZATION OF THE INEPT UNDER INDUSTRIALIZATION

The preceding relationships merit further testing, but it is also worthwhile here to consider how they should be qualified on theoretical grounds. For even if all societies and nearly all collectivities do protect the less able, and even if failure to protect them will usually reduce output, it is equally clear that the protection of ineptitude can also *reduce* the effectiveness of the group. Certainly the evidence from societies with a high protection of the inept, such as caste or feudal systems, suggests that a high degree of protection is typically associated with low production. How does the utilization of the inept affect output?

The earlier sections of this paper anticipated that question by offering the hypothesis that social structures embody a tension between two factors, the protection *of* the inept and the protection of the group *from* the inept. At the psychological level this may be viewed as a tension between the frustration of the more able, and the degradation of the less able. Social structures vary in their solutions to this tension. For example, as noted earlier, family systems are far toward the extreme of placing little emphasis on achievement in ranking people, while sports (especially individual competition) fall toward the opposite extreme.

Social analysts have noted these differences, and have generally asserted that, for psychological integration, the individual cannot operate solely in activities whose criteria for reward are mainly those of performance. Everyone must at times retreat to other areas, such as friendship or the family, or perhaps religion and recreation, in which people are somewhat more protected from group downgrading or expulsion by a relatively lower frequency of public rankings, and the lack of refined ranks.[38]

This paper has focused, however, on the social structures which support nonachievement behavior *and* values even in groups or organizations whose rhetoric emphasizes achievement criteria. Some of the resulting protection of the inept is necessary if the collectivity is to produce effectively.

Yet such a hypothesis does not answer the question of how *much* protection of the inept is necessary for the highest efficiency or output. It is obvious, however, as a partial answer, that the modern industrial system outproduces all prior social systems. Is this the result, as so many have claimed, of giving freer scope to the highest talent and skill, and from rewarding more by merit than other societies have done?

That possibility cannot now be rejected, but I wish to sugest an alternative hypothesis, which emerges from the basic focus of this inquiry—how social structures handle the problem of what to do with the less competent. My alternative hypothesis is that the modern system is more productive because its social structures *utilize the inept more efficiently*, rather than because it gives greater opportunity and reward to the more able.

At one level this alternative explanation is merely self-evident. The two most significant tools of industrial society are the rationalized bureaucracy and the factory; their relation to ineptitude is the same. Both are based on a high division of labor, with fairly precise definitions of the task. As a consequence, a wide range of talent can acquire the skill necessary to carry out most jobs. Within any job level, some people will be much less competent than others, or than others whose job levels are lower, but they *can* do the job. Both the machine and the bureaucratic system lower the chances of catastrophic individual failure by the inept. They embody a control system which diminishes the range of possible error on the part of the individual worker. And, as so many essayists have noted, they also diminish the advantages that high talent would create, by narrowing the scope of free action. Then too, modern egalitarian ideology encourages men to feel valued as persons, providing motivation to all.

By contrast, the caste or feudal society gave great scope to talent, but only if the talented man was born to high position. Relying on placement by birth, such societies gave much protection to the inept, but gained little from it. Their productive technology was not organized into sub-tasks or sub-units or carefully articulated job assignments, which would maximize the productivity of the less able. The less competent in high places could do more damage, and the inept in lower positions could not contribute as much, as in modern society.

Variation Within Industrial Society. Evidently societies vary in their solutions to this problem, as do smaller units (sports teams, churches, and so forth) within each society. However, even with similar types of work organizations some variation is observable. In the French bureaucracy, for example, very little freedom of action is given to the outstanding, or for that matter even to the chief, and the lower echelons are still more controlled. On the other hand, from time to time an imaginative new organizational system is evolved by the very top men in the bureaucracy.[39]

In the Japanese system, entrance is granted to those who do well in competitive examinations, but of course that success is strongly determined by ascriptive criteria. Belonging to the right families guarantees better training for the tests.[40] Once hired, they move upward by seniority rather than merit, and people are rarely fired. However, the supervisor of a work unit gets credit for any ideas generated by people in his group, and precisely for that reason he need not attempt to stifle ideas. Granted, the more able man receives little advantage in promotion, but he does receive group esteem and some of his talent is put to use. Individuals are protected, and there is a correspondingly high degree of group loyalty. One result is that the organization as a whole is much more productive and creative than the United States observer would predict from the simple statement that nonachievement factors play a large role in the Japanese factory and bureaucracy.

In the American bureaucracy, perhaps the worker can obtain more individual credit for his contribution than would be likely under the Japanese system. Both factory and bureaucracy in the United States seem to change more easily than in France. The American system has become more decentralized, and more autonomous at the lower levels, than either the Japanese or the French. Superiors consult more easily with subordinates in the United States than in the other two countries. This pattern may increase somewhat the chances of obtaining an advantage from the contributions of the more able, but also yields less protection to the less competent.

CONCLUSION

So brisk a set of comparisons does not aim at a full answer to the question of optimum production or efficiency, but rather serves to illustrate the fact that apparently similar types of structure may give more or less protection to the inept, and more or less protection *from* the inept. The answer, if we were able to obtain it over the next few decades, would yield a still more useful by-product: how to create sets of social structures in different areas of action, to correspond more closely with our own values. In these relations, as in much of our social life, we may *will* some of the proximate social patterns without approving their ultimate result. If we knew better the full consequences of given arrangements for protecting the inept, we might decide to change these structures.

With reference to such values, I have ignored a number of issues that would have to be faced in a more extensive analysis. One, of course, is whether a society can or should reward equally those who are known to be less productive.[41] On a different level of values, though we may feel the less able performer ought not to be given more rewards, some of us may also assert that the performances properly to be rewarded are not those of automobile production and billboards, or even moon-rockets, but the far less easily measurable performances of warmth and loving, truth—note that the problem here is not one of ineptitude but simply a total lack of demand—beauty and taste, laughter, compassion, courage, generosity, or the support of variety in men and women.

We would ultimately also have to examine not only our own values about the equality of opportunity, and the degradation of those who would inevitably fall behind,[42] but the more complex consequences for every sector or sub-system of the society. In doing so, we might have to take on a significant but nearly neglected task of an imaginative theory of society, the analysis and creation of utopias,[43] based on our widening and deepening knowledge of how social systems really operate. What kinds of societies are in fact possible, other than those which have existed?

Perhaps, by ascertaining both our values and the possible organizations for achieving them, we might learn that the costs of many contemporary patterns are too great. I do not agree with the many critics in sociology who hold that our dominant theory is merely an extended Panglossian commentary, proving this is the best of all possible worlds. Doubtless, whatever is, is possible, and whatever is may have to be, but we can, I believe, go beyond those powerful laws and demonstrate, as other sciences have before us, that many desirable but presently nonexistent arrangements *are* also possible.

6. *Violence*
Between Intimates

INTRODUCTION

THE SUCCEEDING ANALYSIS IS ONE OF A SERIES OF PROJECTED PAPERS ON THE ALMOST ENTIRELY NEGLECTED THEORETICAL PROBLEM OF force and force-threat in social life.* Space does not permit an exposition of my views on this topic, which contain methodological and conceptual subtleties more difficult than in most other aspects of social behavior. Sociology has for long glossed over this realm, because it was thought to be the proper task of political science, which also failed to tackle it, except with reference to violence among nations, and revolutions. Very likely, however, we ignored it because the traditional sociological conception has expended more of its intellectual energy on an exploration of voluntary action in the narrow sense. Since people were socialized to believe in the norms and values of their group, they were perceived as conforming because at some level they wanted to do so. We exploited the wisdom that social systems, political regimes, groups and institutions could not survive unless they were *legitimate*, that is, people accepted them as right, just, and moral. No such social system could be based on force alone.

But though that wisdom was correct, it postulated a false dichotomy: no system can rest on force alone, but not even a *legitimate*

---

* The only other one that I have published is "Force and Violence in the Family," *Journal of Marriage and the Family*, 33, 3, 1971.

social system can survive if it is not also based on force or its threat. We may not perceive this truth, because we *see* so little force being used, but that does not tell us that force and force-threat are not powerful. Indeed, the opposite: it is precisely because they are *powerful* that we observe so little violence being displayed. People do not use open force much upon one another in a civil society, and a civil government does not often use violence on its citizens, in part because in a civil society people know very well that they will not escape punishment easily if they openly violate the laws or resist the government with violence. This truth is displayed spectacularly in those pockets or ghettoes or even a civil society where open violence is more common: there, by contrast, people can get away with the open use of force upon one another, and policemen cannot count on the support of ordinary citizens.

Here, however, I have not tried to develop this broad view, but only to deal with a small segment of force and force-threat, specifically the open violence between intimates. Since I have avoided much explicit theory formulation, it may be useful to comment on the view from which this analysis proceeds.

First, although the social behavior being analyzed is legally criminal, I have not viewed it *as* criminal. I have rather supposed that the dynamics out of which violence between intimates grows are the same for perhaps all of us. Consequently, I have not felt as much trepidation as perhaps I should, in entering upon a topic in which criminologists are certainly more expert.

Second, although the analysis does take note of emotions and passions, inner debates about possible actions, the sense of injustice, and so on, the theoretical sense is not at all psychological. The violence of emotions is not used here to explain violence in social behavior; rather, emphasis is constantly on the social interactions in which the surrounding society, the victim, and the culprit contribute—usually unwillingly and almost always unknowingly—to the outcome. Social forces define and shape these feelings and actions, control or encourage their expression, or offer alternative solutions to the individual's problem.

Furthermore, I have cast the analysis in a somewhat unusual framework for violence: exchange theory. It is not, of course, that people exchange murder for an insult, although some have done just that. It is rather that much of violence is not only *followed* by rationalizations and exculpations, whose aim it is to obtain sympathy or a lighter sentence. It is also *preceded* by a smouldering or explosive sense of *injustice*: the other person has paid our goodness and fairness back with injustice, heartlessness, and selfishness.

Indeed, the analysis throughout underlines the powerful role that norms and values play in the generation of violence: the scaling or evaluation of how violent we have a right to be, in response to a range of provocations; the support or discouragement of violence by others; the definition of which obligations others owe to us; others' social disapproval of the person who backs down; and so on.

The exposition also takes account of the "field-effect" of others' violence on any potential assault. This can be analytically distinguished from the "culture of violence," for the latter simply refers to the values and norms of a local group, neighborhood, ethnic group, or class. People in a contemporary ghetto neighborhood live in a social atmosphere in which they perceive themselves as more often under threat, less protected by either the police or other citizens, less likely to be ostracized or disapproved if they resort to violence, more likely to witness assaults on any given day—in short whatever other *cultural* or social variables in their lives are conducive to violence, the very field of *social* forces in which they live potentiates the overt and criminal use of force still more.

Class differences are also observable in crucial structural aspects of exchanges between intimates: not that one gets more than the other at higher class levels, but that toward the upper strata people have more resources for working out pacific relationships with others, new experiences, and alternative solaces. These resources include especially verbal skills for solving or glossing over conflicts, and the help of experts in ending a relationship.

As noted in Chapter 2, some of the political attacks on sociology stem from a perceived contrast between the deplorable conditions that research reports, and the lack of pleas for correcting the situation. The charge has been hurled against functionalism, that is, sociology since World War I, that it merely explains in great detail why nothing *can* be done. Here, I have left in my suggestions for change, but am aware that the most important of them would not arouse much acceptance among most Americans. Even the relatively modest suggestion, that we remove hand-guns from citizens now, and gradually from policemen as well, could not survive a vote in a single legislature. To suggest that we change the class system so that those in the lower social strata enjoy more rewards and suffer less humiliation and insult is even less welcome to the American populace.

As I urged in Chapter 2, such policy suggestions, whether calmly or passionately expressed, need not bias the empirical analysis. In fact, in this instance I would argue that they underscore the hypotheses in that analysis, since the predictable opposition to these proposed policies demonstrates how much more tolerant our people are of violence than they are of the changes in the social system that would be necessary to reduce it by much.

In the standardized murder mystery, the plodding detective stubbornly tries to pin the crime on the husband, wife or good friend of the victim, while the imaginative super sleuth through a dazzling skill in intuition or reasoning proves that a seemingly unrelated individual plotted the dark deed. Bureaucratic lack of imagination and the authoritarian forces of the police are thus exposed to ridicule.

Real life does not imitate art that closely. In ordinary life, when the homicide squad encounters a crime of violence there is no murder mystery at all. Several people already know who was the criminal. If not, some patient questioning of close friends, lovers, or spouses reveals who the culprit was. The best guess as to "who did it" is that an intimate of the victim was the culprit. In one half to three fourths of the homicide victims reported on in various studies, the murderer and his victim had at least some previous association.[1] Why do intimates commit violence against one another? Perhaps the most powerful if crude answer is that they are *there.* Most automobile accidents occur within 25 miles of the home because that is where the cars *are* at the time. Home may not be as dangerous as mines or ski slopes, but more injuries occur there because people are there more of the time. It cannot be surprising that more violence is directed against those with whom we are in more intimate contact. We are all within easy striking distance of our friends and spouses, for a goodly part of the time.

Moreover, again crudely but reasonably, we are violent toward our intimates—friends, lovers, spouses—because few others can anger us so much. As they are a main source of our pleasure, they are equally a main source of frustration and hurt.

What they do affects us more directly and painfully than what most strangers do.

At this simple level, then, *why* most murders and a high but partially unreported percentage of violent acts are aimed at intimates appears to contain no mystery at all. Nevertheless, from the earliest myths to the latest plays and novels, the theme of violence between those who are emotionally close has fascinated human observers. From Cain and Abel to Othello; from Clytemnestra to Lolita, our literature (like that of the East) has been written in blood, because the theme entranced both writer and audience. Indeed, as a literary theme, violence between *strangers* is pallid and uninteresting. It must be supposed that all of us respond in darkly atavistic ways at the deepest levels of psychological impulse to the idea of killing or maiming those who are emotionally close to us.

If the human response is so common, and the primal impulse to do violence to our intimates is so ubiquitous and powerful in the human animal, must we also accept the widespread belief that man is by nature a killer, by his very biological predisposition prone to attack his fellow man? And if he is, does this mean that we must despair of ever pressing him gently or firmly onto the paths of civility, restraint, or at least a lower propensity to violence? If the gloomier interpretation of man's biological nature is correct, then why intimates kill one another is even less of a mystery. If we are natural killers, put together in the same cages and habitations, then surely many of us must die.

Certainly man must plead guilty to part of the accusation. From Homer to the present, social philosophies have denounced our savage deeds. We now know that over a million years ago our man-like ancestors in the Olduvai Gorge had already become the scourge of the animal kingdom. Clever at killing both small and large prey, our ancestors included members of their own species among their victims. Doubtless, until man sinks into the abyss of eternity, he will continue this ancient practice.

By contrast, man's anthropoid cousins, the gorilla, chimpanzee, gibbon and orangutan, began to follow a separate line of evolution 15 or 20 million years ago and remained largely herbivorous and pacific while we become omnivorous and warlike.

However, we are not only unlike our closest relatives in this respect alone. We are also unlike all the animals as well. First, because man makes tools he is unlike the great killers in this: almost *any* adult human being can kill any other human being with stone or club, knife or split bone or obsidian, gun or poison. The weak can kill and hurt even the strong, can equalize the differences in strength or skill that nature or training has granted to the superordinate. The lion or leopard, weasel or shark, that is smaller or less competent in attack must learn to accept the dominance of its superiors, but the oppressed, frustrated, or merely angry human being can work out a successful plan for eliminating any of his fellows.

In the wild state, as so many animal ethologists have reported, animals do not kill members of their own group or species. But the weak ones *cannot* do so, and when whipped they submit. A whipped man or woman can by contrast bide his or her time until an opportune moment for redressing the balance of power.

Man's violent urges are less controlled or controllable than those of animals not because he has an "instinct to kill" but because he has no instincts at all. Although some adult animals will eat the unprotected young of their species, and under stressful circumstances (mainly in captivity) some mothers have eaten their own young, no species has any instinct to kill other members of its own species. Inherently self-destructive, such an instinct would have been an intolerable burden for any type of animal in its fight for survival. Indeed, if Conrad Lorenz is correct, the killer animal has counter-instincts against any dangerous intraspecies aggression, which include both limitation of the types of attack and rigid patterns of submission when one animal is defeated.

By contrast, man has no biologically prescribed "solutions" to standard environmental problems: he has to learn all that he knows or does. Thereby he is the most flexible of animals in searching for answers to environmental challenges, the most open to new procedures for adapting to social or biological pressures.

But precisely for that reason, what he has learned is not sufficiently compelling to overcome his aggressive impulses if his fellow men do not inhibit his violent urges socially; no built-in biological restraints or instincts exist that would keep his actions within even the bounds of civility that lions or wolves respect. Untamed by instincts, man is frequently not gentled by his childhood or adult learning experiences either.

Indeed, in this set of learning processes, man achieves at best a precarious, paradoxical balance. If in fact others succeed in implanting in him a deep and passionate concern for others so that he might cherish them, their actions become thereby so important to him that they can arouse a murderous anger in him. If he cares little or not at all, he may not feel much concern or guilt when weighing the advantages of getting rid of others.

The same precarious and paradoxical balance may also be observed in man's dealings with outsiders, strangers, or foreigners. In a warlike, primitive society, strangers are not brothers, and the society may exact only a minor penalty for killing someone who hardly belongs to the human race. Western explorers and settlers displayed such cool sentiments in South Africa, in the South Pacific and the New World. Natives were able, at times, to return the compliment. Again, however, when groups become more important to one another, and their welfare is more dependent on other's actions, they also begin to be more indignant about what others do and thus more willing to kill or hurt.

Thus, in its rearing and controlling process, the civil society aims at a balance between caring too much about what others do, and being indifferent to their fate.

That few men do kill or maim others seems to refute the notion of a biological urge or instinct to murder. Whatever man's aggressive impulses, obviously most men learn to control them. Much more compelling, however, are the great differences in homicide and assault rates among nations, regions within nations (e.g., the southern United States or Italy as compared with the north), classes and ethnic groups, the two sexes. The differences are so great as not to be explicable, except by reference to *social* factors. This fundamental conclusion also gives some support to those who aim at reducing man's violence toward his fellows. If different social patterns create high or low rates then perhaps we can find out why, and build toward social structures that will generate less violence.

Since broad social differences affect the relations among intimates, they also lower or raise the frequency of violence between intimates and we must examine them in this analysis. However, it seems likely that the peculiarities of intimate emotional links among human beings have their *own effects within* the general and pervasive pressures from great cultural factors. In this analysis, those peculiarities, as mediated by the larger social-structural pressures, will be the main object of our attention.

Before considering some of the broad regularities that govern the outbreak of violence between human beings, we should at least take note of the range of variegated forms that violence may assume among intimates. Clearly no theory or interpretation can encompass all of them, and any classification is subject to criticism. These overlap here and there, and the motives for them vary considerably.

As a major category, we shall place most emphasis on various forms of homicide and assault. Within this, of course, we shall have to consider the smaller case of murder accompanied by suicide. To include various forms of assault with homicide may appear to confuse the issue somewhat, but we must keep in mind that many forms of homicide actually appear in court as aggravated assault and many whose anger stimulates them to an act of homicide claim later, in all sincerity "they did not mean to do it." Many fail, in turn, to murder and only maim another when their real intention was to kill. In addition, all of us are enough aware of our own emotions under periods of great stress to know that though we were inhibited from an actual attack, our deepest impulse was to destroy, to eliminate our opponent. All who have observed opponents in a furious contest of merely verbal debate will recognize the intensity of anger that may well up, and intuitively can understand how—given different circumstances—one or another of the opponents would cheerfully crush the other. Thus, the overlap within this broad category is very great. It is safe to say that many children engaged in an ordinary fight have a strong wish to kill at the moment, even though they would recoil in horror at the reality itself. Thus, the overlap within this set of complex legal categories is extremely great and they do share a considerable common root, an intense murderous emotion.

Violence among intimates must also include the wide range of behavior under the general category of forcible rape. We shall later on present some of the data that indicate how frequently this type of case involves people who have had prior or even very close contact with one another. More important, it is safe to say that rape is like assault in that a very high proportion—even a majority of the cases that actually occur—never come to the attention of the police. Certainly this would be true for cases of attempted rape, or the use of force to achieve a sexual end, even when it ends in failure. The steps by which men and women move consciously or unconsciously toward this type of confrontation will be dealt with later on.

Of course, any examination of violence among intimates must include fights and homicide among friends, drinking companions, and adult and juvenile gangs. These include both the enmities that exist between chronic opponents as well as the transformation of friendship into momentary hate, not to mention the simple arguments that result eventually in a fight. We shall also have to consider the extent to which such networks of friendship actually stimulate one form or another of violence.

One of the more troubling of the cases we shall have to consider is the case of child abuse, a phenomenon that has occupied the attention of welfare workers for many decades, but which has received little public recognition until recently. Without any question, child abuse is far more common than most believe, and those who have published reports on it have had to face the relative disbelief of others in their data. In individual cases, welfare workers or physicians have been reluctant to invoke public authority or legal powers to save the child from further hurt.

That type of case overlaps psychologically in turn with cases of matricide and patricide, as well as the case of parents killing their older children. The complex swirl of emotions within the small family is usually difficult to understand or even to untangle, but we must at least attempt to see what light can be thrown upon such cases.

It is clear, of course, that many cases of child abuse and homicide or assault within the family between parents and children often grow from severely neurotic or psychotic personality structures. The extent to which families maintain their common residence, even when one or more may be dangerous, is a problem we must also examine. Such cases overlap in turn, of course, with the more general case of the mentally ill person who murders or assaults someone who is close to him. This may include a good friend or helpful neighbor as well as a member of the family. We cannot, of course, unravel here the transformation of psychotic impulses into homicidal impulses, though we have progressed enough in the past 50 years to be well aware that psychosis only rarely leads to homicide. The "mad murderer" is a common enough newspaper phrase but psychoses themselves are not specifically homicidal in character.

Finally, of course, we must consider somewhat separately—at least analytically separately—the case of the *calculated* murder or assault against an intimate, when material advantage is the aim. These include the instances of homicide for insurance or inheritance, the removal of a spouse or lover who is blocking the way toward a satisfactory new life arrangement, the murder of a competitor, the attempt to "persuade" a competitor in a business or illegal racket, and so on. It may be somewhat less productive of understanding to consider these cases, since they seem to approximate a simpler case of jungle warfare. What makes them somewhat more interesting is that often they involve two people who have not only intimate relations with one another, but sometimes apparently friendly relations with one another. At a minimum, some simulated friendship may be utilized as a way of achieving the objective of destruction. In addition, we need to consider why people are willing, in the face of the known risks, to attempt so hazardous a course for the achievement of what seem to be quite ordinary goals.

But though we shall wish to consider some of these types of cases separately, all of them could be crowded under the broad category of "homicide and assault" and much of our analysis will therefore focus on this most general category, for whatever the motives or backgrounds of those intimates who hurt one another may be, they issue in violent attacks, some of which end in homicide.

As we noted previously, the peculiarities of human relations that grow from closeness and intimacy alter and shift the characteristics of violence in many ways, but these in turn form part of a broader category of violence in our time. Homicide between strangers is different from violence between intimates in some ways, but both are subject to the broad social pressures that generate or reduce the rate of homicide or assault. In a society with a general low rate of homicide, there will, of course, be fewer homicides between intimates. We must therefore give at least some passing attention to the general distribution and incidence of violence. Those data are relevant here, since they constitute the broad framework of forces within which violence between intimates occurs at a higher or lower rate.

These broad patterns are also of use to the analyst, because they help to guide him toward possible *causes*. Unfortunately, as all researchers in criminal behavior have noted, official reports do not help us much in understanding the social and psychological causes of crime, because they contain only the information that is necessary to the policeman in keeping his own records, and to some extent in formulating the case for prosecution. The law is much less interested in the forces that created crime, and far more in setting the stage for demonstrating what crime actually took place and who was responsible for it.

On the other hand, these reports do contain some evidence as to where violence is most likely to occur. The categories that are typically used are not *causal categories*. They are often what the sociologists call "status variables" such as age, sex, region, class, etc. They are not themselves the causal influences, but they help us locate such causes. Thus, for example, the status category "Negro" is not, strictly speaking, a racial category, but is a social one. Much more fundamentally, however, it says nothing about cause per se; it merely directs us to look at the social factors within the lives of a disadvantaged group, to ascertain why the rate might be high or low within that group. Similarly, we know that women are convicted far less than men of almost any category of crime except shoplifting and prostitution but we do not suppose that we have located a biological cause. Rather, we are directed to look again at the social constraints, the manner of socialization, the allocation of energies, the differential opportunities, and so on that may lead to a lower rate of criminal conviction, and possibly also a lower rate of criminal activity.

We shall not even attempt here an adequate summary of these broad patterns, but merely make reference to a few of the findings that by now have been validated in many studies. For our purposes they constitute only the background or framework within which violence among intimates takes place. Perhaps the most general of these is the finding that among industrial nations, the United States is perhaps the most violent. Although of course legal definitions vary greatly from one nation to another, to the point that the category of "assault" is almost useless for comparative purposes, and "homicide" can be compared only very loosely, it is unlikely that any standardization would change this general ranking by much.

This finding has been widely discussed by commentators and criminologists for many decades. Americans, it is claimed, begin with a frontier tradition and though the frontier itself included only a small percentage of the total population after the first settlement, its patterns affected all of the United States. On the frontier, men had to depend upon their own mastery of violence in order to survive, whether against lawless intruders or Indians. Courage was useful in such a social structure, it is asserted. The ideal of a man facing the threat of death unafraid became embedded in myth and folklore. Moreover, some would argue that those who settled here were primarily not from the more civil, polite layers of European or Anglo-Saxon society, but lower middle class or lower class people, accustomed to violence in their own country.

In addition, there is at least some reason to claim that Americans have been more restive under authority than the population of Europe, more prone to local revolts, riots and feuds. Colonists evaded English law before independence, and dissidents of all types refused to bow to the yoke of legality. As a consequence, we must face the fact that from the beginning of American settlement, our cultural tradition has leaned toward the solution of personal and social problems through the use of force, more than the nations from which the settlers came.

It is not surprising then that various studies over the past generation have disclosed our homicide rate (by various modes of calculation) is typically from 3 to 10 times as high as that of other Western nations. For many American cities, the present rate would come close to 9 or 10 per 100,000, while that of, say, Amsterdam or Berlin would be 1 or less.

Doubtless, the comparison between the United States and such Western cities and nations is the correct one to make, but it should not be forgotten that other nations almost certainly have rates equally high. Certainly many Latin American nations have extremely high rates of assault and homicide and some Eastern nations also fall into that category.[2]

Moreover, as against the frequent gloomy analyses of the present, almost certainly this rate has not risen over the past half century. The "rising tide of violence" is almost certainly a fabrication of newspaper excitement, moralistic preaching, and changes in police reporting. In an earlier period, most assaults never appeared in the police court, and far more killings did not, for they were viewed as relatively private, local affairs. It is true that people fear for their safety in American cities now, but this has been true in the past—and once was true in London too.[3]

The importance of this general set of facts is, however, that all of us live to some extent in an atmosphere of greater violence than in other nations whose technological development is close to that of ours. Consequently, the propensity to violence among intimates is also likely to be higher here than in other countries.

The same may be said with reference to *regional* differences within the country itself. Here, of course, the most obvious difference is to be found in the *southern* regions, i.e., the South Atlantic, East South Central, and West South Central States, whose rates of both homicide and aggravated assault vary from two to five times as high as those of other parts of the country. Here again, essayists and even casual observers have noted the cultural differences. Southerners are much more likely to carry guns. They have maintained, longer than in others parts of the United States, a resistance to authority and a cultural emphasis on a man's right to solve some of his personal problems by direct intervention rather than recourse to the law. This grew partly out of a rural tradition, but also out of a tradition that gave great weight to the ideal of the cavalier who had a right to bear arms and a duty to uphold his own honor.

Apologists for the South have sometimes urged that the extremely high rate of homicide and aggravated assault was caused only by the high percentage of blacks in the South. According to this argument, blacks are an especially violent part of the American population; they are not only more emotional than whites, but are subjected to fewer restraints. Lacking adequate socialization in the home, it is argued, they are unable to bear frustration and vent their rages immediately without thinking of the consequences. Thus, the rate of *general arrest* among blacks is about three times that of the white population. If we confine the cases to criminal homicide, the black rate is about 4 times that of whites. Cities with a higher percentage of Negroes have higher homicide rates.

Unfortunately for this kind of explanation, Southern *whites* also have a higher rate of homicide than the rest of the nation. One could, then, argue that since it was the blacks who were the immigrants, and who have learned their cultural patterns from the whites, in fact they have done no more than acquire the propensity to violence that characterizes the Southern white culture.

Nevertheless, by almost any type of criterion, the rate of homicide and aggravated assault is higher among blacks than among whites, both men and women. The black rate is lower in areas where the white rate is lower, but it is nevertheless higher than that of the whites. This general fact is important, again, as a guide to understanding the dynamics of violence among intimates.

For many decades it has been known that women commit homicide less than men do. Among blacks, the ratio is somewhat less, perhaps as much as 1 to 4, and for whites as much as 1 to 9, but the ratio is high in all reported studies, in this as in other countries. One study of nearly 20 years ago suggests that where the rate of homicide is low, the difference between men and women is less.[4] Nevertheless, by almost any comparison, women are much less likely to commit homicide than are men. We shall examine some of the reasons for this difference later on.

Although official police reports do not include class differences in homicide rates, when assault or homicide is distributed on city maps by census tracts, it is clear that the higher rates are found in the poorer areas, and the lower rates in the suburbs. This finding accords, of course, with commonsense and with ordinary observation, though again the dynamics are not equally obvious. In such poorer areas, a higher percentage of blacks is also to be found, but higher rates are also recorded in poorer white areas as well.

It should be kept in mind, however, that poverty per se is not the causal variable. It is true that the South is poorer than the rest of the nation, and has higher homicide rates, but poorer counties in Idaho or Iowa will not exhibit rates as high as those in the somewhat wealthier urban counties in the New York City sprawl. Poorer areas in the United States are more likely to be rural, but rural areas do not have rates as high as urban regions do. Thus, we must interpret class variables as referring to various kinds of social and cultural dynamics, not merely to mechanical relationship between poverty and violence.[5]

Such broad differences suggest that people in different social settings acquire different *predispositions* to violence, and are restrained more or less by the *social networks* within which they live. Since violence between intimates must be shaped or generated by such factors, it is necessary to consider first the patterns of socialization, the ways by which the kin and friend networks, and later the school, attempt to mould the child to fit the demands of the society.

In perhaps the simplest of socialization models, the infant is a bundle of unformed desires, and the parents from their first interaction with it are occupied with trying to inhibit most of those desires, and to implant more civilized ones. By punishment and reward, parents (and others, later on) "teach" the child that crime does not pay and that virtue does. In the ideal case, the child learns "what is right and what is wrong," which does not mean only that he can describe what his parents want, but that he comes to feel deeply the same values they have been urging on him.

The child, in this ideal version of what happens, becomes an autonomous individual, who refrains from violence, revenge, or crime not because he can not get away with it, but because it is wrong in itself, because his conscience would bother him, because he is not even tempted to kill or rob. He has learned a distaste for crime. From an inarticulate, savage beast—fortunately, helpless at birth—he is transformed into a civil adult, pleased to obey the laws.

Of course, it is recognized that some people are not so transformed, and in this description the criminal is viewed as one whose impulses were not inhibited. He remains at some primitive or childlike level, and at best learns that others will punish him, so that he had better be careful when he breaks the law. His parents were ineffective, or he associated with evil companions who persuaded him to flout the civil rules of his society.

The dynamics of socialization seem to be more complex than the above description suggests. Children do come to acquire the values of their parents, but it is not clear just how or why.[6] Often they do so only because both parents and children live in the same neighborhood, class, and ethnic group.

We also see more clearly that most of us can be tempted by crime at times, and indeed a rather high percentage of people actually do engage in it.[7] Professional criminals *are* different in some ways from the rest of us, but all those who commit crimes are probably more like the rest of us than different. Few of us are so completely socialized as to feel no impulse to aggression. We do feel committed to legal order, civility, nonviolence, and similar virtues, but we are also quick to spin out a chain of moral justification if we are tempted by their opposites.

Moreover, it is clear that some part of the process toward criminal behavior is a "labeling process," by which the young person is gradually *typed* by others as a criminal, is treated differently, and responds differently. In harmony with our previous comments on cultural differences, we also note that the criminal—and these comments apply, as we shall see, to much of assault and homicide among intimates—has more *opportunity* to engage in crime, and is more likely to associate with others who are part of (or who at best do not object to) a criminal subculture. We shall later see at which points some of these general processes are relevant for violence among intimates.

However, more fundamental for our present inquiry is the extent to which we are all trained to some extent *for* violence, including aggression against intimates. Let us consider this process briefly.

In general, social science has neglected force as a factor in social interaction. The economist postulates a civil society in which people obey the laws, and only now and then recognizes that force protects the telephone company against an intrusive competitor, the heiress against the predatory embezzler, the wife against the threats of her husband. Typically, the economist does not even touch on the sprawling criminal enterprises of the country. Similarly, the sociologist or psychologist analyzes the value commitments and motivations of people, but ignores the ways by which force or its threat may shape decisions, actions, and even wishes. The pupil may respect the teacher, but is also aware that the teacher is (in the lower grades) stronger or can call a policeman to remove the obstreperous from the classroom. The parent can call on force to impose his will on the child, and either spouse can invoke outside force to protect himself or herself.

This underlying factor in social relations is usually neglected, because we *see* little force, and because our own impulses to use force are concealed—often even from ourselves. Nevertheless, this concealed variable is of considerable importance, and not the least in intimate relations. Napoleon is said to have remarked that one can do anything with bayonets except sit on them: People must be persuaded, not merely forced. Nevertheless, force is *at least an ultimate deterrent*, and its threat colors many aspects of our private lives.

We must view the outbreak of violence among intimates as not merely an example of *failed socialization*, a case that shows the individual received a poor or inadequate rearing as a child. Many people are capable of homicide or assault whose earlier experiences could not be distinguished from those of the law abiding.

Next, we must not suppose that violence, even among intimates, is a simple function of association with others who are criminal or addicted to violence (although that experience *does* have its impact). It is not only criminals who support the social patterns of violence.

We must rather understand that not all of the socialization experiences mould the child *against* violence. Indeed, in many ways what happens in the earlier years is a training *for* violence. It supports violence more in some groups than in others, but few groups can claim that the entire content of their rearing and social control techniques press toward peaceful behavior.

First, of course, the child learns from the earliest years that force *is* effective, and does in fact prevent others from carrying out an act that is disapproved. Although observational studies of child rearing are rare, any observer can see that American parents characteristically use force on their children, from the earliest ages on. Certainly they use far more force than parents in most primitive societies do. Their contrast with the less violent Japanese parents is especially striking.[8] Although hundreds of articles over the past 20 years have denounced John Dewey's notions of progressive education, Dr. Spock's earlier advice to punish less and love more, and the various forms of "permissive" child rearing, in fact none of these theories was ever put into effect. American parents *do* whip their children less now. Teachers also use less force on their pupils than a generation ago. But love and peacefulness as parental or pedagogical techniques have not been tried. Indeed, since the adult generation has had so much childhood experience with the ultimate effectiveness of force, it would be surprising if its members even *could* put such a philosophy into action.

The child learns, then, that when *he* does something that displeases others who are stronger, they will deter or punish him if they can. This is a simple and powerful lesson, and is clearly not limited to strangers, since it is first learned within the family.

He learns from observing his own parents that males are stronger than females, and when they lose in a verbal battle they can have recourse to violence. Even if his parents do not fight physically, he may observe (even in middle class households) that his mother is frightened when his father is furious. He learns that even grown men who are neighbors may goad one another into fighting. Here again, he will experience more violence in a lower class than in a middle class street, but he will be conscious of these flares of temper anywhere. At a minimum, he sees his father threaten violence to another driver who has bullied his way through traffic; or sees his father avoid a threatened battle with another driver.

Of course, parents do preach nonviolence to their children, and so do teachers, but both sets of authorities, like policemen, exhibit their *own* belief in the efficacy of force when used on intimates, and impose their will through the superior deployment of violence.

The child learns several things from these experiences, which become part of his adult personality, forces in his own psychodynamics. First, of course, he learns that violence *can* be useful, and that many get away with it. Very little of the aggression he observes is ever punished in the courtroom, and force is often successful in protecting one's rights, or in imposing one's will on another.

Second, he learns the various *gradations* of violence, fitted to different types of situations, frustrations, insults, or people. Part of this is, of course, simply learning the *costs* of different grades of violence. A man learns to judge (erroneously or not) how tough other men are, so that in various encounters he knows when to retreat and when to stand his ground. Each individual is also taught a complex set of cost *contingencies:* A boy is punished more for using violence on a girl than on a boy, on a younger boy than on a boy his own age, on a teacher than on a stranger; more for imposing his will by violence than for defending his rights; etc.

The adult has also acquired, as part of his emotional dynamics, a set of values and attitudes that rank violence differently according to the action that potentially stimulates it. Until recently in Texas, for example, not only did courtroom practice support the outraged husband who killed his wife and her lover when he caught them in *flagrante delicto*—this could be a calculated *cost*—but men were socialized to *feel* that degree of outrage, to feel so dishonored that they could not without shame treat the event nonchalantly. In an earlier era in the United States and in Western countries generally, certain types of confrontations required a duel, and men who called themselves gentlemen felt shame if they avoided one.

So extreme a set of cases merely points up the central fact that we come to respond with different intensities of emotions to the different actions of our friends, spouses, and lovers, and thus we learn gradations of violence with which to respond to those actions. Almost no one as parent refuses violence as a tool, to put down the violence that a child directs against *him*, but some parents will ultimately refuse to use violence against the verbal attacks from their teenager children. At an earlier age, such an attack would have been met with violence. Middle class husbands do not often use fists on their wives, but I would venture that most have at least slapped their wives at some point in their married lives when the provocation seemed great.

Of course, no rule in contemporary society approves of homicide as an answer to even adultery, but many informal rules are applied, that show how we are trained to respond with different degrees of violence to different types of action. These may be observed both in the results of jury trials, where "folk values" often soften the rule of law, and in neighborhood gossip about a given act of violence. For example, few men will condemn outright a man who shot his wife's lover when he came to the house to take her away, and both men and women "understand" a woman who after much physical abuse stabs a husband who threatens to kill her. Similarly, people will not approve, but they will at least sympathize, when they read of a father who used force on his high school daughter who announced her intention of staying out all night.

We acquire, then, a set of values and attitudes toward others' actions, by which we are guided in violence. Simply put, some actions anger us more than others, because in our value system they are more important: some cause us material losses, but others cause us shame. In a society in which romantic love is central, almost all of us feel violence when our love is threatened. In a subculture in which male honor requires courage and competence in confronting others, certain types of challenges and insults are dangerous. Where the mother is venerated, at least as a theme in the culture, the taunt "Your mother!" calls for violence.

At the same time, parents and the larger society do attempt (and much more publicly), to inculcate in everyone a repugnance to the actual use of violence. However, their real lesson is more complex: they show a partial approval or lesser disapproval of certain types of violence, and thus we learn not to reject violence under all circumstances. We hide our own impulses not only from others, but also from ourselves. We even try to hide the extent to which we *do* grade the degree of violence to fit the acts that arouse our anger, for we say publicly that all violence is "wrong." Nevertheless, what the society grades as unimportant most of us also view as trivial, while almost everyone comes to respond more violently and aggressively—even when he controls his counteraction—to acts that are rated as more serious.

Finally, of course, as part of the socialization *toward* degrees of violence, we acquire a range of *rationalizations* that justify our own lapses into physical aggressiveness. Few people are so deprived intellectually as to be unable to create a moral or ethical justification for their assault on another. As we shall note later, it is not at all certain that most of these rationalizations are cynical or morally obtuse. Indeed, in most intimate relations the balance of the ethical books is not at all clear. But what is significant in this context is the deeper fact that the gradations of insults or hurts that lead to gradations of violence are based on a set of values, and these in turn can be used to "explain" why we lost our heads in anger, or succumbed to a blind fury. According to *our* values, which we learned from our parents and our own society through our socialization experiences, the other person was in the wrong, and we had a *right* to be angry, or even to use violence.

We are emphasizing, then, that although the main official thrust of socialization in modern society opposes the use of violence, and especially when directed against intimates, many themes, forces, and processes in family, neighborhood, and school convey a somewhat *different* message in support of some violence, under some circumtances, against some individuals.

This range of factors emphasizes the degree to which individuals have a greater or lesser *predisposition* to use violence in certain types of situations, and to that extent introduces the victim *as a causal agent*. That is, what he does also affects the outcome. We cannot consider only "the" aggressor or murderer as an isolated figure. The dynamics that produce violence between intimates requires special attention to the offender-victim relationship. This direction of inquiry has been neglected in the past, (1) because official records contain few usable data on the actual processes through which violence was generated, (2) because of our propensity to find a guilty party, and of course (3) because the social researcher cannot easily locate a sample of violent acts for field observation.

This neglect will continue in the future because of research difficulties, but by now a goodly number of analysts have at least brought to our attention the importance of these dynamics, especially in cases involving intimates. Indeed, some have come to use the term "victimology" to underscore the contribution of the victim to his own demise. It is not necessary here to review the work of Mendelsohn, von Hentig, and others, in which they urged this type of focus.[9] Nor is it useful to debate who first suggested the idea.

In fact, of course, the *idea* that the victim contributes to his victimization is frequently expressed in the socialization experience, since it is part of folk wisdom. Every child has been shocked at some time by the refusal of his parents to give him sympathy for having been hurt, and by the harsh question, "But what were you doing with him, anyway?" The terse phrase, "served her right" conveys not alone retribution, but is also applied to the individual who entered a situation which a really innocent person would avoid.

When applied to the relations among intimates, however, this notion must be narrowed somewhat. We *can* not avoid all intimate relations, all friendships, all family ties, all interaction except with strangers. Perhaps we should not have acquired *this* spouse, *this* set of in-laws, this set of friends, but we do not all have the option of choosing wisely, and violence occurs between people who once seemed to be reasonable human beings. The question can and must include the problem of *entering* the relationship when we consider the case of forcible rape with intimates, but even there the dynamics of generation seem to be more important than the original choice of a companion.

In Schafer's recent report on a Florida inmate population, about sixty percent had been incarcerated for violence committed against a stranger, but this included theft with violence (the largest single category). Most studies, as noted before, report that half or more of various acts of violence were committed by people who were at least acquaintances. In a study of 588 homicides in Philadelphia, Marvin Wolfgang found that close friends (28 percent) and family associations (25 percent) formed the two most frequent types of cases, and "paramours" accounted for another 10 percent. Indeed, strangers were killed in only 13 percent of his sample, for the other categories include such types as homosexual partners, paramour of the offender's mate, sex rival, enemy, or acquaintance. In the Uniform Crime Reports of 1965, 31 percent were killings within the family, and 21 percent were outside the family unit but were lovers' quarrels or involved in a romantic triangle. In the District of Columbia Crime Commission report, only 19 percent of the aggravated assault victims were not acquainted with their assailants, and indeed 20 percent had had confrontations with their assailants before. In a national survey designed to ascertain the amount of unreported crime, as well as attitudes toward the police, respondents were also asked why they did not report the crime. Some of these answers ("did not want to harm offender," "afraid of reprisal," "was private not criminal affair" suggest that the victim had some kind of relationship with the offender. In other answers ("police wouldn't want to be bothered," "did not want to take time," etc.) there is at least the possibility that the response conceals some knowledge of the offender.

As noted earlier, a high but unknown percentage of assault, forcible rape, and attempted rape cases are not reported to the police, and they are not reported because the victim would prefer to avoid being questioned about his or her part in the generation of the violence. Especially in incidents of assault, as in schoolyard fights, it might be difficult ever to disentangle the contribution of the conflicting parties to the outbreak. Certainly a decision as to who was hurt the most would not do as evidence, as often it would not in homicide. Both von Hentig and Wolfgang have documented in some detail the frequent case of the victim who was originally the offender, the bully who is killed in a fight, the wife beater who is finally knifed. Homicide is fairly reliably reported, since such cases are not easily hidden, but it is safe to say that most unreported cases of assault fall into this category of battles between people who have at least known each other before. Those who are involved know that the police sergeant, like their parents, will begin to ask them how they got into that situation in the first place, and a truthful answer will reveal that both contributed some share to the conflict.

Both black and white males are more likely than females to be killed by a close friend, while women are overwhelmingly killed in a family or lover relationship. Men spend more of their time outside the home, and thus are more likely than women to be killed by people outside the family. On the other hand, white male victims are more likely than blacks to be killed by strangers, because far more are the victims of a robbery. This, of course, is more likely because whites are more likely to be proprietors or managers of a business place, and more likely in any event to look like a lucrative prospect for a robbery even on the street.

Although women exhibit a much lower homicide rate than men, when they do kill they are more likely to kill their husbands than any other category of persons. Since men have a wider network of acquaintances and are involved in other types of emotional ties, their victims are more widely distributed, and wives make up 10 to 15 percent of their total.[10]

Because both homicide and assault are highly personal relationships, those who hurt one another are likely to be of the same class, roughly similar ages, the same race, and from the same neighborhood. Various studies, a few of them of doubtful validity, also suggest that in a very high percentage of cases one or both parties were drinking. Detailed arrest records and being known to the police are usually not included in analyses of violence, but studies confirm what the ordinary respectable citizen darkly assumes, that victims and offenders— especially the latter—have some prior history of violence. Although those who commit homicide or assault are not comparable to professional criminals, and typically are not engaging in violence for profit, their offenses are not usually the only one they have committed.

Indeed, if we allow for the variegated forms that violence takes, a substantial percentage of cases will fall into a general category which the middle class citizen is concerned about in only an abstract way, as an index of how much the social fabric is dissolving. When newspaper editorials comment on the "rising tide of violence," and the citizen deplores the state of the nation, they are referring to acts and events that are confined to a relatively small part of the population.

They are concerned that some part of this violence might touch them, but it has little direct bearing on their lives or their emotions. They guess what the data roughly show, that a substantial part of the violence which is expressed in deeds is to be observed among the brawling, drinking poor, among the lower class blacks and whites whose weekend drinking is climaxed by anger, conflict, and fighting.

However, those who are killed are dead just the same, though poor, or black, or brawling lower class whites. The processes that lead to their violence are similar, if somewhat lower in frequency, to those among the more respected. Lovers, children, and spouses mourn for them as well. If this epoch is to tackle the problems of poverty, deprivation, race discrimination and hatred, and psychological disturbance, because we have decided that we *are* our brothers' keepers and cannot pass them by under the belief that they caused all their own problems, then we can do no less with violence. For some of the factors that produce the former set of problems also generate violence. And if a large part of it is directed at each other (as, indeed, is theft: the poor stealing from the poor), we cannot even then avert our eyes from a problem that must concern us as well.

Let us then probe more fully the processes by which violence is generated among intimates, within the broad set of forces we have been analyzing.

A perceptive Cornell University investigator of automobile collisions once noted that the primary element in any such accident is *surprise*. Had the driver predicted accurately what was to happen, no one would have been injured. When a conflict between intimate issues in assault or homicide too, one or both are surprised. Why?

If we begin with the climax, or the denouement, it is because the beginning is like any other interaction. On their way to a killing, people take the same road at first that others travel in an ordinary argument or disagreement. The fights that culminate in serious injury or death are at first like the arguments and fights that others have. Although all of us harbor some hostility in our hearts and doubtless the world would soon be depopulated if all of us could, by pressing a button, eliminate undetected any other person, a relatively small percentage of offenders fully desire to see their victims dead or maimed before them, and certainly few wanted to face all the consequences of the act.

But even more obviously, neither did the victims desire that end. Again, why did neither take another way out? In the simplest formulation, why did neither break off the interaction before it reached such a crescendo? An answer tells us more about man than the hypothesis that we are inherently bloodthirsty.

Few of even the predatory animals kill one another in the wild, in part because when one begins to lose, he submits or runs away. Caged animals sometimes kill, but there the loser cannot easily break off the interaction. Man shares with a few of his domestic animal creations (e.g., pit bulldogs, gamecocks) a considerable unwillingness to submit or escape. It is reported that under special circumstances rats (caged, as it were, in the same building) will also make war, but if so they are the only animals that share this unlovely trait with man. Again, however, war also exhibits man's unwillingness to submit or escape.

Several factors combine to support this pattern, which, it must be emphasized, is not so much a predilection for violence as a willingness to risk it rather than back down. We have already alluded to one such source, the socialization experience in which values are inculcated in the growing person. There we focused on the values that approve various degrees of violence. However, we must here take a broader view in order to underscore the fact that man's whole existence is guided by values. Men have—in radical distinction from other animals—been willing to die for their religious or patriotic values, their views of personal honor and their political philosophies, far more frequently than for their narrow self-interest. Indeed, what is so striking about man is that through his socialization experience he comes to believe that his self-interest is identical with such abstract values and to deny them is more abhorrent than to risk his life. Far fewer people will endanger their lives for money than for honor as defined by these fundamental values, that after all give meaning to human existence.

But such definitions of what is right, good, honorable, beautiful or decent also guide social relations among intimates, whether friends, spouses or lovers. Any two people who become emotionally close to one another are drawn together in part because they share common definitions of what is appropriate behavior and because their psychological needs mesh to some extent. The wider their shared experiences, the more they learn about each other's values. In an ideal case, they enhance the significance of each other's lives by supporting each other's values, attitudes, and opinions.

In any continuing intimate relationship, the sharing of values is expressed in and buttressed by an unending series of transactions. Some of these may be thought of crudely as "exchanges" and a couple may so describe them. For example, when a husband states his *right* to be given respect and a clean household in exchange for his financial contribution, he may use such a rhetoric. Most transactions are not described that way, except when one of the couple violates their common, unspoken understanding, and then the other angrily refers to what he "owes." A wife may prepare a special meal on Sunday and her husband expresses his thanks or admiration for her cooking. A friend agrees indignantly that his buddy was shabbily treated by his boss, and his buddy reiterates their solidarity. Relatives exchange babysitting or Christmas presents or appear at each other's solemn occasions, such as weddings or funerals.

In such transactions, a rough balance is to be observed when both sides are content. Although the contributions may not seem to be equal, both sides feel they are about equal, because they place similar *evaluations* on what each other does. Money may, for example, flow in only one direction, from husband to wife, but if he evaluates highly what she does he may consider the bargain "fair." One friend may "pay out" far more deference than he receives from his partner, but if he feels his partner's friendship and companionship are worth that much, he will not feel he is unfairly treated. In the ideal case, then, both participants in an intimate relationship reinforce one another's values, affirm the other's significance and worth, and feel that continuing the interaction is worth more than possible alternatives.

But the vicissitudes of life sour many partnerships, and one or both members come to feel they are being cheated, betrayed, or wronged. The husband who loved his bride enough to tolerate her nagging loses his ardor, and the cost of staying together rises too high. Evaluations change, because social positions alter. Thus, the coquettishness that was attractive during courtship looks like promiscuous flirtation after marriage. The drinking companion comes to believe that his buddy is too quick to anger when bested in an argument. A man is at first pleased that his brother-in-law has had a bit of success, but later feels he takes advantage of it by trying to dominate his relatives.

From time to time all have the experience of being put down by others, of being pushed about, of feeling diminished by those to whom we are emotionally close. As Norman Mailer has commented, "threatened by the extinction of our possibilities, we react with rage." We are confined in the relationship, but cannot redress the balance, or open the door to a new set of inviting prospects.

When both are wise, one of them discusses his reasons for resentment and persuades or is persuaded. But perhaps most of us are not wise, and follow other roads. One is to nurse the annoyance, and now and then engage in sporadic outbursts over an unrelated slight. Friends may gradually avoid one another while keeping up the pretense of civility.

Intimacy survives an argument more easily than the corrosive fester of suffering a continuing imbalance in reciprocities. Such an imbalance is most difficult to redress, because the other person will rarely concede, and honestly does not perceive, the injustice. Accustomed to one set of transactions, or gradually adjusted to his own pattern of behavior, he is more inclined to believe that his own contributions are already sufficient—or, at best, the cost of giving more is too great. If each values what he gives more than what he receives, then neither can, without losing face or feeling an even greater loss, concede still more.

It is in such a state that many people find themselves. The rules of polite society are arranged not to solve such problems, but to gloss over them. At a cocktail party we engage in chit-chat rather than probe to a level where we or the other person will be hurt. We learn to break off a conversation in the office when we perceive the other individual is becoming angry or resentful. Such rules vary in form among different circles, cliques, classes and personalities, but all serve the function of easing social interaction while avoiding a real intimacy that might only increase anger and violence.

In a sense, these modes of behavior become "masks" which we present to one another. They are not our real self, but then we do not wish most others to know our real self. Social philosophers of love have often deplored such barriers to communication, and have urged that everyone open himself and bare his heart. This has become an especially pervasive doctrine among hippies in our generation, and many applied psychologists have organized training sessions to encourage a greater openness. Nevertheless, ordinary people in every society rejected this message, and instead followed the intuition that it is dangerous, or at least uncomfortable, to drop their defenses. Only with intimates is it safe to expose one's true self, and even there the intensity and frequency of hurt proves that the pleasures of emotional closeness are sometimes dearly bought.

In an intimate relationship, as noted, one or both persons can come to feel (suddenly in a flaring argument, or over time) that the other is unfair or wrong but a redress of the imbalance is difficult to achieve, because both are convinced that they have already overextended their resources, and already done enough for the other. There is no more to give out without making the exchange even more unfair than it is. Being emotionally close, each is vulnerable, and knows how to hurt the other, while neither can easily retreat to the comfortable, civil formulas and masks that are permissible and common with mere acquaintances or strangers.

Many people cannot easily choose the equally obvious solution, breaking off or letting go. This fact is often overlooked, because we observe the continual formation and dissolution of human ties. However, most of these are not intimate, and do not carry a high voltage of emotional intensity. More important, when we review in our memory the shattering of past love or friendship bonds, most of us will recognize that breaking off was hurtful and difficult.

Letting go is painful, because both individuals once fed each other's emotional needs, and the need remains, while no other person is exactly a substitute. Breaking off is hurtful also because one or both may feel that the other is getting away scot free without a just revenge being inflicted, without a fair and final balance of the emotional books. One or both may not wish to let go without one more attempt to wound, to pay back, to justify one's behavior.

One consequence is that many people remain in a relationship which they have come to detest and which they know may even be physically dangerous. In a bitter marital situation, all the above factors may combine with still others to prevent one or both from letting go; one or both spouses may still need the other emotionally; one or both may feel guilty *and also* feel the other has behaved unfairly;

one or both may still be trying desperately to pay back his old hurts and injustices. In addition, the pressure of friends and the sheer practical difficulty of starting and maintaining a new household can seem insurmountable. Even now, when divorce is thought to be easy, it is taken for granted that spouses do not finish their fighting when they divorce: we still take note of the unusual cases by commenting, "they are being very civilized."

Locked in but suffering from it, couples may engage in fighting that is savage and even lethal. Many men and a goodly number of women have finally come to the conclusion that homicide is a cleaner, neater solution than the dragged out, acerbic destruction of ego and dignity that is inherent in breaking off.

Another solution is even perhaps more difficult than the foregoing: accepting one's losses. Having observed over time that in the intimate relationship one is constantly losing, the odds are poor, and change is unlikely, few people can simply shrug their shoulders and decide that there is no point in worrying or brooding over the past. One could either accept the new set of bargaining terms, or leave in the secure knowledge that one should not continue to throw good energies and emotions into a bad investment. Several factors combine to make this solution difficult for all but the most philosophic. One of the most fundamental is an insight derived from Skinner's Theory of Random Reinforcement. When an animal has been trained to perform a set of acts, a schedule of random rather than regular reinforcements will generate a greater propensity to continue that behavior pattern. Comparable to some extent is the gambler's addiction, or perhaps that of the sports fisherman. In the face of a low but random payoff, the individual now and then receives some reward, so that he is never quite willing to abandon the enterprise entirely. In any intimate relationship, even one that has become corrosive and hateful in many respects, the habitual patterns of interaction do yield from one day to the next a few rewards—a memory of fun shared together once, a quick understanding when some outsider makes a foolish statement, a casual pat on the shoulder. These do not outweigh the hurt and the sense of injustice, but they continue to give some hope that things might be improved. Few intimates can be so totally bent on constantly hurting the other that they will not stop from time to time to support the continuance of the relationship for yet a while.

Moreover, though the payoff is low it is one relationship in which there is *some* payoff, and alternatives are not obvious. New relationships are risky, and casual ones do not yield the same satisfactions.

When an intimate is finally seen as a person who will continue to do wrong, to betray, to be overbearing, one might suppose that the other might simply cut his losses and leave. If a man learns that his wife is sleeping with another man, or a lover learns that he is betrayed, or a mistress learns that she is betrayed, it might seem to be wise to say, in effect, who wants a person like that? If the person is really to be labeled unworthy or inadequate, then a serene person might be able to accept the fact and sever a relationship that does no honor to either person.

However, the values that give meaning to the relationship also prevent most people from being able to accept the losses, as suggested before. If a man knows that he has been betrayed, the loss is too great to accept as it is. At least part of the solution must be some hurt, and at the deepest levels of emotion among peaceful as well as violent people, this hurt must be physical and destructive. If the roulette wheel is crooked, then we wish to smash it, not merely walk out. We may not smash it because we fear the consequences, but the urge to do so is strong in all of us. Indeed, the greater the sense of betrayal, which ought to show that the other person should be cast aside easily, the stronger the demand for the most vigorous counter-payment in hurt that we can safely manage.

An additional factor is sometimes overlooked in the violence among intimates, Who is the victor in the war of words? The conflicts among friends, lovers, and spouses is never action alone or physical battle alone. It is most pervasively a war of words, and this always means arguments about who is wrong and right. Unfortunately for the distribution of justice in the cosmos, the person who is least fair may not be the least competent in verbal skill. On the average, of course, women are somewhat more skillful than men, but each person develops his own rhetorical abilities in order to justify his behavior or his wishes. The guilty one may win the argument and the other person thus feels doubly wronged. He or she has not even had the satisfaction of redressing the balance by stinging words.

One small factor in the distribution of homicide by sex should be noted here. Women are socialized to use far less physical violence than men, but typically do not feel that the words they use justify violence against them. Men are trained differently and recognize far more clearly that certain degrees of verbal violence will have a high probability of eliciting a physical counterattack, not only a verbal counterattack. With a different perspective, women are far more frequently surprised by a physical counterattack when they use stinging words.

Another element of importance in the battle of words as it leads to physical violence is a peculiarity of all conversations. As ethnomethodologists have documented so fully by now, all societies have a set of implicit rules as to how to begin the conversation, whether among intimates or strangers. Those who violate the rules will often be rebuffed, or they will merely puzzle the other person. Certain settings permit easy initiation of conversation, while in other settings we understand the rules do not permit it.

Similarly, whether in casual telephone conversations or serious discussions in a conference, there are implicit rules of order as to when a conversation is finished. We give small cues to one another, in tone, gesture, and actual words, to indicate that the conversation is completed. However, there are no recognized rules that define when a conversation of a violent character is completed, and especially such a conversation between intimates. Clearly it is not finished when there has been no resolution and typically there is none. As long as the other has something that he desperately wishes to express, he feels that conversation should not end and among conflicting intimates there is usually no limit as to the emotions yet to be expressed. In addition, violent arguments between intimates continue to move toward higher pitches, and in all such progressions the natural ending is attack, not calm and peaceful analysis. To leave the scene immediately is to lose face; to back down from a violent argument with a friend is likely to make one feel cowardly. Thus, in the intense verbal conflict among intimates, the very lack of orderly and adequate rules for ending the conversation forces the dispute toward a more total confrontation.

All of these factors combine to offer only two fundamental reactions: crush or run. Both participants feel a deep need for resolution; the transaction is not adequately finished, but the various open avenues are awkward, dishonoring, unsatisfactory, or impossible. The animal emotions that arise in such fights between intimates—and on a psychophysical level, these are the same among the most well-mannered members of the middle class and the most violent of the lower class—are fight or flight. But flight, as we have just noted can come to seem a less desirable alternative than the risk of violence. Since neither knows exactly at what point the other is likely to express his anger in hurt or homicide, both are tempted to continue to press the other to strike once again verbally, to taunt, and of course one or both may make a substantial and catastrophic error. The anger that boils up is murderous in all of us, and at least generates the desire to crush. As we have noted earlier, it is easier to run at an earlier stage in the battle, to avoid the later surprise when actual violence erupts, but running away is more likely to be a flash of rationality, a recognition of the objective dangers, rather than a satisfying solution.

It will be noticed that in this analysis of the dynamics of conflict between intimates, we have referred from time to time to various kinds of precipitants, which are sometimes labeled "motives" in discussions of homicide and violence. Typically, the category of motives has included the reasons for a final fight as recorded in a police investigation. By and large, these do represent *precipitants*, that is, the final triggering events. Sometimes, of course, the category of "motives" will include "reasons why." Such lists are varied, and usually unproductive. In using such motives as examples in our previous discussion, we do not assume that these are the real motives. As recorded, such motives include adultery, being cheated by a partner in business, a falling out among thieves, a family fight that began in a dispute about who contributed the most money to the support of the parents, and the conflict about who had the right to a deceased aunt's bracelet, and so on.

In the strict psychological sense, of course, these are not motives. They are not basic psychological needs. They are merely the events that generated either a final conflict or a continuing action pattern that contributed to the development of anger and hurt. It is not likely that either victim or offender could adequately describe his motives in the psychological sense, for most would not have sufficient clinical insight to know the structure of their own personality dynamics. Such continuing psychological needs doubtless create a major part of the clash between intimates, but the analysis of homicide and assault in a psychological framework has not yet advanced that far.

At a simpler level, of course, the conflict is the immediate outcome of primitive emotions rather than motives: rage and anger and the urge to destroy. But, as we have noted, that denouement must be traced back to the dynamics that generated it. All of us feel these emotions from time to time and are inhibited from expressing them fully. But they are the outgrowth of our psychodynamic heritage. Thus, the reasons that people give for violence against those close to them are to be taken seriously, but only as guides for finding where the sense of outraged injustice began to grow.

A concrete tabulation of such answers is likely to be infinitely broad. The reasons for killing are all the reasons for living. Hurting others is, for many people in a tragic situation, a life-affirming act, though, of course, only rarely as life-affirming as other acts might be. This is especially so for violence between intimates. With a stronger ego, one could get out; one could ignore the social loss of face and the internal sense of lessened worth; one could start a new life. But, like most neurotic solutions to life problems, violence is easier, given all the restraints, assumptions, pressures and sense of injustice each person feels. All of us can envision killing or crushing as simpler than solving an apparently impossible problem and, of course, as we have seen in the dynamics of conflict among intimates, those who are emotionally close "help" toward this outcome by forcing another individual into that violent solution—tempting and taunting, not letting go, exacerbating the conflict, winning the verbal debate while committing other hurts, refusing to cooperate, etc.

Hurting aims at redressing an imbalance as the aggressor sees it by a means which also seems efficient at the moment. Violence is, as noted before, often socially supported although officially deplored. It is at least a *deterrent*, even when it is not very effective in engendering positive actions. At the least, it stops the other individual from what he is doing now. It is satisfying in anticipation, and possibly sometimes after, because the aggressor is then also the agent of vengeance. Against the impersonal fate that has given another person the advantage in action or argument an opportunity to cheat or betray, and against the evil that one's friend or spouse has committed, one can take part in the cosmic redistribution of goods and pleasures, and restitute by forcing one's will on another person. To this extent, one must see violence as one "solution" for an ideological problem that creates overwhelming emotions. Nothing is so violent as passion in the service of ideology and values, whether it is the outraged husband killing his wife for betraying him, or a demagogue inflaming the masses to loot and burn the enemies that are exploiting them. It seems likely that even the calculating murderer, rationally plotting to kill for material gain (insurance, inheritance, to avoid blackmail) manages to convince himself most of the time that he has a "right" to the money or advantages he seeks by the homicide.

This account of the dynamics of violence among intimates also explains to a considerable extent why so much of assault is not reported and why it is so difficult after a serious conflict for the outsider ever to ascertain precisely what took place—not merely all the motives, reasons and pressures, but even the objective sequence of events. Neither participant can bring to bear an undistorted perspective on what took place, or when it all began.

Illustrative of certain events in the foregoing analysis is Wolfgang's finding that women are homicide offenders in the kitchen first and then in the bedroom, in order of frequency. Over one third of females were killed in the bedroom.[11] He links this location with the somewhat lopsided distribution of offender and victim, that over four-fifths of all female victims are slain by males, and when females slay, four-fifths of them slay males. In a high proportion of these, of course, arguments are concerned with sex, love and family matters. It is especially the bedroom where unresolved conflicts are likely to burst out because when finally both have gone there for the evening: neither can have an adequate excuse to leave or break off the conversation. To a lesser extent, of course, this is true for the kitchen, which in many lower class dwellings is where family members are likely to spend a good bit of relaxed time. Not being in contact with one another during the working day, they confront the dilemmas and distasteful solutions finally in the rooms where by social definition this is the only unresolved business.

The few data on homicide-suicide also support the general perspective we have sketched here. Primarily, it is confined to a relationship between a man and a woman; very few cases exist of male-male or female-female relationships. Of course, this means that there are few cross-racial cases. Furthermore, if one tabulates homicides by whether they were accompanied by excessive violence—repeated stabbings, shootings, beatings—husband-wife slayings are much more common than any other category of intimate relationship.

Perhaps of deeper significance is the fact that wives rarely commit suicide after committing homicide; the combination is most often carried out by males. Wolfgang suggests that the husband is likely to feel more guilt and remorse than wives do.[12]

There are at least some data that bear partially on this pattern. Perhaps the most significant come from studies of husband-wife attitudes, and from analyses of the dynamics of divorce. In all studies, women feel that they do most of the adjusting in marriage (and some data suggest that that, indeed, is correct) and are more likely to feel somewhat abused in the relationship.

This does not mean, on the other hand, that women are more likely to seek an end to the marriage. Indeed the data suggest the opposite. Because men are less likely to make their marital relationship the center of their lives, because they move about far more and establish other relationships that are meaningful, and because they can go much further in new and alternative emotional relationships without serious criticism or control, men are more likely to try to get out of the marriage first. Indeed, it may be suggested that they pursue unconsciously or consciously a strategy of making themselves sufficiently obnoxious (within the limits of permissible or approved conduct in their social circle) to the point where women are really convinced the marriage should end.

Although those factors in interaction may generate some hostility on the part of the male, they also leave him with some considerable residue of guilt. He may engage in violent behavior as an expression of his wish to end the relationship, but also feel guilty that he has, as it were, added insult to injury. One must suppose that when women finally do commit homicide (as, doubtless, when they commit assault) they are much more inclined to feel that they have been goaded to it and thus feel relatively innocent. That this may represent a partial reality may be seen in the fact that husbands are less often acquitted than wives. This fact is only a partial confirmation, because we must keep in mind that our society makes an assumption that women will in fact be less violent and that only when they have been driven to it will they engage in serious attacks on others. The courts are not inclined to view the verbal attacks or the nagging of women as an adequate justification for assault or homicide, though the injured man may feel differently.[13]

One further qualification ought to be introduced here, which also has a broader application. As noted earlier, far more men commit homicide than do women, and more men kill one another than kill women. We have considered at several points the factors involved in this differential but one more ought to be noted, since it bears especially on the problem of the successful act as against the assaultative emotion. Specifically, men are technically better equipped to kill each other, or to kill women, than are women. The differential may be seen in several areas. Men can strike harder, pound for pound, than women can. They are far more skilled in the use of all tools, and have had far more training in combat and body contact sports from their early childhood. More of them can shoot accurately and even own guns. Any attack by a woman is much less likely to issue in a homicide case, even when her emotions are as extreme, her urge to destroy as intense, simply because what she does is less effective.[14]

A very small part of all homicide is committed by the psychotic. However, we should at least note that although the ultimate, fundamental generation of the psychosis cannot be located in the immediate situation where the homicide or assault occurred, when psychotics do kill people who have been emotionally close to them, the dynamics of target fixation, and the generation of resentment against particular persons is not greatly different from that of ordinary people. Their reactions are sometimes more extreme, and laymen read with avidity the bizarre details of their behavior, but the clinical work of the past half century shows all too clearly how similar are the psychodynamic patterns of the normal, the neurotic, and the psychotic.

There are no "murder psychoses." There is no specific psychosis whose resolution is inevitably assault-homicide. Doubtless the classic paranoic and the paranoid schizophrenic are more likely to commit assaults than other categories. Their delusions of reference by which they suppose all sorts of unrelated activities by other *do* aim at them, their sense of great self-importance, their feeling of being beleaguered and thus their hostility, doubtless generate more aggressive feelings. On the other hand, this aggression often takes the form of self-aggression, and the dynamic do not specifically *aim* at murder *per se*.

In any event, although the psychotic may be in error as to who has harmed him (if anyone) and who threatens him, and in a technical, legal sense he is often held to be not responsible for his crimes, in fact most psychotics do know what they are doing when they commit assault or homicide, and have (within their own version of reality) the same kinds of justifications for it that ordinary people have, when they succumb to the temptation to attack their lovers, friends or spouses. And, of course, all the factors that prevent an adequate or wise resolution of their life problems are to be found in these cases to an even more extreme degree. Those against whom they aggress, whether or not they themselves have contributed greatly to the exacerbation of the conflict are, in turn, even less capable of understanding the behavior of the mentally disturbed person since they simply do not have any relevant clinical techniques.

In this extended analysis of violence between intimates, we began with various differences in behavior, by race, sex, class, region and relationship between offender and victim. These led to a consideration of differences in values and in the socialization process by which those values are inculcated. All of these can be roughly categorized as ways by which differential predispositions to violence get generated, a differential willingness to use violence in a dispute. These different propensities to use violence do increase or lower the chances that someone will resort to homicide or assault.

In examining the dynamics through which violence is generated, we were turning to various alternatives among which people can choose when they engage in disagreements with friends, lovers, and spouses. Those who can choose or are helped to choose some of these alternatives are less likely to resort to violence. Since assaults of all kinds are more common among the young than among older people, we can suppose that experience does teach some to opt for other roads than attack.

At all points in the decision to act, of course, people do calculate the costs, as we have noted before. Doubtless few would ever kill if all were certain to face a public execution as a result. But that outcome is rare, and the press of immediate anger or long-suffering resentment is great. Moreover, the "costs" of nonviolence include, we saw, many undesirable sequels *other* than official punishment—degradation, loss of face and honor, continued maltreatment and so on.

In addition it is clear that if *one's predisposition* to violence is high and if one's evaluation of various courses of action is different from that of other people, one may therefore be more inclined to rank a violent confrontation above most peaceable alternatives. We have continued to explore these various differences in evaluation, precisely because they figure as elements in the calculus of cost, whether that computation is carried out in the heat of rage or alone and slowly in the quiet of the night.

No kind of analysis can explain adequately why one man kills another, while a different person kills no one even under great provocation, but we can lay bare some of the factors that create higher or lower chances of violence among people of different characteristics, as we have been doing.

To continue our analysis, we must consider at least briefly some of the *social pressures* toward violence. We introduced some of these at an earlier stage when we considered the "subcultural" differences among regions or even districts of a city, in which a greater or lesser approval of violence could be found, and also when we discussed the socialization patterns by which people learn the appropriate degree of force to use when answering different intensities of provocation. Implicitly, then, we were pointing to just such social pressures, but let us take note of them when they appear in a more direct form.

Everyone as a child has observed the common practice of boys who egg on two of their playmates who are engaged in a bitter quarrel. Often, neither would have struck the other had there been first of all no audience and secondly if the audience had not attempted to cut out all avenues of retreat. Youngsters do this physically by surrounding the two potential combatants; they do it socially by taking sides and by articulating clearly the possible loss of face or the charge of cowardice if either backs down. If one does back down, the group will taunt him so that everyone learns the costs of retreat. If one person strikes the other, the other cannot easily decide to run, in the face of so much pressure to do battle.

In the above paragraph we have deliberately used an innocent vocabulary, appropriate to a playground situation in which young chil-

dren are pushing one another about. At a later age, and in tougher
sections of the city, the encounter can be lethal. Weapons can be and
are used, from broken bottles to zip guns. Two groups can move toward a battle that parallels the one between the two combatants.
These battles take place, as so much research has already documented, between gangs in different turfs, or subgroups within the
same neighborhood. Sometimes they are friends, but of course more
often they are simply well known to one another but enemies just the
same.

A similar type of social support to assault, even an attack that may
lead to death, occurs when two drinking buddies engage in an antagonistic altercation. They are not likely to be pressed hard toward violence if they are strangers to one another among strangers. On the
other hand, when they are close friends and other companions are
around, the support for violence may become relatively strong. To
some degree, of course, this is no more than a thirst for drama, for
excitement. At a deeper psychological level, of course, it is also an
expression of each person's reservoir of hostility, his desire to participate vicariously in the striking of blows. To a smaller extent, one or
more of the group egging the combatants on may simply want one or
the other to be hurt. Whatever their motives, the two antagonists feel
the pressure, and see fewer alternatives to an attack.

Such pressures are, of course, greater in an urban district of high
violence. The standards of physical reaction to provocation vary
greatly. Two middle-class friends in a violent altercation in a fash-
ionable bar might simply walk out in a huff. If they did not, but
seemed to be edging toward a physical attack, the management would
intervene. It is considered unseemly to engage in battle in a respectable bar. In a lower class bar the bartender would not want the battle
to occur within the bar itself, because his license might be threatened,
but he might be quite tolerant if the couple moved out to the street to
"settle" their argument. Similarly, violence in most middle class circles, whether between men and women or between friends of the
same sex, is so frowned upon that those who commonly express their
anger in physical attack are likely to be ostracized. The social pressures are very strong in subjecting others to this kind of violence.
Proper people restrict it to situations when they are alone.

We ought also, however, to keep in mind that within a given

neighborhood, and within a group of friends, one may observe different fields of "violence potentiation," i.e., aside from the immediate differential pressures in different neighborhoods and districts. There are different "fields" in different areas and social circles, which may be expressed by saying that even when no immediate pressures are evident, everyone knows that one or more has engaged in some physical battle recently. Much of the gossip is about the threats and dangers that are encountered daily. Each person observes some violence each day, though often nothing with which the police have been concerned. Friends disappear for a few hours or a few days to be sewn up at the emergency clinic or to recover at home from a fight. The reverberations of this atmosphere of violence may be as pervasive and as generating of additional violence, as the immediate social pressures in a combat situation. Living in a kind of jungle, human beings become alert, hypersensitive to provocation, quick on the trigger, swift to retaliate. This affects greatly not only the relations between strangers, but the intimate relations between friends or between men and women who care for one another.[15]

Again, such a field of potentiation does not mean that everyone engages in battle, but it does mean that those who live in it are more likely than others to be affected by it and a major consequence is the lowering of the threshold of violence. Each person is less likely to be inhibited in the expression of his own hostility, to be less restrained in using physical attack or counterattack as a way of settling differences. In such an atmosphere, a smaller provocation is necessary than in others to stimulate individuals to a physical attack and, as already noted, this powerful effect may be observed in the interaction among intimates. The same dynamisms operate that have been analyzed earlier, but when the field of potentiation is especially intense, those dynamisms will more quickly express themselves in physical assault.

Although we had earlier noted that assault and homicide are more common among the lower classes than among middle or upper social strata, we focused there far more upon the differences in the subculture, the differences in the socialization experience. Most treatises that focus on class differences in violence take note of the fact that the lower class person is less inhibited in his expression of violence (though not less constricted psychologically), and is less willing to offer gratification now in exchange for a somewhat bigger payoff later. Thus, the middle class person is more likely to calculate correctly the costs of engaging in violence and to avoid it. He is taught as a child to disapprove of violence.

However, we just took note of a very different type of factor that separates the lower class experience from the middle- or upper-class pattern, which may be characterized as a difference in *structural position*. We noted, for example, that there is much less likely to be a highly intense field of potentiation of violence in middle class social strata, and that the social pressures against it are strong, to the point of ostracism against those who give vent to their hostilities by physical attack.

But let us consider a few additional differences in structural position. A fundamental difference in the class position of the lower social strata is that they have far fewer alternative sources of pleasures or contentment. Essayists have long attempted to praise the virtues of lower class and rural life, pointing to harmony, quiet, lower aspirations, the serenity of limited horizons and so on. It is notable that few such essayists join the lower strata or their rural cousins and Benjamin Franklin long ago expressed his skepticism about that argument, by wondering why so many writers spent energy on *proving* the virtues of poverty: surely if the advantages were so obvious, one would need no additional argument.

However, we need not argue the relative contentment of people in different classes, though the empirical data do support the common sense suspicion that to be rich is better than to be poor. All that we are emphasizing is that when the relations between middle class intimates become somewhat painful or a festering sore, usually both participants do have a wider range of alternative sources of pleasure from the theater to being warm in their apartments; from the sensuous delight in a well-cut coat to the fascination of travel. Granted, these do not give happiness, but they do drain away some part of the anger and hurt in the intimate relationship.

By contrast, the lower class person has far fewer resources with which to achieve his aims, whether in an intimate relationship or in interaction with outsiders. He has less prestige, money, and power so that his sense of frustration and bitterness are greater than a member of the middle classes. One consequence is, of course, that when an additional frustration occurs in his intimate relations, he may feel tempted to displace them onto even a person he cares about. The lower class father brings home far more hurt than does the middle class father and sometimes those about him suffer from it.

These resources also permit greater independence within the middle and upper social strata. Individuals can move about more freely, make far more decisions that do not depend so intimately upon their friends or spouses. Although it is a common observation that everyone feels poor in all social strata, the objective differences remain, and are not erased by the higher consumption aspirations toward the higher social strata. Spouses *can* take vacations separately from one another, whether these are only a few hours of shopping in pleasant stores or some days at a resort.

Another important difference is to be included here, although it derives ultimately from the different socialization experience in different classes: the development of a wider range of peaceful techniques for dealing with disputes. The middle and upper strata are far more articulate, and indeed, much of their school training is aimed in that direction. The differences in IQ between lower social strata and middle strata are not great, but the differences in verbal skills are substantial. The middle-class child is taught far more intensively to mediate, to talk out difficulties, to suggest or initiate alternative arrangements for alternative role relationships. Where the lower class husband and wife are typically relatively inarticulate in their sexual relationship, so that neither may know except vaguely that the other is dissatisfied, middle-class couples are much more likely to discuss their sexual problems openly and to utilize both counseling advice and sex manuals for achieving a better adjustment. Middle class households are much more likely to read about, to discuss, and to use the latest psychological advice on how to get along with one another.

Thus, even aside from a greater inhibition in matters of violence and a higher evaluation of nonviolence in intimate relations, the middle and upper social strata have far more rules of manners, civility, avoidance, escape and discussion available to them in their habit structure, which will mitigate somewhat the normal hostilities that grow out of their intimate disputes.

A final structural difference overlaps with a somewhat peripheral topic that should be discussed at this point: The role of police in disputes between intimates. Although this topic will reappear briefly in the later section on policy recommendations, it is relevant at this point too. The effect of the police is multiplex, but in at least two ways it increases the frequency of violence between intimates.

The most obvious effect has been noted for well over a generation. Although middle and upper class people are much less likely to be arrested, and will be treated more gently if they are arrested, this large generalization must be qualified in several ways. In a street dispute between an obviously lower class man, especially a black and a white man in a middle class neighborhood, the chances are high that if anyone is arrested, it will be the black. The police are much firmer in protecting the lives and homes of middle class people than lower class people.

On the other hand, in part because in lower class districts there is so much violence and near-violence the police take a somewhat lenient attitude toward anything short of real injury. Moreover, serious assaults and even homicides are not likely to be punished as severely, in part because such events are usually shown in court to be the outcome of an altercation in which both sides contributed considerably. The police feel surrounded by a considerable amount of potential violence, and feel that they cannot stem the tide fully. All that they can do is to control the most obvious manifestations. To that extent, the police exhibit a somewhat more permissive attitude toward violence in lower class areas, so that the inhabitants are less likely to take as seriously the legal consequences of physical aggression. This permissiveness extends, of course, to violence between husband and wife, lovers, and close friends.

In addition, in lower class areas, a high percentage of the population feels angry toward the police as representatives of exploitation, as people who are physically threatening, as sources of further degradation and insult. Both blacks and whites, but especially blacks, feel the insults of the social system as frequently coming through the harsh voice, strong arm, and blazing revolver of the policeman. One consequence is that the relations between men and women and between close friends of the same sex (but especially men) carry a heavier emotional burden. They must console more, be more effective in redressing the emotional imbalances of the day, than similar relationships among the middle or upper social strata. It is not necessary to over-emphasize the role of the policeman in engendering the hostility that is expressed in intimate relations, but far too many personal accounts of life in lower class districts have expressed this theme, to ignore it here.

It should also be added, that one further consequence of this complex linkage is the high chance that policemen themselves may at times bear the brunt of this greater hostility, when they are called upon to intervene in a dispute between husband and wife, lover and mistress or close friends. When the outbreak becomes violent because the sense of wrong has risen to intolerable levels, and a policeman is called, the overflowing anger may be displaced onto the policeman. Indeed in one recent report, it is asserted that "one of every five policemen killed in the line of duty dies trying to break up a family fight."[16]

Commonly in a family dispute, one or both of the antagonists will turn on the policeman, eager to show that at least in that encounter he can come out honorably, though he has failed in doing so within the more intimate relationship. The policeman is an especially fine target, because in American society he is likely to be cast in the role of a local, unofficial judge. He is called upon to settle minor disputes, calm down combatants, to stop bloodshed, and to the extent that he prefers (as the society wants him to prefer) to soothe and mollify rather than lock up people, he may well antagonize one or both disputants. In endeavoring to calm down an angered husband, the policeman may attempt to overpower or dominate when the husband has reached the end of his ability to bear any more domination, with the result that the policeman's life may be in danger—and, of course, a greater chance that one of the combatants will be killed.

A complete analysis of violence between intimates should include the case of forcible rape, but we shall deal with it only briefly here, and primarily to clarify a few elements in its dynamics. Most people can empathize to some degree with ordinary assault, because they can remember their own angers in the past, though perhaps many would deny that their rage was murderously intense. Almost all men have participated in assault at some time, if only as a child. By contrast, few men would admit, at least in ordinary conversation with friends, that they had attempted rape at some time in the past. Indeed, understanding of the case is hampered somewhat by the usual stereotype of the rapist, who is pictured as a sex-crazed pervert who waylays a lone and innocent woman on a deserted street, and then drags her into a dark alley. The term "sex offender" covers a wide variety of extremely different cases, from child molesters and fetishists to relatively ordinary heterosexual males.

In the United States, forcible rape is an urban phenomenon, with an overrepresentation of blacks, lower class whites, the young, and those who live in districts characterized by a high frequency of violence. The overwhelming percentage of rapes are intraracial. Contrary to most white fears, the victims of rape are mostly black girls. Although studies report somewhat different percentages, something like half of the victims had some prior association with the offenders.[17] As Amir has shown, in approximately half of the cases actual force was not used to subdue the victim, although of course a mixture of seductive words and threats make that category somewhat empty.[18]

If we confine ourselves to the cases of rape between intimates, we confront first of all great gaps in information, for obvious reasons. Violence itself is a continuum, ranging from a mere push through serious verbal threats, to the use of knives, clubs, and guns. And though rape is by definition a completed act, various degrees of approach to it do occur, from being forced by superior strength to submit to mere petting, to being subjected to various kinds of sexual humiliation. A substantial but unknown percentage of women have at least experienced a forceful attempt by some male to press her toward sexual intimacy. In two studies done on the college campus in the 1950s, for example, about one-fifth reported some forceful attempt at intercourse and 6 to 9 percent reported that someone they had dated had used "violence or menacing threats or coercive infliction of physical pain" in order to achieve sexual intercourse.[19]

Various studies have asked men whether they have committed various delinquencies in the past, and a substantial minority admit an attempt to use some force in an erotic situation.

It should be remembered that these college girls form a sample of women who are least likely to be aggressed against, so that their report is a minimum percentage. We would suppose that a random sample of lower class girls would report a much higher percentage of such experience.

In Amir's study, approximately one-third of the forcible rapes that were actually reported were committed by close neighbors, close friends, or boyfriends, family friends or family relatives. Whether one should, within the context of the present analysis consider all of these "intimates" is not clear, but the figures do suggest a substantial minority of cases in this category.[20]

A substantial percentage of actual rape remains unreported, and especially that between intimates, since in the majority of instances, the rape was preceded by at least some stages of erotic intimacy. And, of course, as young men have complained in court, at least some charges of rape are false, since there was consent first, and then a later denial of consent.

Because a real sample is difficult to obtain, and because most analyses are confined to police and court records, it is difficult to probe deeply into the motivational patterns of rape between intimates. However, a few points seem clear enough beyond those noted above. One is that the cases seem to fall primarily into two large cases, those of multiple rape (pair rape or group rape) and rape by a single person. In the former instance, intimacy is less likely but in more than half of these cases the victim had at least some prior contact with the offenders and in a small number of cases had actually been intimate. Very common is trying to persuade the girl, with the support of some intimidation or threat, to have relations with a friend as well, or a "bargain" is made by which the girl is told that if she submits to one boy, the others will not rape her—a bargain which is typically violated.

These cases are interesting in their own right, but primarily as part of the general syndrome of multiple rape, which has been relatively little analyzed, though it may well represent, as Amir argues, over two-fifths of all cases of rape. More relevant to our explorations are the instances of rape between people who are steady dates, close friends, or at least persons with whom the victim could suppose herself reasonably safe. Unlike the multiple rape situations, which are overwhelmingly planned, these are most likely to be rapes by a single person, and the victim is typically not transported from one place to another. Instead the rapist simply takes advantage of a situation in his own or the victim's residence, or while on a date in an automobile.

Most of these cases occur in a social structure in which there is no shortage of females, so that sex ratio is not a serious factor in the generation of this offense. Moreover, there is no reason to suppose that such men are especially perverted in their psychodynamics, or are unable to obtain sexual favors by ordinary seduction.

They do, however, enter the situation with a set of understandings which is at least widespread in lower class areas. One of these is the principle that if anyone has a duty to control the situation, it is the female's alone. The male is permitted to go as far as she will permit. If her permission extends very far, then it is her responsibility.

There is the further principle, widely shared by most males, that women are to be exploited if possible. Part of the code of *Machismo*, the intense glorification of specifically male characteristics, such as courage in battle, recklessness, independence of family ties, etc., is a contempt for female characteristics, and a philosophy that urges the use of women as a mere instrument of pleasure. To be dependent on a woman, and especially to show her tenderness and consideration because she deserves it as a human being rather than because it is a useful device for overcoming her resistance, is thought to be foolish. It is taken for granted among such men that women are trying to tame their men, trying to catch them in the toils of matrimony, and indeed they have good reason to believe that.

It is also a principle of lower class male society (and increasingly at all levels of American society) that sexual intercourse is expected if dating continues. With each successive date, the male will try to go as far as he can, and will judge the dating series to be a failure if there is no progression toward full sexual intercourse. Any previous stage of erotic intimacy must be followed by a forward step. The male is likely to feel cheated and betrayed if there is a backward step. Indeed he is not likely to continue dating, unless he actually falls in love seriously, or persuades the girl to engage in sexual relations with him. Needless to say, the establishment of a sexual relationship may or may not mean real intimacy. His aim was to exploit, not to become involved. Within his group of male friends, he would assert, with their approval, that he owes her nothing, and feels no need to continue the sexual relationship if he has better alternatives.

This set of values and attitudes is supported by male friends in their gossip and philosophic exchanges about girls and it also occurs in a milieu in which—as we have analyzed at some length—violence is common. Men should not be as violent toward women as toward men but mainly because it is not necessary: they are much weaker.

It is meaningless for the stern moralist to argue that the young woman should not get herself into that situation to begin with, because it is in such situations that most raped girls live. Moreover, we are talking only of the situations in which a previously intimate relationship existed, so that the young woman had at least some reason to suppose that the danger was low.

Here, however, we enter a most murky set of patterns. Most important is the problem of communication. If young men enter a dating situation, or even visit a close friend at her house, with such a set of understandings, it is likely that he will interpret almost any acquiescence as a signal to proceed. Moreover, he is also likely to become angry when he is blocked: he is being "cheated."

Still more important, in his experience force is an almost legitimate technique for getting his way, and not least with women. Few would wish to admit that they could obtain sex only through force, but men at all class levels, from fraternity boys and college football players to ghetto dwellers, can brag from time to time that they used a bit of forcible persuasion on a date, especially when they could do so safely. In Amir's cases, it is clear that violence was more commonly used when a single person raped some woman with whom he had a fairly close relationship, than one who was a stranger. This is partly an artifact, of course, since the very intimacy would have permitted an otherwise ordinary seduction had it *not* been frustrated.

However, common in such situations is a reciprocal failure to communicate. Beginning with the ordinary pleasantries and exchanges of friendship or affection, the male feels that he can go further, and at least hopes that her apparent unwillingness to engage in sexual intercourse is only an effort toward appearing "respectable," while the young woman in turn feels that their previous relationship established an agreed upon limit to the intimacy permitted, as well as a trust that her rejection will be accepted. The male, in turn, often hopes that if he uses a modicum of force, and is ultimately successful, the mutual enjoyment will persuade her to relent, and to forget this temporary unpleasantness. In addition, of course, the very struggle itself is likely to be not only somewhat exciting to the male, but its very excitement persuades him that the girl feels similar emotions. Indeed, it may be said that the sexual appetite is the most projective of all drives: it is difficult for someone who feels a sexual hunger to believe that that person does not reciprocate at all.

Consequently, the patterns of communication, coupled with the lack of adequate techniques for deflecting the aggression, may well lead to still more violence and even brutality, along with the rape itself. Pervasive in such episodes is a strongly aggressive element, which is frequently a factor in lower class sexuality, but possibly to some extent in a high percentage of male seduction. We need not pursue the psychodynamics of this aggressiveness far except to note the extent to which males view females as sources of frustration as well as pleasure; as persons who refuse to give what is so easy to give, who balk the spontaneous expression of appetite—and, of course, this pattern has its own roots in the much earlier infant and childhood experiences with the mother, who so frequently appears in psychiatric analyses as a source of emotional fulfillment that was denied.

NEED FOR DATA

Throughout the foregoing analysis we have made many references to the paucity of data. Most studies of violence are hampered because they are confined largely to official records, and the criminologist has had little access to the offender at a point in time close to the offense itself. For obvious reasons, most offenders do not care to expose the details of their crimes to outsiders, especially prior to the trial. Interviewing prisoners fills only part of this gap, because the events occurred so far back in time that the individual has lost many details and in any event has managed to fabricate a consistent story from what may have been a set of confused events. The sample of prisoners, in any event, omits a high but unknown percentage of violent confrontations between intimates, especially when they were assaults that were not reported to police. Thus the sample itself is likely to be biased.

Most important, of course, is the lack of systematic interviewing of both offender and victim. In homicide this is a natural gap, but considerable light would be thrown on the cases of assault if both could be systematically interviewed.

Such data would be especially useful in obtaining a better understanding of *process*: the dynamics by which such aggressive acts are generated, whether they end as homicide, assault, or rape. Process must include not only a specific act of violence, but also a *longitudinal* collection of data on successive confrontations, many of which were not violent in themselves, in that they did not include physical assault, but many of which threatened violence and did over time contribute to its generation. We do know that a high percentage of offenders have previously been guilty of some assaultive acts against either their last victim or other people. It would be useful to know the pattern of generation in those successive acts, as well as the gradual process by which violence became an accepted mode of procedure for dealing with others.

Most important, we need wider samples of people who live within the same milieu, but who have *not* participated in such acts of violence either as victims or as offenders. Our present sociological and psychological tools do lead us to the areas and situations in which violence among intimates is more likely, but these are crude devices, that permit only the most general statements. We cannot chart either the psychodynamic characteristics or the social patterns that lead to violence, other than the most general of factors. Thus we need larger, more representative samples so that we can examine more precisely the differences between those who engage in violence and those who manage to avoid it *within* similar social structures.

POLICY RECOMMENDATIONS

It seems worthwhile, after this small scale exploration of violence among intimates, to comment briefly on policy recommendations. Much violence occurs between intimates, but it is hardly sensible to recommend that people not enter intimate relations. Many men and women are killed in bedrooms, just as most people eventually die in bedrooms, but it seems this statistical fact cannot be the basis of a policy recommendation that we all avoid bedrooms.

We can, however, make a few suggestions. Not all of them can be easily implemented, and some can be implemented only by changing the society radically, but all of them deserve some attention.

Perhaps, since our earlier comments suggested that the total effect of the police is likely to exacerbate the amount of violence between intimates, we might begin with this important subgroup of our society. Here, one important policy recommendation can be made briefly, since it has been put into effect in one city, New York.

Here the Police Department has set up, under the training supervision of a psychological center, a police unit whose specific task is to intervene in dangerous family quarrels in upper west Harlem. As against the gloomy comment from the Federal Bureau of Investigation that one of every five policemen killed in the line of duty was attempting to stop a family fight, the Family Crisis Intervention Unit in the 30th Precinct has not sustained any injuries at all in its first 15 months of operation, during which it has intervened in more than 1,000 individual crises.[21]

Since policemen are in fact called to intervene in the entire range of domestic quarrels, and indeed in most quarrels among intimates that end in violence, it would seem the part of wisdom to train policemen to handle such problems more effectively.

Our earlier analysis of the dynamics of violence between intimates suggested the kind of emphasis necessary in police intervention: showing respect for the combatants; avoiding any show of force; de-escalating the anger by informality, listening to both sides and discussing with sympathy the arguments on both sides; conceding explicitly the man's masculinity; permitting both antagonists to talk out their problem at length, suggesting alternative solutions; etc.

A more obvious policy recommendation has been so widely discussed within the past year, that little addition seems necessary: strong gun controls. By now the data are relatively obvious, although those who wish to continue present American practice have hardly budged in their intransigeance. Here the cultural complexities are great and the difficulty of persuading people to give up their guns is great, but every serious analysis shows that a reduction of gun ownership would substantially reduce the rate of homicide.[22]

It is difficult to make precise estimates, because it is not known how many homicides were committed out of previously worked out and steady intent. One would expect gun control to have less effect upon *this* category than on the wider category of homicide, but it seems unlikely that more than a very small percentage of homicides between intimates would fall into that category. After all, they include gang killings, insurance murders, etc.

However, the substantial elimination of especially hand guns would have a further effect that is rigorously predictable from sociological theory, although a numerical estimate cannot be made. Without question, the reduction of hand guns in the nation would deescalate the atmosphere of violence, just as the gradual elimination of guns from the hands of police would do so. Here, we return to the comments made earlier about the social potentiation of violence—the creation of an atmosphere in which each person is subject to some threat and thus prepares himself for that threat. The existence of an intense field of violence in Southern cities creates a lower threshold to violence and a greater desire to carry or own hand guns, but since everyone knows that a high percentage of others *do* carry such guns, they have a reciprocal effect upon that field. The simple knowledge that other people are armed persuades some that they should be equally forearmed, and equally quick to protect themselves. The obvious social consequence, which is only common sense, is that the tools of violence increase the potential for violence not only directly (since more people *can* kill) but also by generating a higher tension and anxiety, and a greater readiness for violence.

Much more utopian would be the recommendation that a concerted attempt be made to introduce in American child-rearing practices a greater concern with peaceful modes of solving disputes and confrontations. However utopian, it should be kept in mind that American parents have over the years actually changed their child rearing practices in part, to conform with expert opinion, and over the last decade this pattern has extended increasingly beyond the middle classes to the lower social strata. At the present time, insufficient attention is paid to the problem, and parents merely yell harshly at their children to "stop fighting!" It seems especially worthwhile at this point in our history to urge the inclusion of peaceable techniques of social interaction, since so many confrontations are occurring in which a large number of issues are labeled as "nonnegotiable"; force is viewed as a legitimate tool for blocking others; many groups deny the right of others to be respected; and so on. It seems very likely that we are entering upon an era in which there will be more violent confrontations than in the past. Consequently, though our primary concern here is with the reduction of violence between intimates, and we have suggested some of the patterns which ought explicitly to be made part of the socialization experience of a child for dealing with such battles: in fact, such a childhood training would be salutary for issues and problems outside those arising in intimate relationships.

Far more fundamental, however, and of course far more difficult, is the suggestion that if we really wish to reduce violence between intimates or violence generally, we must reduce the frequency and intensity of insults that the social system pays to the members of the lower classes, both white and black but especially black. We have taken note of the structural differences by class, the different childhood experiences, the dissimilarities in value patterns, and the great likelihood that some disadvantages, the degradation, and humiliation suffered especially by blacks in our society will be displaced onto intimate relations. Far too great a burden is placed on such relations in the lower class. They cannot discharge all the hostility that is generated by the daily experiences; they cannot generate enough consolation to redress the emotional imbalance created by the hurts that come from the society. The much higher divorce rate among the lower classes is in part a function of the intolerable burden that such marriages are forced to carry. The black male cannot act as an adequate role model for his sons, because they see all too clearly that he is not respected.

Space does not permit us here to present an organized plan for restructuring our society toward the end of paying more respect to the lower classes, toward incorporating blacks into full membership in the society, though in other works I am indeed pursuing that problem. However, from our earlier analysis of the dynamics of violence among intimates, and of the structural position of those who occupy the lower social strata, it seems likely that the frequency of violence between intimates would be reduced if this policy recommendation were to be put into effect.

III. SOCIOLOGY
OF RELIGION

7. Religious
and Economic Action

INTRODUCTION

THE ANALYSES IN THIS SECTION HAVE BEEN DRAWN FROM A SINGLE LARGER WORK AND I WISH TO COMMENT ON ALL OF THEM TOGETHER, on both chapters in the section. They contain mainly descriptive data, in an effort to avoid generalizations by fiat and, therefore it seems useful to sketch the broad view that guided the larger inquiry, and thus the more limited investigations presented here.

The sociology of religion has tantalized perhaps all the theorists in our discipline, however we may judge the power of their results. On the one hand, as Weber noted, sociologists have no "ear" for religion. They are likely to be nonbelievers or apostates, not to be numbered among the faithful. Consequently, they typically lack a sense of religiousness that might correspond to their sense of familism, bureaucracy, or political action. Since they do not continue their religious observance as adults, they have few opportunities to observe others who are believers. They segregate themselves socially from believers, and thus have little chance of interviewing them, unless they engage in a specific research project in the field.

On the other hand, ever since the gradual crystallization of our conception as to what the task of sociology is, religion has been accepted as a major, if murky, set of variables. They are quintessentially *sociological*, since they are so far removed, at least on the surface, from the rational, technical, or economic variables that sociologists believe are the central buttresses of the society. Sociologists cannot contrast what people believe with "the reality," since there is no way to observe the supernatural. All that we can do is relate religious behavior to apparent religious beliefs.

A long line of distinguished sociologists and social anthropologists have, therefore, attempted to ascertain what the connections are between religious behavior and beliefs on the one hand, and the other social processes on the other. The line is especially long, since many distinguished scholars in other fields have attempted sociological analyses as well—in history, the classics, philosophy, and psychology.

Many of them, like Durkheim, supposed that by examining *primitive* religions, they could locate more easily the prime underlying variables that would be equally powerful in understanding religion in contemporary life. I do not believe that that search for "pure variables" was successful, but I continue to believe that a comparative perspective should include not merely our own society or the historical tradition of the Western world, but also other major civilizations of the past and present, and all of the societies, primitive or not, whose religious systems and religious behavior we can describe accurately and in adequate detail.

Ideally, our inquiry ought to grant equal intellectual and scientific importance to the religious systems of the Dahomey and the Augustan Romans, the Lacandones and the Unitarians. The fact that some religions have had a great impact on our personal lives, because they form part of our group tradition—the Hebrew, for example—does not make them more fundamental for our understanding of the part that religion plays in society.

Doubtless, sociology increasingly excluded primitive societies from its analyses until recently because it has utilized to an increasing degree the research survey as its prime tool of inquiry. As I noted earlier, however, now that sociology has developed more confidence in its own tools, it is becoming in recent years more comparative, and indeed many younger sociologists are carrying out researches among peoples that would once have been labeled "primitive societies." In addition, we can now observe even a resurgence of interests in the development of a theory of societal evolution. Hopefully it will be anchored much more firmly in empirical data than the grand edifice of evolutionism that collapsed so swiftly at the turn of the twentieth century.

In a comparative perspective, religion has been intellectually tantalizing, because (like the family) it seemed not to fit easily into any grand evolutionary pattern. Specifically, the comparative social analyst could show a line of apparently necessary sequences in technological advancement, but they do not parallel in any obvious way the religious systems of the world. Some theologies under a highly developed technology are relatively simple, while some societies with a very low technological development have had extremely complex religious systems. As the knowledge base of a technologically developed society grows, it rejects many of its older beliefs as "superstitions" but we now know that superstition, magic, and religion continue in many forms in all great civilizations. Societies with high technologies and those with less developed ones are also similar in that they both contain unbelievers and atheists. Moreover, we cannot suppose any longer, as many sociologists have in the past, that primitive societies and primitive religions change very slowly while the literate or "developed" ones do not. No one has managed to measure the rate of the change in religious belief within any society, primitive or not.

The most fundamental observable belief pattern in primitive religions is almost universal among the religions of great civilizations, especially at the level of folk belief: the faith that the supernatural entities or gods are "anthroposocial," that is, their "personalities" are like those of members of the society. In more specific terms, at the level of folk belief, primitive or "civilized," the deities take notice of men's actions, act broadly to further man's welfare, desire human attention and are pleased by honor paid to them, but displeased by neglect, punish men for disobeying the rules of society, sometimes have moods and whimsies that can be destructive, and so on.

However, the examination of religious beliefs, like the examination of religious objects, has not been fruitful in understanding how religious forces operate. Over the past two decades, the more fruitful line of inquiry has been to focus on the *social* aspects of religion, for instance, the examination of religious organizations as bureaucracies, the study of power and influence between parishioners and their clergymen, the relation between class and participation or leadership. Unfortunately, sociologists have been in the main more successful in understanding religion to the extent that they have ignored its specifically *religious* and *sacred* character, and instead focused on social behavior. The succeeding analyses also single out social behavior in religion. Specifically, these inquiries link the role demands of religion with their consequences for other realms and processes within the society, such as the economy, the policy, and the family.

Essentially, the guiding view is the common sense one, that the institution of religion does nothing, but the believers in it do everything. If anything is to be done, people must somehow be motivated by payoffs, the avoidance of punishment, deprivation, or prestige to do it.

Thus we can examine the kinds of role prescriptions not so much of belief as of performances, which are defined in the society as specifically religious, whether paying tribute to a deity or organizing a ritual. These in turn may be viewed from another theoretical perspective—if Sir Ghost (a man's ancestral spirit) among the Manus, a Melanesian tribe, enjoins a particular ceremony upon his ward, that ward must engage in much economic activity in order to carry out the command. This underlying view is, of course, applicable to almost any kind of action. We may view the movement of food from kitchen to the dining room as a purely physical act, to be measured in terms of mass, velocity, or work, or we may view it as a psychological process, motivated by the host's sense of inferiority and his need to placate someone else. We may instead view it as part of the broader pattern of commensalism in society, or it may be viewed in religious terms, for the meal may be a Seder.

So similarly, we can examine in great detail any set of role transactions within a religious system as being simultaneously governed by beliefs and norm commitments, but also as economic or political in consequence.

From this view, religious action is to be viewed as occurring primarily in this world, not the next, whatever may be its sacred or spiritual meaning. Not only do the punishments and rewards meted out by the gods occur in this world, but the various religious performances have an impact on other social realms, in this instance those of economics and political behavior.

When we examine these transactions in great detail, as they are here, we see that the older sociological cliché that religion "supports" the social system is neither sufficient nor entirely correct. Certainly in the sense that all religious action somehow "contributes to the survival of the society" it is partly incorrect. For example, many religious injunctions require the destruction of capital goods as well as consumption goods. Others are simply waste, as when a religious ceremony requires a vast accumulation of food, which is then distributed to the same people who contributed it in the first place.

On the other hand, some of these redistributions may indeed give food to those who had less. In any event, there is often no way of tracing out the impact of these religious patterns on the long term "survival" of society. That question may indeed not be a very fruitful one theoretically. However, when we examine any two such realms of social behavior, such as religion and polity, or religion and the economy, we see that social institutions are to some degree like human beings, that is to say they are in competition with one another. Individuals invest more of their energies and talents in one institution than another, and thus perceive correctly that they can aggrandize their position by aggrandizing the institution. Religious organizations seek, and sometimes achieve, considerable control over other realms of the society. In our own era, perhaps, religious organizations are less powerful than two centuries ago. The decline or rise in the range of its influence is doubtless worth considerable close historical analysis. Here all we can do is to note these kinds of competition, the modes and procedures by which each institution uses the other—again directed by and mediated through the individuals who are enjoined to carry out these behaviors.

Religious institutions must of course support to some extent the political or economic system, because otherwise they cannot survive at all. The organization requires investment and contributions, and it cannot obtain them if it is simply in total opposition to the other organizations of the society. On the other hand, priests and fervent believers may press for more command and authority. The actual allocation of men's energies to various of these institutions is a resultant of this continuing competition among the organizations of the society for the power and wealth that the society yields. Again, this can be expressed, as it was in the earlier chapter on role strain, by noting that the continuing and apparent stability of these social organizations and institutions is a resultant of the pervasive and detailed strains that are generated by the range of demands made upon each individual by the social networks in which he lives. If he contributes too much to one of them, he will usually be pressed by other role demands to diminish that contribution, and to make inputs in other realms. From this view, not all people in primitive societies are "religion"-dominated, but vary greatly among societies and within societies. Some invest far more of their talent in aggrandizing their political power, while others seek to accumulate goods for various purposes. Rulers in primitive societies can cunningly use religious commitments and role behaviors of their subjects for their political ends, as modern and historical rulers have also done in the Western world. In short, we must ask about the competition and strains among institutions, as mediated through their members.

The economic and sociological aspects of human action may be viewed as different levels of integration and emergence.[1] Economic action enters or could enter without any other person being involved, since the allocation of scarce means for given wants is found in any individual's action system.[2] That is, "an economic element enters in only in so far as the comparative scarcity of alternative means to a given end becomes relevant to the choice between them."[3] This fact limits an economic discussion in several directions. The technological thereby becomes peripheral. For this would involve the concept of "efficiency," not that of "cost." One need not analyze in detail the technical efficiency of one type of fishing, or of baiting hooks, or of the tools used, or the methods of manufacturing in a given society. A study of techniques is not a study of economics.[4]

This problem of economic choice assumes the ends to be achieved. Classical economics would have fallen into a hopeless morass of complex problems had it not generally attempted to exclude the problem of *how* ends are set at all, or of the source of goals.[5] One important proposition which is implied by this fact, however, is that the economic analyst cannot then claim that the ends which a given society strives for are "irrational."[6] Since in an absolute sense, and without any value judgments, all goals are "irrational," or at least non-rational, the category itself has to be abandoned. Also abandoned is the claim that a given economic pattern is "irrational" because it does not strive for a maximum monetary return. Rationality may enter as a concept, *when the choice of allocation is made*, the judgment being made on the basis of available means, overabundance or insufficiency of means allocated for a given end, allocation of scarce means to immediate ends because of lack of foresight and inability to think of important goals (in the person's own value system) in a future period, etc. Consequently, a maximum monetary reward may actually be "irrational," since in many societies the currency would have only a curiosity value.[7] It is only in societies where a maximizing of money means at the same time the greatest increase in means that a failure to work for the highest monetary reward can be classed as irrational. And, even then, if the values one holds highest are not to be achieved with money, such a pattern of action could not be classed as irrational.[8] Actually, the use of a price system allows values to be expressed in terms of one factor alone: money.[9] In a complex society, Firth remarks, "the existence of a price mechanism allows of an adjustment between supply and demand, by giving indices to producers and consumers of the pressure of wants and the level at which they can be satisfied."[10] Furthermore, it is evident that "the existence of some standards of measurement and some mechanisms of control of supply and demand are necessary for the operation of any economic system."[11] Consequently, the lack of the price system in the economic systems of some primitive societies will mean other features: "(1) Multiple standards of evaluation, particularly when services are measured against goods. (2) The absence of any fine adjustment of supply to demand on a large scale even if market conditions obtain. (3) A tendency to work for things directly and not for the medium by which they are procured."[12]

Because of the general latter-day extension of information about other societies, no effort need be spent in destroying common misconceptions of the primitive man, held so dear and so long by orthodox economists. Over three decades ago, Firth found it necessary, for example, to spend some time to point out that Seligman had used many preconceived erroneous notions of "primitive" man in his economic discussions, particularly the assumption that in a self-sufficient economy there is no necessity of barter or exchange.[13] This is no longer necessary. Nor is it necessary to devote attention to a refutation of some unilinear plan of social or economic evolution, such as "collector to hunter to herdsman to agriculturist."[14]

Anthropology is indebted to Firth, trained as an economist, for a clearer understanding of the theoretical problems of analyzing the economic system of primitive tribes, just as economics may well be indebted. Being competent in both fields, he is not guilty of maintaining that the "mentality of the primitive" is incapable of seeing his own advantage,[15] or of maintaining, as does Warner, that a primitive tribe has no separate economic structure, being dependent on other social institutions to regulate economic processes.[16]

TIKOPIA

With reference to the Tikopia, a Polynesian society not far advanced technologically and with a relatively simple economic system at the time of his study, Firth notes:

There is a scarcity of the means available for satisfying wants, these wants are arranged on a broad scale of preferences, and on the whole choice is exercised in a rational manner in deciding how the means to hand shall be disposed of. The employment of the factors of production is governed by some recognition of the advantages of the division of labour and specialization in employments according to differential skill, and economies of scale are also secured in an elementary way in agriculture, fishing, and other cooperative work. Productive equipment and other goods are accumulated specifically to engage in further production, so that one may speak of the employment of capital, though it does not fulfill all the functions of this factor in a modern industrial system. Moreover, there is an implicit concept of a margin in the use of the various factors of production, as in the transference of labour from one area of land to another according to variation in its productive capacity, or from one type of fishing to another according to the conditions operating at the time, or in the tendency for the size of the working group to vary directly with type of employment. . . . There is some realization of the operation of the law of diminishing returns. . . . There is a system of property rights. . . . Notions of value can be said to exist with the forces of supply and demand as a regulating influence . . . though . . . not expressed through a . . . system of exchange of commodities, or a price system. . . .[17]

Though an economic analysis does not have to explain the choice of ends, the general analysis of an economic pattern must note their existence, so as to make clear what the group is attempting to achieve. As this relates to the Tikopia, it becomes clear that the ends which are sought are for the most part social in the broadest sense—i.e., there is social emulation more than economic emulation. Firth characterizes the Tikopia economy by saying that it is "non-competitive," or that labor is "a social service, not merely an economic service." He expresses it further in the form of three propositions: (1) the economic relations are personalized; (2) the profit-motive is prevented from free operation by "other psychological (in the terms of this study: sociological) factors concerning the social role of the accumulation and use of wealth"; and (3) economic transactions are governed by a broad code of reciprocity, but this is part "of a wider code which obtains for all types of social relationship(s) which . . . receive much more overt and institutionalized expression than in our type of society."[18] Furthermore, Firth found it necessary to examine ends, without attempting at all to explain or justify their origin, for he had to indicate why certain economic decisions were made, such as a failure to use productive equipment at a particular time (mourning). The explanatory factor of "maximization of satisfactions" as used by the economist had to be broken down into *different types of satisfactions*, since there are different types of satisfaction possible. The explanation becomes meaningless "an an aid to the changes in demand, or differential application of the factors of production" if it applies only to the maximization of money.[19]

As in most societies, food is a primary goal of production in Tikopia, and therefore a prime factor in the economic processes. This follows from the commonsense and pragmatically obvious notion that in order to live one must eat. However, beyond this, not only is the Tikopia economy related to food: the social system itself is so oriented. The reason is not far to seek, taking into account several situations which have been previously described. It is not the nutritional value of the food which plays such a dominant role. It is rather that food is necessary for hospitality, in a culture given to dancing and visiting. It is a means for repaying obligations of various kinds, for showing respect to a chief, or acknowledging his suzerainty. It binds kinship units. It is, furthermore, a means of making religious offerings.[20]

It is at this point, therefore, that the system of ultimate values and beliefs called religion makes a pronounced impact. For just as, in another connection, religious elements impinge on the economic system through the political,[21] so here the emphasis is on the non-nutritional aspects of food exchange, production, and distribution, as well as the conditions surrounding all these. That is, ritual obligations and rules, impulses and beliefs, set certain ends, and aid in fixing means and conditions to these ends.[22]

Perhaps the most obvious relationship is expressed in the division of important food plants among the four principal chiefs, each one under the care of the peculiar deity of that chief, who is in turn responsible for rites (and therefore food production and offerings) in honor of that deity. Thus, the Ariki Kafika has control over the sacred yam, "the Ariki Tafua over the coconut, and the Ariki Taumako over the taro, and the Ariki Fangarere over the breadfruit. Each chief has his own set of rites to secure the prosperity of his food."[23] The rites of the last three are performed separately, but those for the sacred yam are the focus of much of the religious ritual of Tikopia, forming part of the seasonal cycle, the Work of the Gods.

Its importance is not simple and direct, however; it is only a small part of the total yam crop which must be fitted to the cycle. All but one type (not a distinct variety) may be planted and harvested at will.[24] It is of economic importance partly because it is a durable food, which can be kept over many months even in a tropical climate. However, its explicit and analytic importance does not lie in this, but in its relationship to the deity of the Ariki Kafika, to his position as chief and therefore as chief director of economic enterprises on the island. Furthermore, these integrated rituals are important for the food which must be produced for them and for the communal (and therefore intensified) endeavor which is set off and directed by such goals. Consequently, the significance of the yam extends beyond the Ariki Kafika and his direct relationship to the yam. This may be investigated in both these directions, and with a broader reference than to the Kafika chief himself. For substantially the same pattern holds true for other rites as well.

This is clearly shown in the case of the canoe rituals, which also call for increase and prosperity, such as in a formula used by Ariki Taumako:

I eat your excrement Tafaiata! (his title for the Atua i Kafika, when in
  his canoe court)
Turn to your timber is anointed there (the rite of oiling the canoe)
Anoint with power
Anoint for welfare
To ascend a flying fish on to your canoe.[25]

It is clear that this ritual is being used to obtain fish, asking the help
of the deity in the production of fish for food. But it must be noted,
also, that the reference is to "your canoe." The deity will simply not
obtain suitable offerings if he does not furnish food in quantity and
quality. The interest becomes more than merely selfish on the part
of the Tipokia native, and his interest in fishing with renewed endeavor, in order to fulfill his obligation to the deity, is indicated.
Thereby, also, an impulse is given to apply energy and time to repairing the equipment used in fishing. Firth suggests four main aims
of this ritual activity: (1) the deities are brought again into contact
with the canoes made by tools furnished (ultimately) by the deities;
(2) the deities are stimulated to help to provide for their own worship; (3) the relations between the deities and the kinship groups are
strengthened; and (4) the material fishing equipment is ritually
charged again with *manu*.[26]

As to function, he remarks, "And in so doing, the ritual secures that
these items of equipment, particularly the canoes, are in fact overhauled and made technically more effective. Moreover, the ritual provides a socially unifying occasion . . . the total result is an integration in technical, ritual, and social terms."[27] The description of this
work, constituted by the productive and ritual parallels, indicates
clearly how the presence of others in the group at a religious ceremony influences the individual to respond with alacrity and skill.[28]
This is even more definitely the case than is at first apparent, when
it is remembered that the gods are thought to demand promptitude
and speech in their rituals. When the oven must be begun extremely
early in the morning, in the ritual at Somosomo, the Pleiades are used
to judge the time, and some individuals are deputed to wake others.[29]
Speed and energy (the two concepts are close in Tikopia thought, as
they are in Dahomey) must be characteristic of the worker for the
gods. This is suggested even more strongly in the case of the first
fruits ceremony for fishing, related to the repairing of the canoe men-

tioned above, and having as constituent parts certain formulae such as that given immediately above. The situation is thought of in symbolic terms. The gods of the (sacred) adze insist on receiving recognition for their aid to men (the tools ultimately came from the gods, and are used for repairing the canoes). But if men are slack in performing the ceremony, or do not obtain fish for the ceremony, these gods will become angry. The adze then will strike among men instead of among fish.

Hence there is always some haste to get the ceremony over, and if bad weather prevents the fleet from going out or if the catch is poor, uneasiness is felt in all the villages. It is during this time that the mats lie open in the canoe court and everyone is relieved when they are folded up; it is a sign that the due rites have been completed.[30]

The people of Kafika perform the ceremony three times at least, and if the catch is not good enough to include a large fish, the most desirable being a shark, the ceremony is again performed in Uta, the most sacred area in Tikopia. Thus the ritual sanction furnishes a strong push to perform the rites with dispatch. But the ceremonies depend upon the allocation of time and energy as well as equipment and rituals, to fishing. The deities will not be satisfied, and therefore fishing will be poor, unless proper offerings are made. These can be made only if the necessary repairs are made, work is expended on fishing, and many members of the clan cooperate and compete to achieve these goals. Besides the purely secular pride and admiration attached to an efficient and fast worker, the gods themselves approve. And the competitive context of the ceremony induces a greater expenditure of labor.

Even when competition is not a dominant motif, the ritual conditions may create a situation where a greater amount of work is demanded. In the plaiting of mats at Somosomo[31] by the women, for the "recarpeting," a more efficient situation is possibly created. At least, the energies of the women are not distracted from production. This is not a *purpose* of these ritual restrictions, but a latent or implicit function of them. The purpose is, of course, to emphasize the ritual sacredness of the action, which is imbued with religious feeling.

Because of respect for the sacred area of Uta, which lies close to the glade of Somosomo, the women must turn their backs to the seacoast and their faces toward Uta. Even though they worked in groups, and the Tikopia are given to light chatter and gossip, they were not supposed to speak at all, except for technical discussions about the actual plaiting.[32] Besides this tabu of silence, the elders warned the women not to stop or slow the work down, no matter what happened. At the time, a light shower had begun, but the task was too sacred to be stopped. Furthermore, no one was to approach the workers. The function of these ritual restrictions becomes clear, then, since the work would be speeded up greatly.

Some suggestion has already been made that the act which initiates the period of excitement, hard work, routine, and tapu (Work of the Gods) focuses on the chief as central religious head, and constitutes both an economic and a religious act. After the firestick has been thrown, the main question asked is an economic one, even though the context is sacred: how many days will be allowed to cut and plait the coconut mats?[33] The answer is a formal one,[34] but with this answer the ritual-economic period begins with hard work on the mat-making. Likewise, he initiates the collecting of food for the making of the sacred roi,[35] used at the kava ceremony preceding the lifting down of the adzes for the ritual canoe (and fishing) ceremonies. The ritual resacralization and actual repair of these canoes, discussed above, is also under the aegis of the chief. And, in a similar fashion, the change to intense fishing as an economic activity is instituted by the ritual necessity of fish, particularly a shark, for the fishing welfare invocations of the chief, which were mentioned above. As ritual head, then, the chief initiates a diversion of economic activities in channels serving religious requirements, particularly the demands of the deities. Partly, also, he diverts energies to the replacement of perishable objects or productive capital (canoes), this being placed in a religious context. As a consequence, the significance of the chief is very great. Both the economic and the political headship of the Tikopia chief stem from his relation to the religious realm, in the thought of the Tikopia. As representative of the deity of his clan, or, in the case of the Ariki Kafika, of the whole tribe, he owns the land. But more important than this "ownership," which is nominal for most ordinary purposes, is his function as organizer and director of economic enterprise. In this, there are several phases at which the element of the sacred is introduced, since much of such enterprise is related to the wishes and plans of the gods, not merely of men, and the aid of the gods is obtained through the chief.[36]

The most obvious economic function served by the chief in his ritual capacity is to divert energies toward preparations for sacred ceremonies, for which great quantities of food, bark cloth, and coconut mats are needed.[37] The Throwing of the Firestick begins a period of keeping the fishing equipment as well as the gardens in working shape. Actually, much of the diversion of energy is "wasted," in that energies are spent on both productive equipment and purely sacred objects (e.g., mats). Nevertheless, there is an imperious immediacy to the religious demands, preventing procrastination; and the integration of the community's forces as initiated by the chief is an important result.[38] An important political function may also be served, in that the several chiefs are thus again joined ritually, while the supreme place of the Ariki Kafika is emphasized.

Attention will be later directed to the politico-religious interrelationship at the points where the chief prohibits the use of one or another commodity or area, and no detailed discussion need be given here. However, it should be emphasized that this is a pattern of saving, induced by religious demands. Certain foods are consumed in smaller amounts, or not at all, while others become dominant in the diet. The function and purpose are the same, to save foods for the religious or secular ceremonials, particularly the former. Thus, Firth summarizes in tabular fashion these shifts in patterns of economic consumption, and it is noticeable that all but one of the shifts are caused by the tapu of the chief in particular.[39] This one is the individualistic restriction, to his own use, of the cultivations of a given person. Others may be noted: (1) the Throwing of the Firestick stops the felling of sago palms for nearly two months; (2) funeral prohibitions on: a. richer foods, b. plucking coconuts, c. reef or canoe fishing, cause a change in consumption habits by which some few reserves are accumulated, poorer foods are eaten, and production shifts from sea to land; and (3) restrictions on taking coconuts, which cause a diversion partly to other foods, and allow the accumulation of coconuts which can be used for creaming the ceremonial foods used as gifts or offerings. These are backed by religious sanctions, thus delineating sharply the close interrelationships between what would seem to be realms diametrically opposed.

This close integration of production and economic decisions, by the chief in his capacity as religious head, with sacred goals, can be seen most clearly in the manufacture of turmeric. This spice is related most closely to the Atua i Kafika, and thus to the Ariki Kafika, though turmeric is also manufactured by the other chiefs. The religious element is seen in that the food importance of turmeric is comparatively little, and the coloring matter is used only in making a mark of ritual significance. It is considered attractive to the gods, and is used as a dye to color the bark cloths made as "toppings" or "coverings" for important food gifts to the Ariki Kafika.

As in the case of many other phases of the religious cycle, this is initiated by the Ariki Kafika, when he plants turmeric.[40] Firth witnessed the turmeric extraction of the Ariki Tafua, who is considered a turmeric expert. That he should be an expert is significant, since in this type of production great emphasis is laid on technical skill, as distinct from sacred power.[41] However, it remains true that the grinding and washing of the plant roots must be done every year by the chiefs, as a religious obligation,[42] while a commoner who produces at all will do so much less often. Even in the case of this technical procedure based on skill, it is thought by the Tikopia that the expert cannot rely on such skill alone. He must also use ritual formulae. For it is by his deity that such an expert obtains success in the separation of the pigment. Each will have a different deity, though it is understood that the ever-present Atua i Kafika is thought to preside over the process or season as a whole. It is also understood that the "chief in accordance with his rank and esoteric functions, is always leader of the first unit in his own *nuanga*" (turmeric extraction),[43] the same order of precedence being maintained in the units throughout the procedure. The first batch of pigment is considered valuable, and is the chief's.

Here, again, capital equipment is renewed as a ritual necessity, while it is also a necessity for efficiency. The aqueducts are repaired or overhauled, being sections of split areca palm. The cutting of the first palm for this use is preceded by a short appeal to the particular deity of that *nuanga* unit, and later a libation and a food offering are made to the Kafika deity, informing him of the presence of a sufficiency of water. The deity is thus ceremonially notified that the secular aim has been achieved.

The ritual implications of the turmeric extraction are more clearly seen once the first grating of the roots begins, for it is from that time that a number of restrictions and prohibitions begin. The situation is well incorporated by the phrase, "living in the *nuanga*," as opposed to "those at the back."[44] Here, again, the imposition of the regulations is thought by the Tikopia to be of a merely religious nature, but the result is greater efficiency, for one of the important tabus is against sexual intercourse. To assure the efficacy of the prohibition, women and men separate both at night and for rest during the day. Affairs of sex might hurt the health of the people, or ruin the turmeric (it will be soft). Connected with this explicit bar against sexual intercourse is a series of prohibitions against certain postural positions: men must sleep on the back, while women must sleep on the face, and one may not squat with the knees hunched up, while it is permitted to "sit with crossed legs, or recline with the legs straight out in front."[45] These are considered less suggestive, sexually.

Similarly, there are food prohibitions, most of which attempt to induce the turmeric to become hard, by a symbolic process. Semi-liquid foods, or mush foods, or even sugar, must not be eaten. A less clear regulation insists on those "within the *nuanga*" eating only "hot foods." Those who eat the one must not come into contact with those outside, who eat "cold foods"; otherwise the turmeric will not be satisfactory.[46] The remnants of the *nuanga* ovens, which would ordinarily become the cold food of the next day, are not thrown away, though this might be expected as a possibly symbolic rite. Instead, they are passed out from the *nuanga* into other households "outside." These rules are, it may be observed, significantly close to a magical pattern, though Firth does not remark on it. For a breach of these tabus is not punished by a deity presiding over or playing a part in the *nuanga*. The breach is rather the beginning of a (seemingly) cause-effect chain. Further, these are not tied to ritual formulae or any relationship to the deities, but are rather sanctions running "fairly evenly throughout the whole process."[47] Even children must obey the rules about food, which would not be expected if the sanction were less personalized. The impersonal pattern must be followed. This is particularly striking, since Tikopia children are usually allowed many breaches of tabus, being only gently (though repetitiously) admonished.

After the grating of the roots and the building of the filter stand for the funnel-like filtercloth of palm fiber, the extraction proper begins. Even though the expert is skillful, this is such an important point in the manufacture of the pigment that one could expect some ritual. At the time when the first batch of grated turmeric roots are being thrown into the filtercloth, the chief is given a cue by the one emptying the bowl, and then begins a formula called Fishing for Success.[48] It contains the usual metaphors of abasement, with several symbolic references to the turmeric, by the mention of redness in several connections. It is supposed to induce the greatest amount of turmeric from the materials being worked. The appeal is partly to the vanity of the deity being involved, who is Tuna, the Eel-God (who controls the fresh water used in filtering). This is related to other ceremonies in Tikopia, where there is a direct relationship to economic production, in that in each case the deity is told to help because the work is being done for him.

In spite of the insistence on genuine technical ability, the sacred (and partly magical) character of the whole process, noted before, continues to obtrude itself in this economic affair. That is, the expenditure of skill and energy on the process is not considered sufficient: the favor of the gods must also be obtained. For the final proportion between the edible, though less valuable, extract and the vermilion pigment is "believed to be not simply a physical relation, but one governed by spirit action."[49] This spiritual assistance is believed, in the Tikopia pattern of thought, to manifest itself in three main ways: (1) aiding the precipitation of the pigment; (2) transforming the edible portion into the vermilion precipitate; and (3) stealing pigment from others while guarding the home supply. This latter is done by the spirits, not by men, and the thieving is not to be done on the island, but elsewhere.

Somewhat the same phrasing is used in other formulae brought in later, in that a pattern of inducing the turmeric to be plentiful and well solidified is repeated. At every stage in the production of the pigment some ritual elements enter, some having a demonstrable function in increasing, or shifting the emphasis of, production, others (like the spiritual assistance petitioned for above) having none. In terms of the Tikopia ideology, each is necessary, and the Tikopia is not always conscious of the effect of the ritual, in economic or technical terms. Thus the enclosure to hold the bowls of turmeric while settling is tabu, once the bowls are filled, serving to leave the mass undisturbed during the precipitation.[50] Also, the sacred character of the pigment ensures a greater care in the handling of it, so that the actual production is greater.[51] This care is even more marked in the case of the first cylinder of turmeric from the oven of the Ariki Kafika. That is, the ritual motivation induces great care in production itself. This follows from the critical position of the chief. He is the initiator of the whole phase of turmeric manufacture, and leads the various units in beginning each step in the procedure. As the person most closely connected to the supreme deity of the island, who in turn is the deity of all most interested in the production of turmeric, it is felt that his pigment is crucial: ". . . if his pigment turns out well it is believed that this is a good augury for all the rest. . . . The Ariki Kafika himself, imbued with his responsibility, said that he recited formulae not for his turmeric alone, but that the nuanga of the whole land might be successful."[52]

Thus it is that the world of the supernatural and sacred, whatever its "illusory" qualities, actually interacts with this economic realm in definite, concrete ways, by shifting the ends to be achieved, and by furnishing a more imperiously immediate motivation for certain economic goals. The ways in which these ends may be achieved are conditioned by ritual sanctions which in some cases impair efficiency, in others increase it. In still others there is no perceptible way in which either could occur, the ritual sanction either having little effect, or consisting in a ritual formula which merely occupies an interval of waiting during a technological process. The demands of the sacred, then, divert scarce resources of time, energy, and capital equipment to certain activities at certain periods, changing eating and working patterns at the time, usually causing an increase either in the accumulation of wealth for later expenditures or, by repairs, in the heavy capital equipment of canoes, canoe sheds, turmeric equipment, adzes, etc.

It would not be expected that ritual elements would play such a directive role in economic production, without at the same time performing some distributive and exchange functions. That is, we should expect to find that the determination of the direction of distribution and its quantity would follow, at least in part, from ritual status, sacred obligations, and religious demands. It would also be expected that the focal point for such distribution or exchange as takes place must be the chiefs, in both a secular and a ritual capacity.

That is, he receives gifts as political head, and as representative of the clan deity.

Even the chief of the Kafika clan works in Tikopia. No one is a true member of the "leisure class," though it is true that the Ariki Kafika is allowed to work less, in terms of actual production, than other individuals. He is not, for example, allowed to shoulder burdens. Without a court or army to consume the gifts he receives, it becomes obvious that he must be a constant giver as well as recipient. This is even clearer in view of another fact, that his own possessions would more than cover his requirements and those of his family.

Stated briefly, he is the recipient from his people of periodic gifts of food and special types of raw material which, sporadic in the case of any individual contributor, nevertheless form *in toto* a steady stream of additions to his wealth. But . . . a great deal of what he receives he redistributes, and with his family's help he must reciprocate the initial gifts, though not necessarily to an equal extent.[53]

These gifts come from the chief's clan, but also come from people living nearby though from other clans, as well as those who are in other clans though closely related to the chief. The food gifts usually are constituted by a large basket of creamed pudding, or of fish, with "a mass of baked taro or yam tubers, breadfruit, or bananas."[54] They are also reciprocated soon afterwards. The reciprocating gifts usually come, of course, from contributions made by still others, thus forming a steady stream of income and outgo.[55] Besides the "first gifts," large fish are supposed to be brought to the chief. Further, "the border of the path is the orchard of the chief," that is, the food growing near the edge of the path may be taken by the chief, unless the owner takes it first. There are also food gifts indicating specific kinship ties, particularly the relationship to a common ancestor. These may be made when the chief is ill, or even in mourning.[56] Moreover, there are gifts which chiefs make to other chiefs when they attend ceremonies together. This is only one phase of his traditional role as a fountain of generosity, emphasized even more in other connection: "Toward poor commoners . . . a chief is expected to be generous without necessarily getting anything in return."[57]

Besides these sources of income, which are essentially secular, even though in many cases partly ceremonial, there are a great number of strictly religious rituals which include gifts to the chief, in particular to the Ariki Kafika. Such gifts include the *monotanga* of a sacred canoe, the *fonakava* from the recarpeting of a temple,[58] both given by commoners; *monotanga* of the very sacred canoes to the Ariki Kafika (given to him only), "the path of our ancestors (from Taumako to Kafika only), food from rebuilding a temple, and, possibly, the exchange of gifts at certain ceremonies, all the latter being gifts from other chiefs.[59] This does not include certain of the chiefly feasts, at which the chief composes songs to his deities, or at which the gods are brought in to witness the accession of the chief. . . . All of these call for return gifts of some sort.

It is not necessary to describe all these in detail, since the pattern is much the same. The quantity of food is large, an effort being made to express a general abundance. It is of the best quality, and is usually accompanied by something which is "extra," or "topped" by some contribution such as bark cloth. It is often redistributed at that point, or at least soon afterwards. The offering or gift is made when a particular ceremony is going to be performed, and is made at the place of performance, usually at a temple. The gift is made in view of the religious relation between the chief and the clan deities. Such a pattern is represented by the *fonakava*, mentioned immediately above.

Thus, the *fonakava* acknowledges the overlordship of the chief over the temple of the kinship groups in his clan.[60] As part of the Work of the Gods, the kava houses are reconsecrated. These are used by elders or chiefs on various occasions during the year. Even though the suzerainty of the chief over these several temples is only formal, the gift is considered very important. In the eyes of the Tikopia, this contribution made twice yearly is expressive of a fundamental connection between the gods of the chief and the deities of the kinship groups in the clan, and thus between the chief and the same groups. The ritual of reconsecration differs from case to case, since the characteristics of the different deities vary. Such an expression of relationship is involved in the ceremonies at Nukuora, when at one phase of the sacred ritual only the two chiefs of Fangarere and Kafika are present, with two helpers.[61] The Ariki Kafika makes the kava, while the temple itself belongs to the Ariki Fangarere by virtue of an ancestor buried there, who was saved by the Ariki Kafika at the time of the slaughter of the people of Ravenga.[62] Many libations to various gods were made at Nukuora, as well as thirteen offerings of roi, one for each god and ancestor, each on the proper mat. The morning previous to the setting out of the sacred roi, similarly large food gifts had been brought to Nukuora, though these were not of the sacred roi and were instead contributions to the Ariki Kafika as fonakava. This was again an acknowledgment of the relationship between Fangarere and Kafika, and a link forged because of the aid of the Kafika chief long before. This particular tie was made even more evident by the preparation of the roi, mentioned above, in the Kafika oven, and by a "coconut kava" on a grass plot between Kafika temple and the oven, but near Nukuora. In all this procedure, the economic function is not recognized by the Tikopia as being central at all. The most important goal is the reconsecration and recarpeting of the temples. The recarpeting is also economic, of course, since it is thus that the sacred property continues in good repair (unlike Polynesian temples elsewhere since the coming of white men). The distribution of food is also economic in character. But neither is thought of in such terms, the motivation for the economic processes being ritual and social in nature. The deities would be insulted, and the power of sacred objects would be destroyed, if they were not periodically refurbished, repaired, or renewed. This is consonant with both the attitude of the gods that men should be energetic and efficient in the ritual labor, and with the notion that some ritual objects lose their power when not "fresh." This is true of the several *tapu* knottings of palm leaf, as well as the circlets used by the chief when performing a ceremony.

It must be remembered that exchange for a concrete object of a secular nature is, though not pervaded by sacred elements, nevertheless noncompetitive and traditionalistic, somewhat like the food "exchange" which has been described. Here, using the concept of "equivalence,"[63] it is noticeable that certain objects are typically traded for one another, and that there is a graded series of "equivalents," even though the objects are not on the other hand expressible in terms of a universal medium of exchange. Furthermore, though this realm of exchange in a purely secular context is not so heavily motivated by sacred patterns, some few carryovers may be noted. Among these is the very set of concepts used to describe objects which are valuable.

The term, *mafa,* is used to describe the "degree of ritual sanctity attaching to names of the gods, formulas and ceremonial institutions."[64] It does not mean precisely that in this connection, of course, but rather emphasizes an importance in the economic pattern. Even here, however, it happens that this economic importance is often related to the importance in the ritual scheme. Some objects, as we have seen, are important in production and in sacred ceremonies, such as turmeric bowls and equipment, the sacred canoes, the sacred adzes, etc. Furthermore, the same objects which figure largely in this secular exchange, such as sinnet, fish hooks, bowls, bark cloth, etc., are also those which are very important in the ceremonial exchanges at a funeral.[65]

Of all the objects which do play a role in this exchange, the most valuable, in terms of equivalents, are turmeric cylinders, canoes, and bonito hooks. The first two, as is known, are connected closely to sacred rituals and to a high social status. Turmeric and canoes are typically the property of the chief, whose relationship to them is not in terms of property and ownership but in terms of his function as religious officiant and representative. It must be confessed that the exact status of the bonito hook is not clear in either secular or ritual terms. It is true that the bonito, as a large fish, is wanted as an offering at the time of the repairing and reconsecrating of the canoes. However, as has been noted, the chief expression of desire is for a shark, while the shark hook is put by Firth in a secondary position of equivalents, less than the bonito hook.[66] Part of its high value lies, of course, in "its ritual use for funerals, for atonement, etc."[67] but this sacred value would seem to be derivative, not primary. One possible explanation is that Firth is simply not clear as to the relationship of the shark hook and the bonito hook. Thus he does not make clear where the shark hook is related to the several "spheres" of values, except to say that ". . . the sinnet for the shark-hook is next to the bonito-hook, while next to it is the mat."[68] It may be that the two are the same thing, since when a bonito hook is given, the sinnet accompanying it is not "bonito sinnet," but "shark sinnet" or a "shark line." Further, as "weighty" goods the sinnet cord figures, but "that for catching sharks only." However, since Firth also remarks that the bonito hook "is primarily, after all, an instrument for catching bonito," the question must be left unanswered for the present.[69]

The exchange of most of these articles is fixed. One type of object calls for another object, or the same type, within its own sphere of equivalence. Food, of course, does not figure as an object of ordinary secular exchange, since most of such food exchanges are ceremonial in character, and not the result of someone coming to desire an object not now possessed. Furthermore, food is not durable. But, more important, *food is simply not an equivalent* of such objects as bonito hooks, shark cord, turmeric cylinders or canoes. In the case of these objects, "when the transfer of them from one individual to another takes place the situation is usually charged with emotional significance. Turmeric cylinders are broken over the body of a dead chief, bonito-hooks are hung round his neck, or in the lobes of his ears, a canoe is handed over to his mother's kin, as part of the payment for his burial."[70] These are, clearly, closest in their relationship to the sacred, while the next removed is the series of objects which Firth calls the bark cloth-sinnet group, which are sometimes used for ritual presentation. However, for the most part they are used for specialist skill in canoe or house building, for timber, bowls, damage to valuable tools, etc. The pandanus mat is "its highest expression."[71] Food is, of course, the ordinary payment for arm rings, the loan of a canoe, ordinary labor, paddling, and so forth. Its function in a genuinely religious context has already been discussed. In each case the equivalents are not derived from what we would call a market—Firth himself created the only situation comparable to a market, during his stay—or profit situation, but from traditionalized patterns which designate certain objects as occurring in the same sphere of values. These spheres nevertheless increase in value by degrees, as they approach objects which are peculiarly the property of the chiefs[72] and are sacred in many contexts. The economics of ordinary market competition cannot strictly fit this set of circumstances, even though there is emulation in the matter of work and efficiency, and in the effort to "live up to one's status," as well as elsewhere.[73]

Competition is limited, then, and Firth notes three main types of limitations to the "individual greed and acquisitiveness" characteristic of sharp competition. These are:

. . . firstly, there is the force of tradition, the binding obligations of kinship, respect for rank, and magico-religious taboo. Secondly, there is the lack of the means for individual economic assertion, the low level of material culture and the limited range of possible satisfactions. And, finally, there is the difficulty of evasion, the fact that in a small island community public opinion is hard to deceive, easily mobilized and effective by reason of the close and intimate nature of the personal bonds uniting the members of the community.[74]

Two of these types, it is seen, are personalized in nature, ranging from the effect of public opinion to the sanctions of the gods. The other merely expresses a lack of opportunity.

8. *Religious and Political Action*

WE CAN ANALYZE SOME ECONOMIC CHOICES BY CONSIDERING THE AC-
TIVITIES OF A SINGLE INDIVIDUAL, ISOLATED ON AN ISLAND IN A CLAS-
sical Robinson Crusoe fashion. At such a level of analysis, political
problems are not visible. However, when two or more men interact,
social conflict emerges as a possibility. Their ends may be compatible,
but they may need the same, limited means to those ends. Or their
goals may be the same objects, which are themselves limited. Or, a
further possibility, the goals themselves may be in contradiction.

Whatever these possibilities, the problem of "order" inevitably
arises. Conceivably, an individual may attempt to use others by
means of force, manipulation, or domination. He may rationally select the most efficient human means to his ends. Indeed, we may
know of individuals who seem to do just that. Yet this can not be the
foundation for a society. If such attitudes are generalized throughout
the group, as Hobbes so brilliantly demonstrated, chaos would result.

The ultimate structure which prevents this chaos is that of com-
mon-value integration. Nevertheless, the phenomena of power, conflict, and political order are aspects of social action requiring their
own level of analysis. This is also true of economic phenomena as
well, and in both cases we can assume the basic integration while
holding to one focus as far as is possible.

An obvious debate then threatens: Do preliterate groups have "government and law"?[1] This is partly a matter of definition. There is, indeed, a temptation to claim that it is *only* a matter of definition. In some final, Pickwickian sense this is perhaps true. Such a sense is hardly adequate for science. We must, rather, attempt to relate our own focus to that of others, not only in order to communicate, but also because there seems to be some homogeneity in the phenomena.

The suggestion was made that conflict between individuals must be prevented or controlled. Differently phrased, *power and authority must be regulated institutionally*. As power dominates a geographical area, we usually call it *political authority*. In technologically developed societies, with a formal definition of political authority, we frequently call it *government*. The *state* then becomes a groupal structure centering around and claiming a monopoly over the legitimate use of coercion. Such an organization may develop a set of practices called a *system of law*, perhaps even a *court system*. We expect to find this latter phenomenon in formalistic, rationalistic, secular, and urban societies far more frequently than in their polar opposites.[2]

Let us make a few distinctions beyond these. A society will exhibit the phenomenon of political authority, or *power*. This may imply the existence of *law*, which again requires some description. Now, a law, or legal system, is surely not to be equated with the total complex of social custom or *mores*.[3] Nor is it useful to restrict it to court phenomena alone.[4]

Perhaps scientific convenience can guide us in the choice of definition, concept, or category.

Let us approach the matter from the concept of power, or authority. We then see that "the legal" is not a characteristic inherent in any particular group of *acts*, such as murder, quarrels, adultery, etc. It is rather a quality observable in a situation involving a broad, impersonal, societal norm which is threatened on the one hand, but which on the other is also protected by public coercion or its threat.

Several points are implied here. One is that a legal rule, as Malinowski correctly points out, is not usually called into play. The norm has been inculcated in the growing individual, and has become part of his value system. Moreover, the norm is "baited with inducements."[5] We refrain from murder because, for the most part, we have been reared to feel no such conscious inclinations, and we also derive some advantages from being law-abiding.[6]

Let us note further implications. *We expect conflict with the norms,* for the socialization process does not make the individual a complete conformist. Moreover, when such a conflict arises, the sole recourse is not a reliance upon the individual conscience: resort is made to force, as well. Following this out further, the matter is not a matter for the injured party to settle alone, *as an individual.* In addition, the application of the public coercion is in support of the societal norm. This implies the existence of *systematic pressure,* and the possibility of sociological *prediction.*

This prediction will deter some individuals from committing legally deplored acts, knowing the consequences. Beyond this, the public backing of the force makes the coercion *legitimate*: the creation of *authority.*[7]

We do not, then, speak of *all mores,* or customs, even though all have some social sanction behind them.[8] We must rather confine ourselves to the "formal and legitimate assignment and maintenance of legal authority, and the rules governing this patterned social activity."[9]

The existence of a social system presupposes, then, a power system. The converse is likewise true. Genetically, its chief aspects are achievement or ascription; functionally, they comprise the maintenance and exercise of power. Deposition, of course, is merely achievement or ascription in the eyes of the new officeholder.

Furthermore, the power-holder is not so dominant in this situation as he seems. However their philosophies conflict, leaders pay service, lip or other, to group values. Characteristically, they claim to be preserving the group from destruction, physical or moral.[10] In an efficiently ordered power structure, the ruler may assume his followers believe that he embodies their group values. In point of strategy and fact, he will do well to steer clear of both charge and refutation, and the clever ruler may manage to do so by making that embodiment apparent.

The point is further documented by the inability of even despots to break far from the pattern of values which the group generally follows.[11] The charismatic leader has a greater chance to do this, but even he must then remain a "constant deviant"—deviating in ways previously accepted by the group—in order to maintain his flock intact.[12] By the very act of group-value integration, the power holder is himself limited in his scope of action, precluding for the most part the coexistence of complete individual arbitrariness and a social system. The leader is dominant not because of his uniqueness, but rather because he is much like the rest of his followers, who find in him some symbol of, as well as a means to, their values and ends.

It would follow from these remarks, then, that any political system as a continuously operating unity is *legitimate*. In so far as the power system is not based on force alone—and none has functioned long on that basis—it derives its strength from being legitimized by the values which it upholds. Consequently, a *de facto* system as a going concern must become legitimate. Part of its struggle to become dominant, and most of its efforts to maintain itself, are to be catalogued under appeals to legitimacy—its *right* to possession. The traditional system has no such open struggle, disguising it in various ways.

It becomes evident that all societies have one or more central foci of political power. It is, then, significant to ask about the *explicitness* of the connections between legitimate power and other social phenomena. There is always a power structure, but it may be far more implicit than explicit.[13] And the extent to which other structures are explicit will vary. Such a formalized structure delineates *specific procedures* for attaining power. Further, power limits become more *stabilized*, in that the symbols for verbal and open resistance, or conformity, are closer to hand. ̄*Social distance* is made more definite, reducing the importance of personality (charismatic) factors in the exercise of politics. Further, the structure comes to be partly autonomous, since it may not embody the ultimate authority at all.[14] This may vary independently of another factor within the structure, that of *inheritance*, or *ascription*, of political power. This is important, since it is related to defined classes or castes within the group; to social mobility (and therefore with religious prophets); to the necessity of removing a dynasty (Dahomey) or entire status instead of a particular person in order to change the political structure; as well as to the different types of socialization involved in the preparation of a child for his inherited or achieved position.

Moving from this point, the most significant orienting proposition is one iterated previously, that religious action takes place in this world, even though many of its ideas are directed to another. This means that most religious action has concrete effects in this world.

One sins, for the most part, in this world. One is also, for the most part, punished here. Repentance and expiation, as well as exhortation and supplication, occur in this world, and the proposition holds for political action.

This means, then, that there will be some limits to the variation of world goals as they relate to the sacred direction of interest. In concrete terms, the goals of political action must integrate somewhat with those of religious action. There are always some mainly political ends which are partly gained by religious means.[15] There may be religious ends achieved by political means. Problems of authority and control may arise, since a clear-cut division may not exist. Since power is potentially capable of extension and generalization, the political official may at times be threatened by the power of religious officials or personalities. Legitimacy may be achieved through religious means. This legitimation may even be made formal as, e.g., when a ruler is formally accepted by the religious leader or sacred beings. Further, a proposition which seems likely, though difficult of proof, some emotional release through religion may function to divert attention from the repressions of political rule.

DAHOMEY

It would be in Dahomey, the culture of great secular and sacred specialization, that we would expect the religious pattern to be most difficult to find at work in the political sphere.[16] The same difficulty, to a greater degree, appears in the attempt to analyze religion in our secularized Western society.

Before proceeding to less obvious interrelationships, the more evident might well be noted. The religious pattern in Dahomey, as among the Murngin, includes many magical patterns as well. The yehwe, or *vodun*, include the *azizan* who gave *gbo* fetishes, thus forming part of the magico-religious interweaving. There are a large number of such *gbo*, variant in concrete physical structure, but more especially in function. One curious type of *gbo* figures in a crucial fashion here. The *ordeal itself is a gbo*.[17] It is, like other magic, owned by a practitioner, and it distinguishes the guilty from the innocent. There were many such ordeals in Dahomey, most of them entirely comparable to those in our own past: if administered properly no one would ever be innocent. Some of these were placing a red-hot machete on the tongue of the accused (to see whether it blistered); taking an *adjikwin* seed from a pot of boiling oil (to see whether the oil burned the hand); placing a pepper under the eyelids (to determine whether the eyes would become inflamed); requiring the accused to kneel on broken palm-nut shells (to find out whether the skin was abrased); etc. Others were more primarily supernatural from the Western point of view: two magically treated seeds (*ago*) tied to a cord and lightly buried, the cord then being thrown about the neck of the accused to find out whether he could lift it; a similar test with pots; crossing the wrists, to determine whether the accused could separate them at command; washing the face in cold water, on the theory that if guilty his eyes would inflame.

As would follow from the preceding analysis, there is little if any difference among these in social definition. In each case, it is the supernatural power which creates the efficacy, and it then becomes irrelevant whether, by reference to Western cause and effect, one group inevitably causes guilt to be adjudged, while the other results in innocence.[18] The magical, supernatural power is being used in the interests of justice.[19] Such ordeals were performed under the supervision of the village chief, who was and is the central figure in Dahomean political life.[20]

As is usual in a hierarchal political structure, the right of appeal existed. Thereupon the king could annul the ordeal, both as supreme political head and as possessor of superior magic: the religio-political parallel. His own ordeal then put the whole village to a poison test, begun by administering it to a representative of a quarter, then a compound, then the individuals, the actual poison being given to a cock (recovery meant innocence). The accused himself did not undergo the ordeal personally. If the original culprit was again determined to be guilty, his punishment was even more severe, while if innocent he was free again.[21]

Similarly, two other types of trial may be noted, again using supernatural forces, this time definitely not magical. When the accused happens to be a member of a cult-group, he may be required to take an oath of his innocence, the retribution being death for false swearing. For he is to swear that if he be guilty he should die on the day his god "comes to his head."[22] Refusal, as in the case of ordeals everywhere, is a clear sign of guilt. A comparable type is the oath by which the individual takes earth in his hand, after saying, "If I am guilty, let the King of Dahomey take my head. Here is the earth of Dahomey." He then calls on the spirits of his sib dead, and eats the earth. If guilty, he will die in seven or sixteen (both sacred numbers) days. Calling on the sib dead is not to be taken lightly, since they are so close. The pattern is again followed, for men only, in an oath by Gu (god of iron), made when the man scoops up sand on a knife and swallows it. Rather than swear by the earth, the warrior will confess. This intrusion of the political into the religious, and vice versa, is entirely understandable in terms of our own culture, for not all the evidence is known to the whole group, and there is enough individualistic patterning and secularization for a very solemn and grave ordeal to be necessary.

The village chief, though apparently considered more as judge and conciliator than arbitrary ruler, was very powerful. On the other hand, he had to bear in mind one important source of *sacred limitations on political power*.[23] For "if the inhabitants of a village were members of one sib, then the representative of the sib-head in that village . . . exercised a considerable restraining influence on any untoward exercise of power to which the village chief might be tempted."[24] This is understandable not only from his position as head of an important group of people, but even more comprehensible from his semi-sacred character. The sib-head, who was and is the oldest male member, constitutes a link between the dead and the living. This is carried to its logical conclusion, in that his usually early death after assumption of office (explicable to us as a function of his age) is explained as a result of his contact with the dead. His religious duties include "establishing" the dead as deities, and if he forgets any, the forgotten soul will cause his death. Thus he was in a religious office, and likely to die. However, by virtue of that very contact which would kill him, he was in a powerful position from which to limit or deal with the more secular official, the chief.

Considering the intimate relationship held to exist between the gods and daily life in Dahomey, as elsewhere, it is not surprising that the village chief would often have duties which extended into that realm. Not thinking of disease as a primarily medical problem, the society required him to act officially when epidemics occurred. At that time, he had to call his diviner, to find out which gods had caused the situation, as well as which gifts would influence them to take back the misfortune. He thereupon acted as an official sacrifice collector for the gods in question, assessing the villagers the amount of animals needed, ". . . and would then set the date when the animals with the magic palm-fronds, or the foodstuffs required, were to be brought to the chief-priest of the deity in that village."[25] ". . . The chief is seen as the one who crystallizes action in order to propitiate a supernatural power who, discontented with some occurrence in the village, had endangered the lives of its people."[26]

In Dahomey, property in land is not held to be inalienable in any ordinary sense as is the pattern among the Murngin. Consequently, titles may have to be validated. This situation may be one where the political relates to one small element in the sacred complex. The sib-head or head or collectivity may hold in trust a field or palm grove for a group of heirs. If a division is to occur, the chief presides over the division, first seating himself on his stool as a ritual act establishing legality. The measure is in terms of bamboo lengths. However, this measure is not merely noted in a secular fashion. There is an official to watch the proceedings, one element of which he watches particularly. At the boundaries of the bamboo measures either a sacred tree, *angya*, or "an equally sacred bush called *desilisige*" is used as a mark. This bush or tree then becomes the validating mark of the title, there for future generations to use as an unquestioned boundary.

As in any autocratic political system, the political administration insists on having control over and knowledge of all occurrences and all activities of the kingdom. Various devices were used to insure an adequate census, the collection of the honey and pepper crops,[27] and the count of livestock, to mention only a few examples. This was partly fiscal, but also it was merely part of a highly complex administrative system, in which every individual was kept under definite control. In most of these cases, the essence of the system was a double count by different persons, one of which was not easily known to the individual concerned. Two interesting examples may be mentioned, where the sacred becomes an adjunct and useful tool to the administrator.

In order to tax the kill of the hunters, there were chiefs of the hunt in each village, every one of whom was known to hunting chiefs at the court (one for fishing and one for wild animals). It was through the village *degan* (hunting chief) that the count was to be made. The actual count was made near Abomey, at the shrine to a spirit of the hunt (Gbwetin). The king came as a warrior, fresh from his annual campaign, sword in hand and (probably symbolically) the head of a conquered king in hand.[28] He met the assembled degan, and ordered them to come back to Djegbe (near Abomey) with the hunters who were officially under their supervision. At that time, these hunters were lined up with the degan for the count. However, the counting process was not made obvious, as it rarely was in Dahomey. Instead, hunters' knives were given each hunter and degan as they filed by. This was followed by a dance and festival, in which the hunters and the king danced, pantomiming the warrior. This seems to have been in honor of Gu, the god of iron, since he (as well as the king) was praised. He is symbolically associated in the Dahomean mind with war and weapons. The dance ended with a drink from a common cup by everyone, the water being drunk from a human cranium.[29] Then the hunting knives were heaped, and reconsecrated by sacrificial blood from bullocks, goats, and chickens donated by the king.[30] The hunters were not present at night, after having celebrated with food and drink from the king, when the chief-priest of Gu reported to the king. This sacred dignitary then collected the knives, taking them to the forest sacred to Gu, *guzume*, located at Ahwagan. There the assistants of the priest counted them, the result being the number of hunters in the kingdom.

It was not only at this point that the same deity figured, however, in the administration of the count. As would be expected, some degan knew why the knives were given out and returned in the ceremonial. To prevent them from concealing the accurate number, the number of knives was known, though it may have seemed an indiscriminate heap to the participants. Therefore, the number of knives taken to the sacred forest had to equal the number originally taken to the festival. When the numbers did not tally exactly, the degan were again called. This time, they were told that the deity of the hunt was aware of the discrepancy. Whatever cynicism they may have had about the source of the information, deity or mortal, there was no doubting the efficacy of the technique for forcing the individual to confess: the verdict of the supernatural, the ordeal. Thus at both points, the administrator utilized the sacred tools as means to achieve entirely secular ends.

This same technique was used for determining the production figures of those smithies which did not make hoes.[31] These figures were obtained, again, through religious dignitaries, the priests of Gu, the deity most closely concerned with iron. The procedure was for the king to set a date for Gu to be given food—"to eat"—at each of Gu's shrines. This food would be cocks, which were placed at the shrines, at the disposal of the chief-priests. This announcement was coupled with the statement that the deity, Gu, would punish any priests who failed to participate in this "feeding" by not taking their share of the birds. "The Dahomeans being devout, the priests invariably obeyed, and since every forge must have its shrine to Gu, the deity especially sacred to forgers, all the shrines were represented."[32] As each official came to the center of fiscal control (where those from outlying areas would have to go), he was to inform the secular official of the number of smiths working at the forge he represented. The procedure then simply consisted in counting the number of fowls taken.

On the other hand, the king could not overlook the power potential of such a highly organized system of religious worship. One aspect of this has already been mentioned, the conflict between Sagbata and the king, antagonism being expressed by the royal family against this cult. It was felt that its very title was presumptuous, besides the fact that several kings died of smallpox. Since the political regime was highly autocratic, proper control would be needed over other elements in this organization.[33] All cult houses, established for the worship of the "public deities" already outlined, were kept under the king's control. The procedure was to require a particular rattle for the chief-priest of any cult house to be established. This rattle could be obtained only through the monarchy. That is, a secular barrier is offered to a free expansion of sacred organizations.[34] Herskovits maintains that "no notation was made within the palace at the time these rattles were distributed, nor any account taken of those to whom they were given," however surprising this may seem.

Nevertheless, at the time of the annual customs,[35] all priests of the ancestral cult had to come to a special ceremony on a certain day. They were to come with the rattles in question. The rattle had to be brought or sent, whether the priest happened to be ill or not. The other cults were not ignored in this process, for still other dates were set for them, when the principal ceremony took place. At that time, all the rattles were displayed. Their presence was consciously ritual and sacred, since this was the time for reconsecrating the rattles. It was necessary to have a rattle if one was to summon the deities. The control kept over the rattles was constituted by a record kept by the planter of the rattle calabashes. Each year he sent forty-one[36] calabashes of this type, and at the same time set aside a pebble for each one. When, at the end of the year, some were returned, it was known how many new rattles had been put in circulation, and, consequently, how many rattles in use there were in all the kingdom. One official counted those at the cult house, thus furnishing a close check on the actual number. A rattle might be replaced without authorization if broken, but two such rattles in the same cult house would weaken— "spoil"—the power of the deity.[37]

Though there seems to be no economic advantage to be derived from this information, a full knowledge of all details of the kingdom was held to be (as it certainly is) necessary for complete political control of the kingdom. Further, the king would then know what preparations to make for occasions of great significance, when the priests were to make sacrifices. More important, however, was the fact that through the cult the king reached more concretely and intimately into the lives of the people. For the chief-priest of each pantheon kept a tally of all the initiates entering a cult, a pebble being dropped, without looking at it or the receptacle, into a pouch, and one being taken away when a cult member died. The King could therefore find out from the chief-priest how many members there were in the cult. In this manner, rapid dissemination of knowledge about an edict could be achieved, while the power of the priests over the cultists could also be put to work. Herskovits expresses this situation concisely:

. . . since about half of all the inhabitants of the kingdom were numbered in the membership of the cult-groups, and the other half of the Dahomean people were related to cult-members and since, also, the religious convictions of these cult members and their relatives required implicit obedience to commands of the priests, control over the cult-houses by the king gave him a simple means of rapidly making known an edict to the people, and of assuring compliance with it.[38]

It is not from such uses of sacred techniques that the king's great political power stemmed, in the main.[39] The kingship was intimately associated with the rulers of the ancestral dead, the kingly dead. His person was actually sacred.[40] Abasement on the part of those who came before him was taken for granted. The royal family itself shared this characteristic.[41] This was accentuated by the enormous amount of ceremony which attended all his movements and those of his court, and by the extremely detailed fashion through which he kept abreast of all occurrences in the kingdom.

These apotheosized ancestors symbolically played a part in the king's very accession. The "grand customs," mentioned previously, which were the funeral ceremonies at the death of a monarch, had to be performed by the new incumbent before he would receive full title to his throne.[42] The actual ceremony of enstoolment is not, to my knowledge, extant in the literature. The ceremony took place in Allada, ". . . where all Dahomean kings had to go to be confirmed in their sovereignty,"[43] but of its wider significance, or relationship to the ghostly deities, I find no record.[44] The conclusion is inescapable that at such a time the incumbent was given to their care, and he was exhorted to follow them, while the subjects were told to obey.

Whatever the imposing qualities of such a kingly inauguration, the kings took much of their awe-inspiring status from their constant identification with their deified ancestors. This was true not only of their ordinary associations, but it was significantly true even of the stories and history of the kings as well. That is, their historical past was kept partially secret, and endowed with sacred implications. Le-Herissé claims,

L'histoire revet, en effet, pour le Dahoméen un saint caractère; elle n'est pas seulement le monument des gloires et des rêveurs d'une tribu fondatrîce d'un royaume, elle touche encore au merveilleux, parce qu'elle conserve la mémoire d'origines mystérieuses et qu'elle enregistre les acts des ancêtres, héros divinisés, protecteurs des "Danhomenou," "gens et chose du Danhome."

Les rois paraissent même avoir vu dans cette conception de l'histoire un moyen d'augmenter leur prestige. Ils s'étaient reservés certain secrets sur leur famille et leurs dieux. Ils ne les transmettaient qu'à l'heritier du royaume et les anciens eux-mêmes les ignoraient, dit-on. Ainsi ils acqueraient la force du mystérieux, la vénération de l'ignorant pour le savant, du simple pour le génie.[45]

Though Herskovits does not attempt to probe precisely this set of relationships on a deep level of analysis, he summarizes several points of interest in this regard:

Just as the King of Dahomey constituted a category apart in the social whole that comprised the population of the kingdom, so the worship of the spirits of the dead kings was a thing apart from the worship of any other category of ancestors. It has been seen how the general class of *tɔvodun* encompasses the *nɛsuxwe*, the souls of the princely dead. Over all these, in the world of the dead as in the world of the living, the souls of the dead rulers of Dahomey hold their exalted position. Their spiritual importance was reflected in the implicit acknowledgment of their active collaboration with their living descendant in the ruling of the kingdom. Thus their cult daily required a sacrifice as a matter of routine thank-offering for the King's awakening in health to the new day. When their advice was desired concerning any matter of policy, or when a remedy was sought for some unfavorable condition in the kingdom, or when a campaign was to be launched against an enemy, or when a crisis of any kind impended, sacrifices proportionate to the issue at stake were made at the tombs that marked their graves, and they were called upon to manifest their wisdom and will.[46]

This situation gave a great deal of emotional continuity to the reigning family. For in this manner the incumbent is not a single individual. The group came before the incumbent, and will make a place for him when he dies. He will receive advice and aid in crises from these deities. Just as they had power on earth, they now have it as supernaturals. They rule in each case, thus becoming "part of the structure of the universe," to the ordinary Dahomean, not to be questioned. The Dahomean came into a world where the king ruled. After death, he expected to go to a supernatural world where the king or his ancestors still ruled.

This was accentuated by the peculiar role which the prince or king played and plays in the rites for the royal ancestors. For the cult of the ancestral royal dead gives to the prince almost the status of an initiate in a cult. Like such cult members, he "may not be struck on the head, or across the cheek."[47] This would be akin to blasphemy. The rights of the initiate are his without the hardships of being initiated. He thus plays an important role in the royal ancestral ceremonies without actually being a cult member. For this cult ". . . approximates the worship of the gods in its following and ceremonialism.

A prince can and does dance for the princely dead, but he is not thought to be serving the spirit of a dead prince, but rather to be representing this designated ancestor at the annual customs. In Dahomean theory, this means that annually, for the duration of the ceremony, the soul of the dead prince will enter his body, and he will not be himself but the dead man brought back from the land of the dead."[48]

It was in such ceremonies that the position of the king, from whom all power came, received its highest expression. In the ceremony witnessed by Herskovits, which must not be considered a greatly attenuated version of the former annual ceremonies,[49] the position was even made geographically clear, since in the large court where the dancing took place an area was laid off (the division was noted by early observers) by forming a rectangular space, delineated by bare palm branches. It was within this space that Behanzin's son, Daha, and his wives were to remain during the ceremony. Priests, members of the royal family, the chief-priest of the ancestral cult, elders, collateral relatives, etc. remained on the other side, approaching the "bamboo" boundary to prostrate themselves and kiss the earth before Daha.[50] Communication from the chief-priest to the "king" occurred by means of an elder wife of Daha, who would face the chief-priest at the boundary line, then carry the message to the chief.[51] To maintain this symbolically, "on one occasion an especially old man took up one of the palm ribs and, holding it before him, came close to Daha and talked directly to him."[52] As usual, animals were sacrificed,[53] the animals being tied very tightly so that their struggles could not impede the flow and catching of the blood. This blood was poured over the *asen*, or altars. A symbolic ritual was then enacted, by which a curtain placed in front of the altars was lowered both during the pouring of the blood and the bringing of food. It has been noted before that the monarch did not allow others (except as a mark of favor, and except for the case mentioned, of the hunters) to see him eat or drink. The lowering of the curtain, while the officiant called out "Zan!" or "Zanku!" (Night!), symbolized this ceremony of the king's meals, when he would be alone, set off from the others. Interestingly, the meat of one goat killed is not eaten, for it is a sacrifice made with a chant asking that the ancestors prevent princes and nobles now ruling from ever being sent away as slaves to foreign countries.[54] Several orchestras, of drums, gongs, and smaller drums, of flutists and singers, chanters with wands, and singers with gongs, played in succession, followed by the women in the palm barrier, who sang in solos and choruses. This was accompanied by body movements, the rhythms quickening. The intent of the songs was to praise the chief and his ancestors, and to call him to dance for the ancestral spirits. This pattern is, of course, highly traditional, the king never being a fine dancer, but rather a symbolic figure. In the ceremony witnessed by Herskovits, Daha finally came forward to dance.[55]

The audience became more excited, and the singing louder, as he danced, one of his wives behind him, twirling his umbrella. He was called back after his first dancing, and again circled the space while dancing. After this, the space reserved for his entourage was narrowed, so that the male performers might have more room for dancing. Other groups outside were later summoned in succession to pay "tribute with singing and dancing to the spirit of the dead King. . . . The ritual itself was complete when the sacrifices had been made and the blood poured on the altars."[56] However, each group offered formulae of obeisance (and dance) during the afternoon. Though not actually part of the "annual customs," being commemorative of Behanzin's burial, it neatly expresses the general position of the king in the Dahomean society, while also helping to strengthen the kingly power. It also suggests the effectiveness of the "Great Customs" and the annual customs in supporting and reemphasizing the far-reaching power and exalted rank of the kingly incumbent, from whom the power of his subordinates flowed. However, it is clear that this is *not mere support:* The political activities also hold the religious somewhat in check.

Thus at many points of basic significance, the political superstructure had a strong foundation in the supernatural sanctions, both minor magic and the greater ceremonies. Several others may be briefly mentioned. One of these concerns the position of the chief-priest, whose position as ruler over the "servants" of a given deity was extremely powerful. It has already been related how some control was maintained over him by the king. More than this was obtained, however, though it occurred only once in the lifetime of such a priest. His position was hereditary, and thus was not easily attacked. Nevertheless, he could not take over his office unless the king confirmed his accession. This was merely an elementary precaution, and thus enabled the king to wield more power through the religious organization.

This type of control, the existence of which emphasizes the potential importance of the religious in crises, and the actual day-to-day significance of it as a possible political power, was further extended by the use of secular officials appointed by the king.[57] These officials were in at least nominal control over the priests and followers.[58] Furthermore, "religious offences committed by priests were judged by a court of priests presided over by the head-priest of *Zumadunu*, king of the royal tɔxɔsu,[59] in the presence of these officers, but offences against the state were judged exclusively by these officers, who were empowered to punish the culprits with beating, imprisonment, enslavement or death."[60]

Furthermore, though the priest was to hold his position until death, and could not be shown publicly as a degraded criminal, the king could remove him for inciting to rebellion.[61] Recognizing further the power of the religious in this world, the political system forbade the existence of secret societies in Dahomey.[62] These might have constituted an even greater threat.

Though the extension of the supernatural into court procedure has already been shown in several connections, an interesting interrelationship arises in the case of Fa, the system of Destiny, by which the will of the gods was to be known to human beings. The practitioners are thought of with great respect by most Dahomeans. It is true that those who have wielded power, the highest class members, are somewhat more sceptical, and condescending. Here, again, however, a supernatural system is used by those in power, understanding the locus of the sacred in this world, and its uses for personal or political ends. Indeed, Herskovits points out,

. . . in native "history" the *bokɔnɔn* (diviners), with their cult of Fa, are held to have been introduced into Dahomey as a means of attaining a more efficient control over society by the rulers, and to overcome the influence of those other divinatory systems which were less well organized and thus less easily controllable.[63]

Even today, all chiefs have a diviner for each of their destinies, and in former times the royal *bokɔnɔn* had great power. There were uses for such a diviner, aside from mere knowledge: Yet while the chiefs and princes and in earlier days the kings consistently consulted their diviners, the fact nevertheless remains that these same diviners in situations where it was politic to offer advice of a certain kind did not fail to pronounce as the will of Destiny what those in power desired to hear, or in mundane matters to read the lots in accordance with the best interests of their patrons.[64]

One more point, again with respect to fiscal policy, may be noted at which the regime was bolstered by the religious officiant. An adequate tax policy required information about the number of livestock, particularly cattle, goats, and sheep. The count of pigs was taken in another manner, but sometimes checked by this. On a great market day a crier made known to the people that a god living in a certain river had announced the coming of an epidemic and a poor harvest. The only way in which this misfortune could be averted would be for every man and woman to bring one caury shell for each head of livestock. These would be put in separate heaps, and the king, who was also part of the kingdom, would then add a great amount of palm oil, all this to be offered to the spirit. Since the predicted epidemic would probably not occur, the king thus received much emotional support for his leadership and economic contribution. Before these shells were taken to the priest of the river god, they were counted, a pebble being set aside for each shell, and placed in separate sacks with appropriate symbols sewn on them.[65]

In a society with such a high degree of formalized legal organization as Dahomey, the identity between secular legal officials and the religious officiants could not be expected to be close. Nevertheless, it has been seen that the hierarchy is bolstered at many important points by the religious system. This is true not only for the highest official, but also for such matters as the administration of justice and the taxation of the people. On the other hand, the potential power of various religious groups was consciously curbed. This recognized the necessity for keeping the political system secure, as well as the possible spread of temporal authority belonging to the priests.

IV. FAMILY AND SOCIAL STRUCTURE

9. *The Theoretical Importance of Love*

INTRODUCTION

GRAND THEORY HAS CONCERNED ITSELF WITH CLASS ORGANIZATION AND THUS WITH POWER, WEALTH, AND PRESTIGE. SINCE LOVE, FRIEND-ship, and affection seem by contrast not to be one of the major axes of the stratification system in any society, sociologists have implicitly agreed that this range of variables can safely be ignored.

On the other hand, folk wisdom has always recognized that this set of variables had great impact on everyone's *individual* fate: unre-quited love is as inescapably, immediately painful as a toothache; a loving wife warms the home; a friendship betrayed is a tragedy; a lucky friendship may guarantee success; and so on.

Sociology has not gone much beyond folk wisdom, in noting that this range of variables is important for individual careers and lives, but without being able to describe how it links *systematically* (as causes or as effects) with other elements in the social structure—if indeed our guess is correct that it does. However, from the fact that many sociologists have discussed this problem with me over several decades without publishing a monograph on it, I would deduce that the task is difficult.

This investigation utilizes the general sociological insight that though dichotomies are useful in preliminary thinking, they are almost invariably false, and examining in detail their falseness will disclose a different social pattern than what we had originally supposed. A good number of social analysts have viewed romantic love as a Western, if not American, aberration. In other societies past and present arranged marriages have been the norm. The dichotomy "love vs. nonlove" or "love vs. arranged marriages" is fruitful in a rough way, but it is also false: the variable is rather continuous, not dichotomous. Love is rather more or less institutionalized in various societies.

The analysis also begins, as did one of Sherlock Holmes's lines of reasoning, by wondering why there is an *absence* of something. That is, why, if we assume that love is a nearly universal psychological potentiality, does it seem to be rare? In sociological terms, we ask, under which kinds of social structures can either the appearance of strong love relationships, or their often deplored consequences, be frustrated or diverted?

As nonconformists have learned in every generation, social structures do not often facilitate individual happiness, but do encourage people (by rewards or punishments) to sacrifice for the larger social grouping, such as the family, lineage, or the society. Strong love ties, like deep friendships, are often a nuisance and sometimes a disaster for others outside that dyad. This study outlines some of those possible consequences for the family system and thus for the position of the family in the class system. Because of these possibilities, societies typically seek some kind of control over where love may strike. It is not a decision that is thought to be wisely left for the young to make independently.

The modes of control are many, but most fall into a small number of categories, described in this article. In some societies with a very great emphasis on family or caste line, marriages are arranged before the threat of love can arise. Others can forego this system by seeing to it that the young associate intimately only with eligible mates.

These linkages also help us to make other predictions. For example, in a society where family honor, line, and property are less important, and individual achievement is emphasized more, the controls over love are weak, so that love as a prelude and basis for marriage becomes typical. Modern industrial societies are a major example, but it seems likely that for many centuries the urban proletariat also enjoyed this privilege. After all, the proletariat had much less to lose if a *mesalliance* occurred.

We would also predict that even within societies where a considerable love freedom is encountered, those families, lines, and classes which evaluate highly their own continuity, property, and rank would apply more strictly the socially permissible techniques for controlling the occurrence or incidence of love.

Although that analysis explains why such social patterns occur, it does not express approval of those controls, and indeed my own rereading of my own implicit biases suggests the reverse: to the extent that my evaluations appear in the problem formulation, they rather show an approval of love. More important, to show how a social pattern is maintained does not *assume* order or regularity for example, but the opposite. For it rather suggests that any existing social structure is contingent, under some threat (in this case, from love); and some investment and organization is required to reduce that threat. We can as sociologists correctly *predict* order, but we must also expect to find that it is always supported by inputs of social action, for it is otherwise precarious.

Because love often determines the intensity of an attraction[1] toward or away from an intimate relationship with another person, it can become one element in a decision or action.[2] Nevertheless, serious sociological attention has only infrequently been given to love. Moreover, analyses of love generally have been confined to mate choice in the Western World, while the structural importance of love has been for the most part ignored. The present paper views love in a broad perspective, focusing on the structural patterns by which societies keep in check the potentially disruptive effect of love relationships on mate choice and stratification systems.

TYPES OF LITERATURE ON LOVE

For obvious reasons, the printed material on love is immense. For our present purposes, it may be classified as follows:

1. Poetic, humanistic, literary, erotic, pornographic: By far the largest body of all literature on love views it as a sweeping experience. The poet arouses our sympathy and empathy. The essayist enjoys, and asks the reader to enjoy, the interplay of people in love.

The storyteller—Bocaccio, Chaucer, Dante—pulls back the curtain of human souls and lets the reader watch the intimate lives of others caught in an emotion we all know. Others—Vatsyayana, Ovid, William IX Count of Poitiers and Duke of Aquitaine, Marie de France, Andreas Capellanus—have written how-to-do-it books, that is, how to conduct oneself in love relations, to persuade others to succumb to one's love wishes, or to excite and satisfy one's sex partner.[3]

2. Marital counseling: Many modern sociologists have commented on the importance of romantic love in America and its lesser importance in other societies, and have disparaged it as a poor basis for marriage, or as immaturity. Perhaps the best known of these arguments are those of Ernest R. Mowrer, Ernest W. Burgess, Mabel A. Elliott, Andrew G. Truxal, Francis E. Merrill, and Ernest R. Groves.[4] The antithesis of romantic love, in such analyses, is "conjugal" love; the love between a settled, domestic couple.

A few sociologists, remaining within this same evaluative context, have instead claimed that love also has salutary effects in our society. Thus, for example, William L. Kolb[5] has tried to demonstrate that the marital counselors who attack romantic love are really attacking some fundamental values of our larger society, such as individualism, freedom, and personality growth. Beigel[6] has argued that if the female is sexually repressed, only the psychotherapist or love can help her overcome her inhibitions. He claims further that one influence of love in our society is that it extenuates illicit sexual relations; he goes on to assert: "Seen in proper perspective, [love] has not only done no harm as a prerequisite to marriage, but it has mitigated the impact that a too-fast-moving and unorganized conversion to new socio-economic constellations has had upon our whole culture and it has saved monogamous marriage from complete disorganization."

In addition, there is widespread comment among marriage analysts, that in a rootless society, with few common bases for companionship, romantic love holds a couple together long enough to allow them to begin marriage. That is, it functions to attract people powerfully together, and to hold them through the difficult first months of the marriage, when their different backgrounds would otherwise make an adjustment troublesome.

3. Although the writers cited above concede the structural importance of love implicitly, since they are arguing that it is either harm-

ful or helpful to various values and goals of our society, a third group has given explicit if unsystematic attention to its structural importance. Here, most of the available propositions point to the functions of love, but a few deal with the conditions under which love relationships occur. They include:

1 An implicit or assumed descriptive proposition is that love as a common prelude to and basis of marriage is rare, perhaps to be found as a pattern only in the United States.

2 Most explanations of the conditions which create love are psychological, stemming from Freud's notion that love is "aim-inhibited sex."[7] This idea is expressed, for example, by Waller who says that love is an idealized passion which develops from the frustration of sex.[8] This proposition, although rather crudely stated and incorrect as a general explanation, is widely accepted.

3 Of course, a predisposition to love is created by the socialization experience. Thus some textbooks on the family devote extended discussion to the ways in which our society socializes for love. The child, for example, is told that he or she will grow up to fall in love with some one, and early attempts are made to pair the child with children of the opposite sex. There is much joshing of children about falling in love; myths and stories about love and courtship are heard by children; and so on.

4 A further proposition (the source of which I have not been able to locate) is that, in a society in which a very close attachment between parent and child prevails, a love complex is necessary in order to motivate the child to free him from his attachment to his parents.

5 Love is also described as one final or crystallizing element in the decision to marry, which is otherwise structured by factors such as class, ethnic origin, religion, education, and residence.

6 Parsons has suggested three factors which "underlie the prominence of the romantic context in our culture": (a) the youth culture frees the individual from family attachments, thus permitting him to fall in love; (b) love is a substitute for the interlocking of kinship roles found in other societies, and thus motivates the individual to conform to proper marital role behavior; and (c) the structural isolation of the family so frees the married partners' affective inclinations that they are able to love one another.[9]

7 Robert F. Winch has developed a theory of "complementary needs" which essentially states that the underlying dynamic in the process of falling in love is an interaction between (a) the perceived psychological attributes of one individual and (b) the complementary psychological attributes of the person falling in love, such that the needs of the latter are felt to be met by the perceived attributes of the former and

vice versa. These needs are derived from Murray's list of personality characteristics. Winch thus does not attempt to solve the problem of why our society has a love complex, but how it is that specific individuals fall in love with each other rather than with someone else.[10]

8 Winch and others have also analyzed the effect of love upon various institutions or social patterns: Love themes are prominently displayed in the media of entertainment and communication, in consumption patterns, and so on.[11]

4. Finally, there is the cross-cultural work of anthropologists, who in the main have ignored love as a factor of importance in kinship patterns. The implicit understanding seems to be that love as a pattern is found only in the United States, although of course individual cases of love are sometimes recorded. The term "love" is practically never found in indexes of anthropological monographs on specific societies or in general anthropology textbooks. It is perhaps not an exaggeration to say that Lowie's comment of a generation ago would still be accepted by a substantial number of anthropologists:

But of love among savages? . . . Passion, of course, is taken for granted; affection, which many travelers vouch for, might be conceded; but Love? Well, the romantic sentiment occurs in simpler conditions, as with us—in fiction. . . . So Love exists for the savage as it does for ourselves—in adolescence, in fiction, among the poetically minded.[12]

A still more skeptical opinion is Linton's scathing sneer:

All societies recognize that there are occasional violent, emotional attachments between persons of opposite sex, but our present American culture is practically the only one which has attempted to capitalize these, and make them the basis for marriage. . . . The hero of the modern American movie is always a romantic lover, just as the hero of the old Arab epic is always an epileptic. A cynic may suspect that in any ordinary population the percentage of individuals with a capacity for romantic love of the Hollywood type was about as large as that of persons able to throw genuine epileptic fits.[13]

In Murdock's book on kinship and marriage, there is almost no mention, if any, of love.[14] Should we therefore conclude that, cross-culturally, love is not important, and thus cannot be of great importance structurally? If there is only one significant case, perhaps it is safe to view love as generally unimportant in social structure and to concentrate rather on the nature and functions of romantic love within the Western societies in which love is obviously prevalent. As brought out below, however, many anthropologists have in fact described love *patterns*. And one of them, Max Gluckman,[15] has recently subsumed a wide range of observations under the broad principle that love relationships between husband and wife estrange the couple from their kin, who therefore try in various ways to undermine that love. This principle is applicable to many more societies (for example, China and India) than Gluckman himself discusses.

THE PROBLEM AND ITS CONCEPTUAL CLARIFICATION

The preceding propositions (except those denying that love is distributed widely) can be grouped under two main questions: What are the consequences of romantic love in the United States? How is the emotion of love aroused or created in our society? The present paper deals with the first question. For theoretical purposes both questions must be reformulated, however, since they implicitly refer only to our peculiar system of romantic love. Thus: (1) In what ways do various love patterns fit into the social structure, especially into the systems of mate choice and stratification? (2) What are the structural conditions under which a range of love patterns occurs in various societies? These are overlapping questions, but their starting point and assumptions are different. The first assumes that love relationships are a universal psychosocial possibility, and that different social systems make different adjustments to their potential disruptiveness. The second does not take love for granted, and supposes rather that such relationships will be rare unless certain structural factors are present. Since in both cases the analysis need not depend upon the correctness of the assumption, the problem may be chosen arbitrarily. Let us begin with the first.[16]

We face at once the problem of defining "love." Here, love is defined as a strong emotional attachment, a cathexis, between adolescents or adults, usually of opposite sexes, with at least the components of sex desire and tenderness. Verbal definitions of this emotional relationship are notoriously open to attack; this one is no more likely to satisfy critics than others. Agreement is made difficult by value judgments: one critic would exclude anything but "true" love, another casts out "infatuation," another objects to "puppy love," while others would separate sex desire from love because presumably sex is degrading. Nevertheless, most of us have had the experience of love, just as we have been greedy, or melancholy, or moved by hate (defining "true" hate seems not to be a problem). The experience can be referred to without great ambiguity, and a refined measure of various degrees of intensity or purity of love is unnecessary for the aims of the present analysis.

Since love may be related in diverse ways to the social structure, it is necessary to forego the dichotomy of "romantic love—no romantic love" in favor of a continuum or range between polar types. At one pole, a strong love attraction is socially viewed as a laughable or tragic aberration; at the other, it is mildly shameful to marry without being in love with one's intended spouse. This is a gradation from negative sanction to positive approval, ranging at the same time from low or almost nonexistent institutionalization of love to high institutionalization.

The urban middle classes of contemporary Western society, especially in the United States, are found toward the latter pole. Japan and China, in spite of the important movement toward European patterns, fall toward the pole of low institutionalization. Village and urban India is farther toward the center, for there the ideal relationship has been one which at least generated love after marriage, and sometimes after betrothal, in contrast with the mere respect owed between Japanese and Chinese spouses.[17] Greece after Alexander, Rome of the Empire, and perhaps the later period of the Roman Republic as well, are near the center, but somewhat toward the pole of institutionalization, for love matches appear to have increased in frequency—a trend denounced by moralists.[18]

This conceptual continuum helps to clarify our problem and to interpret the propositions reviewed above. Thus it may be noted, first, that individual love relationships may occur even in societies in which love is viewed as irrelevant to mate choice and excluded from the decision to marry. As Linton conceded, some violent love attachments may be found in any society. In our own, the Song of Solomon, Jacob's love of Rachel, and Michal's love for David are classic tales. The Mahabharata, the great Indian epic, includes love themes. Romantic love appears early in Japanese literature, and the use of Mt. Fuji as a locale for the suicide of star-crossed lovers is not a myth invented by editors of tabloids. There is the familiar tragic Chinese story to be found on the traditional "willowplate," with its lovers transformed into doves. And so it goes—individual love relationships seem to occur everywhere. But this fact does not change the position of a society on the continuum.

Second, reading both Linton's and Lowie's comments in this new conceptual context reduces their theoretical importance, for they are both merely saying that people do not *live by* the romantic complex, here or anywhere else. Some few couples in love will brave social pressures, physical dangers, or the gods themselves, but nowhere is this usual. Violent, self-sufficient love is not common anywhere. In this respect, of course, the U.S. is not set apart from other systems.

Third, we can separate a *love pattern* from the romantic love *complex*. Under the former, love is a permissible, expected prelude to marriage, and a usual element of courtship—thus, at about the center of the continuum, but toward the pole of institutionalization. The romantic love complex (one pole of the continuum) includes, in addition, an ideological prescription that falling in love is a highly desirable basis of courtship and marriage; love is strongly institutionalized.[19] In contemporary United States, many individuals would even claim that entering marriage without being in love requires some such rationalization as asserting that one is too old for such romances or that one must "think of practical matters like money." To be sure, both anthropologists and sociologists often exaggerate the American commitment to romance;[20] nevertheless, a behavioral and value complex of this type is found here.

But this complex is rare. Perhaps only the following cultures possess the romantic love value complex: modern urban Anglo countries (U.S., Canada, etc.), Northwestern Europe and increasingly the rest of Europe, Polynesia, and the European nobility of the eleventh and twelfth centuries.[21] Certainly, it is to be found in no other major civilization. On the other hand, the *love pattern*, which views love as a basis for the final decision to marry, may be relatively common.

WHY LOVE MUST BE CONTROLLED

Since strong love attachments apparently can occur in any society and since (as we shall show) love is frequently a basis for and prelude to marriage, it must be controlled or channeled in some way. More specifically, the stratification and lineage patterns would be weakened greatly if love's potentially disruptive effects were not kept in check. The importance of this situation may be seen most clearly by considering one of the major functions of the family, status placement, which in every society links the structures of stratification, kinship lines, and mate choice. (To show how the very similar comments which have been made about sex are not quite correct would take us too far afield; in any event, to the extent that they are correct, the succeeding analysis applies equally to the control of sexual behavior.)

Both the child's placement in the social structure and choice of mates are socially important because both placement and choice link two kinship lines together. Courtship or mate choice, therefore, cannot be ignored by either family or society. To permit random mating would mean a radical change in the existing social structure. If the family as a unit of society is important, then mate choice is too.

Kinfolk or immediate family can disregard the question of who marries whom, only if a marriage is not seen as a link between kin lines, only if property, power, lineage honor, totemic relationships, and the like do not flow through the kin lines from the spouses to their offspring. Universally, however, these are believed to follow kin lines. Mate choice thus has consequences for the social structure. But love may affect mate choice. Both mate choice and love, therefore, are too important to be left to children.

THE CONTROL OF LOVE

Since considerable energy and resources may be required to push youngsters who are in love into proper role behavior, love must be controlled *before* it appears. Love relationships must either be kept to a small number or they must be so directed that they do not run counter to the approved kinship linkages. There are only a few institutional patterns by which this control is achieved.

1. Certainly the simplest, and perhaps the most widely used, structural pattern for coping with this problem is child marriage. If the child is betrothed, married, or both before he or she has had any opportunity to interact intimately as an adolescent with other children, then

she or he has no resources with which to oppose the marriage. Neither can earn a living, both are physically weak, and both are socially dominated by their elders. Moreover, strong love attachments occur only rarely before puberty. An example of this pattern was to be found in India, where the young bride went to live with her husband in a marriage which was not physically consummated until much later, within his father's household.[22]

2. Often, child marriage is linked with a second structural pattern, in which the kinship rules define rather closely a class of eligible future spouses. The marriage is determined by birth within narrow limits. Here, the major decision, which is made by elders, is *when* the marriage is to occur. Thus, among the Murngin, *galle*, the father's sister's child, is scheduled to marry *due*, the mother's brother's child.[23] In the case of the "four-class" double-descent system, each individual is a member of *both* a matri-moiety and a patri-moiety and must marry someone who belongs to neither; the four-classes are (1) ego's own class, (2) those whose matri-moiety is the same as ego's but whose patri-moiety is different, (3) those who are in ego's patri-moiety but not in his matri-moiety, and (4) those who are in neither of ego's moieties, that is, who are in the cell diagonally from his own.[24] Problems arise at times under these systems if the appropriate kinship cell—for example, parallel cousin or cross-cousin—is empty.[25] But nowhere, apparently, is the definition so rigid as to exclude some choice and, therefore, some dickering, wrangling, and haggling between the elders of the two families.

3. A society can prevent widespread development of adolescent love relationships by socially isolating young people from potential mates, whether eligible or ineligible as spouses. Under such a pattern, elders can arrange the marriages of either children or adolescents with little likelihood that their plans will be disrupted by love attachments. Obviously, this arrangement cannot operate effectively in most primitive societies, where youngsters see one another rather frequently.[26]

Not only is this pattern more common in civilization than in primitive societies, but is found more frequently in the upper social strata. *Social* segregation is difficult unless it is supported by physical segregation—the harem of Islam, the zenana of India[27]—or by a large household system with individuals whose duty it is to supervise nubile girls. Social segregation is thus expensive. Perhaps the best known example of simple social segregation was found in China, where youthful marriages took place between young people who had not previously met because they lived in different villages; they could not marry fellow-villagers since ideally almost all inhabitants belonged to the same *tsu*.[28]

It should be emphasized that the primary function of physical or social isolation in these cases is to minimize informal or intimate social interaction. Limited social contacts of a highly ritualized or formal type in the presence of elders, as in Japan, have a similar, if less extreme, result.[29]

4. A fourth type of pattern seems to exist, although it is not clear cut; and specific cases shade off toward types three and five. Here, there is close supervision by duennas or close relatives, but not actual social segregation. A high value is placed on female chastity (which perhaps is the case in every major civilization until its "decadence") viewed either as the product of self-restraint, as among the 17th Century Puritans, or as a marketable commodity. Thus love as play is not developed; marriage is supposed to be considered by the young as a duty and a possible family alliance. This pattern falls between types three and five because love is permitted before marriage, but only between eligibles. Ideally, it occurs only between a betrothed couple, and, except as marital love, there is no encouragement for it to appear at all. Family elders largely make the specific choice of mate, whether or not intermediaries carry out the arrangements. In the preliminary stages youngsters engage in courtship under supervision, with the understanding that this will permit the development of affection prior to marriage.

I do not believe that the empirical data show where this pattern is prevalent, outside of Western Civilization. The West is a special case, because of its peculiar relationship to Christianity, in which from its earliest days in Rome there has been a complex tension between asceticism and love. This type of limited love marked French, English, and Italian upper class family life from the 11th to the 14th Centuries, as well as 17th Century Puritanism in England and New England.[30]

5. The fifth type of pattern permits or actually encourages love relationships, and love is a commonly expected element in mate choice.

Choice in this system is *formally* free. In their 'teens youngsters begin their love play, with or without consummating sexual intercourse, within a group of peers. They may at times choose love partners whom they and others do not consider suitable spouses. Gradually, however, their range of choice is narrowed and eventually their affections center on one individual. This person is likely to be more eligible as a mate according to general social norms, and as judged by peers and parents, than the average individual with whom the youngster formerly indulged in love play.

For reasons that are not yet clear, this pattern is nearly always associated with a strong development of an adolescent peer group system, although the latter may occur without the love pattern. One source of social control, then, is the individual's own 'teen age companions, who persistently rate the present and probable future accomplishments of each individual.[31]

Another source of control lies with the parents of both boy and girl. In our society, parents threaten, cajole, wheedle, bribe, and persuade their children to "go with the right people," during both the early love play and later courtship phases.[32] Primarily, they seek to control love relationships by influencing the informal social contacts of their children: moving to appropriate neighborhoods and schools, giving parties and helping to make out invitation lists, by making their children aware that certain individuals have ineligibility traits (race, religion, manners, tastes, clothing, and so on). Since youngsters fall in love with those with whom they associate, control over informal relationships also controls substantially the focus of affection. The results of such control are well known and are documented in the more than one hundred studies of homogamy in this country: most marriages take place between couples in the same class, religious, racial, and educational levels.

As Robert Wikman has shown in a generally unfamiliar (in the United States) but superb investigation, this pattern was found among 18th Century Swedish farmer adolescents, was widely distributed in other Germanic areas, and extends in time from the 19th Century back to almost certainly the late Middle Ages.[33] In these cases, sexual intercourse was taken for granted, social contact was closely supervised by the peer group, and final consent to marriage was withheld or granted by the parents who owned the land.

Such cases are not confined to Western society. Polynesia exhibits a similar pattern, with some variation from society to society, the best known examples of which are perhaps Mead's Manu'ans and Firth's Tikopia.[34] Probably the most familiar Melanesian cases are the Trobriands and Dobu,[35] where the systems resemble those of the Kiwai Papuans of the Trans-Fly and the Siuai Papuans of the Solomon Islands.[36] Linton found this pattern among the Tanala.[37] Although Radcliffe-Brown holds that the pattern is not common in Africa, it is clearly found among the Nuer, the Kgatla (Tswana-speaking), and the Bavenda (here, without sanctioned sexual intercourse).[38]

A more complete classification, making use of the distinctions suggested in this paper, would show, I believe, that a large minority of known societies exhibit this pattern. I would suggest, moreover, that such a study would reveal that the degree to which love is a usual, expected prelude to marriage is correlated with (1) the degree of free choice of mate permitted in the society and (2) the degree to which husband-wife solidarity is the strategic solidarity of the kinship structure.[39]

LOVE CONTROL AND CLASS

These sociostructural explanations of how love is controlled lead to a subsidiary but important hypothesis: From one society to another, and from one *class* to another within the same society, the sociostructural importance of maintaining kinship lines according to rule will be rated differently by the families within them. Consequently, the degree to which control over mate choice, and therefore over the prevalence of a love pattern among adolescents, will also vary. Since, within any stratified society, this concern with the maintenance of intact and acceptable kin lines will be greater in the upper strata, it follows that noble or upper strata will maintain stricter control over love and courtship behavior than lower strata. The two correlations suggested in the preceding paragraph also apply: husband-wife solidarity is less strategic relative to clan solidarity in the upper than in the lower strata, and there is less free choice of mate.

Thus it is that, although in Polynesia generally most youngsters indulged in considerable love play, princesses were supervised strictly.[40] Similarly, in China lower class youngsters often met their spouses before marriage.[41] In our own society, the "upper-upper" class maintains much greater control than the lower strata over the informal social contacts of their nubile young. Even among the Dobu, where there are few controls and little stratification, differences in control exist at the extremes: a child betrothal may be arranged between outstanding gardening families, who try to prevent their youngsters from being entangled with wastrel families.[42] In answer to my query about this pattern among the Nuer, Evans-Pritchard writes:

You are probably right that a wealthy man has more control over his son's affairs than a poor man. A man with several wives has a more authoritarian position in his home. Also, a man with many cattle is in a position to permit or refuse a son to marry, whereas a lad whose father is poor may have to depend on the support of kinsmen. In general, I would say that a Nuer father is not interested in the personal side of things. His son is free to marry any girl he likes and the father does not consider the selection to be his affair until the point is reached when cattle have to be discussed.[43]

The upper strata have much more at stake in the maintenance of the social structure and thus are more strongly motivated to control the courtship and marriage decisions of their young. Correspondingly, their young have much more to lose than lower strata youth, so that upper strata elders *can* wield more power.

CONCLUSION

In this analysis I have attempted to show the integration of love with various types of social structures. As against considerable contemporary opinion among both sociologists and anthropologists, I suggest that love is a universal psychological potential, which is controlled by a range of five structural patterns, all of which are attempts to see to it that youngsters do not make entirely free choices of their future spouses. Only if kin lines are unimportant, and this condition is found in no society as a whole, will entirely free choice be permitted. Some structural arrangements seek to prevent entirely the outbreak of love, while others harness it. Since the kin lines of the upper strata are of greater social importance to them than those of lower strata are to the lower strata members, the former exercise a more effective control over this choice. Even where there is almost a formally free choice of mate—and I have suggested that this pattern is widespread, to be found among a substantial segment of the earth's societies—this choice is guided by peer group and parents toward a mate who will be acceptable to the kin and friend groupings. The theoretical importance of love is thus to be seen in the sociostructural patterns which are developed to keep it from disrupting existing social arrangements.

10. *Illegitimacy, Anomie, and Cultural Penetration*

INTRODUCTION

THE FOLLOWING REPORT BUILDS ON A PREVIOUS ANALYSIS, "ILLEGITIMACY IN THE CARIBBEAN SOCIAL STRUCTURE," BY EXAMINING THE linkages between illegitimacy rates and variations in social structures. The earlier article began with the apparent contradiction between Malinowski's Principle of Legitimacy (that is, the norm that all children should have a social "father") and (1) the high rates of illegitimacy in the Caribbean and (2) the widespread reports that Caribbean society does not usually make any distinction between children born in and out of wedlock. Needless to say, variants of this comment have been frequently made in the past, concerning the black population of the United States.

By contrasting such *general* assertions with the details of field observations, it became evident that the Malinowski principle holds even there, since numerous behavioral indexes of normative approval of "legitimacy" are reported.

However, the theoretical puzzle remains: if people do accept the norm of legitimacy, why are the illegitimacy rates so high? The earlier analysis focused on the micro-structures of the courtship situation, and especially on the extent to which the young lower-class woman gets little support from a family network in her social interaction with men. Unless her bargaining position is strong (for example, she has property, is very attractive, and so on), she will have no opportunity of marrying (as most do eventually) without first entering one or more types of liaisons with men whose primary aim is not marriage, and who indeed feel their social and financial position forbids it.

It is not necessary to continue that analysis, in order to see that a very different *level* of problem is also visible: Are such microstructures observable in *other* regions of high illegitimacy rates, and if so, why are they prevalent? Or: can we find any general structural similarities among the regions of high illegitimacy rates?

Here again, crucial descriptive data help to organize the inquiry, for similar rates may be generated by very different social structures. Indeed, one of the three main regions of high illegitimacy rates underscore our hypothesis about the Caribbean pattern. In the Northwestern European region, rates are relatively high even though courtship took place under community and family controls, and within a restricted pool of propertied eligibles, but the father did marry the mothers of their children. An illegitimate child created no local scandal, because it was correctly taken for granted that the marriage would take place eventually.

In contrast to that integration of local moral norm and social behavior is the widespread social disorganization in the lower-class Indian and black populations of the New World and industrializing sub-Saharan Africa. Both the cultural and social structures that support the norm of legitimacy have been weakened by a major conquest period. The native patterns were undermined in many ways, most strongly of course in the New World, and the subordinate peoples were not encouraged to assimilate the dominant Western social and cultural systems.

The implicit theoretical assumption underlying that inquiry is that in "normal" societies the illegitimacy rates will be fairly low, because people are socialized to believe in the norm of legitimacy, and social controls will keep most people in line who are tempted to deviate. We could also predict that in lower social strata both the normative commitment and the social controls are lower than in higher social strata where there is more concern about maintaining the rank of a family line.

However, that line of theory permits us to make several additional tests of this explanation of high illegitimacy rates in this vast region. (1) If the hypothesis of cultural and social destruction is correct for the New World, we should find that among the populations that suffered the greatest destruction, that is the black slaves, the rates should be higher than among the Indians; correspondingly, the rates should in general be higher where there are higher percentages of blacks. (2) Since the destruction preceded by phases, the rates should have followed. At some point in the past, the Indian rates in the cities should have been higher than in rural regions. (3) Since the undermining of black culture and social patterns was so complete, and did not differ as between town and country, the rural-urban differences should not be great.

But we also know that all these peoples have been undergoing a process of assimilation, comparable to that of White U.S. immigrants. After all, the Indians of the New World are now predominantly European in culture, and the blacks are no longer African. This permits us to reason further in a test of the broad hypothesis. Specifically, *to the degree* that the dominant (Anglos, Iberians, and so on) encouraged assimilation, permitted and rewarded the cultural and social *re*integration of these conquered people into the dominant system, we should observe lower rates. Thus we can make these further predictions as tests: (4) since the first encouragement and facilitation of Indian assimilation and reintegration would occur in the cities, after the initial phases of the destruction, the illegitimacy rates should gradually have dropped below the rural ones, or should eventually drop below them. (5) Where the process of reintegration has not gone far, the rural-urban differences should be less, but the general rates should be high.

Furthermore (6) some Latin American countries have gradually included more of their populations in the national cultural and social systems, with respect to a wide range of civic and economic opportunities and privileges. Those with the higher degree of national integration should exhibit lower illegitimacy rates. Finally (7) some peoples exist who now maintain real communities, either because they were spared the widespread destruction of the past, or because they have managed to reassert in isolation some new community controls. In such subsocieties (usually in mountain regions) the *official* rates may be high, because bureaucrats will follow legal definitions, but the social rates will be low, since almost everyone goes through a so-cially prescribed marriage ceremony before starting connubial life.

So elaborate a set of predictions requires a considerable accumula-tion of indexes (for instance, social and cultural integration at the community and national level) as well as of different statistical breakdowns of illegitimacy rates. A theoretical justification is also required for focusing on illegitimacy, which is more usually viewed simply as a "social problem." Perhaps a different focus, centering on some other type of deviation, might also bring these great structural relationships to light. In any event, this focus does permit us to con-sider the problem of why most conquerors fail eventually to assimi-late the cultural and social systems of the societies and nations they take over militarily.

Our present focus also requires that some theoretical attention be given to the complex relations between social and cultural integra-tion. And even from so broad a perspective it is possible to develop policy suggestions for lowering illegitimacy rates.* It is obvious that if the data support our larger hypotheses, the relatively higher rate of illegitimacy among U.S. blacks can be reduced by offering them the same rewards as those given to members of the dominant white system and thereby facilitating their cultural and social integration into the larger society. Consonant with hypothesis No. 7, the rates would also be diminished if a black subsociety with high integra-tion were created. Although on a large scale that is not likely, I do believe that one social-cultural effect of the Black Muslim and other black separatist movements has been to develop genuine and strong community ties among subgroups of blacks, and one consequence of that integration has been a lower illegitimacy rate than is to be found among the Black population as a whole.

Since the family is a prime instrumental agency through which the needs of various institutional needs are met, and legiti-macy is the keystone of the family system, an examination of family systems with high illegitimacy rates should yield useful data on the

* For an extended set of such suggestions, see my paper, "A Policy Paper for Illegitimacy," in Mayer N. Zald, ed., *Organizing for Community Welfare*, Chi-cago: Quadrangle Books, 1967, pp. 262-312.

integration of societies. Analysis of high illegitimacy rates indeed suggests that some modifications may be profitably made in several segments of sociological theory: (1) the cultural and social conditions under which high illegitimacy rates occur; (2) the classical theory of the assimilation of both native rural and foreign-born immigrants in the United States; (3) effective procedures for destroying cultural and social systems; and (4) the relation between social and cultural integration.

Illegitimacy rates are, or have been, relatively high in three major areas: Northwestern Europe, industrializing sub-Saharan Africa, and the New World, from Tierra del Fuego to the non-white Southern population of the U.S. To consider these in turn, let us note that Iceland and particular regions in Sweden, Germany, and Austria have had rates of about twenty to thirty per cent in recent years.[1] In special studies of native urbanizing areas in sub-Saharan Africa, rates of forty per cent or more have been reported.[2] In the New World, particular provinces may have rates over eighty per cent, a handful of mainland countries have rates over seventy per cent, and a majority of all the political units have rates over thirty per cent. The non-white populations of the Southern states in the United States had rates of twenty to thirty per cent in 1957.[3]

Why did the New World rates become so high? They cannot be "survivals of native customs," since neither the native Indian groups nor the New World immigrants, whether White or African, had especially high rates of illegitimacy.[4] Moreover, they had many *different* family patterns—patriliny and matriliny, low and high divorce rates, polygyny and monogamy—but the rates are *generally* high.

Another common explanation is that the consensual union, out of which such high rates grow, is part of the "development of a new sub-culture." That is, the union without benefit of wedlock is the "native," normatively supported equivalent of a legalized union. Consequently, Malinowski's Principle of Legitimacy, according to which every society has a rule condemning illegitimacy, is to be discarded. This explanation is not satisfactory, either. For at least the Caribbean, where this explanation has been widespread, it has been shown that both mother and child have a lower status outside the legal union, that women prefer to be married, and there is general agreement that the ideal family relationship is that of marriage. More-over, a majority eventually do marry in the Caribbean. The Prin-ciple of Legitimacy is, then, roughly correct. But we did correct Malinowski's Principle in certain respects and described the bargain-ing process of consensual courtship outside parental or peer group controls, by which the young girl, unprotected by a kin network, must risk an unstable union and childbirth in order to have a chance at eventually entering a legal union.[5]

That analysis seems to be generally applicable, with only minor and obvious modifications, to the New World south of the Mason-Dixon Line: the consensual union is not the normative equivalent of marriage. Let us now consider the larger structural conditions under which such rates *develop*, to complement our previous analysis of the processes of individual social interaction which *maintain* these rates. From such a view, Northwestern Europe, urbanizing sub-Saharan Africa, and the New World exhibit very different patterns.

NORTHWESTERN EUROPE: A RURAL SUB-CULTURE

The relatively high rates in Northwestern Europe were the product of a courtship system which permitted considerable sex freedom to the young, under indirect but effective adult and peer group super-vision. The choice of sex partners and of eventual spouse was re-stricted to a pool of eligibles, who were children of farmers. When premarital conception or even birth occurred, the young man was likely to be known as the girl's partner, and both were likely to be acceptable to both sets of parents.[6] Illegitimacy was likely to occur mainly when there was some reason for delaying marriage (e.g., un-availability of farm or housing), rather than because either partner or set of parents had rejected the marriage.[7] Childbirth outside of marriage was not approved. Rather, the exact *timing* of the marriage, whether before or slightly after the birth of the first child, was not a focus of intense moral concern.

This pattern was a "native," rural custom, upheld within an inte-grated social and cultural system of norms which was *not* integrated with those of the dominant national society. Both the national state and Church opposed this pattern for centuries. It is not, then, a re-cent development, an index of "disorganization" in an urbanizing epoch. It is a subcultural difference, which has gradually been disappearing as isolated rural cultural and social systems have become more closely integrated with national cultural and social systems.

CLASSICAL ASSIMILATION THEORY

Studies of United States rural-urban migrants and of immigrant populations in the period 1910–1935 outlined a theory of assimilation and a theory of cultural destruction which fit both these cases of migration but which must be modified to fit the other two great cases of culture contact being analyzed in this paper, Africa and the New World south of the Mason-Dixon Line.

These migrants entered as *individuals* and families, so that their initial social systems were undermined. Thus, their cultural patterns could not be maintained by those social systems and were dissolved by an open-class, individualistic, secular culture which gave substantial rewards to those who assimilated. The in-migrating populations were culturally absorbed by the dominant, numerically larger group. In the transitional period, they also become somewhat anomic: they lost their allegiance to their native cultural patterns but for a while felt no great commitment to the norms of the dominant group. To some extent, in various cities[8] they developed new social subsystems and kept some of their cultural integration by living in ghettos, from which individuals moved out as they became acculturated into the larger society. Younger and older generations were in conflict, since each was oriented to different cultures. Some people lived as "marginal men," being accepted by and accepting neither culture and neither social system fully.

These in-migrants typically entered society in the United States at the bottom of the class structure, where they were somewhat freed from both the older social controls and the controls of the new country. Some customs were difficult to obey under urban conditions and lost their force. Younger people could use either set of norms as a justification for any desired course of action. Generally, the native-born generation became acculturated, and the grandchild generation was *both* socially and culturally integrated in the larger society.

The cultural and social systems of the in-migrating peoples were undermined by these factors: (1) the dispersion of the immigrating social systems, (2) the political power and prestige standards of the receiving populations, which judged the migrants as belonging at the bottom of the class system, (3) the economic and social opportunities in the new system, which gave rewards to those who became acculturated and punished those who refused to do so, (4) the sheer numerical superiority of the receiving populations, and (5) the irrelevance of older customs to the new social situation.

Transitional populations exhibited, of course, relatively high rates of deviation in such areas as juvenile delinquency, adult criminality, desertion, illegitimacy, and so on. Unfortunately, the studies of that time did not make independent measures of "anomie," or "social disorganization," and correlate them with the usual rates of deviation in various areas of action. However, their findings do add corroboration to the modifications of Malinowski's Principle, offered in the paper on the Caribbean: (1) its foundation is not primarily the protection which the male gives the child, but the social importance which a kin or family line enjoys; i.e., it focuses on status placement, and (2) the strength of the norm commitment will vary with the importance of the kin line and thus will be higher toward the upper strata where the proportion of important kin lines is greater and where as a consequence illegitimacy rates will be lower.[9]

AFRICAN ILLEGITIMACY: BREAKDOWN OF THE CULTURAL AND SOCIAL SYSTEMS

Classical assimilation theory was, then, an outline of the processes by which a given "native" system moves from (a) being internally integrated both socially and culturally to (b) being internally non-integrated or anomic *both* socially and culturally and then (c) eventually absorbed. *Individuals* moved from state (a), their original situation in their native region, to (b), losing their position in their native social system, but gaining one in the new United States social system and, for a considerable time, being part of the older cultural system but not part of the new one. Ultimately, of course, they became integrated in the new social and cultural system. That set of phases must be modified somewhat to fit urbanizing or industrializing sub-Saharan Africa and still more to fit the New World. On the other hand, both the suggested modification of Malinowski's Prin-

ciple and the anonymous "bargaining" pattern of Caribbean courtship may be applied to the African situation.

The African anomie is like the older United States rural and foreign immigration in these respects: (a) African individuals have
been greatly dispersed in the urban locations, (b) native customs are
often irrelevant and inconvenient in urbanizing areas, and (c) white
standards and customs have higher prestige. It differs chiefly in these
respects: (a) the original dominance of the white group was achieved
by force, (b) those being assimilated outnumber the dominant group,
(c) the African cultures were much more different from that of the
dominant group than were the cultures of the United States in-
migrants from that of the United States, and (d) because the Afri-
cans face caste barriers, they often cannot obtain substantial rewards
for accepting European ways.

Important political consequences flow from these differences—for
example, the inevitable creation of independent African nations
throughout the continent—but here we shall confine ourselves to the
matter of illegitimacy.

The natives in the African urban or industrialized locations have
come from tribes in which elders were once powerful, marriages were
arranged, and illegitimacy was rare. The skills and knowledge of the
elders are not greatly respected in the urban areas, because they are
no longer effective. Social control is therefore likely to be reduced to
the formal controls of the outside, white society. Although there is
some tendency for people from the same tribe to cluster together, as
happened in urban ghettos in the United States, such groupings
achieve less social control over the individual than do the economic
and political imperatives of urban life, and at every turn the native
is reminded that both his parental culture and community have no
prestige and can be ignored. The kin lines that his family was once
at pains to preserve need not be taken seriously. A young man need
not worry that a girl's elders of male siblings will bring him to account for a pregnancy outside marriage. A girl need not wait until
her sweetheart has saved enough for the bride price; nor is she, unprotected by a kin network, in any position to force him to wait.
White governments in Africa, like those in the United States *ante-
bellum* South, are little interested in maintaining legitimacy, since
by caste definition African legitimacy has no relevance for white

legitimacy. By contrast, U.S. white rural or foreign in-migrants could marry native whites so that public agencies were concerned about their legitimacy patterns.

The African couple need not bother with marriage. Indeed, marriage can no longer achieve its former manifest objectives: (1) it cannot maintain a respected lineage for yet another generation, since the kin line itself has lost its importance and because in an urban agglomeration the young man and woman may well be from different tribes, (2) it does not integrate a tribe by joining two lineages within it, since the tribe itself is disappearing and the tie may not be known to either lineage, and (3) it does not give a fully respected adult status to the young male, since under the Western caste pattern his rank will remain a lowly one, and whatever rank he does achieve will be based on his occupation and not his tribal position or the marriages he enters. Since, finally, both kin and elders have lost the authority on which social control once rested, both the young man and woman can and must make whatever individual role bargain with one another their circumstances permit.

In short, the political and economic dominance of the new urban world has begun to undermine that self-evident rightness of older family values which once guaranteed a legitimate position for the newborn child. The younger urban African generation has begun to feel a less intense commitment to those values, has acquired some opposing values, and in any event does not possess the means with which to achieve the older goals. The anomie of native African urban life in some centers surpasses anything observed in United States immigrant life, because the original culture of the African was more different from the Western culture, to which he must adjust, and his present deprivation is greater than that of the United States immigrant. The latter was already part of Western Culture, so that the cultural destruction he experienced was minor by comparison. The native is at the bottom of a caste system and is no longer part of an integrated social group or cultural system which would permit him to assert his own worth or the worth of the family. Thus, the stigma of illegitimacy becomes minor.

In the urbanizing African areas, the native patterns are neither (1) socially or culturally integrated internally nor are they (2) integrated socially or culturally with the dominant societies. In this transitional period, when the social importance of kin lines has become minimal, illegitimacy is high because of casual liaisons, promiscuity, and delayed marriage. On the other hand, the consensual union has perhaps not become the *usual* pattern of marital unions. The numerical preponderance of the native populations has prevented its being absorbed into white cultural patterns, but modern industrial and economic expansion has prevented the whites from "keeping them in their place," either in the tribes or in the stratification system.[10] As a consequence, the phases of destruction have proceeded rapidly, and perhaps re-integration will occur more swiftly than in the New World.

THE NEW WORLD

The conquest of the New World seems at first to exhibit a very different pattern. First, no case of cultural penetration on so huge a scale can be found since Rome, unless the Islamic conquest be excepted. From Alaska to Tierra del Fuego, aside from a few tribal pockets, the hemisphere is Western in culture. The native cultural systems have been penetrated, undermined, and destroyed, though of course some elements of the older cultures do survive.

Next, two different forms of destruction may be distinguished. One of these, shared by the Southern United States and the Caribbean, was primarily a physical destruction and overwhelming of the native population, together with the substitution of alien slaves, who were so mixed geographically that their social systems were destroyed, and thus they could not maintain their African cultural heritage. These slaves, emancipated for the most part late in the nineteenth century, became Western in culture. Their descendants generally occupy the bottom social strata in the countries in which they were introduced, but in a few countries some occupy higher strata as well.

The second major pattern of destruction, socially more complex, was found on the Latin American mainland, from Mexico southwards. The main attacks were first concentrated on the three great population centers, the Aztec, Mayan, and Inca civilizations. Intent on political conquest and economic exploitation, the Iberians nearly undermined their own aims in the Conquest period by wiping out from one third to one half of their subjects, through disease, over-work, and underfeeding. At first, they ruled in part through native leaders, but by 1600 they had also removed this top stratum from power. Although the church often opposed those actions, its own efforts at destroying native religions were backed by political leaders, so that even when the Church attempted to save native bodies, it persisted successfully in its goal of undermining native cults and substituting some form of Catholicism. The Iberians, like the whites in Africa, were greatly outnumbered by native Indians until relatively late in the Colonial period, but within a hundred years after the first conquests most of the cultural destruction had already taken place.[11] The Iberians imposed their cultural patterns on the natives, unlike the Manchus in China, the Spanish in the Philippines, the Dutch in Indonesia, or the English in India.

Both the assimilation and destruction processes differed somewhat from those in Africa. The U.S. and the Caribbean masters dispersed the (forced, slave) immigrants, but the whites outnumbered them in the United States and did not in the Caribbean. On the mainland, the Indians outnumbered the Iberians, but their social systems were in part undermined by death and partly by forced dispersion and relocation in villages. There was no industrial expansion, and little economic expansion, so that there was little need (in contrast to modern Africa) to use the natives in higher level jobs. Native African customs are essentially irrelevant to the problems faced in urban and industrial situations, but since in the New World the natives or slaves were used primarily in an agricultural setting, their customs might have been maintained had the whites not opposed them. In all these cases, the rule of the whites was based to a considerable degree on face-to-face interaction rather than indirect rule.[12]

The destruction patterns in these major cases are summarized in Table 1.

Before analyzing the consequences of these different patterns, let us comment further on the situation of the mainland natives. Although the Iberian rulers attempted to hold the Indians in economic and therefore political subjection and thus sought to keep a rigid caste line between the two groups,[13] the emergence of two new classes in the stratification system had considerable effect on the subsequent development of the family system. One new class, eventually to be-

Table 1
*Comparison of Cultural and Social Destruction and Assimilation
Patterns: Modern U. S. Cities, Modern Industrializing Sub-Saharan
Africa, and the Past New World*

Patterns	Immigration to U. S. Cities, Rural or Foreign	Africa, Modern	NEW WORLD: PRE-1900 Ante-Bellum U. S. South	Caribbean	Mainland Iberian Countries
1. Physical Destruction of Acculturating Population	No	Some	Little or none	Some	Considerable at first
2. Dispersal of Social Groupings	Yes	Yes	Yes	Yes	Yes
3. Numerical Preponderance of Population Being Acculturated	No	Yes	No	Yes	Yes
4. Prestige Dominance of Absorbing Population	Yes	Yes	Yes	Yes	Yes
5. Caste System	No	Yes	Yes	Yes	Yes
6. Industrial Expansion	Yes	Yes	Yes	No	No
7. Economic Expansion	Yes	Yes	Yes	No.	No
8. Relevance of Native Customs to New Situation	No	No	Yes	Yes	Yes
9. Situation of Culture Contact	Urban	Urban	Rural	Rural	Village and Urban

come the top stratum, was the Creoles, those born in the New World
as legitimate offspring of Iberian families. As in the colonial United
States, these rulers gradually loosened their ties with the Old World
and led the revolutions which, in one country after another, freed all
these possessions, except Puerto Rico and Cuba, from Mexico southwards, during the first quarter of the nineteenth century. The second class, which began at first from illegitimate unions between
Iberians and Indians, were the mestizos, who gradually came to be
a majority of the population in most Latin American countries.
Likely to be intermediate in both appearance and culture between
the rulers of pure descent and the Indians, this class reduced the
strength of barriers against mobility.

More important for our understanding of cultural penetration, the
mainland caste patterns permitted mainly only one form of mobility,
what is called "passing" in United States white-black relations. This
pattern is still found in the so-called caste relations between Ladinos

and Indios in Guatemala[14] and in the Andean Highlands of Bolivia, Ecuador, and Peru. That is, the individual could enter the Iberian world, for the most part in urban areas, only by becoming Iberian in all observable cultural characteristics, by ceasing to be Indian. He might starve as easily being all Iberian as being Indian, but without becoming Iberian the way upward was entirely closed. This structural pattern permitted some upward mobility without softening the low evaluation of Indian culture and without eroding the social barrier between Indian and Iberian.

In the New World, then, the native social and cultural systems were undermined by the steady economic and political pressures of a *closed*-class system, rather than by the open-class, expanding industrializing system of the modern world. The destruction was greatest among the slaves of the ante-bellum South, less in the Caribbean, and least on the Iberian mainland. Southern slaves were "seasoned" in the Caribbean first and were further dispersed on arrival in the U.S. Indians were able, especially in areas of less economic and political interest to the Iberians, to maintain some part of their social and cultural integration for many decades, and a few tribes still exist in remote regions, such as the upper Amazon. An index of the disorganization of Caribbean slaves is their failure to reproduce,[15] so that slave-running continued to be profitable almost until the end of the slavery period. In general, the illegitimacy rates of former slave areas are still higher than the non-slave areas; and on the mainland countries rimming the Caribbean, the coastal provinces where black slaves were introduced have higher rates than the interior.

The caste barriers were most severe in the ante-bellum South, somewhat less severe in the Caribbean non-Iberian islands, and least severe on the Iberian mainland. As Tannenbaum has shown, the Iberian treatment of even blacks was less rigid than the treatment by any of the other New World settlers.[16]

The Iberians also made the most conscious effort to indoctrinate their subject peoples, the Indians, in Western norms, especially those relating to religion. However, in all these cases the inculcation of the new, Western values proceeded slowly and inconsistently. It is difficult to socialize an individual unless he is assured of acceptance as a full member of the social system, but the Iberians refused to accept the Indian anywhere until recently. *Village* controls were weak, because norm commitment to either native or Iberian values was weak and because the local social system was truncated: the locus of economic and political power was in the Iberian world, and the religious system accepted the Indian as parishioner, not as priest. Rewards for becoming Iberian were low or non-existent. For example, the Indian might be exhorted to work hard, but he would be subjected to economic exploitation if he acquired any wealth. Learning to read would help little, since there were few positions open to him if he became literate. The Iberian pressures were directed toward keeping the Indians docile, not toward transforming them into Iberians.

In the slave areas, primarily the United States, Brazil, and the Circum-Caribbean, neither master nor slave had any concern about illegitimacy, since the slave kin line had no social importance: slavery undermines the status of the male as family head, more than that of the female,[17] and it is precisely the male elders who would be (in an independent society) the guardians of the family honor. It was to the interest of the conquerors or masters to prevent the development of native systems of social control, whether family or community, for therein lay a potential threat to their dominance. Even in the twentieth-century United States South, whites have opposed the "pretensions" of blacks in seeking certificates of marriage and divorce. Slavery was abolished only late in the nineteenth century, and we could expect that where the caste barriers against blacks were stronger, especially outside the Iberian regions, concern about black legitimacy among both whites and blacks would develop only slowly.

ILLEGITIMACY AND THE
STRUCTURE OF COMMUNITY INTEGRATION

Our review to this point suggests that it is the *community*, not the individual or the family, that maintains conformity to or deviation from the norm of legitimacy. The community defines and confers legitimacy. The individual decision, his or her role bargain, determines whether illegitimacy will be risked, and both family and individual may lose standing if illegitimacy results, but there is little stigma if the community itself gives almost as much respect for conformity as for non-conformity. Lacking integration, the community cannot easily punish the deviant. In any population, the maintenance of a high individual or family commitment to a given norm or conformity to the norm, is dependent on *both* the commitment of the community to the *cultural* norm and the strength of its *social* controls. In the New World during the Colonial Period and the nineteenth century, as in contemporary industrializing sub-Saharan Africa, both native community controls and the commitment to the norm of legitimacy were weak. Correlatively, neither conquerors nor masters were concerned, since such deviations had little effect on their primary interests, power and economic exploitation.

The failure of community social integration means, then, a high rate of illegitimacy, since (a) it is likely to occur along with a weakening of norm commitment and (b) even if norms are not greatly weakened, controls are weak. However, the nature of this community integration or non-integration must be *specified*. We cannot fall back on the frequent alternative term, "anomie." The classical definition of "anomie," *normlessness*, is not adequate because such a state is so extreme: almost no cases of it, perhaps none at all unless we accept the examples of Nazi concentration camps and of United States prisoners of the Chinese during the Korean War, have been described by modern investigators. Here we can more usefully think of anomie or non-integration as a matter of *degree*. However, sociological theory has not agreed on a clear meaning for "non-integration." Moreover, most analysts have viewed New World villages as "communities," i.e., as integrated. Thus, it is fruitful to specify the *several* structural points where "integration" may or may not exist.

We are asserting that for a period of about two centuries most of the slave and peasant populations of the New World lived in relatively stable, *non*-integrated settlements, kept from integration by United States, Iberian, and other European rulers. They were kept from either being integrated into the Western cultural and social systems *or* establishing independent, *internally* integrated cultural and social systems of their own. Here, of course, we necessarily go beyond the available data, but some of the specific descriptions can eventually be tested.

The points of non-integration can be outlined as follows:

I. These villages were not internally *culturally* integrated. This statement also holds, of course, for the U. S. Southern Negro population, only a few of whom ever lived in separate communities. Without even a geographical basis, cultural integration is most difficult to achieve. This general assertion means:

A. There was a commitment, though relatively weak, to a wide range of norms from *both* cultures: religious elements from both cultures, allegiance to both languages, songs and music, or local and "national" loyalties.

B. There was relatively low norm commitment to various *instrumental* norms, such as literacy, Western languages, skills in economic activities, etc., which might have been useful in fulfilling *other* Western norms to which there was some commitment.

C. Conditions for the achievement of norms in the villages were difficult (contradictions of norms and conditions).
   1. Costs of church marriage were high.
   2. Masters or conquerors were little interested in facilitating formal marriage.
   3. Costs of the *fiesta*, or reception, after marriage were high.
   4. There were few means for economic expansion, literacy, and even learning Church beliefs precisely.
   5. Conquerors and masters opposed native or slave efforts to pretend to the status honor enjoyed by rulers.
   6. European goods were urged on them, but prices were high.
   7. Responsibility for debts or labor was encouraged, but caste prohibitions against mobility were strong.[18]

II. These villages were not internally *socially* integrated. Of course, where there is very low norm commitment, social integration may be low: there is little to be integrated *about*. Again, the Southern black population obviously fits this description, which means:

A. White rulers prevented the development of local leadership or self-rule, thus hindering community controls.

B. Natives were not generally permitted to participate in Church activities as priests or officials (the cofradías may be viewed as a partial exception, but they were organized to ensure proper contributions to the Church).

C. Any local community pressures, decisions, or rules were subject to being overriden by the whites.

III. The village *cultural* patterns were not integrated with "national," white patterns. This means:

A. The two patterns were differently oriented toward various important norms: the value of working and owning agricultural land, the value of living in the city, nationalism-patriotism, or belief in the details of Church doctrine.

B. Whites viewed the native or black patterns as alien, rather than as merely lower class or a variant of the dominant culture.

   C. Whites viewed the native or black people as requiring acculturation or training (even when they wasted little energy on the task), not as having a different culture of equal validity.

IV. The villages were not *socially* integrated with the dominant social system of the whites or the larger social system of the nation.
   A. Natives did not generally feel part of the nation and had little interest in the changing political fortunes of the elite.
   B. Relatively few inter-community relations existed.[19]
   C. The native was not viewed as a "citizen" everywhere in the nation, and many barriers to free movement existed.
   D. The economic system was locally oriented, for the most part.
   E. The wishes of the local villages were little taken into account in national planning or action.

All four structural connections have been specified, in order to avoid needless debate as to whether these populations were "anomic," or "non-integrated." The outline is thus partly a summary of the preceding analysis but emphasizes the special character of the non-integration of these populations, which also applies *mutatis mutandi* to the black population of the Old South in the United States. The caste pattern of India is different in that the local village is *internally* both socially and culturally integrated; and it is culturally integrated with the larger Indian cultural pattern, in that the local caste norms and patterns are viewed as a legitimate part of the national moral fabric. It seems doubtful, however, that until recently such local village castes were *socially* integrated with the national social system except through a lengthy series of intermediate steps. Under such circumstances, social control remains strong locally and so does the commitment to the norm of legitimacy.

   Consequently, in the New World from the Old South in the United States to Cape Horn, the non-whites assimilated only slowly into the social and cultural patterns of the West. They accepted the superiority of these patterns or at least did not assert the contrary. However, the barriers to integration into the nationally dominant patterns and the forces arrayed against local social or cultural integration failed to yield the rewards which are necessary for effective acculturation, so that the process did not accelerate in most countries until the twentieth century.[20] Consequently, both low norm commitment to legitimacy and weak community controls maintained relatively high illegitimacy rates.

PHASES OF ASSIMILATION:
RURAL-URBAN ILLEGITIMACY DIFFERENTIALS

Although the foregoing outline of nonintegration in the New World seems both theoretically and descriptively correct, it goes far beyond available data from individual community studies, which would test whether any large proportion of existing or historical villages were in fact non-integrated. However, some further conclusions can be derived and tested in this analysis, so that we are not left merely with speculations.

The first of these concerns the *phases* of non-integration. If the line of theory pursued so far is correct, then in the conquest period in the Iberian world the illegitimacy rates first began to increase in the urban centers where contact was first made and the primary undermining of the Indian patterns began. Thereafter, however, because urban centers were the source of Westernizing forces and the urban Indians were more likely to assimilate, the norm of formal marriage was more likely to be followed. In addition, of course, the cities contained Iberians who would usually follow this norm. Thus, while the rural areas were kept in a relatively non-integrated state or forced gradually into it as Iberian dominance spread, the urban regions moved toward Western norms.

We should, therefore, suppose that in most cases the urban illegitimacy rates would now be *lower* than the rural rates, even though the modern rapid urbanization of Latin America may be creating all those disruptions of social and cultural patterns which have elsewhere been recorded when rural peoples enter an urban milieu.[21] In Table 2 on the following page, the rural and urban rates are presented.

As can be seen, the conclusion is validated, except for Paraguay. If our theory of phases in disintegration and reintegration is correct, this means that Paraguay, the socio-economically least developed of independent Latin American countries, has not yet entered the phase in which urban rates have begun to drop below rural ones. It should do so in the future. Correspondingly, of the seven independent Iberian countries with very high rates (over 50%) all are little developed, and still show very low differentials between urban and rural rates.[38] Finally, in the more advanced countries, such as Uruguay and Mexico, the differences should *diminish* in the future.

Table 2

Differences in Illegitimacy Rates Between Capitals and Remainder of Country,
Mainland Independent Countries South of the Rio Grande

POLITICAL UNIT	YEAR	FEDERAL CAPITAL MAJOR URBAN PROVINCE	PER CENT	REMAINDER OF COUNTRY (23.8% FOR WHOLE)	HIGHEST RATE IN ANY DEPARTMENT OR PROVINCE PER CENT
Argentina	(1957)[22]	Federal Capital	10.4	27.0	60.3 (Formosa)
Brazil	(1952)[23]	Capital Territory	12.4	15.0 (Total for country as a whole)	
Chile	(1958)[24]	Valparaiso Province	16.3	25.2	30.2 (Coquimbo)
Uruguay	(1943)[25]	Montevideo	18.4	27.5	66.7 (Florida)
Paraguay	(1946)[26]	Capital	62.4	56.5	(No figure obtainable)
Colombia	(1956)[27]	Cundinamarca Section	20.2	30.1	69.1 (Córdoba)
Ecuador	(1947)[28]	Pichincha Province	22.3	34.7	84.9 (Los Ríos)
Peru	(1953)[29]	Callao Department	30.9	43.9	59.6 (Loreto)
		Lima & Callao Departments	46.4	43.0	54.7 (Lambayeque)
Venezuela	(1954)[30]	Federal District	47.2	58.3	74.9 (Yaracuy)
Nicaragua	(1947)[31]	Managua Department	57.5	62.3	70.4 (Chinandega)
Honduras	(1957)[32]	Francisco Morazán	68.4	69.3	80.3 (Colón)
Costa Rica	(1957)[33]	Province San José	14.2	28.1	49.1 (Limón)
Mexico	(1956)[34]	Distrito Federal	12.9	23.9	27.9 (Sinaloa)
El Salvador	(1955)[35]	San Salvador	30.8	59.3	67.6 (Santa Ana)
Guatemala	(1956–57)[36]	Urban Area Urban Areas	64.5	76.1 (Rural areas)	
Panama	(1958)[37]	Urban Areas	64.5	79.6 (Rural areas)	

The mainland *dependent* countries do not fit this phase pattern (British and Dutch Guiana, British Honduras), nor do the Caribbean island countries. Of the three Caribbean countries that have been independent for more than half a century, Haiti, Cuba, and the Dominican Republic, we have been able to obtain rural-urban breakdowns for only one, the Dominican Republic, where the rural rate *is* slightly higher but has become so only recently (65.1%–63.9%, 1958).[39]

In the Caribbean political units, the rural rates are almost the same as the urban and are very slightly *lower* in over half of them. This region differs from the mainland Iberian lands primarily in these characteristics: (1) almost all their population is descendant from slaves. Caste restrictions were more severe against blacks than on the mainland against the Indios; (2) almost all of them have been dependencies until this century, so that there has been little basis for national integration; (3) most important, the phases which apply to the mainland Iberian countries do not apply here, since the initial disorganization *was as intense in rural as in urban regions*. The Indians were everywhere destroyed. The slaves who replaced them were no longer members of a community, and the bulk of them was used in agriculture. We should not expect the Caribbean, then, to follow all the phases of the mainland development, though we predict that the urban rates will become lower than the rural. Several of the differentials are given in the following table. The United States Southern black rates are also included, as following the Caribbean pattern.

Table 3
New World Rural-Urban Differentials in Illegitimacy Rates, Selected Mainland Dependencies and Caribbean Countries[40]

| | ILLEGITIMACY RATES | |
	URBAN	RURAL
U. S. South, Non-White (1957)	18.6–32.7%	18.6–32.1%
Puerto Rico (1956)	34.6 (San Juan)	27.4 (Rest of Country)
British Guiana (1955)	43.8	33.6
Trinidad and Tobago (1956)	47.3	47.4
Dominican Republic (1958)	63.9	65.1
Surinam (Dutch Guiana) (1951)	43.0 (Paramaribo)	38.0 (Rest of Country)
Jamaica (1954)	73.1 (Capital)	71.5 (Rest of Country)
British Honduras (1956)	52.9 (Capital District)	49.8 (Rest of Country)
Barbados (1955)	65.2 (Capital Parish)	59.3 (Rest of Country)

ILLEGITIMACY AND DEGREE OF NATIONAL INTEGRATION

A second conclusion may be drawn from our earlier analysis. The New World countries have succeeded in varying degrees in integrating their formerly Indian or slave populations into the national cultural and social systems. Since their illegitimacy rates are in part a function of this variable, countries which have moved *further* toward such an integration should have *lower* rates. The degree of this

Table 4
New World Political Units According to Their
Degree of National Integration and
Illegitimacy Rates[41]

DEGREE OF NATIONAL INTEGRATION	ILLEGITIMACY RATES (PERCENTAGES)	DATE
A. Higher Integration		
Brazil	15	1952
Chile	16	1958
Uruguay	20	1954
Mexico	22.5	1956
Costa Rico	25	1957
B. Medium Integration		
Argentina	28	1957
Colombia	28	1957
Cuba	30	1939
Puerto Rico	28.5	1955
U. S. Old South, Negro	19–32	1957
C. Lower Integration		
Ecuador	36	1956
Peru	43	1955
British Guiana	34	1957
Paraguay	48	1955
Surinam	34	1953
French Guiana	65	1956
Venezuela	57	1955
Guatemala	70	1957
Panama	71	1956
Jamaica	72	1954
Martinique	48	1956
British Honduras	48	1957
D. Not Classified		
Dominican Republic	55	1956
El Salvador	59	1953
Honduras	65	1957
Nicaragua	62	1945

type of integration is greatly dependent on the extent of industrialization and urbanization, since these variables require more interconnections between different parts of a nation and offer rewards to the individual for entering the cultural systems. Thus, it becomes both easier and more desirable to conform to the norm of legitimacy. However, the rank order of the illegitimacy rates has a Spearman-Brown coefficient of correlation of only .50 with the rank order of urbanization as measured by the percentage of the national population living in the major metropolitan areas.

In the preceding table, most of the New World political units are ranked by the degree to which their formerly slave or Indian populations have been brought into the dominant cultural and social systems. As can be seen, with few exceptions the conclusion holds: in general, where the formerly slave or Indian populations have been more fully integrated into the national cultural and social systems, the national illegitimacy rates are lower.

ILLEGITIMACY AND THE INTERNAL
INTEGRATION OF COMMUNITIES

A third deduction from our earlier analysis can be tested: because of the wide variety of geographical and sociological factors in New World history, some communities have either continued to be *internally* integrated both socially and culturally (but *not* integrated culturally or socially with the *national* systems) or else re-achieved such an integration after the initial dissolution. Such communities would then be the main source of individual or family honor and rank, and would be able and willing to ensure conformity to the norm of legitimacy. Thus, their illegitimacy rates would be low. Their *formal* official rates might be *high*, since the national registration system will recognize only the legal, civil ceremony; but their social rates would be low, since few people will enter a union without a public marriage ceremony of some kind in which both family lines participate. Such communities might be found, for example, in the Andrean Highlands of Peru, Bolivia, and Ecuador, or the northwestern highland region of Guatemala and even here and there in the Caribbean. We should find low real rates of illegitimacy in such villages and high rates in villages where such integration seems weak. In the following table, various places which have been the object of community studies are classified by illegitimacy rates and by the degree of integration, i.e., the extent to which the village forms a self-validating social and cultural system.

Table 5
Illegitimacy and Integration in Selected
New World Communities[43]

	HIGH RATE OF ILLEGITIMACY	LOW RATE OF ILLEGITIMACY*
High Integration:		Tzintzuntzán (Mexico)
		Cherán (Mexico)
		Cruz das Almas (Brazil)
		Tusik and Quintana Roo (Mayans of Mexico)
		Orange Grove (Jamaica)
		Nyame (British Guiana)
		Saucio (Colombia)
		Santa Eulalia (Guatemala)
		Peguche (Ecuador)
Low Integration:	Rocky Roads (Jamaica)	Otóvalo (Ecuador)
	Sugartown (Jamaica)	Chichicastenango (Guatemala)
	Moche (Peru)	
	Tobatí (Paraguay)	

* "Low" illegitimacy means, of course, relative to the level prevailing in the respective countries. Specific rates cannot be calculated from the descriptions.

As can be seen, we find relatively low rates of illegitimacy in specific communities which have achieved, or re-achieved, an internal social and cultural coherence, an acceptance of themselves as the source of prestige.[42] Individuals in such communities are participants in their social systems and presumably also committed to their cultural norms. If prestige is earned within the system, then a family line or the community as whole will insist on conformity with the norm of legitimacy. The communities which form a self-validating social system have low rates, and the communities which are less integrated have higher rates.

CONCLUSION

The present paper has attempted to relate cultural penetration, cultural and social anomie, and illegitimacy rates, by considering the main areas of high rates: Northwestern Europe, urbanizing Africa south of the Sahara, and the New World south of the Mason-Dixon Line. In the first case, the community retains control, and though some children are born outside of wedlock, they are likely to be only technically and temporarily illegitimate, not socially illegitimate. In urbanizing Africa, by contrast, Western culture has undermined the native cultural and social systems, and the Western community has not created conditions which permit the native to become a full member of the Western social and cultural system.

This situation is also observable in the history of the Western Hemisphere among both United States rural and foreign immigrants, where however the later phases in such a massive process of penetration have also taken place. The parallels among the United States and Latin American mainland, the Caribbean, and urbanizing Africa are striking, if we allow for the differences which the twentieth century political situation has imposed on Africa. At the same time, apparent differences suggest theoretical reformulations of the assimilation process. We see a conquering people who first rule indirectly through native leaders, and then directly, in Africa and the New World south of the Rio Grande; considerable destruction of native populations and forced migrations; destruction of the native cultures, but the erection of quasi-caste barriers to prevent the full achievement or even complete acceptance of Western norms by the native; the undermining of the *local* community as the source of prestige; bars to entrance into the conquering Western community; and the dissolution of native family systems, without granting the rewards for conformity to the new Western family norms. We have also outlined the differences among these cases.

Behind the New World, however, are four hundred years of assimilation, so that it has been possible to see what happens after the initial period of cultural penetration. It is in the cities that full assimilation of the peasant is possible, and under the later industrialization that assimilation is even useful to the upper strata. Thus, it is in the city that the Indian peasant may become not only culturally but also socially assimilated, while in the rural areas, the encomiendas, and villages he has taken over Western *culture* with less commitment, because he has been denied a part in the Western *social* community, with its concomitant rewards and punishments. Thus, it is in the urban areas that the rule of legitimacy begins to be imposed more stringently by the community, and the mestizo becomes willing to pay the price of marriage, such as the wedding feast which serves as both a community blessing and a ritual of passage.

In a parallel fashion, those countries in which strides have been taken toward integrating their populations into the national community will have lower illegitimacy rates.

And, finally, where the village becomes the cosmos, usually in isolated or mountainous areas, so that the individual in it is participating in both the cultural system and the social system of a genuine community, there again we find a stronger commitment to the norm of legitimacy, and greater community and family concern about marriage. The dominant value system does not set norms which the individuals cannot achieve; there is less contradiction between norms, so that there is a stronger commitment to them; and the coherence of the community permits more effective sanctions to enforce conformity to the norm of legitimacy.

11. *Social Mobility, Family, and Revolutionary Potential*

INTRODUCTION

FACED WITH SO MASSIVE A QUESTION AS "WHY REVOLUTIONS?" WE ARE LIKELY TO ANSWER WITH EITHER A BANAL TAUTOLOGY, "BECAUSE CONDITIONS are so intolerable," or the flippant response, "why not?" As in all theorizing, we do not advance much until we have framed the right question—whereupon many complex and confusing data become orderly and comprehensible. The traditional query may be as badly phrased as the child's puzzle, "why is the sky?"

The following exploration of linkages between mobility, family, and revolutionary potential has not formulated the problem correctly either, but it may contain one fruitful step, the suggestion that we measure the revolutionary potential of *any* country or social system. This aids our inquiry in part because we then enlarge the cases under examination. After all, if we follow very strict criteria for what constitutes a "real" revolution, we can locate only a handful. If we relax our standards to include any change of rulers through force, we enlarge the number.

This widening is especially fruitful theoretically, because a high revolutionary potential may exist without a serious attempt at revolution—consider, for example, the rarity of revolutions over the past century in the British and European-ruled colonies of the Caribbean, where disciplined troops could easily keep the dissidents from gaining power. Or, by contrast, a succession of coups could succeed in a society whose population is apathetic rather than rebellious, or at worst with only a low revolutionary potential.

The analysis also seeks to show that a set of variables usually thought to be dependent or peripheral does have consequences for the grand factors of power, prestige, and wealth that are the focus in most inquiries into revolution. Structurally, family variables may be powerful, for the family is the keystone of the stratification system. One important base of class position is family behavior: who is permitted to marry whom, the control of children's social relations, help given to kin, education in class customs, barring entrance of the able but lowly born *arriviste*, and so on. The theoretical significance of the family is here explored in part by considering a range of speculative alterations in the family system that might reduce the revolutionary potential of a society.

The linkages between family, mobility, and revolutionary potential are especially visible when we consider the *collectivistic* orientations of revolutionaries: they must organize a collectivity, they typically aspire to help others, they seek in especially the more radical or Jacobin overthrows to remove groups and not individuals from power. Moreover, although they are usually young and less encumbered by family obligations, they eventually aim at guaranteeing for *their* families the benefits their political action has won.

Revolutionary potential is here explored as the partial outcome of tensions whose relations are paradoxical: families and, therefore, classes that enjoy great advantages use a wide variety of social techniques for maintaining their power and privilege, whose result they hope will keep out those who push upward from lower ranks; however, precisely to the extent those practices are successful, they generate an even greater malaise, *ressentiment*, and revolutionary potential. In short, if they are successful in protecting their inept, they reap a whirlwind, because the able, aspiring families work harder to achieve the rank they feel the system itself has denied them.

As all students of revolution know, the leaders are not the poor and the downtrodden who suffer most from exploitation. They are rather from higher social strata, but below the top. Families below but near the top feel much more relative deprivation, since they are in a position to observe the rulers and to judge more accurately their failures and their weaknesses. They can and do decide that they are at least as worthy. Realistically, they have more resources (educational, literary, political, economic) with which to mount a coup or revolt. They are also more likely to see the encouraging truth that the position of upper-class families is often insecure, that they can in fact be toppled. For the great *immediate* threat to continuous rule is not the masses, but other families with about the same rank, who fiercely compete among themselves for whatever privileges and emoluments this system affords. As to the lower orders, it is probable that in most societies they are not convinced the system is just, but they also perceive it is too powerful to be overthrown.

The above analysis views social systems as contingent and potentially unstable; it assumes that many people are not greatly committed to their social systems, or convinced of the justice of these systems. The fruitfulness of this view, which is explored in the exposition, must be measured by the results that are expounded here. However, the contrary stance might also be theoretically fruitful, if its logical and sociological implications were carefully examined: Just as the biologist may usefully look upon all organisms as dying (and they do) or as successfully resisting the onslaughts of the environment (which they also do).

Finally, this study considers a set of "revolutions" that have been generally excluded by stricter definitions of the term, the many revolts, coups, rebellions, and revolutions of the New World. Here, I have tried to illuminate the forces at work in them, especially the peculiarly widespread social and cultural disorganization of the New World colonies—a theoretical theme that was analyzed in an earlier chapter on illegitimacy in the New World. However, these patterns of disorganization may not be as peculiar as they first appear, for they may also be observable in many emerging nations of our era. In any event, by drawing on the theoretical analysis of revolutionary potential, the inquiry both extends its hypotheses by examining this set of cases, and thus helps to explain the new world revolutionary patterns as well as those in other regions.

The many contemporary attempts to bring order into our thinking about revolution constitute a salutary step in social science. The topic has been paradoxically neglected in the midst of much analysis that is relevant to it. In the indexes of standard sociological work, including those in general theory, political sociology, and basic texts, the term "revolution" appears rarely, albeit increasingly. The paradox lies in this, that such widely read works typically treat social integration and stability as variables, but do not then ask, What are the conditions under which the revolutionary potential of a society is high or low? By expending so much energy on social stability, they implicitly point up the importance of instability, but then neglect it. A considerable amount of work in the present decade aims at filling that gap.

The Assumption of Instability. Critics have attacked present-day sociology because of its supposed defense of the status quo. It accepts, the dissidents assert, a Panglossian view of social action: everything contributes to the continued existence of current social arrangements, and everything works out for the greatest good. Actually, the dominant sociology has not so much defended existing social structures as explained why they *are* the current state of affairs, that is, why things are as they are. Moreover, one might indeed argue that searching for the main stabilizing factors suggests, on the contrary, that there must be powerful sets of disruptive forces in society; otherwise, stability would not be problematic.

Nevertheless, that analyses of societies so rarely focus *explicitly* on these disruptive forces within does suggest that such critics are correct in part. What indeed are these disintegrative forces against which the stabilizing factors generally prevail? This inquiry focuses on one set of such stabilizing and disintegrative factors in the revolutionary process, the social mobility system, and places special emphasis on a relatively neglected dimension, family variables.

When Has a Society Died? That sociology emphasized social stability explicitly during the past generation was perhaps salutary, since thereby at least one major theoretical orientation was well explored. Moreover, in a rough pragmatic way this view incorporates much of reality, since societies observably *do* maintain themselves from day to day, just as most individuals (often against their better judgment) do much the same things day after day.

But if the massive, observable fact about societies is continuity, boundary maintenance, and stability, just as one startling fact about the biological organism is homeostasis, stability, or defense against disturbing internal or environmental changes, the processes of destruction and dissolution are equally observable. A social theory that ignores either is crippled.

Both great truisms are productive, and if properly studied will lead to the other. The other face of biological homeostasis is death and continuous cellular breakdown.

Moreover, precisely because the analogy with the body is not perfect, it is productive: it reminds us that we have never agreed on a suitable definition of the death of a society: when can we say a society has disintegrated or changed radically? And, as an obviously related corollary, when can we say the alterations are radical enough to constitute a revolution? We concede that Rome fell, but do not agree on any but an arbitrary date. Moreover, whatever date we select, the dissenter can point to elements of Roman culture that continued to exist for centuries afterwards—its dialects in Spain, France, or Romania; its aqueducts and roads; its literature and mythical heroes, or even parts of its social organization.

Even if the analogical attempt fails somewhat, it leads us to locate subsystems, parts, or elements—social roles and collectivities—that definitely ceased to exist, whatever we may argue about the larger social structure of which they were once a part. These would include associations and clubs, individual families, churches, corporations and businesses, occupations and social statuses, and of course governments.

At first glance, an examination of such concrete cases of subsystem dissolution would appear to yield a better social theory. Existing theory has not contributed much to our understanding of how societies disappear, because it had only a few cases to study, and did not study even these. If we examine both the societies that have disintegrated, and the subsystems that have ceased to exist, perhaps we can better comprehend how it is that most societies contrive to exist so long. Indeed, it is likely that we might learn that major adjustments in these subsystems are the major factors that facilitate the continuity of whole societies.

But though the problem of defining how *much* alteration is the death of a society may thereby become more manageable, it is not really solved by focusing on the smaller elements of a society. For some of these elements also endure for decades, generations, or centuries, within which we can see no sharp dividing line between the old and the new, the death of an ancient pattern and the formation of a new one. Is the Catholic Church of Luther's time dead? Perhaps the answer is "yes," but what criteria are used in so intuitive a judgment?

Which criteria to use is crucial, if we are to examine revolutions: we must separate the daily fluctuations, growth, or decay in any society from some types of far-reaching processes of dissolution and rebirth. Unless we can distinguish the phenomenon we are studying from the myriad processes of alteration, we are left with a banal question.[1] If we try to avoid the problem of defining the dissolution of a larger society by attending instead to the disintegration of subsystems, we could of course then treat revolution as one type of such a change. Nevertheless, if we still cannot sketch the criteria for such a dissolution, we have merely moved back a step to smaller changes: We are then only asking, what causes social change—any social change, any alteration—for these are all a kind of death of the older social form.[2]

That question is like the query, "what causes the sea, what causes water, what causes the sky?—or society?" And the answer is equally banal: the banal question inspires, forces, ineluctably leads to, a banal answer. "Change or revolution or dissolution occurs because the forces of change become greater than those of maintenance and stability."

The Classification of Revolution. Such a dead end can be avoided, if we substitute for the global phenomenon a set of processes that can be identified more precisely. A taxonomy of revolution would be an important step, if a fruitful *basis* of classification can be developed. If the variables used in creating the taxonomy are the ones that determine the form and course of revolutionary events, they will yield testable propositions about real events.

The aim of a useful taxonomy is to transform the primitive question, what causes revolution or change or conflict, by asking a more specific one: are there very different causes for very different *types* of revolution? From a multidimensional analysis, Chalmers Johnson offers this classification:[3]

> Jacquerie
> Millenarian rebellion
> Anarchistic rebellion

Jacobin Communist revolution
Conspiratorial coup d'état
Militarized mass insurrection

Such a classification permits us to look for several examples of the same type throughout history, and perhaps to come closer to a set of typical natural histories of revolution, instead of guaranteeing failure by a quest for *the* causes of revolution, or *the* natural history of revolution.[4]

This is one step forward from the traditional question, phrased by Dahrendorf as, "Under what conditions do the conflicts within a society acquire so intensive and powerful a form that they can find expression only in a revolutionary explosion?"[5]

Johnson's classification is also a more fruitful posing of the problem than is achieved by using the *Oxford English Dictionary* (1961) definition of the phenomenon: "A complete overthrow of the established government in any country or state by those who were previously subject to it; a forcible substitution of a new ruler or form of government," particularly if, as is common, the theorist then excludes as coups d'état the " 'Latin-American' types of revolution."[6]

Other conceptual preliminaries besides classification are also necessary, especially the attempt to locate those various parts or *elements* in a revolution, to which we must direct our most intense energies. Among these is Thornton's analysis of terror as a revolutionary technique, with a specification of these major elements in a revolution: (1) actors; (2) targets; (3) objectives; and (4) the responses of others.[7]

One may instead classify the major *techniques* of revolution, that is, what techniques are used to gain control? Janos directs our attention to seven of these (guerrilla warfare, strikes, subversion, and so on).[8] Even his excessively formalistic framework does at least require some consideration of the many different elements within the various arenas of a revolution.

It is not useful for the aims of this paper, however, to criticize or even to summarize such attempts. They are useful for descriptive purposes, and in any event are a recognition that to analyze so complex a phenomenon as revolution, it is necessary to break it down into its constituent elements, and thus to sketch the different types of revolution. Hopefully, among the many suggestions already made in this growing literature will be found the most seminal classification. Science can progress only feebly as long—and the period may be *very* long—as it has not yet located the main elements and processes in the phenomenon it hopes to explain.

Although definitions of revolution vary, most are fairly close to this:

It is a kind of *social force* that is exerted in the process of *political competition*, deviating from previously shared norms, "warlike" in character (that is, conducted practically without mutually observed normative rules), and involving the serious disruption of settled institutional patterns.[9]

Such a definition omits many events now called revolutionary, but it almost certainly includes perhaps all that are called or thought of as quintessentially revolutionary, together with a large enough array of others to challenge even the most industrious of analysts.

Consensus and Conflict. Considering such a definition, one can ask either: why are people willing to risk their lives in order to overthrow their government; or: why do revolutions occur so seldom? Either version should lead to similar answers, if pursued far enough, but let us proceed from the latter formulation.

That formulation brings into relief the various reminders, over the past decade, that a society does not rest on consensus alone: Coser's resurrection of older statements about the "contributions" of conflict; Dahrendorf's repeated insistence that conflict and change are normal; Feldman's comments on the ubiquity of dissensus; and even a few of my own.[10]

The ubiquity of dissensus, both within an individual and among individuals, is a prime cause of the ubiquity of role strain. Recognition of the ubiquity of dissensus complements, without rejecting, the older, Lintonian model of conformity and social structure, according to which individuals continue to do what the society needs to have done, because they have been socialized to want to do it.[11]

By contrast to that model, I have specified certain of the types of strains and dissensus that are common in the action of any individual or any society:

1. Some individuals do not accept even supposedly central values of the society.
2. Individuals vary in their emotional commitment to both important and less important values.
3. This value commitment varies by class strata, and by other characteristics of social position, for example, age, sex, occupation, geographic region, and religion.
4. Even when individuals accept a given value, some of them also have a strong or weak "latent commitment" to very different or contradictory values.
5. Conformity with normative prescriptions is not a simple function of value commitment; there may be value commitment without conformity, or conformity without commitment.
6. When individuals' social positions change, they may change both their behavior and their value orientations.
7. The values, ideals, and role obligations of every individual are at times in conflict—with each other, with the capabilities or the situation of the individual, with the diverse demands made on the individual by different people, etc.[12]

It follows from a consideration of these diverse pulls and hauls on the individual as well as among individuals, that they may also be observed among *collectivities* and *subsystems* of a given society. That observation also reveals that (1) neither the individual nor a collectivity or subsystem can find a sufficient guide to action in any supposed moral or normative consensus (though without doubt *some* degree of consensus exists; we do not know how much, or how much is necessary) and (2) there is much dissensus in any society. More important, however, this view suggests it is in fact the *strains* within the society that hold the structure *together*. Indeed, a society, like any other structure, may be defined by the sets of strains that, working against or with one another, create whatever stability it does possess.

Under this view, individuals or collectivities are constantly pressing in directions which would alienate themselves from others, contribute little to others, frustrate others' goals, or cut off relations with others, but the response to those tendencies is not merely a resistance or repression. Rather, in an ongoing social structure, reciprocal strains, equally alienative or frustrating, and arising from other individuals or collectivities, prevent those tendencies from going very far. Moreover, several counterstrains together may sometimes hold the individual or collectivity in place, even though no one of them is *directly* opposing, because their total resultant *is* directly contrary in effect. If a social structure does break up, it is not only because one or more strains rise, but because adequate counterstrains are not generated.

This view raises, then, the significant question: *Under which conditions may a society continue to exist even though at some crucial nexuses its structure is anomic or disorganized?* For if *any* society has a significant component of strain, dissensus, or noncompliance in it, then perhaps some may exist even with very high indices of anomie. It is partly for this reason that the New World countries are of special theoretical interest, and will be discussed later with respect to their revolutionary potential: I believed that much of this great population segment lived under relatively anomic conditions for well over two centuries.

The view that society is torn with schisms, rent with conflict, at least potentially explosible, is of course ancient. Mazdaism or Zoroastrianism, interpreting the universe as a conflict between light and darkness, expounded such a philosophy some twenty-five centuries ago. Plato's analysis of the transformation of governments from kingship to mob rule and chaos, each stage of one type producing its degenerate mirror image (Kingship: tyranny; aristocracy: oligarchy; democracy: mob rule; and the like) as well as his advice on excluding disruptive forces from the Republic, indicate his awareness that the social structure may be inherently unstable. Hobbes introduced a monarch to keep under control the "natural" conflict among men. Marx's central theme was the class war. Indeed, this view may also be deducible from the Second Law of Thermodynamics.

I believe, however, that the contemporary view is different from all these classical views, in that our own not only asserts the conflict, but also takes it for granted that such conflicts will *continue*, and also supposes that such strains need not mean overt revolution, or even any resolution of the conflict. As is so common, a litterateur, Renan, has said it better: A nation is a daily plebiscite. If Lucien Pye is correct in his assessment of British (in contrast to U.S.) colonial reactions of native revolts, this view was at least partially embodied in British colonial policy a hundred years ago:[13]

Civil disorders spring from "man's inherent and compulsively irrational urge to violence and mischief";

Counterinsurgency against the rebels is, then, properly a police action, not a moral crusade;

It is easy to stir up violence; revolt is not to be interpreted as the last resort of desperate men;

Justice will not prevent revolt, because subject peoples do not understand justice anyway (justice is nevertheless a *duty*).

CONFLICT AND DISSIDENCE AS SOURCES OF REVOLUTION

But this pragmatically calm interpretation again misses important elements, just as did Plato's and Marx's, because it envisions an alternative social system in which all this violence and dissidence need not and would not occur.

Rather, we take the following view: (1) With reference to either their system of government or its goals, some people are dissident. (2) All societies and all governments use violence or its threat to keep their populations in check. No society could maintain itself without violence and its threat, and not alone against criminals. Such instruments have been used to enforce eminent domain when taking land for highway construction, to protect the enclosure movement, to prevent children from attending a public school forbidden to them, to break strikes, and so on.

(3) Although all modern governments claim a monopoly of violence, and especially deny the right of any other collectivity to the use of violence, in fact violence or its threat may be found—albeit almost never studied by social scientists—at times in almost every type of private social interaction as well, whether among collectivities or individuals.

(4) Since all members of a society possess some means of violence, and some opportunity of organizing force with others, against the government, some degree of threat to the government always exists.

(5) Although collectivities and individuals, knowingly or unknowingly, use many tension-management techniques, we have no measures of their overall success, the degree to which people end their day with a feeling of satisfaction.[14] More, we do not know with how much resentment, malaise, unhappiness, or dissatisfaction most individuals

go through their day's social interaction. Nor, still more important for the study of revolution, do we know, except through the prevalence of revolution, how societies differ in this degree, or how high a degree is necessary before a revolution breaks out. Here, especially, modern survey techniques could yield useful data.

(6) Tension-management techniques may not return the system to the *status quo ante*, just as the homeostatic mechanisms of the body do not.[15] Even effective *responses* to any *particular* threat from either the internal or the external environment may themselves create still further dangerous strains, processes, or products. Some of these may eventually kill the organism (or the government). Often, the failure of reform movements is explained as "coming too late," but they may fail equally because they set in motion still other destructive forces (for instance, Cranfield's attempt to save James I, Charles I's efforts to retrench, or Necker's moves to buttress the financial structure of the French monarchy in its last years).

This is *not* the same statement as Marx's Hegelian doctrine, that any system *contains* the seeds of its own destruction. Such a view sees only the initial set of strains, or the gradual development of one of them, to where it destroys the social system within which it was gestating.[16] My own view predicts no apocalypse, but rather emphasizes that the very efforts to contain or to dissipate a set of such strains will, *even when successful*, create new systems, positions, forces, or strains which may eventually undermine the larger body politic.

(7) This view also implies that any society is continuously changing at a degree less than revolutionary, and that part of this evolution is the creation of new statuses, positions, political and social structures or mechanisms, and the like in response to its external *and* social environments. Many or most of these do not survive, but neither does the revolutionary process necessarily yield new structures that will successfully meet these challenges.

(8) It follows from these theses that though each society has some degree of potential for revolution and, as I shall indicate in a moment, each revolution is a response, an attempted *collective* solution, to a problem, few such revolutions solve *that* problem, and none solves the fundamental problem that generated them. Perhaps, however, most do alleviate some of the particular problems their leaders thought they were tackling.

THE FAMILY DIMENSION OF
SOCIAL MOBILITY AND REVOLUTION

The foregoing theses sketch the contingency, the balance of strain, in an operating social structure, but the analysis of revolutionary processes demands a further specification of factors that more directly threaten that balance. Although the examination of any historical revolution uncovers unique factors, the present inquiry will focus on one *general* set of factors, the interaction of family and social mobility processes. These, needless to say, do not predict fully whether or not a revolution will occur, but in perhaps most or all revolutions their impact is important enough to call for serious consideration. To emphasize this set of factors here does not, then, deny the significance of other predisposing or precipitating forces, but does assert that this set has considerable impact.

A revolution is a *collective* act in at least three ways. First and most obviously, it is an organizational instrument, requiring the rational assessment and allocation of resources among those who take part in it, the forging of social links among its participants, the fixing of responsibility and command over groups, and so on. Second, such cognitive steps toward creating a collectivity and thus generating power will inevitably fail unless adequate ideologies, moral imperatives, and normative appeals persuade men that their cause is right, that their destinies are joined by virtue of shared values.

Note that both of these action types are necessary to create any group out of a mere aggregate of individuals, but they are especially crucial in this context because revolution is, after all, *dangerous*. Those who lead must convince others that their collective chances are good, and the arguments must be both rational and normative. In general, the greater the moral indignation among the participants, the less will they demand rational proof of their own greater material resources, actual or potential.

Third, a revolution is also a collective act in its selflessness: Whatever the individual psychological motives, the personality types, or the material aspirations that drive revolutionary leaders to violence against the established government, their acts aim at ameliorating conditions *for others* as well. To get followers, of course, they must do so, but aside from that rational necessity they invariably have this aim independently as a personal and group goal. They wish to eliminate certain injustices for others like themselves, and for still others who they believe will benefit from the installation of a better set of rulers and programs.

Partially contained within this last aspect of revolution as a collective act is the factor of *family*, which is both collective and individual, selfless and self-interested. The most important relationship in this complex set of interactions may be expressed by two great paradoxes. The first is that all family systems contain arrangements by which families can transmit whatever class advantages they possess to their children and other kin. Families give less support to a society that will not grant them some stability in their possessions. No set of families cares that much about the *system*, if it will not pay *them* off sufficiently. They prefer to try to hold on to their shared privileges within a network of similar families.

However, the very success of family efforts to guarantee advantage for the next generation in spite of incompetence, to protect their inept —in short, their collective ability to keep lower-level families from rising into higher ranks—is a powerful factor in the generation of instability, a higher potential for revolution. The very activities that are aimed at permanently securing for the elite families their present gains, are themselves most likely to create violent dissidence. Ironically, then, a greater instability of position among elite families actually promotes a stronger resistance to revolution, and thus promotes the stability of the political system.

The second paradox to be noted is that the revolutionary is not only against something; he is also *for* something. Those who lead the revolution will no longer tolerate the lower place their *families* hold. The goal of a revolution is to remove from power and pelf not alone those *individual* men who enjoy those privileges, or the system that permits them such advantages, but also their *families*. Specifically, the thrust of the moral indignation, the force, and the political creativity is against the efforts of the rulers (1) to prevent some families from rising in the hierarchy and (2) to hold the privileged in high place even when they are less meritorious, by achievement or ascriptive criteria.

But whatever the selfless rhetoric of revolutionaries, their efforts aim at achieving the blocked aspirations of their own families, and eventually to guarantee those new advantages to their own children and kin. After the success of the revolution, they try to consolidate their new privileges.[17]

These great paradoxes are an ironic commentary on the contradictory goals men seek, but both emphasize the relations among family, social mobility, and revolution. Revolutions seek to change the social arrangements by which advantage, training, opportunity, wealth, power, and rank are kept the quasi-monopoly of a network of families, a clique, or class.

Several hypotheses may be developed from this major relationship. One is that almost no revolution would occur if all those in privileged position were celibate and without family ties;[18] or if Plato's abolition of the family were to be inaugurated. Doubtless either system would be abandoned; and contemporary theory would also predict that neither system would produce enough adequately functioning adults to man the posts of the society—but those issues are not central here.

A second is that there is little likelihood of such revolutionary dissidence if lower-strata families, especially those close to the top, fail to train many who are able to rise and who believe they are capable. Empirically, this is an unlikely event, since whatever the *percentage* of able people in the strata lower than the top, the *absolute* number of able people is greater than in the top stratum. No system of deprivation has yet prevented *some* able lower-strata men from presenting themselves for higher level jobs, however much they were rebuffed for it.

Third, if the upper-strata families are simply incompetent at excluding the able families that are trying to rise, a violent overthrow is less likely—though, of course, downward mobility would then be high.

Fourth, it would also follow that a system of random placement at birth would be very unlikely to generate much family-based dissidence. Under such a system, the family network would not yield any advantages to its members. Alternatively, however, the re-establishment of a kin-based privilege system might eventually become a rallying cry, based again on (a) the blocked aspirations of their families and (b) their anticipation of future advantages to be passed on to a network of kin and descendants. Still, the case is unlikely.

Several alternative logical possibilities should also be considered here, before analyzing broad theoretical objections to the general hypothesis. One is a system in which few or no families would change their positions relative to one another, but all are steadily improving their material condition. On theoretical grounds this is an unlikely case, since the necessary economic expansion would invariably give a greater advantage to *some* of the abler families not yet at the top. In addition, any observation of mobility dissidence will disclose also that equal improvement in material welfare is not enough: rancor about unequal rank and power is at least as frequent and powerful as rancor about wealth.

Next, another empirically unlikely pattern—though, as in the prior case, one that still underscores the importance of the relations among family, class mobility, and revolution—is a high mobility of *only* the key potential revolutionaries. The inauguration of such a policy would presumably eliminate in advance the most able leaders of the disgruntled. However, no ruler or set of ruling families has ever exhibited so great a predictive wisdom.

A further instrumental weakness in this technique—though again pointing to the impact of the family dimension—is that a high percentage of revolutionaries have been young and either unmarried or only weakly committed to a marital union.[19] The social and psychological freedom to risk everything on the outcome of force is reduced by giving to fortune the hostage of a family. Indeed, the Jacobin Communist type of revolution, which demands far-reaching changes in the class structure, typically develops an *antifamily ideology* that partly counteracts those pulls.

This set of facts does emphasize nevertheless the selfless aspect of the revolutionary impulse: the attack on family privilege promises no *immediate* family advantages for the revolutionary himself. Finally, at the psychological level, it is at least possible that a goodly percentage of revolutionaries developed their drive to power from their resentment at the failure of the system to reward their own fathers adequately. However, if this psychological hypothesis is correct, seducing them by the offer of high posts might be an effective if an unlikely technique.

One further mobility pattern should be considered, which is somewhat more likely than the foregoing. In this type there is relatively high social mobility into the topmost stratum, but it is not based on the criteria that the ruling families agree is proper. The most common cases are the elevation of families through the ruler's whim or favor, and the granting of position or title because of family ties to either the ruler or his favorite (for example, Buckingham under James I). Then other upper stratum families feel déclassés, object to receiving such families as equals, and feel less loyalty to the ruler. (Note that they do not wish to "revolt" against the "system," but rather wish to *return* to what they consider the right system.) The dissident families may not have lost any specific posts or money, but they and aspiring families near the top experience a relative loss because they have failed to get what they believed to be rightfully theirs.

These are, then, instances of fairly high mobility into the topmost stratum, that nevertheless increases the revolutionary potential, though at most it would lead to a revolt against the ruler or his favorites (or, more frequently, a simple assassination). Thus, though the elements singled out in the earlier general hypothesis (the inverse relationship between mobility and revolutionary potential) seem to apply here, too, simple vertical mobility must be believed to be based on the normatively accepted criteria for advancement, if it is to reduce the revolutionary potential. If the relatives of the king's favorite move upward, but the abler families of, say, the upper-middle or lower-upper strata are blocked, the resentment of the established families supports the outrage of the blocked families. Typically, this elevation of favorites and their families creates an "inflation" in honors, and a corresponding deflation in their value: some have been moved up, but there was no natural flow of downward mobility to create places for them. In any event, this mobility pattern blocks the aspirations of key families, and wounds the pretensions of established ones.

One final type of mobility pattern, that of generally low social mobility, but also low integration or cohesion among families, will be dealt with later, but it does not generate a *low* revolutionary potential. On the other hand, only rarely does it spawn a Jacobin Communist or radical revolution, without a long period during which the revolution itself gradually creates an integrated society.

Achievement Values and the Acceptance of Rank. An adequate defense of all these hypotheses would require a full-scale monograph, but doubtless the reader can fill in a considerable body of confirmatory data from his own knowledge of revolution.[20] However, let us consider here a few objections, and attempt to answer them.

The main and immediate objections to the central thesis appear to be these:

1. It suggests, if it does not state, that all societies support a merit system, that is, placement on the basis of universalistic, achievement criteria, whereas most societies have actually given a higher rank to the values of particularism and ascription, for instance, placement on the basis of personal ties and kinship.

2. The hypothesis implies that in all societies most people *object* to the stratification system, and especially to their place in it, and are trying to scramble upward. Some present data, and most social theory, uphold the view that (a) people do not aspire very far upward, if at all and (b) people accept the stratification system, by and large, as well as their place in it. This is said to be especially true in estate and caste systems.

3. Davies's development from the earlier historical work of Alexis de Tocqueville, Lyford P. Edwards, and Crane Brinton states that revolutions break out when a rising level of expectations meet a short period of sharp reversal, a sudden decline in the product received.[21] Both expectation and reality, presumably, may encompass a wide range of advantages. It has been known for decades that the leaders of a revolution are typically the well-off (those who *have* moved upward) not the poor (who have little hope of rising).

Granted, Davies's hypothesis is not designed to explain different *types* of revolutions, or such interesting hypotheses about leadership as that a more radical revolution would be more likely to be led by, say, junior officers or middle levels of society, as contrasted with the type of revolution created by the stratum next to the top.[22]

Still, the hypothesis is roughly correct. Whether stated as a generalization in psychological or sociological theory, it has been expressed in one form or another by a goodly number of predecessors. Machiavelli applies it as a rule in meting out vengeance after taking over power (for instance, immediately destroy those who are dangerous, who will be those who have lost the most power). However, if it is correct, it seems to make an irrelevancy of my hypothesis, because it states that no matter what the family and mobility patterns, the crucial question is whether there have been rising expectations and they have met with a short, sharp declining output from the system.

4. The hypothesis does not face the problem that there may be very different social *standards* or norms for mobility rates. Presumably a lower stratum in nineteenth-century Latvia might have been contented with the amount of mobility in England of that time, while a corresponding stratum in the U.S. would not have been. As can be seen, this relates to objection No. 2, how much do people accept their place in the stratification system?

Let us consider each of these briefly. As to No. 1, whether and how much the population in any society supports a merit system, the problem is complex theoretically and obscure empirically. It is also related to No. 2, to what degree people accept their place in the stratification system.

There is ample evidence that even in work organizations in which universalistic, achievement criteria are the *ideal* basis for hiring and promotion, (a) often these criteria are not in fact applied and (b) some people will object when the criteria *are* applied, especially when the decision is against their benefit; they may plead instead for the criteria of seniority, friendship, loyalty, and so forth.

Conversely, even in societies supposedly characterized by an acceptance of particularistic or ascriptive criteria, merit is almost *never* irrelevant. No society *prefers* ineptitude in its tasks. Rarely or never is there a norm that explicitly states that the society does not mind if a role obligation is discharged ineptly,[23] though of course rules may state that other traits (for example, royal birth, clan membership) outweigh merit.

Societies vary in the degree to which they require merit in one kind of task or another, from canoe-building and salmon-fishing to friendship and high judicial position. A key difference in this variation is, I suspect, whether apparent talent, or *potential* skill, is viewed as a trait to be *cultivated* even in the lowly born, and used as a basis for social mobility. In ascriptive societies, I am inclined to believe, *developed* visible skill is not often ignored, but the potential skill or talent of the lowly born is simply not seen, or is viewed as irrelevant (as has been true in the past in the U.S. attitudes toward blacks).

However, I assert, without fair evidence, that even in a society in which presumably the populace at large *does* accept social placement by birth—until the textbooks are all proved wrong, this was true of Tokugawa Japan, and medieval Europe—or societies in which people are supposed to give jobs to friends and kin whether or not they are less able (classical China), those who are prevented by these barriers from rising but feel they have ability *do resent* the barriers and do *not* accept their lowly position as just. This applies especially to the strata closest to the top.

Although people in all societies know that families do give favors to kin who perform less adequately than outsiders, and in some societies this is in fact the norm, many or most of those who suffer from such particular judgments do not approve them. The literary history of the West is replete with such comments, and I am here asserting that this conscious objection to the advantages conferred by birth against merit may be found in all nations of the past and present, and is a potent factor in the revolutionary potential of a nation.

These structural relations are highly relevant to the question in objection No. 2, How contented are people in the rank where society has placed them? One answer, rarely brought into the open by social theorists, is that *all* stratification systems apply or threaten force—of course, varying from one society to another—to keep people in their place. If we wish to avert our eyes from Selma, or the hundreds of laws passed by Southern legislatures *prior* to the Civil War to keep slaves as well as freedmen in their place; or the constant protection given by policemen to privilege and rank, we may nevertheless note how in India, that supposed exemplar of caste rigidity backed by religion, the upper castes have not hesitated even in modern times to use force to keep the Scheduled Castes in their place. The period from Independence to the present has been dotted with incident after incident in which caste Hindus have used violence to stop other castes from exercising their new privileges.[24]

In fact, those who accept the existing privileges of property and rank think of these as "the law," and violations, of course, call forth an answer by legal force, with little thought that thereby the rank of individuals is being maintained by violence or its threat.

On a more complex level, we suppose that most people in a time of peace do accept, by and large, the publicly defended criteria for social ranking, and at some level of consciousness their own place as well.[25] However, the evidence, though imperfect, also shows that most people would like to improve their position, that even in a caste society they try to raise the ranking of their caste, and that every class below the top expresses a wide array of resentments about the higher-ups, together with doubts as to the justice of their being there.

As to No. 3, whether a sharp reversal after a period of rising expectations is a sufficient explanation, the basic question is, with reference to *whom* and *what* are the rising expectations felt, or frustrated? The *economic* expectations of the *haute bourgeoisie* of the eighteenth century were rising, and were certainly not being frustrated, yet this class initially led the French Revolution. As Elinor G. Barber has shown in detail, it was not so much that their expectations of family prestige were rising, their hopes of consolidating a high rank permanently by entering the network of noble families— although their anticipations *were* high—as that the nobles were gradually closing their ranks against them.[26]

In short, a specification of the increasing *discrepancy* between (a) expectations (whether or not *rising*, contrary to Davies) and (b) reward-output shows that the *type* of expectation has to do with the goal of *family* advantage, so that Davies's hypothesis sets at least one major condition for the operation of the forces we have been outlining. (We do not know, as he himself points out, how *much* rise or how much fall there must be.)

With reference to No. 4, the relativistic objection, that the amount of resentment is dependent on the social standards of the period and place, doubtless that intensity of objection does vary in different societies. On the other hand, it seems likely that all strata lower than the top do come to accept a more or less standard amount of mobility, and that if they grow up under that standard they are not likely to be violently dissident even if it is low.

However, we must be wary of supposing that people can become accustomed to simply *all* degrees of privation or nonmobility, no matter how low. It seems more likely that a low degree of nonmobility is more tolerable, if the avenues to mobility are *open*, and it is simply a low-opportunity society. There is certainly no body of reliable information to indicate that people in low-mobility societies are any happier or less violent about it, when they are being blocked in their efforts to seize the few chances for betterment that may be available, than are people in high-mobility societies. Indeed, poor as the data are, I believe they suggest the opposite.

The relativistic notion that societies may vary in their acceptance of a low degree of mobility does, however, lead to the notion of relativism among social strata, which helps to explain why it is the *higher* social strata who furnish the revolutionaries. They see a *higher* percentage of *their* own stratum move upward, than do the people in lower social strata, and thus in fact have higher expectations and thus (as many studies have shown) they will experience greater relative deprivation.

Needless to say, other factors also create this generally greater production of revolutionary leaders in the strata near the top. They have greater resources of money, power, and skill, and they can, therefore, realistically expect a higher chance of success. They are less likely to accept the rightness of *their* exclusion from the inner ranks, since in so many respects they are obviously similar to the top leaders.

It does seem likely, then, that the relativism of *expectations* also plays some part in this class differential in the origins of revolutionaries.

(Here, without a complex analysis, I should like to suggest also the possibility that those next to the top also have *family* patterns that generate a higher level of achievement motivation. It is possible that this is a potent element in the thrust toward revolution, as it very likely is toward upward mobility.)[27]

What is more important, however, is that there is at present no evidence to indicate that even in a low-mobility society the populace comes eventually to accept the blocking of talent as proper and defensible.

An examination of these class differentials leads to an important set of hypotheses concerning the process by which dissidence is lowered, that is, the reduction of tension through the upward mobility of families. Just as the families ranking near the top are the main source of revolutionary leadership, so is competition *among* elite and near-elite families perhaps the greatest safety valve for the revolutionary potential of a country. The data from China, Sweden, England, and the U.S. show that upper-class families have not maintained their positions for long; and while most did not fall by revolution, that fact itself is telling.[28] The very effort that is required to keep the family position intact must be directed primarily *against other similarly placed families*. They are the greatest threat, because they are more likely to seize each other's power, property, and rank; and in prenationalistic, local wars they were the prime enemy.

Indeed, if I may offer a hypothesis far removed from any data at hand, I venture to predict that the most stable governments of the West, as contrasted with the less stable, have behind them a history in which elite families held their positions for shorter periods of time, a history in which the interfamily competition among the elite weakened or destroyed many families and thus permitted other, lesser families to rise. Certainly the relatively stable governments of China were run by elite families whose hold on top positions seems to have been precarious.[29] Whether this is true of Tokugawa Japan, without qualification I have not been able to ascertain, but I do venture to predict that when we have at hand the mobility data for that period we shall find that in somewhat lower ranks than the *daimyo* the mobility rates were high.

Social Anomie and Latin American Revolutions. The previous hypotheses can now be extended to interpret a set of revolutions that is often laid aside because they are not "fundamental," "radical," or Jacobin Communist, those of Latin America. The cavalier attitude of social analysts toward this group is unfortunate. Granted, the great cycle of revolutions from 1810 to 1825 was simply a set of revolts against the Iberian colonial powers, and the hundreds of rebellions, revolutions, and outbreaks since then have been most closely akin to coups d'état. Yet we should not lightly omit the consideration of a Western subculture that has been so prolific of political changes through violence. We might at least learn something of the kinds of social structures that are most likely to produce them.

For our purposes they may be still more instructive, since, in apparent contradiction of our theses, of the hundreds of Latin American constitutions written since the beginning of the nineteenth century, almost all have been models of liberal, open-class thinking. Almost none has been fascist in character; almost none (if any) sought to create estates or castes, or publicly aimed at throttling individual or class mobility. But against all such regimes revolutions were mounted.

It is, however, striking that most analysts agree that of all these revolutions, only Mexico, though more recently Cuba may be added, has experienced a "genuine" revolution.[30] To explain this prevalence of "revolution without fundamental changes" by simply pointing to the constant interference of the military, as so many commentators have done, is to answer a question with a question. Similar is the explanation that there has been no sizeable middle class, which since the time of Aristotle has been thought to be a source of political stability. José Nun has partly disposed of both these together, by noting that much of the revolutionary activity in Latin America, especially in modern times, *has* been military, but has also been in fact generated by the middle class.[31]

A more radical hypothesis, but one consonant with a link between (a) the revolutionary potential and (b) the tension between the family elements and processes of class mobility and rigidity, and also one in harmony with my earlier statement of theoretical propositions about how societies operate is this: the New World subregion witnessed a rare phenomenon in world history, a conquest which disrupted, undermined, and broke the native cultures, so that for a considerable period of time, upwards of two centuries, these societies lived in a state of disorganization, or anomie.[32] In this respect, they are unlike the Chinese under the Manchus, the Indonesians under the Dutch, the Indians under the British, the Algerians under the French, and so on. The only comparable cases on a huge scale might be the Roman Empire and the Mohammedan expansion in the century and a half after the death of its leader.

In the earlier chapter on illegitimacy in different cultural and social structures, I have analyzed the technical meaning of "cultural and social disorganization," as well as offered actional indices of its degree. Those indices were also linked with the concept of national integration, which has come to be of some importance in the study of new nations.[33]

Although these indices, hypotheses, or facts about the New World apply to the Caribbean populations as well as to the black population of the U.S. in the recent past, they do not characterize all "poor" areas, such as India.[34] There, the local village is internally both socially and culturally integrated, and culturally integrated with the larger Indian cultural pattern. Through a lengthy series of intermediate links, it is increasingly integrated socially with the national social system.

These structural weaknesses in New World emerging countries had many consequences, but important for our understanding of revolution is that these various barriers obstructed the distribution of the *rewards* that are necessary for effective acculturation, or for generating any substantial commitment of the masses to the political system as a whole.

NORM COMMITMENT, FORCE, AND ECONOMIC EXPANSION

These hypotheses raise a most important set of questions for sociological theory, although this is not the place to examine them thoroughly. Let me state only the most important problem for exploration. Contrary to much contemporary social, sociological and anthropological theory, I am asserting that major societies can operate with a substantial degree of anomie. Textbook discussions suggest that this is unlikely. Under the assumption that anomie is not by definition excluded from any society, we can begin to ask at what levels of anomie a society can continue to operate, and at what costs.

If my speculative description of much of the New World is correct, these conditions would explain in part both the prevalence of rebellions and the rarity of Jacobin Communist or radical revolutions in the region. It is at least understandable why there would be a substantial number of dissident people, a high degree of *ressentiment*, especially among the masses. It also seems clear that dissidents would be *tempted* to revolt, knowing that a relatively modest amount of resources would be needed. That is, most potential rebels would not have to be anxious that a mass of people would rise in anger to smash their threat to the existing regime or system. Most people would not care greatly. On the other hand, we could not conclude that the success *rate* of revolutionaries would therefore be higher: lured by the lesser "cost" of mounting a revolution, a much higher percentage of revolutionary groups with far too little resources might make the attempt.

These hypotheses complement the general interpretation of revolution as a response to the tensions between family aspirations on the one hand, and family protection of its members against selection by merit, on the other. Indeed, that tension was and is high in Latin America. They do not, however, explain *each* revolution, because in such a generally disorganized state (again, in the technical sense outlined above) common to most Latin American (and Caribbean independent) societies, a relatively minor incident, a personal quarrel, a local dispute, might *trigger* a new revolution. That is, the necessary conditions for revolution were endemic.

Before commenting further on this point, let us briefly take note of three related factors, often brought into the analysis of revolutionary potential in Latin America in the past: (a) the military; (b) economic stagnation and boom; and (c) civil rights.

Since there has been a low commitment to the regime, the system, or its norms, *force* or its threat has been a primary mode of social control. Indeed, there is little else (for instance, normative consensus) by which to achieve it. This has meant, in turn, the frequent domination by the military, as well as the frequent overthrow of one military junta by another. These were often the only groups who in fact could command that much force, or could achieve control. *Coups* by military groups should, under these conditions, achieve a higher *rate* of *success* than those by civilian groups, and I believe that has been the history of Latin America.

Since a substantial part of the population has not felt any great commitment to the system, they have accepted the legal restrictions against their using violence only so long as and to the degree that they have been forced to do so, or have been paid off by the rewards they received. Since, on the other hand, they have not ordinarily been engaged in a deep *ideological* struggle, they could be persuaded to cease their revolt by modest payoffs from other groups or rebels or the government, when it has had the time to act.

It is a partial corroboration of this view of anomie that the Caribbean nations which have been independent, Cuba, The Dominican Republic, and Haiti, have had very revolutionary histories, while the political units (not, during comparable periods, much less anomic, I think) under the control of strong Western military and police forces have not, whatever the local revolts and disturbances of minor amplitude.

Similarly, because many of the developing nations *outside* the New World are *not* integrated in one or more of the ways specified above, because in fact a moral consensus is very weak, military control should be common there as well—as of course it is.

It is entirely possible that the pervasive failure in national integration throughout much of Latin American history would not have occurred had there been any steady economic expansion.[35] I do not know what current estimates of economists may be, but it is my impression that in most Latin American countries until perhaps the beginning of this century it would be difficult to demonstrate any great increase of Gross National Product per capita from the Conquest period, and nearly impossible to demonstrate any great increase in the amount of product consumed by the average peasant per year.

Aside from the *ressentiment* this fact engendered directly, it meant that there was no steady expansion of job opportunities, few new jobs for new talent to enter, and stronger pressures on the have-families to hold tightly to what they already controlled, rather than open their network to outsiders from lower strata. This set of forces, of course, made even less likely a full integration of individuals or villages into the Iberian or Western pattern. Whether, conversely, a really open system would have itself generated greater economic growth is another question. I am inclined to believe it, but I know of no reliable data to bolster the belief.[36]

Latin Americans, especially below the favored classes, have not generally enjoyed full civil rights in the sense of protection from arbitrary arrest, impartiality in the courtroom, freedom of speech, and so on, in addition to the right to vote regularly with some hope that their votes would determine who next held high office. The guarantees of civil rights have, evidently, a great stabilizing effect on the political system. They reduce the revolutionary potential by creating an open market for dissent, in which (to use Lipset's phrasing) elites must compete for support. Under these conditions, the only way they can achieve power is by evolving solutions for the problems that now make the populace resentful. By thus incorporating into their programs the goals which otherwise would become the revolutionary platform, the potential rebel is left without important issues. Reciprocally, the populace develops a stronger commitment to the system, and is thus less willing to support a rebellion. It is instructive in this respect to reread the *Communist Manifesto* of 1848, to see how modest its demands are: much of its program has been incorporated into modern political platforms or legislation (if often circumvented by administrative reinterpretations).

Yet leaders in most nations believe it violates common sense to permit their opposition to advocate openly the removal of leaders, to spread antiadministration opinion, or to escape punishment if defeated. The lessons to be drawn from nations in which civil rights are protected are hard lessons to believe.

It is not entirely certain, on the other hand, that the common sense of beleaguered and suspicious leaders on this point is wrong. There is not much evidence in a society that is already rent by dissension, by strong ideological polarities, or even by great apathy and little normative order, that the simple inauguration of civil rights' guarantees will ensure stability. Instead, it may be that without a substantial degree of consensus as a precondition, such that any group of leaders can trust almost any other in power, there would be no gain in political stability from so apparently desirable a program.

As a final note, I have been asserting that the lack of norm commitment, the lack of attachment to the system, and a high revolutionary potential, is partially caused by a closed class and/or caste system and closed mobility channels, created on the foundation of societies undermined and disintegrated by the Conquest. That is, along with a lower normative commitment to the system there was a pervading *ressentiment* about the blocking of mobility channels. Fundamentally, the very efforts of top families and top strata at forming a permanent clique or class to guarantee permanency to their privilege, merely created a situation in which high political and social rank was continually destroyed by revolution.

Final Comment. That a high rate of social mobility has contributed to the political stability of the United States has been expressed implicitly or explicitly by a goodly number of writers. Interestingly, Marx's predictions gave some prominence to this factor, but asserted that *downward* mobility among most of the population, and upward mobility (or maintenance) of a few would lead to revolution. Empirically, this polarization did not occur, and there are good theoretical reasons why it has not happened in industrial society—though I believe it could happen in some types of societies.

Nevertheless, his implicit notion that blocked mobility channels would be a precursor of revolution seems likely. Similarly, many have argued that the U.S. frontier offered a chance for upward mobility, thus reducing the dissidence of the population. Since no one had to accept the pressures toward rigidity in the seaboard states, it has been alleged, the class structure there remained more fluid, and the people who moved also could aspire upward.

The present essay has elaborated this hypothesis in several directions, specifying the possible effects of different mobility systems. It has also brought into prominence the key aspect of family variables as they affect the mobility process and thus the revolutionary potential among possible rebels. Interestingly, though rebels may attack the existing system of family privileges, if they are successful they typically attempt to guarantee advantages to their own kin. On the other hand, as noted, the very "success" of leading families in preventing other families from rising, or in protecting their kin who are inept, generates a greater amount of dissidence and likelihood of revolt.

In developing these ideas, some attention has also been paid to alternative theories as to how societies operate, and especially to the place of dissensus, conflict, and anomie in the social structure. As an excursus to illustrate several of the hypotheses in this essay, revolution in the New World countries was singled out for special examination.

V. THE WORLD OF WORK: OCCUPATIONS AND PROFESSIONS

12. *Incentive Factors in a Low Morale Plant*

with Irving Fowler

HERE I SHALL COMMENT ON THE FIRST TWO SUCCEEDING REPORTS TOGETHER, SINCE THEY ARE THEORETICALLY COMPLEMENTARY TO ONE another, and were generated within the same informal group. Both deal with a relatively narrow set of theoretical problems, but the further implications of both are extremely broad: they cast some light on the techniques for exploiting people, and the social effectiveness of letting people take part in decisions that affect their welfare.

The general level of accomplishment has been, I think, higher in the sociology of work than in almost any of our subfields, perhaps because it contains such a fascinating interweave of normative, non-rational factors with an encompassing, rational, economic and technical structure. It exhibits especially well the particular illumination that sociology brings, for instance, that even where we are given a set of predictions based on, say, maximization of income, technical efficiency, a hierarchy of authority, and official rules—all of which seem to afford a good foundation for neat predictions—we can be sure that they will be partly incorrect unless we know the interplay of social variables with them. Conversely, we can select a most anti-normative, deviant "job," such as picking pockets, safecracking, or prostitution, and we shall once again uncover an orderly social pattern. Indeed, the very content of the pattern is remarkably similar among very different occupations both high and low.

Many factors have combined to encourage much research in the world of work that lies within industrial bureaucracy, which has been carried out by both sociologists and social psychologists. Corporations furnished project funds even when foundations and the government were less generous. Perhaps most large corporations have by now acquired at least a small research staff for this range of inquiries. The problems have seemed to be linked with variables recognized as "important," like economic power, command and authority, productivity, and commitment. On the other hand, because Americans— and the situation is not different in most other Western nations— have so accepted the values of efficiency and high output, that they did not feel their research was biased, although a few critical sociologists (myself included) observed and reported that bias over two decades ago.

Nevertheless, productivity *is* likely to be a sociologically fruitful focus, because it is a nexus where the manager's aims and pressures are strong, but where workers may well resist or feel apathetic. Hundreds of researches, and doubtless thousands of pamphlets, speeches and books, have tried to tell managers how they could make their employees happy but productive.

The links between those two last aims is not so uniquely American as one might suppose. Folk wisdom has always guessed that workers who like their work group and work, whose home life is pleasant, and who feel committed to the rules of enterprise, will also be more effective as workers. In industrial sociology, this has been stated as a correlation between high morale and high productivity.

Another value bias in the sociology of work—one which I cheerfully confess to sharing, and which is visible in both the succeeding research reports—is that people enjoy their work and do better work if they can have some voice in deciding the level of output, innovations, choice of coworker, and so on. Here again, however, the bias does not destroy the hypothesis; it may still be both true and fruitful.

In the second of the two succeeding analyses, a step is made toward stating the *conditions* under which that hypothesis is correct. Obviously it is extensible to all political organizations, not alone to work units. Nevertheless, as analysts we must be aware that it does have limits. If, for example, the ruler is more concerned about losing command than losing production or loyalty, he may correctly perceive that participation could be dangerous.

Moreover, even if the ruler, entrepreneur, or leader believes in the hypothesis, but begins with recalcitrant or apathetic subordinates, he must not only risk short-term losses, but must also invest a good many inputs of rewards, encouragement, praise, and even socialization in order to reap the benefits of such a policy. Nevertheless, it is clear that the common sense of leaders has not yet tested the limits of this broad insight, and sociological analysis still seems more practical than their policies.

The present analysis is concerned with informal social relations in a small urban feeder plant of the automobile industry. The report contains three major sections: (1) Directions in which research of this type is shaped by the values of the society; (2) The structural position of such a feeder plant, together with implications of that structure; and (3) The informal social relations within the plant which are the response to this structural position.

It is a truism to state that the direction and focus of research are channelized and shaped by the biases of our society. It is again a truism, though less often kept in mind, that such biases need not affect perceptibly the validity of research results. Two values of importance in the present context may be noted as affecting present-day "industrial sociology." They have, of course, affected various specific researches and the field of social psychology generally. These two values may be stated as themes or propositions: (1) That groups whose members stand in harmonious relationships to one another turn out considerably more production (it may be remarked parenthetically that of course the value of high production itself has probably structured more research in American industrial sociology than perhaps any other single value, frequently causing it to be classified by some as managerial sociology),[1] and (2) by a process of home-town nostalgia, familiar in content to most urban sociologists if not analyzed as process, the small plant and its informal social patterns are thought to be the model industrial unit from the standpoint of pleasant social relationships. It may be suggested, however, that the general neglect of field research in such informal relationships is reinforced by still further biases. These may be listed briefly, without elaborate comment. They are: (1) Our interest in power foci, as represented by huge industrial plants; (2) a belief, usually only implicit, that by describing informal social relations in smaller work teams within large industry we are at the same time describing the relations to be found in the small plant;[2] and (3) a tendency to identify the modern small plant with the "ideal-typical" small plant in the literature of economics, where it appears as a phase in the development of the industrial revolution, before the rise of mass industry.

It is with reference to this third bias, the identification of the small plant with an evolutionary phase of industry, a sort of social fossil, that the *second section* may be introduced, the economic aspects of the structural position of the modern small feeder plant. To do so, however, requires a clarification of the meaning of social structure, and its relationship to action.

Sociological analyses contain frequent references to "informal" and "formal" social structure. As is the case with many major concepts, they are used in a variety of senses. There is no need to discuss all of them at this juncture.[3] The meaning most central to the present discussion of the economic relationships, and of the pressures imposed upon the factory by those relationships, stems from the familiar conceptual set, "structure-function." For structural purposes, one needs to present statically the major elements in a configuration, and the functional aspects are best treated in terms of the effects of those elements upon each other. The former aspect treats composition, trait or element listings; the latter deals with process and interaction.[4] The structural components in any integrated whole allow considerable variation in "informal" behavior,[5] but they do impose strains on certain types of action, and facilitate others. This is true, of course, for the structural components of any configuration. The many possible variations of activity within a given structural nexus suggest the need for considerable study of the ways by which structures impose such strains or facilitate such actions.

Within the larger structural pattern of economic action there is a social structure of lesser magnitude within the factory itself. The latter may not effectively dovetail with the former, although there are several possible social structures which can do so. Informal action may, in turn, fail to serve the explicit goals of this smaller structure, and indeed a number of observers have devoted some attention to the ways by which the informal behavior of workers may actually frustrate in part the formal structure of a given plant.[6]

Nevertheless, the possibility exists that the informal behavior of a group of workers may conform to these formal demands, and that this may be the case even where there is disharmony or low morale within the social group. It is suggested that this situation may occur if the following conditions are met: (a) the goals are simple and are clearly defined; (b) the skills for attaining those goals are well known and possessed by the individuals in the group; (c) the functional roles are made clear; and (d) the external pressures toward conformity are strong.

The position of the small feeder plant in modern industry is often such as to approximate these conditions. This type of plant has only an external resemblance to the beginnings of industry in the nineteenth century, and in terms of numerical importance is becoming an increasingly larger proportion of the small plants in our economy.[7]

The external similarities of the modern small plant to the ideal-typical small plant in the literature of economics are obvious. Both were presumably begun by an entrepreneur who has amassed capital, often risking his own. He has some technical ability, a considerable amount of capitalistic enterprise, and frequently has absorbed much of the capitalistic ethic described in textbooks. Further, the number of workers is small, and he knows each of them by first name. The workers see each other daily, and they joke among themselves and with the owner. At times, the latter may step in and work with the production group, as supervisor or laborer.

However, the economic context of such a plant is different from that of its nineteenth century predecessor. It has arisen as part of the modern physical decentralization of industry. This decentralization is not alone an attempt to avoid high wages. Physical centralization was a historic answer to the fact that technical knowledge, skills, and markets were themselves concentrated. The cliché that physically centralized production is necessarily more economical derives from a failure to see that varying dispersal patterns are more or less efficient, depending on which of the production variables is less subject to manipulation.

Correlative with this physical decentralization is a financial decentralization of a specific kind. The prime example is the automobile industry, although it is likely to be exhibited in other mass assembly industries, and of course many examples may be found in agriculture. This financial decentralization may be described briefly: A small plant, organized independently or with the aid of a parent company, is a contractor or feeder plant for the parent company. All its production goes to the parent company, and is tailored specifically to the needs of the latter. It has no choice over the products, and naturally has little opportunity to gear its production to a broader market. It is, thus, dependent on a larger organization which fosters competition and consequent price cutting and which does not concern itself with the labor relations of the small plant or its wage policies.[8]

It is seen that this feeder plant structure is different from the textbook picture of the small plant in the past. However, its spread to many regions, and its increase within existing industrial areas, indicate a need for analyzing the resultant social relationships in such a plant, in particular their orientation toward saving, speedup, and "stretch-out."

White Company is one of some 80 electroplating plants in the city of Detroit, nickel and chrome plating automobile parts. Its workers, non-union, number from 15 to 50, depending on fluctuations in the automobile industry. Begun since the war, it is now financially successful against strong competition.

This plant was studied in three observational shifts covering the entire working day, by as many researchers. One of the investigators had previously worked for a period of three months as a semiskilled laborer in the plant, before the study began. During this period he made extensive diary observations at the end of each work day. Nine months later, the three observers entered the plant under management auspices, explaining to the workers what was being done. The observers made systematic notes of social processes within the plant. In addition, personal interviews were arranged, sociometric diagrams were drawn, and a modified morale test was given at two separate points in the period of observation. The managerial group was interviewed both formally and informally, and production and personal records were studied intensively. Interviews with the entrepreneurs laid the basis for a description of the plant's history.[9] The investigation continued over a period of four months.

In spite of technical and personnel changes since the original participants observer's diary observation, it was soon clear that essentially the same patterns of social relationships continued as before. This plant did not use semiautomatic electroplating equipment, although such machinery is found in electroplating plants with a larger capital investment. Nevertheless, the production level of such plants is only about 12% to 14% higher than for White Company.[10] Few personnel records were kept. There was a standard policy of firing anyone who showed any interest in unionism. Hiring and training practices were not formalized and the number of workers varied widely from day to day, depending upon immediate contracts. There was practically no job training. No more than a few minutes were spent in pointing out workers' duties and in introductions to co-workers. Workers exhibited considerable animosity towards the owners as well as the production manager. In addition, clearly evident clique formations divided the workers into small groups, usually with only a grudging acceptance of one another. In spite of some suspicion that the observers were hired by management, workers soon made explicit their grievances and even their personal troubles.

An unformalized but clear system of cost cutting was evidenced in two main areas. One of these was constituted by five explicit managerial practices, all of them effective answers to the pressures inherent in the position of the plant in the economic structure. The other main area lay in the character of speedup and stretchout induced by the informal social structure of the workers themselves.

The character of these managerial practices sets the stage for the social relations within the plant, in which internal and external pressures toward work combined to push production upward in spite of low morale and social disharmonies. They would be called "poor" personnel policy by many, but the savings from these measures are obvious.

1. *Repairs* were neglected, and workers were expected to make up for this mechanical ineffectiveness.

2. *Personal equipment* was not quickly replaced, forcing the workers to take special care of safety equipment.

3. Many *safety practices* were neglected, such as measures of protection against acids and high temperatures.

4. *Hiring and training* were fitted with a situation of high turnover, so that new workers were given little training, and fired if they did not quickly learn to turn out a standard amount of production. The new worker received a beginner's wage long after he had learned to produce at a standard rate.

5. *Over-all wages* were so low that the most highly paid workers

received only average union wages for the industry. In addition, the workers did not receive the usual union fringe concessions: vacations with pay, paid holidays, rest periods, etc.[11]

As to the wage pattern:

The comparison of wage rates is based on the two following sources. First, the rates of average workers in a "typical" union plant in January, 1948: These rates were for 52 forty-hour weeks per year.[12] Second, the wage rates of White Company's most highly paid workers, its "key" personnel: The computed rates were those for June, 1948, and were for an indeterminate number of forty-hour weeks per year. These rates were pieced together from the company's crude pay-roll records. The earlier (and lower) wage rates in January, 1948, were never carefully examined. But they indicate that many of the workers gained increases of five to ten cents about that time through individual bargaining. If these earlier rates were compared with the "typical" union plant, the contrast would have been the more striking.

Wage Rates in a Typical Union Plant
and in White Company

LABOR CLASS	AVERAGE RATE PER HOUR FOR WORKERS IN UNION PLANT, JANUARY, 1948	RATE FOR "KEY" WORKERS, WHITE COMPANY, JUNE, 1948
Polisher and Buffer (days)	$1.545	$1.50 (lower)
Polisher and Buffer (piece)	1.775	
Plating Leader	1.595	1.45 (lower)
Shift Leader	1.495	
Operator	1.345	1.40 (higher)
Racker (male)	1.145	1.25 (higher)
Racker (female)	1.145	1.10 (lower)
Inspector	1.245	1.20 (lower)
Packer	1.195	
Trucker	1.215	1.25 (higher)

These practices, important in themselves, also helped to structure social relations in the plant. The resultant was a set of informal social pressures which pushed toward high production at all times.[13] These social pressures represented an interaction between the type of worker hired and a social structure channeled in the direction of "stretchout" and speedup.

The types of workers may be grouped into two main social categories, (1) *high turnover personnel*, and (2) *key* workers. (1) The high turnover personnel in turn may be divided into several groups. The first of these can be characterized as *part-time* workers, some of whom were students seeking temporary employment. Other part-time workers were friends or relatives who worked briefly in order to help key personnel or to tide themselves over a period of unemployment elsewhere. A second group of *high turnover* personnel were experienced workers from other companies who used the plant while they were on strike or layoff. In addition, there was a third group, just entering the labor market. It will be immediately noted that all of these high turnover workers would or could adjust to personnel policies which might incite considerable resentment in larger, unionized plants over a longer period. Even the experienced workers in this category, nearly all union members, did not overtly object, since their future employment and plans lay with other plants elsewhere. It may also be noted that this was true whether one considers wages or working conditions.

However, it must be obvious that the selection of such workers could not constitute a working force in itself. Any social group selects, but it must also socialize.[14] By a process of *adult* socialization not sufficiently described in the literature, these people must be made a part of the work organization. This function was mainly performed by the group called *key personnel*. Key personnel in this plant seemed to be extremely heterogeneous. However, closer analysis revealed a number of common characteristics. First of all, most of them were in a poor competitive position. Several of the women needed jobs desperately in order to help dependent males. Other workers had various physical defects which would prevent or hinder their employment at a large plant with less flexible hiring practices. Second, many of them had been with the plant since its beginning. Third, all of them had been tested by repeated managerial demands for extra, over-time, or holiday work and had met this challenge. Fourth, almost all of them could perform nearly every task and could constitute for an absent worker without great difficulty. Fifth, it was they who made the decision as to the acceptability of any workers into the informal group activities.[15]

The position of the plant in the economic structure imposed strains toward high production, and management attempted to push the workers toward this end, substituting labor for capital. The selective characteristics of these workers suggest the type of informal work process which developed. It should be noted that although informal social relations can be pleasant to the worker, if in a small plant they are *not* so, there is then no room for escape without quitting the job. Informal practices of speedup and stretchout were followed even without explicit suggestions by foremen. In each such case, one or more key workers would initiate a work pace which the high turnover group had to follow. Those who did not follow such a pace were exposed to reprimand by word, gesture or look from their co-workers. If they continued this lack of cooperation, informal pressures on the foremen by the key workers would eventually cause their discharge. If a worker was absent, it was understood without any necessity for explanation that each man would have to contribute more to the work process during that day. Because of the timing aspects of electroplating, frequent bottlenecks occurred. However, these bottlenecks did not necessarily mean delays in production. They rather meant that at such times the key workers would attack the bottleneck with increased energy and, with the spontaneously induced help of the high turnover personnel, would erase the difficulty. If this in turn produced a piling up of units at a later phase of the plating process, then the key personnel utilized the same practices and again the bottleneck was relieved.

It must be understood that these key personnel accepted the definition of management in such *actional* terms, but not internally. One must speak here of alternatives. The alternative to compliance with high production demands was discharge; and in the case of a number of workers, employment elsewhere would be difficult. The status and power of the key personnel were higher than those of the high turnover personnel, and of course they obtained some recognition from owners and foremen. Expressions of resentment against management were, then, fairly common; and from time to time a given worker would utilize one of several techniques for evading the speedup.[16] He might, for example, spend a considerable amount of time in the washroom, or delay his return to work from lunch, or indulge in horseplay. At times he might refuse to cooperate in relieving a bottleneck. All such practices, however, were temporary and unsystematic. Even when the workers felt that management had no interest in them as people, there was little choice as to alternatives. The constant appearance of foreman and production manager, frequently working side by side with the production personnel, offered little chance for escape.

Thus, a particular type of small plant, increasing in numbers, is found in an economic structure demanding high production. The reaction of the personnel in this particular plant is not the only possible one. However, the reaction fitted well the pressures of that position.

Further, it is clear that major structural components apparently necessary to effective action in the face of disharmony or low morale are to be observed here: (a) clearly defined, simple goals; (b) skills are well known and are possessed by the group; (c) functional roles are made clear; and (d) pressures toward conformity are strong from outside the group itself.[17]

As a consequence, a selection process put into key positions those individuals who fitted the structural demands. These key workers helped to indoctrinate or weed out the new workers. And the informal relationships which developed were such as to maintain pressures toward high production in the face of considerable animosity toward the owners and among the workers themselves.

It is thus seen that there is no simple relationship between harmony, morale, and production; between informal relationships and worker harmony; or between formal structural patterns and worker reactions. The shaping of research by certain value orientations has left a number of areas still undefined and in need of considerable empirical investigation. The feeder plant is one definable type of small plant, increasing in number, which lends itself to the study of these relationships.

13. *Work Incentives in a Self-determined Group*

with Nicholas Babchuk

ANALYSIS OF SOCIAL RELATIONSHIPS IN WORK UNITS HAS SEEMED TO
MANY SOCIAL SCIENTISTS A FRUITFUL TASK BECAUSE SUCH UNITS ARE
not only "natural" (if not quite spontaneous) but also more amen-
able to the types of experimental controls necessary for a scientific
sociology. The problem of experimental controls cannot, however, be
reduced to one of locating groups whose characteristics are sufficiently comparable to approximate a satisfactory classical design for
controlling variables. It is also a problem of locating the variables or
patterns of variables which *need* to be controlled.

The present report concerns one of a series of studies whose aim
was to locate patterns of variables important in group motivation
within the industrial structure.[1] The research proceeded on the assumption that no simple, high, and universal correlation among the
social factors in work situations is to be found. It is precisely because
there are so many social factors in interrelationships that we frequently find low correlations in social research. As is the case in
other scientific fields, such low correlations may mean that (1) The
relationship is a spurious one; (2) One or both of the items between
which we correlate is a complex item; or (3) a *system* of interrelationships is involved so that Correlation X, though real enough, is
not high except under a closely defined set of circumstances. Much
of our fumbling, as well as much of our self-castigation, derives from

one of several sources: (a) We have not been sufficiently precise in our levels or types of abstractions; and thus (b) We have failed to evolve a research design which would delineate adequately the crucial variables. In addition, however, it is possible that we have (c) failed adequately to exploit the possibility of hewing fairly closely to the concrete, but have attacked the problem directly in interrelational terms. In short, the research problem must be met by an *adequate location of what is important,* not alone by exact measurement and tight logic in the research plan.

The present research, like the previous study, attempted the location of crucial variables, and corroborated the results of that study in these respects:

1. Morale and high production do not have a simple correlational relationship.[2] Aside from the almost unavoidable ambiguity in the terms at this stage of the study, it seems possible to conclude that (a) High production may occur even with fairly low morale; and (b) High morale and high production often do occur together, not necessarily because of traditionally accepted reasons, but because many of the physical and social conditions which produce the one are also those which are important in the creation of the other. The sets of conditions overlap but are not identical.

2. Although specification of numerical weights must wait on better tools, it is necessary to introduce the *external* situation, both economic and social, in so far as it is one set of interactional factors limiting the range of possible behavior within the analyzed situation.

3. Small group work behavior is not a simple pattern of rejection of managerial needs and demands. Under certain patterns of social conditions the clique will strongly work to enforce managerial demands, and even to enlarge or change their meanings.

4. It follows from (3) that under a more specialized set of interrelationships the work unit or clique may assume the right to make and execute decisions ordinarily considered managerial.[3]

Let us see the concrete meaning of these complex propositions within the research situation.

DESCRIPTION OF THE WORK UNIT

In this study, the work group was a selling unit composed of 18 persons, of whom 14 men and one woman constituted the sales force. A manager, assistant manager, and a stock boy made up the rest of the section, engaged in selling men's clothing in the basement of a department store. This store, Ryme Company, calls itself "the largest cash and carry store in America," with over 1500 employees. During depression and prosperity, Ryme Company has been successful in a very competitive field, coming to occupy several large buildings in downtown Detroit. Although the company does sell quality merchandise, its reputation is that of a low-price store. Its management has shown considerable ingenuity in the field of merchandising, and would be classed as "liberal" in its personnel policy. It was one of the first large department stores in the city to bargain collectively with its employees, and has consistently paid higher wages than other comparable stores.

The work group in this study was unionized and was made up of skilled sales personnel. The department itself is rated one of the most desirable work areas in the Ryme organization. There is comparatively little turnover, and management has in the past often recruited its assistant managers from this unit. The individuals in the work unit had an average tenure of 12 years with Ryme at the time of the study, and were generally placed in this section as a reward for "good work." As a consequence, the sales personnel had above average seniority rights, in addition to union protection. Their base pay is and was one of the highest in the store. This economic security is related, in turn, to the fact that both seasonally and secularly there has been a steady and strong demand for the merchandise, men's basic clothing. Further, the commissions are higher than the average for the store as a whole. There are, then, high status and pecuniary rewards for the members of this group, and the individuals are and have been "high producers" in their task of selling.

A THEORETICALLY IMPORTANT CONTRAST

So far, this description holds for the time of the study.[4] The description is, by report of the respondents, also accurate for an indefinite period in the past, including a period prior to 1941, when there was comparatively low morale. (The development of low morale at that time will be noted in a moment.) The apparently anomalous fact of "good" working conditions and low morale should be presented in three separate steps: (1) a contrast with White Company, described in an earlier article,[5] which might have been expected to exhibit low morale, considering its working conditions; and (2) a brief analysis of the structural strains within this selling unit which temporarily created a state of low morale. Following that, we will note (3) a social innovation developed by this group, creating and maintaining a state of high morale.

Perhaps a synoptic contrast between Ryme and White Companies is most useful as the first step. Selecting some of the salient factors in any analysis of the work unit, the contrast might be as follows for the periods of low morale:

Work Unit Variables	White Company (Total Group)	Rhyme Company (Basement Group)
External economic situation	Feeder plant in auto industry; unstable demand	Men's basic clothing; steady with a secular rise
Command of skill	Individuals had adequate command of the low skills	Command of fairly high level skills
Significance of job	Manual labor: Semi-skilled job status	White collar: selling
Intra-plant job security	Extremely low	Very high
Union status	Non-union	Unionized
Intra-plant prestige	Fairly low, even for the dominant clique group	Select group in the organization
Intra-plant social relations	Expressions of personal antagonism	Expressions of personal antagonism
Personal relations outside the plant	The data indicated personal problems	No data
Group self-determination	Almost none	Almost none
Fit of personality job demands	Situation too unsatisfactory to isolate this factor	Members liked the type of work
Economic rewards (other than security)	Wages lower than union scale	Among highest paid in the city or store
Engineering factors	Makeshift and inadequate engineering (supply, heat, safety devices, etc.)	Adequate except during intergroup conflict

In spite of unavoidable terminological ambiguities, the contrast is clear. Taking into account the job expectancies of the industry, low morale in this Ryme Company group appears anomalous, while we would expect low morale in the White Company work force. Yet both exhibited low morale. It is, of course, just such apparent anomalies which are often productive of theoretical clarification.

It will be remembered that in the article which this parallels, the suggestion was made that there might be high production with low morale under specified conditions: (a) Goals are clearly defined and simple; (b) Skills are well known and are possessed by the group members; (c) The functional roles are made clear; and (d) Pressures toward conformity are strong from outside the group itself. This type of situation is not uncommon, although it is clear that the conditions need greater specification. In the case of Ryme Company, the goals are not simple, but in terms of the level of skill possessed by the members they were easy to achieve. Functional roles were fairly clear, in spite of contrasts, and the pressures toward conformity existed as rather high individual rewards (money and intra-organizational prestige) along with supervisory pressures. It must be emphasized, however, that these conditions only *permit* high production with low morale; they do not *guarantee* high production.

In synoptic contrast with White Company, then, this work unit would seem to have been "ideal" in 1941. Nevertheless, this group unanimously cited that period as one of discontent, bickering, conflict, and dissatisfaction. Were the dissatisfaction and intra-unit conflict caused by a loosening of group standards regarding rewards and work conditions, following the classical analysis of Durkheim? The answer seems to be a negative one. What we observe rather is two sets of conflicting pressures fairly common within industrial society, particularly in the area of selling, each of them demanding different work habits and different sets of social relationships. Specifically: there is a set of rewards, punishments and values which emphasize group action, group needs, cooperation, mutual help, etc.; and there is a similar set in the direction of individual production, self-help, individual ratings and bonuses, etc. The apparent paradox of these broad themes, both widely accepted throughout the society, is explained away by the ethos of our society, within which the claim is made that *it is through individual competition that the highest cooperation is achieved.*[6] Whether this latter claim is well founded needs empirical study.

We can, however, note that for the case under study the claim must be rejected. The period of low morale was one in which these contrary pressures were accentuated. In order to retain employees who might have wanted to leave the store for better-paying defense jobs, management introduced a new wage plan.[7] Under the old system, there was a base payment plus a commission of 1%. Under the new system, the employee had the option of the old system or a straight commission of 6% on all final sales, depending on which was the higher figure for the week. Since the highest individual ratings and bonuses were given to those with highest sales total, the sales personnel began to use a number of expedients for achieving this goal, "Sales grabbing," for example, was a common accusation, and covered a number of practices such as taking a customer who seemed to be heading for another salesman. A salesman might be busy with one customer, but attempt to prevent a second customer from going to a second salesman—a practice called "tying up trade." In order to have adequate displays of needed merchandise, both display and stock work (sorting, arranging, ordering, checking, etc.) are required, but the bonus-oriented salesman was charged with avoiding such time-consuming work. "High pressure" selling was common, and there was considerable bickering and quarreling during and after consummation of a sale. During this period, *production continued to increase* (possibly due to purely external demand forces) although employees and management in the unit were dissatisfied with the straight commission system which had been put into practice. Take-home pay had become sharply differentiated as among the employees. Some of the men earned relatively and consistently less than their coworkers under the new plan; while others earned a great deal more pay in certain seasons and never less under the new pay plan as contrasted with the old one. Most of the informal group relationships, as well as the informal rules, which ordinarily prevent selling practices from becoming completely individualistic, had broken down under the economic pressure of the straight commission plan, in the early part of 1941. Thus it was that even under "ideal" working conditions there was low morale.

A SOCIAL INNOVATION MADE BY THE WORK UNIT

This work unit merits considerable attention, however, since it thereupon *created a social pattern which tended to eliminate low morale without visibly affecting the already high production.* Its practical consequences were very great, and they are suggestive theoretically as well. This social innovation, called "pooling," was introduced in the latter part of 1941 by two employees with the cognizance of a lower-level manager. The plan was not officially permitted or recognized until all sub-units in the department had informally established the plan. Informal pooling began with a distribution of stock work in one of the sub-units. The members decided to cooperate with one another by dividing the stock work equally. Soon the originating members agreed to cooperate in all work areas. However, this forced them to equalize sales volume among themselves, so that as a consequence each might receive equal pay. This was accomplished by setting a quota for a period of time, comparable to the industrial "bogey." As noted previously, level of skill was high, so that there was only minimal suspicion that any given individual might not be able to contribute his share. When a member was low in sales, as seen by checking the cash register, others would feed sales to him. Any person below quota would be given supplementary credit, so that tallies would be equalized, until everyone was selling an equal volume of goods. If the quota was made by all members in the unit before a given time period had elapsed, then a new quota was set.[8]

The apparent success of pooling soon led other departments to join the system, until all units had been incorporated. The immediate supervisor was the only representative of management in favor of the idea at first, but after all units had joined, top management took over the task of handling the bookkeeping and other formal details. At the present time all persons in this section receive an equal pay check at the end of the week, regardless of individual cash register readings. Subsequently, pooling spread to other selling units in Ryme Company.

CONSEQUENCES OF THE INNOVATION

The problem which this innovation was designed to solve is a common one in industrial society: unlimited individual competition creates many personal antagonisms. The group typically develops informal rules to prevent the complete acceptance of managerial pressures toward the highest possible individual output. Under certain conditions, in this case the introduction of a straight commission plan in a boom period, these rules break down and (in accordance with classical sociological formulations) the members of the group are dissatisfied. They may even be ineffective in certain work areas for which no direct reward is given (display work, stock work, refunds to customers, etc.).

The solution offered is, however, an unusual one, and its consequences deserve comment. The solution was, first of all, a *self-determined* one, and secondly, was in the direction of establishing a *group* pattern for handling the various tasks in the work of selling. Further, and central to the present exposition, the group thereby began to make and execute decisions ordinarily called managerial.

The consequences may be variously classified, but most of them may be subsumed under the headings of (a) division of labor, (b) distribution of work tasks, (c) planning, (d) communication, and (e) discipline. Since the individual earns the same amount as his fellow-workers each week even if his sales tally is low, he can devote more attention to tasks which he likes. There is no economic loss for seeing to it that good displays are made or that sizes and types of merchandise are adequate. The greater increase in effectiveness, however, is caused by a more efficient distribution of labor. When one salesman is waiting on a customer, he has no incentive to "tie up" a second customer. He need not "invade" the territory of the second salesman, and can merely hand over the entire transaction to the other salesman, if the customer wishes to purchase an article in the territory of the second salesman. If one group of articles is in great demand at one time, other salesmen help in attending to customers. If, because of heavy sales, the stock has become disorganized, or in short supply, a salesman can be detailed to take care of the situation with no fear that he will lose by helping the group. Such a decision may be made by the supervisor, but may easily be arrived at by group consensus, on the basis of work distribution at the moment.

Since the individuals become oriented toward the need of the group as a unit, planning on a unit or departmental basis is seen as a useful activity. Common problems are not handled on an individual basis or by referring them to management.[9] Since each individual will be affected equally if sales are poor, bottlenecks develop, unsatisfactory merchandise is bought, etc., there is some pressure on everyone to contribute to the needed solutions. The decrease in personal

conflicts arising from "sales grabbing" and other hostile sales practices permits greater communication, and the gradual recognition by
management of this group orientation permits a much freer flow of
ideas and information both upward and downward in the hierarchy.

As noted in the case of White Company, the small group can be
an effective disciplinary agent. At this ultimate level, there is no escape from surveillance, and one's fellow workers cannot be easily
fooled. Malingering cannot be explained by glib excuses to the boss,
and a consistently poor job cannot be blamed on others. Similarly, in
the case of Ryme organization, where pooling has become an official
plan justifying discipline of the poor producer, everyone is his brother's keeper. When the completely individualistic plan was in effect,
in the early part of 1941, complaints were made, but the individual
could attempt to justify his actions in terms of an individualistic
ethic. If he grabbed sales, it was in order to "make more money," an
acceptable if not highly rated goal in our culture. If he failed to cooperate in work which led to no individual sales, he could answer by
admitting cynically his single-minded interest in the pay check.
Management, in turn, was giving rewards to just such individualistic
competition. An occasional rebuke for failing to cooperate would not
lead to group-oriented action as long as rewards were being paid on
the sole basis of individual sales tallies.

The effectiveness of group discipline now lies precisely in the fact
that the question of individual advantage cannot be raised cynically.
Most of the hostile sales practices have been eliminated, because they
help no one. On the other hand, if the salesman attempts to avoid
work, there is no escape from criticism, and he is actually reducing
his own pay check. Work problems turn from "Whose advantage?"
to "Which is more effective?" Failure to cooperate hurts the shirker,
in pecuniary rewards as in social relations. The managerial areas of
work planning, supervision, and discipline are also problem areas for
each member of the group, since through their impact upon the
group they affect each individual.

In terms of total group sales, "production" has increased since the
plan was finally put into effect. High morale did not exist before the
inauguration of pooling, but prevailed after that point. In intensive
interviews, not one employee believed that the present selling plan
should be changed. Such statements as the following were common:

"I'm willing to work harder because I feel better." "Ever since we started pooling, I don't have to worry about my job outside the store. When I leave work, I can forget about it." Or, "We don't aggravate ourselves. No one cuts a throat."

Perhaps a warning should be appended at this point. The study offers some corroboration of an earlier investigation which suggested that (1) morale and high production are independent variables; (2) outside economic and social pressures limit the range of reactions within the work unit (in this case, allowed experimentation, since the company was not economically marginal, and the period was one of boom); (3) small work units will under certain conditions put pressures on individuals to conform to managerial demands; and (4) under further specified conditions, the work unit may make and execute decisions ordinarily considered managerial. However, because of the dramatic character of the present case, there is a temptation to take a further step and conclude that (5) self-determination of work conditions is the prime determinant of high morale.

Although this is a tempting conclusion, let us look at it with some reserve. Sometimes called the "democratic" or "human" element, this variable has usually been discovered to be necessary for high morale and, often, high output (whether measured by units produced, problems solved, etc.). Here let us recognize our biases. Any research design we are likely to create, however conscientiously we do so, will not adequately test this element as against its usual polar opposite, "authoritarianism." The person we choose to be the authoritarian will probably not create the most effective authoritarian situation, because he has not been socially trained to do so. Moreover, he will not be a socially recognized leader, etc. (It is possible, too, that for similar reasons we cannot create the polar opposite, the "democratic" leader or situation.) Further, we cannot factor out the importance of this element, since all our subjects will have been reared in a culture which values "democratic" patterns highly, and thus will not always respond to the authoritarian situation or leader.[10] No amount of "psychological trait control" for purposes of experimentation will isolate its importance, as long as we choose subjects only from our own culture. This cultural limitation on the range of the experimental design must be recognized, if we are not to extrapolate unwarrantedly from our American data. However, it may be true that in *our* culture self-determination is significantly related to high morale.

In addition to this general warning as to self-determination and morale, it must be remembered that the individuals in the selling unit described here were skilled in their craft, with high prestige, union backing, job security, and long experience. It seems unlikely that an unselected group of workers could have so seized the initiative in order to ameliorate their unsatisfactory work situation; or, having seized it, could have effectively executed it. Knowing their craft meant that many mistakes of a practical order would be avoided. Their secure status meant that they were not afraid of losing their jobs when and if management discovered the plan and objected to it vigorously. Further, with regard to conclusion (2), we note not only the original impact of the straight commission plan, but also the fact that Ryme management is noted as "liberal," working cooperatively with union officials and having developed a "modern" personnel policy even before collective bargaining began. Finally, still with respect to conclusion (2), but even further removed from the work unit, none of these elements would have been sufficient if the product-demand had not been steady and high for many years.

We cannot, then, accept without further question the notion that the self-determined work unit is necessarily the one with highest morale. We will rather confine our conclusions to the basic four already outlined. A suggestive practical notion may, of course, be seen in the data: the material benefits which management may derive from such self-determination. Further isolation of the crucial patterns of variables will be necessary, however, as we probe more deeply into the aspirations and motivations of men in industrial society and their responses to the different group structures in which they participate.

14. *The Theoretical*
Limits of Professionalization

INTRODUCTION

THE EXTENDED ANALYSIS THAT FOLLOWS IS CONCERNED WITH ONE MA-
JOR REALM OF OCCUPATIONS, THE PROFESSIONS, IN THEIR RELATION-
ship to the larger society. It represents the crystallization of some
theoretical tasks to which I have returned many times over two decades, in much published and unpublished work.

Here, as I have done in previous commentaries in this volume, I
shall try not so much to summarize the complex set of propositions
offered in the article that are linked theoretically, but rather to lay
bare or emphasize some of the underlying orientations, biases, and
lines of reasoning that generate the larger analytical structure.

The problem of professionalization appears from the outset to be
fruitful, because we already know that in an industrializing society
the professions come to play a larger role. The category of *professional and technical workers* increases substantially. Much of the industrial apparatus depends upon the contributions made by a wide
variety of professional occupations. Although there is no evidence, in
spite of many prophesies to this effect, that professionals acquire
much political power outside their own interests, we can at least perceive that many of the decisions about policy are made by a tech-
nical-political set of committees and work units. Illuminating the
processes of professionalization would appear to cast some light on
the larger processes of social change, and the quality of large-scale
interaction within the social system.

An underlying conception that guides this as well as most of the inquiries in this volume, is *comparative*. That is, the propositions that are enunciated purport to apply to most societies. Even when the immediate context is the contemporary United States, not only are many concrete examples from other societies looked at, but the generalizations expressed have been again and again qualified by an implicit reference to other types of societies. This is not so much an anthropological bias, as it is rather an acceptance of Durkheim's dictum of half a century ago that sociology *is* (that is, should be) comparative sociology. My own sociological training emphasized this dictum, since in it no important theoretical distinction was made between the data from social anthropology and contemporary sociology.

The analysis also emphasizes, as increasingly sociology does these days, the contingency that is inherent in any social structures. The position of one occupation or another may appear to be remarkably stable over decades, but we observe that it is held intact by a great input of organization, money, political machination, and socialization. Professions are competing among themselves for all the rewards the society offers. They are constantly striving to exclude or to destroy upstart occupations or semiprofessions that wish to take over one or more of the tasks a given profession already maintains as its monopoly. Occupations do rise over time, and others do fall.

On the other hand, we must constantly keep in mind that processes that appear to be very similar may be different in both quality and quantity as between individuals and organization or subgroupings. Thus, the article begins with a consideration of competition among occupations, but soon moves to make clear that the competition among individuals for social mobility contrasts structurally at many points with the competition among occupations and professions.

This analysis is also guided by "economic" conceptions from exchange theory, a few of which were enunciated in earlier chapters. Our view here is that one can look at the competition among professions for power and privilege as taking place within a larger structural context, in which the terms of bargaining are set by preexisting evaluations accepted by members of the society. These exchange processes occur not between any two occupations that are aspiring to the status of professions, or between two professions that are competing for rank, but between an aspiring semiprofession or profession and the society. Granted, the terms of this exchange are not enunciated clearly, and the parties are not individuals. Nevertheless, by examining the cases in which the claims of the aspiring occupation are rejected or affirmed, we can ascertain what the bargain is. Consequently, I have asserted that the profession is not given a monopoly over a particular set of problems, or great freedom in its training, or privilege in its dealings with clients, unless it can claim to have set up procedures for controlling its own members.

Another implicit theoretical bias enters the analysis of the exchange, a bias which is at least fruitful even if it is in part incorrect, that a group can only with great difficulty delude the society or its public into believing that it is worth more than it really is, as measured by the values of the society. Members of an aspiring occupation can write hundreds of articles, deliver many speeches, and present dozens of television programs that are aimed at convincing the public of its vast wisdom, its efficacy in producing cures of all kinds, and its high dedication to service, but all that endeavor will not convince the society very much unless the group also improves its performance. More crudely put, the society will not give any group the power and privilege of professional status unless it manages to prove the quality of its performances in the several realms that are sketched out here.

This is a bias, of course, since we can observe that advertising does pay at times. People can be convinced that useless beauty aids, badly designed automobiles, and foolish politicians deserve to be supported by money or votes. On the other hand, I think it is very difficult to convince exploited people that they are receiving a fair share or that an occupation commands great knowledge when it does not. At least, when people have some opportunity for observing results or performances, they believe much less readily and less completely the propaganda emitted by those who seek support. Moreover, other competing occupations do their best to puncture any such illusions, when they are presented by aspiring semiprofessions or occupations. Thus, it may well be that the most important result of the public relations activities of aspiring occupations or professions is not to convince the public, but to enhance the community cohesiveness of the profession itself, and to exhort its members to raise their own standards of performance.

Another viewpoint implicitly shapes the analysis in part, the no-

344 The World of Work: Occupations and Professions

tion that social relations, evaluations, and norms, are as real as rocks, and that although these vary from one society to another, not all change is possible. The very title of this analysis suggests that view. Accepting the pervasiveness of contingency does not mean that all speculatively conceivable social systems are possible. Very few of the aspiring occupations or semiprofessions will become accepted as professions.

Moreover, in any detailed examination of the underlying *generative* factors in the process of professionalization, it becomes clear that an even tinier segment of the total range of aspiring semiprofessions or professions will ever achieve the particular kinds of professional-client relations, prestige, and influence that the great traditional professions achieved many centuries ago and have maintained ever since.

To emphasize this fundamental point, I have noted the kinds of inputs that might be necessary to raise the performances of one occupation or another to high rank, and have argued in most cases that the necessary inputs or investments would not be forthcoming. This is relevant to a still larger problem: I believe, as I have stated elsewhere, that if we are to develop practicable alternative social systems, we must be good enough sociologists to perceive clearly which kinds of social changes are possible, and in any event what their various alternative social costs might be.

A further theoretical conception is observable in the succeeding analysis, although I have nowhere called attention to it, since it is not a proposition. It is simply a blind faith, justified in other fields, that if one can locate the right variables, they seem to generate a substantial number of linked propositions or hypotheses. On the other hand, and by contrast, attempts to create "natural histories" generally fail. Both statements may seem somewhat surprising, in view of my conjecture here in this volume and elsewhere that we may be engaged in a chimerical search if we hope for some grand overarching theory in which a tiny number of variables will explain most of our phenomena, as once occurred in celestial mechanics; and by contrast, we may in fact follow in the future the model of biology, which has instead worked out a large number of small subsystems in which the interaction of a larger number of variables is shown to have orderly relations.

"Natural histories" have been a recurring task of sociologists over many decades. Unfortunately, unlike the natural history of an organism, they are extremely time- and place-bound. The sequences of phases of a decision to enter an occupation, the growth of an occupation, the birth and death of a religious sect, firm, or club, the life cycle of the family—these are crude or erroneous at the worst, and at best a skeleton on which some descriptive data can be hung. They contradict our own observations at too many points. Much more fundamentally, we are almost never able to generate from them any propositions of wider validity. The interlocking of phases seems arbitrary. More fundamentally, we cannot locate within them the underlying forces that drive or shape the successive stages in the natural history, even when it seems roughly correct. By contrast, it is the experience of most fields that a wide range of empirical observations become relatively orderly if we can locate the fundamental variables that are at work. The resulting propositions *apply* to processes, and illuminate them in many ways, but they are essentially timeless.

Here, I have examined in considerable detail the two great generating variables in the process of professionalization, for instance, the knowledge base, and the dedication to service, laying bare the many subsidiary or subvariables that make up these two factors. However, I have also suggested that a powerful cross-cutting variable, *the substance of the problem itself*, distinguishes one set of professions from the rest, and the substance of the problem itself permits us to range most of the professions and aspiring occupations along a continuum that is expressed by their *personal* relations with the client's world: that is to say, the extent to which the professional must "symbolically or literally 'get inside the client' and become pirvy to his personal world in order to solve the problem that is the mandate of the profession." This is a continuous not a dichotomous variable, but I have used it to develop a substantial number of propositions, which essentially hinge on the extent to which the substance of the problem requires this type of personal relationship.

Of course, some of these hypotheses may turn out to be incorrect, but I believe that the reader will perceive at once that not only does the use of this variable prove its fruitfulness by the propositions it yields, but that the reader's familiarity with a number of occupations and professions will convince him that they contain at least a modicum of truth. By examining this list of hypotheses and subhypotheses, we are then able to see that although the society as a whole has expanded its category of professions and semiprofessions, most of the expansion has taken place within the higher level, managerial, and scientific-technical professions and occupations, not within the four great traditional *person* professions.

Social theorists have attempted to explain why an industrial society is a professionalizing one, and in fact the percentage of the United States labor force that is *professional and technical* does increase each decade. How far can this trend go? An exploration of the theoretical limits of professionalization should illuminate both sets of processes that create this trend: how a profession comes into being, and how a society facilitates or impedes the development of professions.

Such an inquiry leads to the conclusion that many aspiring occupations and semi-professions will never become professions in the usual sense: they will never reach the levels of knowledge and dedication to service the society considers necessary for a profession. Such occupations include school teaching, nursing, librarianship, pharmacy, stockbroking, advertising, business management, and others.

Further, most of the occupations that do rise to such high levels will continue to be viewed as qualitatively different from the four great "person-professions": law, medicine, the ministry, and university teaching. This view will correspond to a social reality, for they will be less *professional* in such traits as cohesion, commitment to norms of service, percentage of members remaining in the profession throughout their lifetime, homogeneity of membership, control over professional violations, and others. In this narrower sense, then, the occupational structure of industrial society is not becoming generally more professionalized, even though a higher percentage of the labor force is in occupations that enjoy higher prestige rankings and income and that call themselves "professions." An examination of these limitations should clarify somewhat the general place of the professions in modern society.

COMPETITION AMONG OCCUPATIONS

All societies are systems of competition among individuals. Each makes his demands on the money, power, or prestige markets, and these are accepted or rejected. But each is also a member of a stratum, occupation, or of various groups whose members are in similar positions, making similar demands. Leaders and their followers in a given occupation work out (consciously or not) strategies and tactics for aggrandizement on the basis of whatever amateur social science engineering they can command. Whether these people are united, as in a labor union, or merely a social aggregate, their total collective failure or success in these exchanges has a continuing effect on the terms of *individual* bargaining in the next phase, and on the rise or fall of occupations.

But though mere aggregate effects are of some importance, doubtless folk sociology is correct in its ancient assertion that a united group can gain what an individual cannot, or that an individual's investment in a group may ultimately pay off. Skill and time invested in the formation of a guild might, for example, yield an occupational monopoly from which great individual advantage could be wrung. Raising the educational standards in medicine in the decade 1910–20 required the expenditure of power, money, and friendship,[1] but that investment raised the prestige ranking of the physician, the power of the profession in legislation, and the income level of the average M.D.

Such group efforts may also fail to yield any perceptible rise. Men invested enough to organize a Swine Breeders Association, and even wrote a code of ethics for its members, but that movement—like that of hundreds of other such organizations for which codes have been written—doubtless paid off more in friendly interaction among its members than in power or prestige in the larger society.

These processes by which an occupation tries to rise constitute a set of transactions among the occupation as a collectivity, its individual members, other related occupations, and the larger society. In the stratification of occupations, as in that of individuals, each actor decides what the other is worth and finds out what it or he is worth through the outcome of a continuing set of exchanges, of demands or offers made and acceptances or rejections received. However, for the most part these evaluations are based on values and norms each already accepts, and only over time are they created within those transactions themselves.[2]

Members of an occupation give a higher prestige ranking to it than do other members of the society; thus, they try to get more deference than others will concede. They are forced to accept less money than they want, and achieve less in protective legislation than they seek. They are held in place by their closest occupational kin (e.g., one of the various building trades will not rise much above the others), and by the refusal of others in the society to agree they are worth that much.

Economic supply and demand, shaped by such factors as monopoly, entrance restrictions, shifts in tastes, and the like will determine how high their incomes will be, but supply and demand operate in the markets of power and prestige as well. An occupation can command more prestige only if the society, applying its evaluative criteria, perceives the performances of the occupation to be better than before or higher than those of similar occupations. An occupation can enjoy more power if it can exchange some of its friendly relations, income, prestige, or political influence for legal privileges or controls.

Occupations that seek recognition as professions engage in transactions within all three markets—prestige, power, and income—with varying success. Most will not rise far or achieve professional status, but those that do rise *must change themselves.* Self-advertisement may create self-delusion but will hardly persuade others. They must be able to offer more on one or other of these markets, in order to gain more in return. In order to be accepted by the society as a profession, an occupation requires special transactions in mainly the prestige markets. If these are successful, they can be used to obtain more power and money.[3] However, merely clever transactions that yield power and money for an occupation are not sufficient to achieve acceptance as a profession.

The advantages of being accepted as a profession are obvious. However, few of even the privileged occupations can or will pay the costs of transforming themselves enough to become accepted.

Is the Professions Market a Zero-Sum Game?
Although people and occupations do compete with one another for

the rewards of the total society, whether this competitive action system can be viewed as a zero-sum game depends on the time perspective. Over the relatively long time period of a generation or so, an occupational system as a whole may produce more goods, as it may also produce more prestige or power, so that a wide range of occupations (theoretically, perhaps all) may benefit: all may rise. In such a perspective, it is not true that what one occupation gains, another must lose. In a declining social system, correspondingly, all could fall.

However, in the shorter time perspective of, say, a few months, there is only so much money, power, or prestige to be shared. If blue-collar workers succeed in raising their wages substantially, white-collar workers must lose somewhat. For example, over the past one hundred and fifty years of automation of several kinds, workers have generally assumed that each job eliminated by machinery would create that much more unemployment, and they were wrong (it was not zero-sum). But they were and are correct (because the individual has but one life, his time perspective is short) in their fear, for at any given time there *were* in fact only so many jobs: the worker knew personally some men who had lost their jobs to the machine (in the short run, it is zero-sum).

These facts are significant in the general processes of interoccupational competition, but more important for our specific concern with professionalization is that some of the actions by which a semi-profession seeks to improve its position (guided by its leaders' folk sociology) are likely to increase its own prestige or income as well as that of the society. To that extent, these actions are not a zero-sum game. Obtaining a monopoly will, of course, yield an economic advantage to the occupation and not to the society, but raising the competence of entrants, imposing quality controls over members' work, establishing centers for developing improved techniques, and so forth will yield greater production for the society, and very likely a modestly greater amount of prestige for the semi-profession as well.

Thus, over the longer time perspective in which a profession becomes recognized, its greater eminence is not likely to have been taken away from that of another profession, but has rather been earned independently, through transactions in which in fact it has begun to contribute more to the society.

Individual Compared With Occupational Competition

At more than one point we have compared individual mobility and that of occupations, as a way of clarifying the process of professionalization. A few additional relations should be added briefly. Metaphorically, perhaps one might say that the competition among occupations lies somewhere between the passivity of commodities on the market and the conscious activity of jobholders, but we can state the patterns more precisely.

1. An important contrast is that thousands of *individuals* have the same type of job, and thus compete directly; but no two *jobs* claim exactly the same charter, so that the competition is somewhat more oblique. Many jobs have overlapped sometimes, amid charges of encroachment and incompetence. Some claim part of a task, while their competitors claim it all. Some claim the right to carry out a task, but also reserve the right to delegate it to another occupation, under supervision. A few of the overlapping jobs will remind the reader of these patterns of oblique or direct competition:

> Lawyer—notary public.
> Medical doctor—bonesetter—midwife—pharmacist.
> Airplane pilot—engineer.
> Sanitary engineer—plumber.
> Plumber—steamfitter—sewer layer.
> Veterinary—farrier; farrier—blacksmith; blacksmith—
> 　armorer.
> Coppersmith—tinsmith.
> Priest—psychiatrist—clinical psychologist—social worker.

2. Although a substantial percentage of *men* rise from blue collar origins to high positions,[4] almost no occupation has risen from a low rank to the top. Midwifery did not, for example, "rise" to become gynecology. Perhaps concert artists have risen more than any other group.[5] More commonly, an occupation destined for professionalization appears at a fairly high level, and then rises somewhat, if at all.

The following patterns are more likely than the great upward movement that is observable in individual mobility: (a) a semi-profession arises from a *non*-occupation, e.g., social work from individual philanthropy or "doing good to the poor"; (b) a semi-profession claims to have a special "package" of high level skills, e.g., the city planner; (c) a profession specializes in a task that another had considered partial, e.g., psychiatry; (d) a professional specialty is built on new instruments and techniques, e.g., cryogenics or laser engineering.

3. As in transactions among individuals, competition is strongest among similar or overlapping occupations, because to some extent they are substitutable: one can be chosen; the other rejected. Especially in an expanding economy, neither an individual nor an occupation is likely to push another out by simply taking over the other's work. The rising individual rarely rises by actually pushing another out of his job, but rather gets a post another man had hoped to enjoy. Similarly, the rising semi-profession is less likely to destroy another directly than to create a new package of high-level skills (social worker, marital counselor, management consultant, architect) that other occupations possess only at a lower level or only in part.

4. In a specialized technology, most occupations (of the more than 25,000 listed in the *Dictionary of Occupational Titles*) engage in few direct transactions with the society and thus are not even known to the public. They come into existence and disappear in response to changing industrial techniques. Their members feel little collective identity and make little concerted effort to rise, other than as members of a large industrial union.

5. Especially in a local market, both men and occupations can rise to high levels of income without an equal rise in power or prestige. In the early 1960s, some school building superintendents in New York City were able to earn six-figure incomes. Mark Twain's classic foray into the sociology of occupations, *Life on the Mississippi*, describes in detail the high income and (he claims) high prestige of the steamboat pilot.[6]

Effects of Competition Among Occupations. Before analyzing the more specific elements of the narrower area of professionalization within the general pattern of competition, let us consider briefly some of the consequences of a social structure in which occupations freely fall or rise. First, the outcomes of the exchanges between occupation and the society alter the terms of *individual* bargaining. For example, the rising prestige and income of university professors as an occupation will affect the new contracts that are made. The new terms will also affect the cost—reward calculations of potential recruits, and so affect the flow and allocation of talent within the occupational system.

Second, like a lineage or family, caste or class, organization or social institution, an occupation must expend some of its collective resources even to maintain its position. Its rank is constantly threatened. Activities may range from proposing laws to the occupation's advantage to founding schools for the improved training of recruits, from publishing encomiums of the profession to establishing higher ethical controls over members.

Third, because the individual shares in the rise of his occupation, some people must decide how much of their personal resources to invest in this corporate enterprise. If the individual has himself moved upward occupationally, he may foresee an added increment from such an investment. In addition, of course, the organizational efforts of the occupation may offer still more opportunities to some individuals for prestigious leadership posts and activities.

Fourth, the total effort toward maintenance of position and the jockeying for additional rewards is a large part of the total allocation of energies and resources in the society. These aims and activities determine in part the establishment of schools, licensing commissions, research agencies, and inspection units; the granting of honors and posts; legislation concerning many areas of life; changes in technology, and so on. Such goals also shape in part the inputs and outputs of social institutions and organizations of the society; they are part of the major competitive processes that constitute much of human behavior.

Fifth, the efforts of all occupations, but especially the semiprofessions and professions to rise or to maintain their positions are a *source of social change*. As is clear from the foregoing discussion, these social changes—the research that becomes the foundation of a new profession, or a useful tool for an older one; the alterations in graduate education and post-college education in industry; legislation to protect a profession against new threats or to consolidate an emerging profession in its new privileges; the distribution of manpower—all arise in part from the efforts of various occupations to increase the various rewards they obtain from the society, to gain recognition, or to protect their privileged position from other aspiring occupations, semiprofessions, or professions.

If various occupations do try to rise, however—and many succeed to some extent, thus contributing to social change—how far can the process go? Various analysts have described a natural history of professionalization, the sequence of steps by which a semi-profession, through its transactions with the society, is transformed into a recognized profession, but these statements are neither empirically correct nor theoretically convincing.[7] Wilensky offers these steps:[8]

> Full-time activity at the task
> Establishment of university training
> National professional association
> Redefinition of the core task, so as to give the "dirty work" over to subordinates
> Conflict between the old timers and the new men who seek to upgrade the job
> Competition between the new occupation and neighboring ones
> Political agitation in order to gain legal protection
> Code of ethics.

Most of these social processes are going on simultaneously, so that it is difficult to state whether one actually began before another. For this reason, such a sequence is both time-bound and place-bound and thus accidental rather than theoretically compelling. To mention but a few examples that do not fit: the American bar, true enough, had no published code of ethics before the American Revolution, but it was well-educated and tightly controlled in its professional behavior; British barristers did not establish university training schools, but continued to train recruits through the four Inns of Court. Medicine and dentistry did not publish a formal national code of ethics until the twentieth century, but in the 1840s men were expelled from their associations for violating their respective codes. Lobbying for protective legislation has been continual in the history of occupations. The ministry still has no formal code of ethics.

In the present era, people are likely to create a formal occupational organization in order to solve problems, so that a profession emerging now is more likely than one rising a century ago to use such an association at an early phase of its existence, but it is also likely to develop a code of ethics rather early. Even when a formal code is not written, a set of such ethical understandings is likely to be widespread. At present, such a concrete set of "steps" as Wilensky's is really a description of the many *areas* in which an emerging profession must participate in its transactions with other occupations and the society.

Moreover, and much more fundamentally, these formal steps miss the essential elements in professionalization. They do not separate the core, *generating* traits from the derivative ones. Many occupations and activities have tried all or most of these steps without much recognition as professions. It is unlikely that a list of the specific historical *events* in the structuring of a profession will yield the organic sequences in its development.

The Generating Traits of Professionalism

An inclusive list of the occupations whose claims to professional status have been announced very likely would total as many as one hundred. The term is loosely used in popular language: I would hazard the guess that a majority of adults would accept the label *profession* when applied to as many as forty or more white-collar occupations.

Nevertheless, both laymen and sociologists do use various objective traits in making evaluative distinctions among these white-collar *jobs*; moreover, speakers at thousands of *professional* meetings have made hortatory and self-congratulatory references to similar traits. When tabulated, in fact, the characteristics attributed (however incorrectly) to various occupations in order to prove that they are professions show a satisfying similarity, suggesting that their foundation is a shared observation of reality.[9] The lists of traits also contain a hidden similarity, which I shall later analyze at greater length, that all of them derive from an ideal—typical conception whose closest concrete approximation is medicine and the priesthood. Ignoring variations in language, such lists report: high income, prestige, and influence; high educational requirements; professional autonomy; licensure; commitment of members to the profession; desire of members to remain in the profession; codes of ethics; cohesion of the professional community; monopoly over a task; intensive adult socialization experience for recruits, and so on. However, it seems worthwhile to abstract from such lists the core, or generating, traits, and those which are a predictable outcome of core characteristics.

It would be generally agreed, I think, that the two central generating qualities are (1) a basic body of abstract knowledge, and (2) the ideal of service.[10] Both actually contain many dimensions, and, of course, each subdimension is a continuum: with respect to each, a given occupation may fall somewhere toward the professional pole or not; and one may ask *where* along that sub-continuum any occupation may be found, even if clearly it is not to be considered a profession. Necessarily, too, at present we have no adequate measure for any of these subdimensions, and must be content with reasonable assertions about where a given type of job may fall. Let us examine each subdimension of the two core traits in turn before weighing the limits of professionalization for a given aspirant semi-profession, or for a range of professions.

Professional Knowledge

With respect to knowledge seven major characteristics affect the acceptance of an occupation as a profession. They are:

1. Ideally, the knowledge and skills should be abstract and organized into a codified body of principles.
2. The knowledge should be applicable, or thought to be applicable, to the concrete problems of living. (Note that metaphysical knowledge, however well organized, may have no such applicability.)
3. The society or its relevant members should believe that the knowledge can actually solve these problems (it is not necessary that the knowledge actually solve them, only that people believe in its capacity to solve them).
4. Members of the society should also accept as proper that these problems be given over to some occupational group for solution (thus, for example, many do not as yet accept the propriety of handing over problems of neurosis to the psychiatrist) because the occupational group possesses that knowledge and others do not.
5. The profession itself should help to create, organize, and transmit the knowledge.
6. The profession should be accepted as the final arbiter in

any disputes over the validity of any technical solution lying within its area of supposed competence.

7. The amount of knowledge and skills and the difficulty of acquiring them should be great enough that the members of the society view the profession as possessing a kind of *mystery* that it is not given to the ordinary man to acquire, by his own efforts or even with help.

The Service Ideal

The ideal of service, sometimes called a *collectivity orientation*, may be defined in this context as the norm that the technical solutions which the professional arrives at should be based on the client's needs, not necessarily the best material interest or needs of the professional himself or, for that matter, those of the society. Again, this may be defined somewhat more specifically by its subdimensions:

1. It is the *practitioner* who decides upon the client's needs, and the occupation will be classified as less professional if the client imposes his own judgment.

2. The profession demands real sacrifice from practitioners as an ideal and, from time to time, in fact. (For example, the student–professional must defer the privileges of adulthood for several years after his nonprofessional contemporaries have come to enjoy them. In each profession there are junctures or different situations in which the individual should expose himself to threats and even dangers from the larger society if he is to live up to the highest ideal of the profession: the lawyer defending the unpopular client, the military man sacrificing his life, the scientist persisting in expounding the truth against the opposition of laymen, and so on. The profession must also allocate some of its own resources and facilities to the development of new knowledge—with the result that some of the knowledge of its practitioners becomes obsolete— and to the recruitment of the most talented youngsters available, though in fact this increases competition within the field.)

3. The society actually believes that the profession not only accepts these ideals but also follows them to some extent.

4. The professional community sets up a system of rewards and punishments such that "virtue pays"; i.e., in general, the practitioner who lives by the service ideal must be more successful than the practitioner who does not.

It is not necessary to spell out in tedious detail just how these two core, though multifaceted, elements generate the commonly recognized traits of the established professions. A brief statement should suffice.

The income of professionals averages higher than that of other occupations because their services are needed (they have the knowledge to solve a problem) and there are no satisfactory alternatives. In simple supply–demand terms, they have a monopoly over a valuable product. On the prestige market, too, their product is valuable because of their dedication to the service ideal, because their education is high, and because their performances are above those of average people.[11] Professionals usually have a monopoly because they have persuaded the society that no one else can do the job and that it is dangerous to let anyone else try. They are permitted autonomy more frequently than members of other occupations (professionals, not laymen, are more likely to judge performance), both because others are not sufficiently knowledgeable, and because others cannot be trusted to be as concerned about the client's interest. The shaping of legislation, the manning of control and examination boards, and standards for licensing are all more likely to be in the hands of professionals for the same reasons. Because professionals must learn to abide by a code that is different from that of the larger society, a period of adult socialization is more necessary than in other occupations. Because the rewards are high and a period of adult socialization (in which professional commitment is inculcated) is more likely, members are less willing to leave the occupation, and are more likely to assert that they would choose the same work if they were to begin again. A code is necessary to implement such service ideas, but it is also an expectable correlate of any subcommunity.

THE ASPIRING OCCUPATIONS

Any predictions are subject to all the hazards of peering into the future, and especially so with respect to the problem of predicting that a given occupation will not develop a sufficient knowledge base for professionalism. Speculation will, however, serve as a vehicle for discussing further the dynamics of professionalization. These estimates divide occupations into three groups: some have become professions, some will become professions, and some will not. Later, we shall want to distinguish *among* the successful ones those which are closer to the four great *person*-professions.

These occupations have become professions in the last generation: dentistry, certified public accounting, clinical psychology, and certain high levels of the scientific and engineering fields, such as electronic engineering, cryogenics, aeronautical engineering, and so on.

These semi-professions will achieve professionalism over the next generation: social work, marital counseling, and perhaps city planning.[12] An unlikely category is that of various managerial jobs for nonprofit organizations, such as supervising principals and school superintendents, foundation executives, and so on.

The following occupations will not become professional: within the medical situs, none will achieve it, with the possible exception of veterinary medicine. Osteopathy is gradually being absorbed into the ordinary status of physician. Nurses have been pressing hard toward professionalism, but will not move far. Chiropractic will remain a marginal or quack occupation, as will podiatry. Pharmacy will not change its status much. Next, school-teaching will not achieve professionalism, nor will librarianship.[13] Many articles and speeches have argued that business management, public relations, and advertising are, or should be, professions, but none of these will achieve such a status.

This is not to say that all of these will retain their present positions relative to one another. Teachers will doutbless move upward in income relative to other semi-professions, and so will librarians and nurses. I am merely asserting that though perhaps all of these will move somewhat towards improving their economic and prestige positions, the journey will not be long and the movement upward not great.

Let us now examine some of the elements or factors involved in the process of professionalization, using various occupations to illustrate the process.

THE DEVELOPMENT OF PROFESSIONAL KNOWLEDGE

On both the prestige and the economic markets, the aspiring profession must be able to offer its control over a more substantial body of codified, applicable knowledge than that controlled by other occupations.[14] However, to express doubt as to whether an occupation has a sufficient knowledge base to be accepted as a profession is likely to arouse considerable emotion among its practitioners (a test of this assertion is easy, if hazardous, to make). Any doubt expressed on this matter undermines the basic claim of any occupation to respect or pay from the society.

Such arguments are difficult to settle because three complex facts or relationships make any measurement difficult: (1) every occupation knows *some* facts or can do some things better than a supposedly higher-level profession (TV repairman–electronics engineer; pharmacist–medical doctor); (2) admission to every occupation or profession of any importance is so hedged about with rules that the entrant must learn far more than he will typically apply in the course of his practice, and there is much overlap in the abstract knowledge base of adjacent occupations (e.g., the physical principles relating to ultra high frequency waves are relevant to a wide range of occupations and professions); and (3) it seems at least speculatively possible to build a broadly scientific foundation for almost any job, i.e., it may be possible to develop a great deal of organized abstract knowledge applicable in any task, whether acting or typing. How much reality must there be, then, behind the public concession that the knowledge base of a given occupation is of professional quantity and quality?

Of course, how much knowledge the profession possesses is defined in part by the society itself. The witch doctor may have very little valid knowledge, but by the canons of truth of his society he may have a great deal. But we need not move so culturally distant as the witch doctor; the physician until the late nineteenth century is an equally good example. And certainly the validity of much psychodynamic knowledge of our time rests on shaky empirical grounds.[15]

Actually most professionals do not use much of their abstract knowledge and perhaps for most problems do not really apply principles to concrete cases, but instead apply concrete recipes to concrete cases. The physician learns much but utilizes relatively little of it in his normal practice. Similarly, it is not possible to obtain a journeyman's license in most of the skilled trades in large American cities without learning a great many skills and principles that are almost never used. One may almost say that practitioners are typically overtrained; on the other hand, such over-training is a partial guarantee (because they will also forget much of what they have learned) that they can at least handle with ease the run-of-the-mill problems.

Because of this overlapping of knowledge between subordinate and superordinate occupations, an intermediate medical occupation developed, both in Germany and in Russia, between the nurse and the full-fledged physician: the *Feldscher*, who handled many simple medical problems. In U.S. military life, too, the corpsman often has to act as the near-equivalent of a physician. Moreover, the suggestion has been made at times that one way to improve health in underdeveloped countries is to reduce the usual long training required to become a physician, as most ordinary medical problems can be solved by someone with far less training.

It might therefore be argued that professions have persuaded a gullible public that all members must command an unnecessarily large body of abstract knowledge, that practitioners do not need that much knowledge in their daily practice, and that occupations exist or could be developed which would carry out most of their tasks with a lesser amount of knowledge. A brief consideration of this knowledge overlap clarifies further the nature of the knowledge base that is believed to be required.

Although much of the knowledge demanded for entrance to any profession may not be used frequently in its daily practice, this is also true for any highly-trained occupation. Consequently, in ranking the various occupations by their knowledge, the society can consider only the amount of learning required for admission. That is, if the physician uses one-third of the knowledge he had to acquire to become a doctor, and the electrician has roughly the same experience, then their actual applied knowledge ratio remains the same, i.e., the M.D. still has much more.[16]

In addition, just how much knowledge is required by society for acceptance as a profession is in part a function of how much the public believes is needed for crises. With reference to the major professions, the social pressures within the profession as well as the larger society demand that *all* the available knowledge be mustered for crises, or at least be on call. The man in jail, or with an abscessed tooth, will accept any reasonably competent practitioner, but he would prefer the highest level of skill he can command. A departmental chairman may have to accept lesser talents in his or her competition with other universities, but he or she would prefer to obtain the best physicist possible. Even if intermediate-level medical occupations, or similar ones within any of the professions, were to develop, the society would continue to recognize the highest level of the profession as responsible for *all* of the available knowledge.

Moreover, to the extent that some part of the professional's knowledge becomes so routine that it can be mastered and applied by a secondary occupation with much less training, such ancillary occupations do develop, but they are harnessed to facilitate the work of the professional. They are given what Everett C. Hughes calls the "dirty work," the tedious, less interesting, preparatory, or cleaning-up tasks —ranging from preparing the patient for the X-ray machine to educating the junior college student who has little chance of entering a university. Often, indeed, such helping jobs are even defined legally as subordinate, in that people in them are not permitted to practice except under professional supervision.

It seems likely, then, that one cannot assert that a profession is simply a type of occupation that requires its students to learn some knowledge in the form of codified, abstract principles.[17] In fact its members must acquire a good bit more knowledge than other workers, so that a lengthy education is needed, not only in a *practicum* but in book learning.

Another hypothesis may be presented from these notions: at any given phase of development of professionalism in a society, the successful aspirant occupations must demand that their trainees learn about as much as the trainees in the recognized professions. The nineteenth century dentist, architect, or engineer had to learn less than the accepted professions of their day and enjoyed a correspondingly lesser rank. The physician, granted, knew much less than the modern physician but did have to learn more (much of it incorrect) than most other occupations. After the American Revolution, the intellectual demands on U.S. lawyers were lowered and the profession suffered a corresponding loss of standing.

It is interesting, and perhaps significant in this connection, that all four of the oldest professions in Western society have maintained their high knowledge standing since the Middle Ages and have not been displaced by the new knowledge of the Renaissance and modern eras. Of the four (law, medicine, clergy, and university teaching) only medicine was scientifically technical in content when it arose, and even it always had (as it still has) a large element of human relations in its practice and principles. What one must say, rather, is that in fact these four constituted the highest intellectual levels to be achieved at that time. They required the longest study and the closest supervision by teachers over the acquisition of knowledge. To this extent they attracted the ablest of students and commanded most respect. In important ways to be noted in a moment, they remain the core of a sub-class of professions that differ from others.

The contrasting cases of librarianship and dentistry illustrate the importance of the knowledge base. The latter has certainly achieved a professional status in our generation, and I have asserted that librarianship will not achieve it.[18] It is only recently that dentistry began seriously to build adequate scientific foundations both for general practice and for the specialties within dentistry. Correlative with this change has occurred a rise in income as well as in prestige. It was always possible to develop the general biological knowledge on which modern dentistry increasingly rests, but dental problems were not defined as important enough to require that much investment in research.

It is an amusing quirk of fate, too, that dentistry is the only one of the medical occupations to achieve professional standing without being taken over by medicine. The ancillary medical techniques such as anesthesiology or radiology became medical specialties, and thus still under the jurisdiction of medicine, when their knowledge base became sufficient to justify independent professional life. Dentistry, on the other hand, achieved its body of knowledge as late as the past generation, after the relationship between the two occupations, medicine and dentistry, had become relatively crystallized, i.e., the physicians considered the dentists not to be worth incorporation because of their low ethical standards and their merely artisan skills.

By contrast, though individual librarians have been learned, and librarians in general are as dedicated to knowledge as they are committed to service, the public is not convinced that there is a basic science of librarianship: the skill is thought to be only clerical or administrative. The university librarian's most significant reference group is the university professor, who believes his mastery of his own field is superior to that of the librarian, as is his knowledge of related areas. Nor does the average professor have the experience of being saved from a serious difficulty by the scientific knowledge of the librarian.[19] Moreover, there has been little research and thus little accumulation of knowledge relative to the central professional task of librarianship, the organization and codification of library materials and the development of principles concerning the retrieval of that information.

The school teacher (especially in the primary schools) has a similar relationship to her knowledge base, which is not so much the curriculum content—most adults believe that they could master that after a short period of study—but the technique and principles of pedagogy. This content is, however, relatively small in amount and shallow intellectually. More important, because the crucial matter here is the interaction of public and occupation, even in the area of teaching techniques the teacher is not thought to be a final arbiter. Most college-educated Americans believe they understand such techniques about as well as the average teacher. Nor does it seem likely that the body of pedagogic knowledge that is the teacher's area of prime responsibility likely to grow much over the next generation.

Nevertheless, perhaps all occupations depend on general natural principles, and these can be discovered. Consequently, one can speculate that every occupation may claim that to understand his task fully, the recruit must study all of the relevant general knowledge. Claiming such a deeper knowledge base, any occupation could then demand a higher prestige ranking. For example, the electrician would have to be an electrical engineer, learning the most advanced physical principles of electricity. It is at least true that as new knowledge accumulates, the occupation may have to change its training practices somewhat. The captain of a modern passenger liner and the international airlines pilot must engage in the formal study of general scientific knowledge as well as learn their practical applications.

The crucial point seems to be the claim of the occupation to the most highly developed body of knowledge in the relevant field, i.e., who is in possession of that body of knowledge. In medicine, it is the physicians themselves, together with men working in the basic biological sciences; in law, it is the lawyers themselves and law professors who are working on the analyses of cases; in engineering, it is the engineers themselves, together with men working in the basic physical sciences. By contrast, even the skilled worker in the occupations of electrician, plumber, TV repairman, and so on have no immediate contact with the sources of their knowledge, or those who develop it, nor has the ship's captain or the airline pilot. The society, in effect, gives the authority of knowledge to the professions as the centers of knowledge from which the knowledge used by subordinate occupations will flow.

A further complexity in this relationship to knowledge may be brought out. Granted that one need not be a sanitary engineer in order to do plumbing or an electrical engineer in order to wire a house, this additional knowledge would certainly not at all be a handicap. If all waiters had to obtain advanced research training in social science and the organic chemistry of foods, they would not on that account do a less adequate job. Against this possibility, however, is the unwillingness of the society to invest great sums in either the development of such formal schools and scientific knowledge, or to pay the much higher incomes that would be necessary to balance the added cost of that investment.

This judgment as to the worth of developing an extensive body of scientific knowledge applies to most occupations. Conceivably, extensive research could be devoted to the tasks of almost any occupation, so that it would be both the master of a body of abstract principles and the source from which additional knowledge would come. Ultimately such research and accumulation depend, however, upon how much support the society is willing to give for the additional knowledge, and how much it will pay for services with such a base.

The key element in this continuing set of decisions is whether the society believes it suffers great costs because members of an occupation do not have sufficient knowledge. Greater investments in research and training will be made only if people feel that important negative consequences follow from the lack of a great knowledge base in the work of, say, typists, nurses, chauffeurs, or teachers. Doubtless, too, potentially positive consequences will count. If the society will not support such an accumulation, the occupation will not become the master of such a highly developed body of principles as is necessary for acceptance as a profession.

Management, whether in school administration, business and manufacturing, or philanthropy, is especially interesting in this context because a considerable body of scientific knowledge can be organized that would be applicable to its problems. Because corporations do calculate costs and even pay for research, many studies have actually aimed at discovering general principles of management, most of them in sociology or psychology.[20] However, not only the society but managers themselves believe that success or failure is not dependent on having been trained in these principles and that a good manager can be an intuitive master without knowing them at all.

The medical occupations illustrate a related principle, that it is the profession which is to be the *judge* of valid knowledge. The case is interesting because medicine deals with problems that are of great concern to everyone, so that precision of control, however expensive, is thought never to be sufficient. As a consequence, the society is willing to pour large amounts of personnel and money into research. However, this added knowledge becomes a base only for new specialties within the medical profession, not for independent medical professions in anesthesiology, pathology,[21] pharmacy, nursing or midwifery. The physician remains the judge of valid knowledge and the added data for greater precision are put into his hands, not those of the nurse or pharmacist. The latter two retain a watchdog function, but the society judges their knowledge and their right of judgment to be ancillary.

As any profession accumulates knowledge, perhaps a larger part of its knowledge comes to be developed by men essentially outside the profession, i.e., by specialists in the subsciences.[22] At the same time, more practitioners *within* the profession become researchers as well.

Power relations also determine which occupations develop and control the knowledge base. A sufficient public will hire quacks to permit them to continue existence if laws are not enforced, and correspondingly some individuals will give money to quacks to "develop their knowledge." Especially in the realms of health and mental disease, almost any kind of research program can obtain *some* support. The established profession, however, retains control over the crucial junctures at which knowledge is transmitted to the next generation or required in examinations. As a consequence, the "knowledge" developed by such aberrant research activities is likely to have a relatively short life.

Who Are the Relevant Groups?

Even if the aspirant occupation moves somewhat toward the development of as much knowledge as is considered adequate for professional standing in a given society, it cannot easily persuade other related occupations of its new achievements. The most closely related occupations have more to lose by such a concession and are also more likely to be able to affect the standing of the occupation with the general public. In a mass market and a growing economy, some part of the public may grant the new claims, but general recognition will likely not occur unless allied occupations also concede them, even if grudgingly, and thus validate them to a larger public.

To implement their own skepticism, the established profession often has legal as well as informal powers. Previously we noted this relationship in discussing the blocked position of the pharmacists, who are, as Adam Smith pointed out long ago, "physicians to the poor at all times, and to the rich whenever the distress and danger is not great." The legal and social controls in the hands of physicians would render profitless any attempt by pharmacists to reorganize greatly the areas of their knowledge. The librarian is not blocked legally from independence, but his most important reference and validating group—university professors—is not likely to alter its judgment of the knowledge base of librarianship.

Public relations and advertising, like management, both have access to a considerable body of social science knowledge, but all three are viewed by the general public as well as by their most relevant reference groups—other businessmen and social scientists—as possessing or needing little more than concrete experience to guide their solutions. In addition, of course, their solutions are thought to be primarily determined by reference to profit, not the needs of the client.

In contrast with these instances are the power and evaluative relations among social work, psychiatry, and clinical psychology.[23] For the past generation, social work has moved steadily toward acceptance as a profession. It has done so primarily because training standards have risen substantially, and its knowledge base has widened and deepened. Not only have social work schools utilized the newest scientific knowledge from sociology, psychology, and psychiatry, but they have also been carrying out research programs of their own.

Rising in evaluation because they are in effect offering more on the prestige market, social workers have also been favored by having no strongly entrenched opposition. One consequence is that at this time it is likely that most of the psychotherapy in this country is being done by social workers, not by psychiatrists or clinical psychologists. Social workers have seen most of their clients in settings where no psychiatrist directly supervised their work. Most social workers have been women, who have not fought hard against the claims to control made by psychiatrists, who, in turn, have consequently organized few counteractions or bothered to set up a pattern of surveillance. Surely of equal importance in the failure to establish legal controls is the fact that the people whom social workers help are not likely to be potential clients of psychiatrists; psychiatrists, therefore, have had little economic stake in a system of legal controls. Now, however, it seems likely that psychiatrists could not regain this control even if they tried to do so.

Clinical psychology overlaps with both social work and psychiatry, and here again it developed in a context in which the medical specialty could not effectively withhold recognition or legally block it from independence. Clinical psychology developed as an offshoot from a firmly-established professional status, that of university professor and researcher. It could claim some respect from related occupations and the society for its general scientific base, psychology, and for its new scientific findings in a specialty. This battle has been relatively strong, but because clinical psychology enjoyed both an independent organizational position and its own body of applicable learning, it could command full professional recognition in a short time.

AUTONOMY, SERVICE, AND KNOWLEDGE

Occupations, like people, claim the right of autonomy and usually fail to get it. Professional autonomy—in a bureaucratic era, this means having one's behavior judged by colleague peers, not outsiders—is a derivative trait and is based on both the mastery of a knowledge field and commitment to the ideal of service. Clearly, an occupation cannot claim independence unless it also asserts that no related occupation possesses superior knowledge of its tasks. However, the autonomy cannot be granted without trust, and members of the society are therefore not willing to concede autonomy unless they are persuaded that the profession can and will control the work of its members in the interest of their clients. Finally, even if the body of knowledge is thought to be adequate, and the aspiring profession proclaims the ideal of service, members of the society will not grant autonomy unless it is persuaded that the occupation *must* be trusted if it is to do its work properly.

Indeed, this last requirement is what sets apart one sub-category which we call *person*-professions, from the rest, a group which is closer in many respects to the older established ones. Moreover, as we urged at the beginning of this paper, in an apparently professionalizing occupational structure, this important sub-group is *not* growing at a rapid rate. In this narrower sense, then, the occupations and the society are not moving much toward professionalization.

Within this set of dependent relations or tensions among autonomy, service, and knowledge, there are three extreme outcomes which aspiring professions try to guard against, but over which they have little control: (a) the occupation may achieve some cohesion, but expend this greater strength in merely improving incomes with little concern about the ideal of service; (b) the occupation may, as its knowledge base grows, simply split into numerous sub-associations, so that little cohesion develops; and (c) because the occupation can be supervised by a bureaucracy and the *substance of its work* requires little autonomy, it is simply absorbed into high-level bureaucratic positions. All three outcomes, of course, undermine the claim to trust and autonomy that is one basis of professionalism.

The first outcome, cohesion with self-seeking, is perhaps best exemplified in the labor unions or the medieval guilds, although all professional associations engage in this to some extent. Any operative code of ethics can be read either as a set of protections for the client or a coolly-executed plan for serving the ends of the profession. For example, competition is frowned upon, as is the exposure of fellow incompetents; advertising is forbidden, even if the professional's skill *is* superior; prices should not be lowered; and so on. Any relatively cohesive group is likely to arrange for its best interests to some extent if it is permitted to do so. The principle of cohesion and brotherhood in the profession tempts the organization to ignore the societal mandate under which it receives privileges but imposes self-controls. Nevertheless, this possibility of cohesion only for the purpose of self-seeking seems not to have occurred in the major occupations seeking professional status. The sporadic efforts of some engineers to develop unions during the 1950s were not successful. Of course, some high level occupations with little claim to professional rank have been able to obtain considerable financial and other concessions from their employers or the society when economic conditions favored such concessions. We noted earlier one dramatic case, that of the Mississippi River steamboat pilot, whose knowledge requirements were immense, though never abstract, and who was able to command a high income in the 1850s. Similarly, the International Airline Pilots' Association has been able to command incomes at the average of professionals. The pilots' cohesion has been high and so is their technical training. No one claims that they should have autonomy any more than a truck driver or a steamship captain. They serve the needs of their employer for hire, and indeed passengers would be somewhat alarmed if they thought that such matters as destinations, speeds, altitudes, or fares were to be decided independently by the pilots who direct their planes.

The second extreme outcome is that the aspiring profession or occupation fails to develop any substantial cohesion, and instead splinters into many sub-groups. This occurs especially in the engineering fields, where in spite of a considerable amount of energy and money devoted to organization, the pattern of splitting into specialty associations (exhibited in the earliest periods of professional engineering associations in the nineteenth century) continues apace. In these fields, the operative code of ethics is likely to be the ethic of science, although the paper code follows closely the usual professional codes.

The rapid growth of knowledge and its organization into specialties encourages each sub-group to focus on its own interests, while members in the broader profession do not believe that they lose much by their lack of cohesion. The typical client (usually a corporation) can measure or have measured to a considerable extent the competence and performance of the engineer, so that the client is in relatively little danger of being exploited; but, as a corollary, the engineer—or any person whose training lies in similar areas—can do as well in the market without the monopoly that a cohesive professional association claims. Engineering associations have not succeeded in maintaining a monopoly over their fields, and indeed many practicing engineers do not bother to obtain state licenses.

This second type of outcome of the tension among autonomy, service, and knowledge overlaps with a third, perhaps the most characteristic professionalizing pattern of this epoch, the absorption of high level occupations and aspiring professions into a bureaucracy, largely because the substance of its work requires little autonomy. Educational and philanthropic administration,[24] librarianship, the engineering specialties, scientists in industry, school teaching, advertising and public relations—all are likely to work in a bureaucracy and to have their work supervised or guided by non-professional bureaucrats or laymen.

The factor of bureaucracy is not the key element here. Indeed, professionals have *typically* worked in bureaucracies. Clergymen and university professors always did. Medical men and lawyers did when they were in orders. True, the bar left the Church in the thirteenth century, and the physician-cleric by the end of the Renaissance, but a high percentage of both now work in bureaucracies. A military structure is a bureaucracy. The crucial difference then, is not, whether members of a profession work within a bureaucracy, but whether *they* (clergymen, military, university professors, physicians, lawyers) or nonprofessional bureaucrats *control* its essential work.

The certified public accountant also works within a bureaucracy, though of course he may instead be chief of a bureaucratic organization. When, however, he is engaged in his most important work, i.e., the tasks for which he is *certified*—dealing with fiscal matters which he then certifies to the public—he is subject not only to the bureaucracy but also to the outside society as well. In that work, he must meet the standards of fellow professionals, not merely the commands of his bureaucracy. Indeed, he may be held legally responsible for certain derelictions of duty in accounting, even though he has been carrying out the orders of a bureaucratic superior.

If professionals, not laymen, judge each other's work even in a bureaucracy, cohesion is likely. Cohesion is needed, for without it the profession as a collectivity is not strong enough to impose acceptable controls of its own. If it cannot impose such controls, the society will not grant autonomy to the profession. Each of these relations is dependent on the others. Without such controls, the occupation cannot protect its own members, and thus will have little cohesion. Thus, as noted previously, the cohesion of engineering specialty occupations has been relatively weak, because competence can be measured more accurately than in other fields, and as a consequence the engineer can succeed in his field without belonging to an association. The profession must also be able to protect its members, even against public attack, when they live by the code.

The correlation of both autonomy and protection in librarianship may be strikingly seen in the fact that not only do librarians avoid controversy in their communities by failing to purchase books which might arouse antagonisms, but a higher percentage of the members of the American Library Association than of nonmembers do so.[25] Their cohesion is so low as to guarantee them no protection against the public, even when in the long run their best professional decisions and ideals would be to the advantage of the society.

Autonomy and Vulnerability

In this analysis we have emphasized what we believe to be a crucial *structural* element that is operative in this set of relationships, that the claim to autonomy or trust loses its point unless the client or society can *in fact* be *harmed* because of unethical or incompetent work by the practitioner; and because of the substance of the problem certain professionals cannot do their work unless they are *able to do harm*. That is, the professional *has* to be trusted if he is to do his work.

Let us consider the first point separately. How high do the stakes have to be for the society to judge that controls, whether imposed by the society or the profession itself, are necessary? Veterinary medicine is a doubtful but interesting case. At present, the level of training and knowledge required for veterinary medicine may be as high as that for several other professional occupations, but very likely the society will continue to decide that the stakes are not high enough in this case to grant professional recognition and autonomy in return for professional control over unethical or poor performance.[26]

Note, too, that the stakes cannot be very high if the aspiring occupation does not have a sufficient command of knowledge and skill to be dangerous in its incompetence. Marital counseling falls into the general group of therapies, and thus the stakes seem to be high. The counselors' work is largely not under anyone else's supervision. However, most people feel that the marital counselors do not know enough to be harmful when they fail to perform well. Those occupations that are somewhat closer to this emerging profession, with its knowledge base resting primarily on sociology and psychology and for the most part growing from the organizational activities of university professors, feel differently.[27] Much of their therapeutic work is psychiatric and psychodynamic, so that the elite of the occupation seeks to impose stricter codes of performance before state governments do.

At present, certainly, the stakes may not be high simply because most who go to marital counselors have marriages with a low chance of survival, and thus have little to lose. However, the knowledge base and therapeutic skills of marital counselors will develop further, and tighter professional controls are likely to be imposed by the occupation itself.

The image of the librarian is primarily deprecatory, not threatening: he is thought to be able to help, but not to harm. In the public view, there is little reason to give the librarian any autonomy or trust, because he can do his job perfectly well without it. At only one point is he viewed as threatening—the selection of books—and that matter is taken out of his hands with respect to nearly all doubtful cases.

PERSON PROFESSIONS

Most of the newer aspiring or recognized professions are technical—scientific or managerial; an industrializing society is also professionalizing in that sense, at least. However, the four great traditional professions are different in important structural elements from them, and we shall explore those distinctions now, keeping always in mind, of course, that all of these traits must be viewed as *dimensions* or continua, so that a given occupation may be high or low with respect to it.

The crucial difference, we have urged, is whether the substance of the task *requires* trust, and therefore autonomy, and therefore some cohesion through which the occupation can in fact impose ethical controls on its members.

In the prototypical case, medicine, this difference has been analyzed at length many times.[28] The physician cannot diagnose and cure his patient without making him vulnerable. He must probe, examine, and question in any direction his own judgment dictates, deciding independently the needs of his patient. Neither the patient nor the society would permit outsiders to witness these procedures or to supervise them. The patient permits the physician to engage in explorations he or she would not permit to even a spouse.[29]

If we place the various professions along this continuum—the extent to which the client *must* allow the professional to know intimate and possibly damaging secrets about his life if the task is to be performed adequately—a fairly clear ranking emerges, and some complex structural implications can be seen. At one extreme are the psychotherapies, and medicine generally. Next would be the confessional clergy, and then law. Following those would be university teaching and, somewhat marginally, architecture for private clients. Because both the military and certified public accountancy have *corporate* clients, they fall at about the same point along this continuum. Beyond them is the wide range of managerial and then the technical–scientific occupations.

To grasp the structural implications of this distinction it is necessary to see that some *part* of the work of even the most humane professions does *not* have the attribute of trust. Thus, the real client of the pathologist is another physician, not a patient, and this is especially so when he reports to the doctor or the hospital staff about why the patient really died. (Under the latter circumstances, he is in a position of trust with respect to his examination of that physician's work, and some of the same structural patterns are observable.)[30] The ophthalmologist in his simpler tasks of determining prescriptions for glasses develops a much less intimate relationship with his patient, but a much more emotional relationship emerges in his role as an ophthalmological surgeon. The radiologist hardly sees his patient, while at the other extreme the patterns to be noted are accentuated in the medical specialties of psychiatry, internal medicine, and surgery. The surgeon may have relatively less interaction with patients but the emotionality of the patient is high.

In a parallel vein, some distinctly non-professional jobs share a few of these traits—but not all, because they have little authority from a knowledge base—e.g., personal servants, executive secretaries, masseurs, geishas, and the like. Within a profession, too, this difference may be observed in styles of practice, e.g., some architects believe the professional should explore intimately their clients' family life in order to design the kind of home needed.

Toward the *person* end of the continuum, several structural patterns are more common. One is that clients are more likely to become emotionally involved with their professionals, e.g. the probability of a transference relationship is higher, because the client feels more vulnerable. Second, the danger is greater that the professional will be tempted to exploit his clients, because they are more likely to be faithful believers. Consequently, a set of norms for appropriate client–professional relations becomes part of the professional's working code of ethics. Moreover, he takes some time to teach these norms to his clients. Indeed, fellow professionals will judge him partly on the basis of how effectively he keeps his clients under control. Some of these norms are: the professional should not become emotionally attached to his client; he should not give any special favors to one which may disadvantage another; he should rate his client's needs as primary, and should not even be seduced by the client's description of his own needs into following procedures that run against his real needs; he should keep the relationship within the limits of the task to be done; and so on.

Because client–professional relations in this sub-category of professions are more likely to become emotional than in others, and their clients feel more vulnerable, these professions are more likely to be socially *salient*: they are universally known, unlike technical-scientific specialties; they figure in novels; stereotypes are created about them; they are more definitely recognized as distinct occupations.

In a parallel fashion, these professions and the men in them are more likely to live in a swirl of gossip and ambivalence. It is difficult, for example, to end a group conversation that starts with one person's account of "my doctor. . . ." The university professor is the intellectual glory of his country, but in the United States he is also the long-haired fool, as well as the dangerous dreamer. Indeed, I would offer the hypothesis that the more closely a professional's life style approximates the ideal of his profession, the greater the amount of ambivalent gossip generated about him, within the circles that know him.

The client's vulnerability stems from both his exposure under diagnosis and the lesser technical control that the professions at the human end of this continuum enjoy over their problems. All patients die; half of the law cases are lost, as are almost half all battles. Many students do not learn much, even when professors do their best. Psychiatric patients terminate therapy eventually, and psychotherapists (like parents) have a touching faith that their patients have improved, but this outcome is often debatable.[31] And how many sinners have clergymen really saved from eternal damnation?

One of the important structural consequences of this is that in these professions more than others the inept can be more easily protected.[32] Indeed, if clients are treated well as human beings, they are less likely ever to question the competence of their professionals.[33] In any event, as we have already noted, the structural fact is that there are no easily available techniques by which the client can test his professional's competence.[34]

Because the client cannot measure performance accurately and is vulnerable, and the profession itself has less technical control over its own problems, the only point at which assurance can be created is the *commitment* of the profession and the professional to the needs of the client whether private or corporate. Because essential behaviors may not be observable by clients or the society, and sometimes not even by colleagues, the internal controls on the professional must be stronger, as must colleague controls when internal controls weaken. One consequence of this structural relation is that ethical problems loom larger and are more frequent in the professional lives of occupations at the *person* extreme of the continuum.

Although we have not exhausted the implications of this great dimension, we must consider the theoretical problem we glossed over in the last paragraph. We have essentially said that ethical controls are stronger because they must be. But to invoke "need" or "must," even in a nonevaluative sense, expresses a faith that sociologists can no longer afford. Societies, like people, "need" a great many things they will not get. At best, if a social structure "needs" something, that will mean no more than that opportunities will be seized if they appear, not that opportunities will in fact appear.

My own view, which I emphasize is essentially unprovable at this phase of theoretical exploration, is that this relation is a *corporate bargain*. The profession is given a mandate to obtain potentially dangerous information about its clients because in fact there is no option: the client otherwise cannot be adequately helped. For three of the four traditional professions, society also imposes a restriction, i.e., the clergyman, lawyer, and medical man are not permitted to disclose professional secrets. As part of that bargain, in exchange for a considerable freedom in obtaining possibly threatening data and for the mandate to practice, the profession itself proclaims its intention of preventing its members from exploiting its clients. For example, it enlarges and specifies still further the restrictions on professional secrets, establishes control systems, and may censure or even expel members for unethical behavior. By contrast, toward the technical–scientific end of the continuum cases of ethical violations are only rarely the subject of discussion in professional councils.

Such a corporate bargain cannot be made or carried out unless the profession is cohesive enough to be able to impose such controls. Specifically, this means that it must be able to organize practice in such a fashion that the more ethical practitioners are, in general, more successful than the less ethical men.[35] Exceptional cases do occur—in academic life, the professor who takes over the work of a brilliant student, the researcher who fudges his data a bit or who alters his conclusions to fit the wishes of an employer, the teacher who exploits the emotions of his students, and the like—but it is notable that such cases arouse considerable moral indignation. They are not simply treated as incompetence or as violations of an ordinary commercial agreement. In academic life, as in other professions, most cases do not become officially known, but the informal network of judgment does operate in all of them.

We cannot treat at length the conditions under which this kind of cohesion is generated, but a brief comment is necessary beyond our earlier discussion. First, the group feels the need of some kind of protection, i.e., precisely because its professional work creates so much emotion, it is also vulnerable. Second, group cohesion usually grows as well from a set of shared experiences that other members of the society do not have: one further structural consequence is that some part of professional training is likely to be a type of apprenticeship. For the clergy, medicine, and the military, where perhaps the differences in shared experience are greater, the apprenticeship contains a period in which the trainee essentially lives apart from the rest of the society.[36] The closest similarity is psychotherapy, where the most highly valued training includes a long period of very personal apprenticeship, usually a didactic analysis of some type.[37] Third, both as students and as professionals, men in these more vulnerable occupations see one another in informal social interaction more than men in other occupations. Their success is more dependent on each other's judgments.[38] Indeed, because precise measurement is difficult, the professional will have much less validation of his competence from his visible mastery of the problem itself, and therefore must get it in interaction with his peers.

A further consequence of these relations is that men in these professions are less likely to abandon their *métier*, and are more likely to say that they would choose the same profession if they were young and faced that decision again.

A few additional relationships may be stated in a more laconic form, since by now the underlying social dynamics are somewhat clearer:

A. The greater the need for the professional to know about his client's private world, the greater is the amount of social interaction between client and professional, and the higher the possibility of intensity of emotional involvement between the two; and the greater is this possibility or intensity,

1. The more *explicit* are the ethical codes, both formal and informal, in specifying appropriate relations between client and professional;

2. The more explicit and stronger are the prohibitions on accepting close relatives or friends as clients;

3. The more heavily do status variables (age, sex, ethnic membership) count in professional–client relations;

4. The greater is the possibility of (a) using the client's emotions as a means in the solution of his problem, or (b) exploiting him through his emotional involvements;

5. The more likely it is that legislatures will consider possible resolutions or laws relating to the profession.

B. The greater the technical control of the profession over its variables, and the greater the precision of its calculations, the less need there is to obtain intimate data about the client in order to solve the problem; and,

1. The more closely does the client–professional relationship approximate a contractual one, with a specification of price and definite results as part of the agreement;

2. The less will be the personal authority of the professional, and the more likely is his advice to be of the form, "if you do so and so, these will be the results," rather than "you must do so and so";

3. The more likely it is that clients will demand proofs of competence, and the less likely that they will demand proofs of devotion to their interests;

4. The less the professional needs the client's confidence in order to do his best work;

5. The less important will be the problems of communication between client and professional, or the difficulties of learning "how to be a client";

6. The less frequently will failure in a case be rationalized or explained away in personal or unique terms ("This was the judge's first case"; "You misunderstood my exposition of the theorem"; "After the operation he did not seem to want to live.")

From the foregoing analysis, it seems clear that a considerable number of consequences hinge on this crucial variable of trust which distinguishes the *person* professions from the rest.

ACADEMICS, THE MILITARY, AND CERTIFIED PUBLIC ACCOUNTANCY

It should be emphasized that we are distinguishing a category of professions, and that doubtless over time other occupations will arise, especially of the healing type, which will take on these traits. Thus, we are not so much describing a few concrete occupations as a set of relationships.

However, three of these occupations do not exhibit so obviously as the others all the relations we have described. Let us consider them briefly. Two have a corporate client: the career officer serves the nation, and the certified public account serves (usually) a corporation. The third, the university professor, is ambiguous, because it is not clear whether he has a corporate client (the society or the university) or an individual one. Many humanists argue that the client *ought* to be the student, but some might assert that the professor has no client at all.

The first two cases are at least conceptually clear, and most of the relations we have outlined do apply wherever the proposition is not altered beyond recognition by the insertion of "nation" or "corporation" instead of "person." The military must inquire deeply into many weaknesses and strengths of the nation (production, morale, age structures, sedition, political agitation), and indeed their knowledge is potentially dangerous to the nation. Professional socialization is isolated and intense.

The temptation of exploiting the nation's vulnerability must be guarded against by an ethic that emphasizes the ideal of service, even to the point of death, and of course history is also replete with violations of this ideal. The military is both glorified and feared. Because of its cohesion and its successful assertion of autonomy within its peculiar *métier*, its incompetents are more easily protected. Proofs of devotion and loyalty are valued highly, status variables (age, ethnic membership, class) count heavily, and outsider–laymen do not often try to test the skill of the insider-professional.

Thus, where it makes sense at all to apply these general propositions to a profession with a corporate client, most seem to hold. We would expect them to be observable in certified public accountancy, as noted earlier, only at the junctures where the crucial variable we are analyzing is relatively high, i.e., not in the ordinary work of bookkeeping, but only at those points where the professional must enter into the corporate secrets of a firm, diagnose and analyze its internal and external circumstances and actions, and bear the responsibility—*certify*—to outsiders, such as stockholders, law courts, appraisers, buyers, or the society at large, for an accurate statement.

Because, on the other hand, the substance of his task falls somewhat closer to the technical-scientific end of the continuum than that of the older professions, we would expect that all the relations we have presented would be much weaker. For the present, however, these assertions remain hypotheses not descriptions, as they may apply to certified public accountancy.

Precisely because the temptation to analyze the academic at length is strong, I shall stifle it, and instead simply locate the problem. Academics are accustomed to eliminating the professor from discussions of the client–professional relationship, not because they believe the university or the society is the client, but because they feel they serve the cause of learning, not an individual person (as the priest serves God, not merely his parishioner) and because the student does not pay professors directly. Moreover, academics do not think of themselves as having a code of ethics, because for the most part theirs is the ethic of science and scholarship, which they have so fully absorbed that they do not see it as a set of rules, but as a set of norms which are relatively unquestioned. Indeed, only when they begin to see ambiguities in the ethic, as occurs in the social sciences in modern research on human beings, do university men consider whether they ought to have an explicit code, forgetting that they already follow a set of ethical rules.

Professors are also likely to think of the recurring emotionality (both love and hate) in their relations with students—and the gossip about themselves—as adventitious and unique, rather than as a structural trait of the occupation. Academics use their authority and these emotional relations in order to guide the student toward his best future, and professors feel they have the responsibility to help define their students' ends for them, rather than simply to carry out the students' wishes or serve student-defined goals. If an academic recruit is talented but exploitative or unethical, his colleagues not only press him to reform, but will refuse to recommend him to others if he persists in his violations.

In short, with respect to most of the relations outlined, the academic fits rather well, but the professor typically does not see them as organized structures, as common conditions, but as individual decisions and commitments. On only one major trait does this pattern fail, that of organizational cohesion, but this is compensated for to a considerable extent by the frequency of interaction among academics, and the informal exchange of information and judgments.

CONCLUSION

It is not possible to summarize adequately this complex analysis, but its main lines of progression can be stated briefly. Concerned with the general process of professionalization within the society and within individual aspiring occupations, we have noted the two traits that generate all the other characteristics that are considered typical of the established professions. These two, the knowledge base and the ideal of service, were specified in considerable detail, so as to lay bare their major aspects and dimensions. Much of this paper was devoted to analyzing why some aspiring occupations have risen, and others have been unable to rise: because in their transactions with the society or other relevant occupations, what they offered on (mainly) the prestige market in these two major areas was viewed as sufficient or not. Among the occupations analyzed by reference to these generating traits, and the transactions concerning them, are social work, veterinary medicine, the military, architecture, clinical psychology, marital counseling, advertising, educational administration, the management of business and philanthropy, and Mississippi River steamboat pilots.

But though the outcomes of these transactions—these bargains between an aspiring occupation and the society or relevant other occupations—do determine both the larger structure of modern occupations and the social acceptance of an occupation as a profession, we have analyzed at length a further variable that cuts *across* these two main generating variables: the substance of the problem itself. We have noted that the four great established professions of the clergy, medicine, university teaching, and the law retained a number of traits that have to do with the *substance* of their problem, rather than simply with the how high they are ranked. Specifically, we suggest that a category of occupations is set apart by a primary variable, upon which a considerable number of structural consequences hinge: whether the professional must symbolically or literally "get inside the client," become privy to his personal world, in order to solve the problem that is the mandate of the profession.

I have examined at length the close sociological dependence of these structural consequences on this variable, and have analyzed their varying form in several professions. I have analyzed to what extent these hypotheses may be correctly applied to two professions that have a corporate client, but which must nevertheless obtain what is in effect "classified knowledge" in order to serve the needs of the client. We have noted the points at which the academic profession exhibits the social patterns we have outlined, although the individual professor may not see these as structures, but as individual and unique decisions and attitudes.

Finally, it is clear that this last sub-category of professions, whose core is the four great, traditional *person* professions, has not expanded much to include many new professions, in contrast with the higher-level managerial and scientific-technical professions and semi-professions. In this much narrower sense, then, it is not entirely clear that the industrial occupational structure of the society is generally professionalizing. Relatively few professions are arising that require trust and autonomy and that can obtain it through transactions with the society.

Notes

CHAPTER 1

1. For the close ties between such theological assumptions and the actual search for physical laws, see Robert K. Merton, *Science, Technology and Society in Seventeenth Century England*, New York: Fertig (1938), 1970; or Carl Becker, *The Heavenly City of the Eighteenth Century Philosophers*, New Haven: Yale University Press (1932), 1959.

2. For discussions of the general place of historical data in sociology, see Werner J. Cahnman and Alvin Boskoff, eds., *Sociology and History. Theory and Research*, New York: The Free Press, 1964; Edward A. Tiryakian, "Structural Sociology," in John C. McKinney and Edward A. Tiryakian, eds., *Theoretical Sociology*, New York: Appleton-Century-Crofts, 1970, pp. 111-35; Seymour M. Lipset and Richard Hofstadter, eds., *Sociology and History: Methods*, New York: Basic Books, 1968.

3. The ritual genuflection of the scholarly to the Heisenberg Principle is not in order here. That principle asserts that we cannot simultaneously measure both the position and the momentum of very small things, because the energy stream needed to accomplish the one will distort the measurements of the other. More generally, we learn that the process of measurement affects the measure; and that the instruments used for measurement include the observer, too. But we sociologists cannot escape by so general an exculpation. To be blunt, sociologists cannot measure *either* position or momentum, much less both. Next, the Principle does not deny the correctness of most measurements; in technical terms, for most measurements the Principle would explain almost none of the variance. In our field, a considerable part of the variance is likely to be explainable by the curious antics of the observer, i.e., sociologists, or the dismayingly complex responses of human subjects to the sociologists' attempts to observe them.

4. See, for example, the critical analysis in Charles Tilly, *The Vendée*, Cambridge, Massachusetts: Harvard University Press, 1964; and Lawrence Stone, ed., *Social Change and Revolution in England, 1540-1640*, London: Longmans, 1965.
5. See Thomas P. Wilson, "The Regress Problem and the Problem of Evidence in Ethnomethodology," paper presented at the American Sociological Association meetings, Denver, 1971.
6. For a neat illustration of this feeling even among theorists—and it should be remembered that Darwin himself was one of the most imaginative of theorists—note how Watson and Crick, for all their free-wheeling speculation, continued to check back with the basic "facts" about which molecules *could* link with which, and with the X ray diffraction photographs of Rosalind Franklin (James D. Watson, *The Double Helix*, New York: Atheneum, 1968).
7. For example, only a handful of the two thousand "mutations" that de Vries recorded at the turn of the century in developing his theory of mutations were later conceded to be true mutations; and Lavoisier's correct theory of combustion was based on measurements too crude to serve as adequate proof.
8. See his *Fads and Foibles in Modern Sociology and Related Sciences*, Chicago: H. Regnery, 1956.
9. James L. McCartney, "On Being Scientific: Changing Styles of Presentation of Sociological Research," *American Sociologist*, 5 (February, 1970), p. 32.
10. *Ibid.*
11. For example: Alvin W. Gouldner, "Anti-Minotaur: The Myth of Value-Free Sociology," in Irving L. Horowitz, ed., *The New Sociology*, New York: Oxford University Press, 1965, pp. 196-217.
12. Even two decades ago, these links were outlined in a methods textbook, and the writers did not assume then that they were expressing any original notions; they were merely codifying fairly obvious observations. See William J. Goode and Paul K. Hatt, *Methods in Social Research*, New York: McGraw-Hill, 1952, Chapter 3.
13. Cf. Gideon Sjoberg, *Ethics, Politics and Social Research*, Cambridge, Massachusetts: Schenkman Publishing Company, 1967; Irving L. Horowitz, ed., *The Use and Abuse of the Social Sciences*, New Brunswick, New Jersey: E. P. Dutton & Company, 1971; Eugene Webb *et al.*, *Unobtrusive Measurements*, Chicago: Rand McNally, 1966; Philip Hammond, ed., *Sociologists at Work*, Garden City, New York: Doubleday, 1967; William J. Filstead, ed., *Qualitative Methodology*, Chicago: Markham Publishing Company, 1970; for an excellent analysis of these problems, see Bernard Barber, John Lally, Julia Makarushka, and Daniel Sullivan, *Experimenting with Humans*, New York: Russell Sage Foundation, 1972.
14. For an illuminating analysis of the social consequences of rigor, see

Janice B. Lodahl and Gerald Gordon, "The Structure of Scientific Fields and the Functioning of University Graduate Departments," *American Sociological Review*, 37 (February, 1972), pp. 57-72.

15. In this connection, see the major attack on Talcott Parsons's work by Alvin W. Gouldner: *The Coming Crisis of Western Sociology*, New York: Basic Books, 1970, but compare it with his empirical work, such as *The Wildcat Strike*, Yellow Springs, Ohio: Antioch Press, 1954, or *Patterns of Industrial Bureaucracy*, Glencoe, Illinois: The Free Press, 1954, whose theoretical orientation is not distinguishable from that of mainstream sociology.

16. To be socially identified with the work of Parsons is not to be coterminous with it. His specific formulations of the AGIL phases have not been accepted, and many of his analyses have been either ignored or rejected. Here, I refer mainly to his general reformulation of the broad sociological orientation that began to emerge just after World War I in the analyses of Durkheim and his school; the classicists such as Gilbert Murray and Jane Ellen Harrison; Max Weber; Bronislaw Malinowski, A. R. Radcliffe-Brown and the other "functionalists"; and the Americans such as E. A. Ross, Robert Park, and William Graham Sumner. That is, Parsons did not "create" this broad orientation, but attempted to state more clearly what its theoretical implications were.

It would be only a slight exaggeration to say that Parsons's contribution to the restatement, clarification, and crystallization of this dominant orientation is to be mainly found in *The Structure of Social Action*, that a small increment is to be found in *The Social System* and in his substantive or descriptive essays, and that little of his remaining work has been incorporated into contemporary sociology.

17. Cf. Robert E. Park and Ernest W. Burgess, *Introduction to the Science of Sociology*, Chicago: University of Chicago Press, 1924.

18. The "analogies," of Lévi-Strauss, ranging from linguistics to religion, remind one of André Malraux's comparisons in the field of art (*The Voices of Silence*). For an amusing critique of one such set of oppositions, see Paul Shankman, "Le Roti et le Bouilli: Lévi-Strauss' Theory of Cannibalism," in *American Anthropologist*, 71 (February, 1969), pp. 54-69. See also Claude Lévi-Strauss, *Structural Anthropology*, New York: Basic Books, 1963; and *The Savage Mind*, Chicago: University of Chicago Press, 1966. See also Edmund Leach, *Claude Lévi-Strauss*, New York: Viking, 1970.

19. See, for example, George Herbert Mead, in *Mind, Self and Society*, Charles W. Morris, ed., Chicago: University of Chicago Press, 1952; Arnold M. Rose, ed., *Human Behavior and Social Processes: An Interactionist Approach*, Boston: Houghton Mifflin, 1962, and Herbert Blumer, *Symbolic Interactionism: Perspective and Method*, Englewood Cliffs, New Jersey: Prentice-Hall, 1970.

20. See, for example, Harold Garfinkel, *Studies in Ethnomethodology*, Englewood Cliffs, New Jersey: Prentice-Hall, 1967; Peter McHugh, *Defining the Situation*, Indianapolis: Bobbs-Merrill, 1968; Jack Douglas, ed., *Understanding Everyday Life*, Chicago: Aldine, 1970; David Sudnow, *Studies in Interaction*, New York: The Free Press, 1971; Erving Goffman, *Asylums*, New York: Doubleday Anchor, 1961; *Interaction Ritual*, New York: Doubleday Anchor, 1967; Aaron Cicourel, *Method and Measurement in Sociology*, New York: The Free Press, 1964; and Alan F. Blum and Peter McHugh, "The Social Ascription of Motives," *American Sociological Review*, 36 (February, 1971), pp. 98-109.

21. See, for example, the use of the ethnomethodological observation that conversations (and therefore fights between husbands and wives) require certain procedures for *ending*, as an element in the dynamics leading to the murder of spouses, in William J. Goode, "Force and Violence in the Family," *Journal of Marriage and the Family*, 33, 3 (1971).

22. See, for example, Lionel S. Lewis, "On Subjective and Objective Rankings of Sociology Departments," *The American Sociologist*, 3 (May, 1968), pp. 129-31.

23. Certainly nothing now, and perhaps nothing in the past, corresponds to the genuine center or school of Frankfurt during the 1930's in Germany. The *Zeitschrift für Sozialforschung* was its publication, and it had a strong political orientation. It did emphasize empirical research during its relatively short life, and many of its collaborators enriched sociology.

24. See, for example, Robert K. Merton, "The Ambivalence of Scientists," in William J. Goode, ed., *The Dynamics of Modern Society*, New York: Atherton Press, 1966, pp. 282-97; Marshall H. Becker, "Sociometric Location and Innovativeness: Reformulation and Extension of the Diffusion Model," *American Sociological Review*, 35 (April, 1970), pp. 267-82; and Jerry Gaston, "The Reward System in British Science," *American Sociological Review*, 35 (August, 1970), pp. 718-32.

25. Bernard Barber, "The Functions and Dysfunctions of 'Fashion' in Science: A Case for the Study of Social Change," *Mens en Maatschappij*, 43 (November/December, 1968), pp. 501-14.

26. See McCartney, "On Being Scientific," especially Tables 1 and 4.

27. Elbridge Sibley, *The Education of Sociologists in the United States*, New York: Russell Sage Foundation, 1963, p. 87, reports that fewer than 1 per cent of sociologists who took their doctorates in the period 1957-59 had been majors in either mathematics or statistics. The recent report of Norval D. Glenn and David Weiner, "Some Trends in the Social Origins of American Sociologists," *The American Sociologist*, 4 (November, 1969), p. 301, states that only about 4 per cent of

the sociologists who received doctorates in the period 1958-67 had majored in even the physical and biological sciences.

28. For a discussion and exemplification of such operations, see Joseph Berger, Morris Zelditch, and Bo Anderson, eds., *Sociological Theories in Progress*, New York: Houghton Mifflin, 1966. See also the statement by Zelditch, "Can You Really Study an Army in the Laboratory?" in Amitai Etzioni, *A Sociological Reader on Complex Organizations*, 2nd Edition, New York: Holt, Rinehart and Winston, 1969, pp. 528-39; and Hans Zetterberg, *On Theory and Verification in Sociology*, 3rd Edition, Totowa, New Jersey: The Bedminster Press, 1965, Chapter VIII.

29. E.g., the work of Sigmund Diamond, Sidney Aronson, Gillian Gollin, Lee Benson, Kai Erikson, etc.

30. For example, the writings of Robert A. Nisbet, Alvin Gouldner, Barrington Moore, S. N. Eisenstadt, Seymour M. Lipset.

31. Julia S. Brown and Brian G. Gilmartin, "Sociology Today: Lacunae, Emphases and Surfeits," *The American Sociologist*, 4 (November, 1969), p. 287, state that over the past two decades the percentage of papers in the *American Sociological Review* and the *American Journal of Sociology* that deal with synchronic data has increased from 64 per cent to 85 per cent.

32. See, for example, Robert M. Marsh, *Comparative Sociology*, New York: Harcourt, Brace and World, 1967.

33. See, for example, Gerald Suttles, *The Social Order of the Slums*, Chicago: University of Chicago Press, 1968; Erving Goffman, *Asylums*; Karl Wieck, "Systematic Observational Methods," in Gardner Lindzey and Elliot Aronson, eds., *The Handbook of Social Psychology*, 2nd Edition, Vol. 2, Reading, Massachusetts: Addison-Wesley Publishing Company, 1968; William J. Filstead, ed., *Qualitative Methodology*, Chicago: Markham Publishing Company, 1970; Howard S. Becker, *Sociological Work*, Chicago: Aldine Publishing Company, 1970; Glenn Jacobs, ed., *The Participant Observer*, New York: George Braziller, 1970.

34. Brown and Gilmartin, "Sociology Today," p. 288.

35. *Ibid.*

36. Jonathan Cole in a private communication denies this contrast between sociology and the physical sciences.

CHAPTER 2

1. Alvin W. Gouldner, "The Sociologist as Partisan: Sociology and the Welfare State," *American Sociologist*, 3 (May, 1968), p. 106.

2. *Ibid.*, p. 112.

3. Thomas Ford Hoult, "Who Shall Prepare Himself to the Battle?" *The American Sociologist*, 3 (February, 1968), p. 7.

4. Martin Nicolaus, "Remarks at the A.S.A. Convention," *The Human Factor*, 8 (November, 1968), pp. 37-40.

5. Martin Nicolaus, "Remarks at the A.S.A. Convention," *The American Sociologist*, 4 (May, 1969), p. 155.

6. Alvin W. Gouldner, "Anti-Minotaur: The Myth of the Value-Free Sociology," in Irving L. Horowitz, ed., *The New Sociology*, New York: Oxford University Press, 1965, pp. 198, 206. I cannot resist quoting Gwynn Nettler's answer to this plaintive query: "It deserves the same reply given the minister who asked, 'If there is no God, where do my morals come from?'" in "Using Our Heads," *The American Sociologist*, 3 (August, 1968), p. 201.

7. Howard S. Becker, "Whose Side Are We On?" *Social Problems*, 14 (winter, 1967), p. 245.

8. I use the absolute "*no* sociologist," fully aware that somewhere someone has nevertheless propounded one of these doctrines. At this writing, nevertheless, I have searched long and assiduously, with the help of others equally motivated, without finding any instances. At the most cautious, it must be conceded that the number of exceptions must be small.

9. Allan Mazur, "The Littlest Science," *The American Sociologist*, 3 (August, 1968), p. 195.

10. This classical dilemma is perhaps first illustrated by the ancient Cretan Paradox: if a Cretan says that all Cretans are liars, then obviously we are not to believe him; but then if we don't believe him he must be telling the truth; etc. It is succinctly presented in Gresham Riley's answer to Howard Becker's article ("Whose Side Are We On?" pp. 239-47): "Partisan and Objectivity in the Social Sciences," *The American Sociologist*, 6 (February, 1971), pp. 6-12. This is also the classic dilemma of the sociology of knowledge.

11. Gouldner, "Anti-Minotaur," p. 196. "Knowing surely," because within a few pages he notes that Weber himself wrote of many junctures where values do affect scientific work. Weber did not claim science could be value-free.

12. *Ibid.*, p. 197.

13. The belief is widespread that political courage guarantees worldly failure, and doubtless is responsible for generating the erroneous notion that "C. Wright Mills never became a full professor" (e.g., Alvin W. Gouldner, *The Coming Crisis of Western Sociology*, New York: Basic Books, 1970, p. 15).

14. Gouldner, "The Sociologist as Partisan," p. 108.

15. Obviously, these are but two cells of a four-fold table. The other two would be the "great works," which are politically *and* intellectually important, and the much larger cell of the trivial reports, which are neither.

16. See, for example, his essay, "The Meaning of 'Ethical Neutrality' in

Sociology and Economics" and " 'Objectivity' in Social Science and Social Policy," in *The Methodology of the Social Sciences*, trans. Edward A. Shils and Henry A. Finch, Glencoe, Illinois: The Free Press, 1949. See also the brief discussion in William J. Goode and Paul K. Hatt, *Methods in Social Research*, New York: McGraw-Hill, 1952, Chapter 3.

17. The technical question of whether it is possible to *prove* "causation" would seem to be answered in the negative, just as Hume did two centuries ago; nevertheless, working scientists do not hesitate to use this vocabulary and obviously believe in "cause" whatever its metaphysical status.

18. See Gideon Sjoberg, ed., *Ethics, Politics and Social Research*, Cambridge, Massachusetts: Schenkman Publishing Company, 1967; Irving L. Horowitz, ed., *The Use and Abuse of the Social Science*, New Brunswick, New Jersey: E. P. Dutton and Company, 1971; Eugene Webb *et al.*, *Unobtrusive Measurements: Nonreactive Research in the Social Sciences*, Chicago: Rand McNally, 1966; Bernhard Barber, John Lally, Julia Makarushka, and Daniel Sullivan, *Experimenting with Humans: Problems and Processes of Social Control in the Biomedical Research Community*, New York: Russell Sage Foundation, 1972.

19. Cf. James L. McCartney, "On Being Scientific: Changing Styles of Presentation of Sociological Research," *The American Sociologist*, 5 (February, 1970), pp. 30-35; see also Robert K. Merton, "Social Conflict Over Styles of Sociological Work," *Transactions, Fourth World Congress of Sociology*, 4 (1961), pp. 21-46.

20. Melvin M. Tumin, "Some Social Consequences of Research on Racial Relations," *The American Sociologist*, 3 (May, 1968), pp. 117-24.

CHAPTER 3

1. Robert K. Merton, "Manifest and Latent Functions," in *Social Theory and Social Structure*, New York: The Free Press, Rev. ed., 1957, pp. 19-84; and Kingsley Davis, "The Myth of Functional Analysis as a Special Method in Sociology and Anthropology," *American Sociological Review*, 24 (December, 1959), pp. 757-72.

2. Note, for example, that Hempel's citations ("The Logic of Functional Analysis," in *Aspects of Scientific Explanation*, New York: The Free Press, 1965, pp. 297-330) refer mainly to Radcliffe-Brown and Malinowski among the functionalists, and not at all to the empirical work by which any "theory" is properly to be judged. He uses Merton's essay (cited above) as another main source, but that essay is mainly devoted to an exposure of the weaknesses in both those authors and to

the exposition of a "functionalist paradigm" that obviously had not been followed at that time by anyone in the field.

3. Robert K. Merton, "The Bearing of Sociological Theory on Empirical Research," in *Social Theory and Social Structure*, p. 88.

4. See Robert K. Merton, "Singletons and Multiples in Scientific Discovery: A Chapter in the Sociology of Science," in *Proceedings of the American Philosophical Society*, 105 (1961), pp. 470-86.

5. William J. Goode, *Religion Among the Primitives*, Glencoe, Illinois: The Free Press, 1951, p. 30.

6. Robert L. Lowie, *The History of Ethnological Theory*, New York: Farrar & Rinehart, 1937, pp. 239 ff.

7. Notably the work of Alfred R. Radcliffe-Brown, *The Andaman Islander*, Glencoe, Illinois: The Free Press, 1948 (1922, reprinted with additions 1933), and Bronislaw Malinowski, "Baloma: The Spirits of the Dead in the Trobriand Islands," in *The Journal of the Royal Anthropological Institute of Great Britain and Ireland*, 46 (1916), pp. 353-430; B. Malinowski, *Argonauts of the Western Pacific: An Account of Native Enterprise and Adventure in the Archipelagoes of Melanesian New Guinea*, New York: E. P. Dutton and Company, 1961 (1922). However, Radcliffe-Brown's work was done before World War I.

8. Tylor sketched this solution to the problem of time measurement in a lecture given at the Royal Institution in 1869 and then later in an article, "On the Survival of Savage Thought in Modern Civilization," *Proceedings of the Royal Institution*. The idea is expressed in his *Primitive Culture*, and more elaborately analyzed in his article, "On a Method of Investigating the Development of Institutions: Applied to the Laws of Marriage and Descent," *Journal of the Royal Anthropological Institute*, 18 (1889), pp. 245-72. See also R. R. Marett, *Psychology and Folklore*, London: Metheun, 1920, pp. 74 ff.

9. See Richard Hofstadter, *Social Darwinism in American Thought*, Boston: Beacon Press, 1955, for a discussion of part of this development.

10. Cf. Bernhard Ankermann, "Kulturkreis und Kulturschichten in Afrika," in *Zeitschrift für Ethnologie*, Jg. 37 (1905), pp. 54-85; Fritz Graebner, "Kulturkreise und Kulturschichten in Ozeanien," in *Zeitschrift für Ethnologie*, Jg. 37 (1905), pp. 28-53; Wilhelm Schmidt, "Kulturkreise und Kulturschichten in Südamerika," *Zeitschrift für Ethnologie*, Jg. 45 (1913), pp. 1014-1124. Cf. also Fritz Graebner, *Methode der Ethnologie*, Dosterhout: Anthropological Publications, 1966 (1911) and R. H. Lowie, *The History of Ethnological Theory*, pp. 177-95.

11. Of course, in the case of Smith's impact upon Durkheim's thought, we have Durkheim's concession itself (Talcott Parsons, *The Structure of Social Action*, New York: McGraw-Hill, 1937, p. 409).

12. For example, in the work of Hempel and Dahrendorf, or for that matter Merton himself; see also John Rex, *Key Problems of Sociological Theory*, London: Routledge & Kegan Paul, 1961, Chapter IV. An especially striking exception is David Matza's analysis in *Becoming Deviant*, Englewood Cliffs, New Jersey: Prentice-Hall, 1969, pp. 31-62. He focuses on research work, pays little attention to Radcliffe-Brown and Malinowski, cites specific passages—and shows the contributions of some people he identifies as functionalists.

13. These are stated in Goode, *Religion Among the Primitives*, p. 31.

14. E.g., Alvin W. Gouldner, *The Wildcat Strike*, Yellow Springs, Ohio: Antioch Press, 1954 and idem., *Patterns of Industrial Bureaucracy*, Glencoe, Illinois: The Free Press, 1954; Ralf Dahrendorf, *Class and Class Conflict in Industrial Society*, Stanford, California: Stanford University Press, 1965; Walter Buckley, *Sociology and Modern Systems Theory*, Englewood Cliffs, N.J.: Prentice-Hall, 1967; Reinhard Bendix, "Social Stratification and the Political Community," in Seymour M. Lipset and Reinhard Bendix, eds., *Class, Status, and Power*, 2nd Edition, New York: Free Press, 1966, pp. 73-86.

15. Merton, "Manifest and Latent Functions," p. 30.

16. As Davis noted over a decade ago, however, some social scientists thought to be functionalists had indeed carried out studies of social change: Merton's study of science in seventeenth-century England, Wilbert E. Moore's study of labor systems, Marion J. Levy's investigation of the Chinese family, Robert E. Bellah's monograph on Japanese religion, and so on (Davis, *op. cit.*, footnote No. 38).

17. Arthur Stinchcombe proposes that the label "functional causal" explanations be limited to such feedback systems: *Constructing Social Theories*, New York: Harcourt, Brace & World, 1968, Chapter 3, Part 2.

18. Davis, "The Myth of Functional Analysis," p. 771.

19. Peter L. Berger, "Sociology and Freedom," *The American Sociologist*, 6 (February, 1971), pp. 1-2.

20. *Ibid.*, p. 2.

21. *Ibid.*, p. 4.

22. See in this connection the very sharp attack by Allan Mazur, "The Littlest Science," *The American Sociologist*, 3 (August, 1968), pp. 195-200. See, however, the attempt to distinguish the major advances in the field: Karl W. Deutsch *et al.*, "Conditions Favoring Advances in Social Science," *Science*, 171 (February 5, 1971), pp. 450-59.

23. For example, in the field of the family alone, William J. Goode, Elizabeth Hopkins, and Helen M. McClure, eds., *Social Structure and Family Patterns*, Indianapolis: Bobbs Merrill, 1971 contains some 9,000 propositions of this kind, and certainly does not cover the field entirely.

24. I should like to note here at least one exception, a doctoral disserta-

tion that does in fact offer a new thesis, whether or not it is adequately proved: John T. Moffett, "Bureaucratization and Social Control," Ph.D. dissertation, Columbia University, 1971.

25. William J. Goode, "The Theory and Measurement of Family Change," in Eleanor B. Sheldon and Wilbert E. Moore, eds., *Indicators of Social Change: Concepts and Measurement*, New York: Russell Sage Foundation, 1968, pp. 295-348.

26. See my article "A Theory of Role Strain," pp. 97-120 in this volume for one such reassessment; as well as "Force and Violence in the Family," *Journal of Marriage and the Family*, 33, 3, 1971.

27. So far, although I have *written* a good bit on the topic, I have published only two articles: "Violence Between Intimates," in Donald J. Mulvihill *et al.*, eds., *Crime of Violence*, a staff report submitted to the National Commission on the Causes and Prevention of Violence, Washington, D.C.: Government Printing Office, 1969, Vol. 13, Appendix 19, pp. 941-77; and "Force and Violence in the Family."

28. Bruno Bettelheim, "Individual and Mass Behavior in Extreme Situations," in *Journal of Abnormal and Social Psychology*, 43 (October, 1943), pp. 417-52.

29. E.g., David F. Aberle, A. K. Cohen, A. K. Davis, Marion J. Levy, and Francis X. Sutton, "The Functional Prerequisites of a Society," in Nicholas J. Demerath and Richard A. Peterson, eds., *System, Change, and Conflict*, New York: The Free Press, 1967, pp. 317-31.

30. George C. Homans, "Structural, Functional and Psychological Theories," in N. J. Demerath III and Richard A. Peterson, eds., *System, Change and Conflict*.

31. For those social scientists who have come to believe that intellectual sophistication requires us to eliminate the notion of "cause," rather than insist upon it, a comment is in order. Well over a generation ago, philosophers of science, including Russell, began to follow Hume in asserting that we have no epistemological warrant for proclaiming a causal relationship among physical forces: all that we can observe are correlations of certain types among pointer readings for measuring instruments. They are correct, but working physical scientists grant about as much importance to this claim as they give to many other epistemological and ontological difficulties in research. In daily language they can use the term "cause" without being distracted by any of its deeper mystical meanings, and in their articles the term can be dropped or used without any confusion. Its technical meaning is, in any event, well enough understood (see, for example, Carl G. Hempel, "Aspects of Scientific Explanation," in *Aspects of Scientific Explanation*, New York: Free Press, 1965, pp. 348 ff.). The advantage of using it is that then we anticipate criticism and to protect ourselves we are forced to be more rigorous. By contrast, if we only assert that X is "involved with Y," or "related to," or "X is functional," we relax our standards.

32. It will be kept in mind that Davis also gives such examples in his 1959 speech, "The Myth of Functional Analysis," pp. 759 *passim.*
33. Cf. *Ibid.*, 11.
34. Merton, "Manifest and Latent Functions," pp. 37 ff.
35. Goode, "The Theory and Measurement of Family Change."
36. Arthur L. Stinchcombe, *Constructing Social Theories*, New York: Harcourt, Brace and World, 1968, Chapter 3, Part 2.

CHAPTER 4

1. I prefer to call this the "Lintonian model" (Ralph Linton, *The Study of Man*, New York: Appleton-Century, 1936), although Linton is not, of course, the creator of this model. Rather, he summed up a generation of thought about social structure in a clear and illuminating fashion, so that for many years the definitions and statements in this book were widely cited by both anthropologists and sociologists. Of course, "everyone knows" these weaknesses, but our basic model is not thereby changed to account for them.
2. For a systematic statement of several earlier models, see Talcott Parsons, *The Structure of Social Action*, New York: McGraw-Hill, 1937, Chapter 2.
3. For an earlier discussion relevant to this paper, see William J. Goode, "Contemporary Thinking about Primitive Religion," *Soziologus*, 5 (1955), pp. 122-131; also in Morton Fried, editor *Readings in Anthropology*, New York: Crowell, 1959, Vol. II, pp. 450-460.
4. For a good exposition of certain aspects of dissensus as they apply to American society, see Robin W. Williams, *American Society*, New York: Knopf, 1956, esp. pp. 352 ff.
5. Charles H. Page has reminded me that role diversity is not confined to modern societies, as the work of functionalist anthropologists (e.g., Malinowski's *Crime and Custom* and Benedict's *Patterns of Culture*) has shown. This empirical fact is of considerable theoretical consequence, especially for the relations between adjacent social strata or castes, or between conquerors and the conquered.
6. This is the label which Talcott Parsons has suggested for the view, generally accepted since Durkheim's *Division of Labor*, that the maintenance of the society rests on desires of individuals to do things which must be done if the society is to survive. *The Social System*, Glencoe, Ill.: Free Press, 1949, pp. 36-43.
7. In the paper, I distinguish role and status on the basis of only "degree of institutionalization": all role relations are somewhat institutionalized, but statuses are more fully institutionalized.
8. Cf. Robert K. Merton, *Social Theory and Social Structure*, Glencoe, Ill.: Free Press, 1957, pp. 369 ff. For its use in an empirical study, see

Mary Jean Huntington, "The Development of a Professional Self Image," in R. K. Merton *et al.*, editors, *The Student-Physician*, Cambridge: Harvard University Press, 1957, pp. 180 ff.

9. Merton's "mechanisms" operate to *articulate* role sets; see Robert K. Merton, "The Role Set: Problems in Sociological Theory," *British Journal of Sociology*, 8 (June, 1957), pp. 113 ff. Here, we are concerned with a more general problem, which includes role sets as a special source of role strain. Moreover, Merton is concerned with only one of our problems, integrating the total role systems of all individuals in a demarcated social system; while we are, in addition, concerned with the problem of the individual in integrating his own role system. Several of our mechanisms, then, are parallelled by Merton's. Compartmentalization partly corresponds, for example, to two of his —observability of the individual's role activities and observability of conflicting demands by members of the role set. Our mechanism of hierarchy or stratification, assigning higher or lower values to particular role demands, corresponds to two of Merton's—the relative importance of statuses and differences of power among members of the role set.

10. This, again, is a general case of which Merton's "abridging the role-set" is a special example (*ibid.*, p. 117).

11. Some structural differences between the two cases, however, should be noted: (1) There are specialized economic *producers*, for example, wheat farmers who offer only one product on the market, but no corresponding sociological positions in which the individual offers only one type of role performance. Some political, religious, military, or occupational leaders do "produce" their services for a large number of people, but they must all carry out many other roles as well in the "role market." Every adult must take part as producer in a minimum number of such role markets. (2) Correspondingly, in the economic sphere all participate in several markets as *buyers*; in the role sphere they act in several markets as *both* sellers and buyers. (3) Correlatively, our entrance into the economic *producer* or *seller* activities may be long delayed, and we may retire from them early if we have enough money, but as long as we live we must remain in the role market: we need other people, and they demand us. (4) We may accumulate enough money so as to be able to purchase more than we can use, or produce more than we can sell, in the economic sphere; but in the role system we probably always ask more on the whole than our alters can give, and are unable to give as much as they demand.

12. The most elaborate recent attempt to state the relations between the two is Talcott Parsons and Neil J. Smelser, *Economy and Society*, Glencoe, Ill.: Free Press, 1956.

13. Again, however, correctness is independent of their origin. It is equally clear that they parallel certain conceptions of psychody-

namics, but again their sociological value is independent of their usefulness in that field.

14. Anthropologists have noted for over a generation that economic theory needs a more general framework to take account of the non-monetary aspects of economic action in non-Western societies. Cf. Bronislaw Malinowski, "Primitive Economics of the Trobriand Islanders," *Economic Journal* 31 (March, 1921), pp. 1-16. See also Malinowski's earlier article, "The Economic Aspects of the Intichiuma Ceremonies," *Festskrift Tillagnad Edward Westermarck*, Helsingfors: 1912; and *Argonauts of the Western Pacific*, London: Routledge, 1922. Also Raymond Firth, *Primitive Economics of the New Zealand Maori*, New York: Dutton, 1929. For a discussion of the interaction of economic roles and religious roles, see William J. Goode, *Religion Among the Primitives*, Glencoe, Ill.: Free Press, 1951, Chapters 5, 6.

15. See the several discussions in Paul F. Lazarsfeld and Morris Rosenberg, editors, *The Language of Social Research*, Glencoe, Ill.: Free Press, 1955, pp. 387-448.

16. Price in an elementary economics textbook, determined by the intersection of supply and demand, requires no such datum (i.e., why or whence the demand is not relevant), and thus the model is simpler than the role model. However, more sophisticated economics, as well as the economic practitioner, must distinguish various components or sources of demand.

17. Doubtless, however, the lessons can be made more explicit and conclusive when the "value" can be expressed in dollars rather than in the equally intangible (but more difficult to measure) moral or esthetic considerations.

18. Cf. Willard Waller's "Principle of Least Interest" in Willard Waller and Reuben Hill, *The Family*, New York: Dryden, 1952, pp. 191-192.

19. Cf. Leon Festinger's Derivation C, in "A Theory of Social Comparison Processes," *Reprint Services No. 22*, Laboratory for Research in Social Relations, University of Minnesota, 1955, p. 123. Also see No. 24, "Self-Evaluation as a Function of Attraction to the Group," by Leon Festinger, Jane Torrey, and Ben Willerman.

20. Note, for example, the potential "seduction" of the mother by the child; the mother wishes to please the child to make him happy, and may have to be reminded by others that she is "spoiling" him.

21. Norman Miller has used data from the Cornell Values Study to show how various combinations of social positions affect expressions of value in *Social Class Differences among American College Students*, Ph.D. thesis, Columbia University, 1958.

22. In an unpublished paper on "doubling" (the living together of relatives who are not members of the same nuclear family), Morris Zelditch has used approximately these categories to analyze the conditions under which the claim to such a right is likely to be respected.

23. This mechanism is akin to, though not identical with, Merton's "mutual social support among status occupants." Merton, "The Role Set . . . ," *op. cit.*, p. 116.
24. I have described this mechanism of institutional integration in some detail in *Religion Among the Primitives, op. cit.*, Chapters 5-10.
25. Perhaps the third characteristic is merely a corollary of the first two.
26. Although the matter cannot be pursued here, it seems likely that in economic terms we are dealing here with the phenomena of the "differentiated product"—ego cannot accept a given role performance from just anyone, but from the specific people with whom he is in interaction—and of oligopoly—ego can patronize only a limited number of suppliers or sellers. Moreover, with respect to certain roles, both supply and demand are relatively inelastic.
27. Cf. C. Addison Hickman and Manford H. Kuhn, *Individuals, Groups, and Economic Behavior*, New York: Dryden, 1956, p. 38.
28. Albert K. Cohen has discussed one example of this special case at length in *Delinquent Boys*, Glencoe, Ill.: Free Press, 1955. It requires, among other factors, special ecological conditions and the possibility of communication among those in the same situation.
29. See Melvin Tumin's discussion of incentives in various non-occupational statuses in "Rewards and Task Orientations," *American Sociological Review*, 20 (August, 1955), pp. 419-422.
30. Partly because of the difficulty of outsiders observing crucial performances within it; partly, also, because of the difficulty of measuring relative achievement except in universalistic terms, as against the particularistic-ascriptive character of familial roles. Note, however, the creation by both Nazi Germany and Soviet Russia of a family title for very fertile mothers (an observable behavior).
31. Note in this connection the case of China, the most family-oriented civilization. In comparison with other major civilizations, the Chinese developed a more complex ranking of kinship positions—and a more explicit ranking of familial performances. (See Marion J. Levy, Jr., *The Family Revolution in Modern China*, Cambridge: Harvard University Press, 1949, esp. Chapter 3). Various individuals have figured in Chinese history as "family heroes," that is, those who performed their family duties exceedingly well.

CHAPTER 5

1. Allen H. Barton and David E. Wilder, "Research and Practice in the Teaching of Reading: A Progress Report," in Matthew B. Miles (ed.), *Innovation in Education*, New York: Teachers College, Columbia University, 1964, pp. 361-398.
2. More cautiously, the chances that the chief of a bureaucracy may be

able to act irresponsibly and destructively are probably reduced. However, (1) the bureaucracy itself generates power, so that his usually limited range of action may nevertheless be more destructive than that of a feudal chieftain could be; and (2) in the event that the chief (Stalin, Hitler) *can* really capture the bureaucracy, his range of destructiveness is multiplied greatly.

3. See Harriet Zuckerman, "Nobel Laureates in Science: Patterns of Productivity, Collaboration, and Authorship," presented at the 61st Annual Meeting of the American Sociological Association, August 31, 1966, especially the comments on the "uncrowned Laureates."

4. As a contrary case, because its members did not form a real group, see William J. Goode and Irving Fowler, "Incentive Factors in a Low Morale Plant," *American Sociological Review*, 14 (October, 1949), pp. 618-624.

5. For one such comment, see Julius A. Roth, "Hired Hand Research," *The American Sociologist*, 1 (August, 1966), pp. 192-193. See also Melville Dalton, *Men Who Manage*, New York: Wiley, 1959, Chs. 7-9. Most analyses of management make such comments implicitly or explicitly.

6. It is noteworthy that, when such ratings are made, it is typically "outsiders" who make them. See, for example, the Teamsters' study of hospital care in New York City: *The Quantity, Quality and Costs of Medical and Hospital Care Secured by a Sample of Teamster Families in the New York Area*, Columbia University, School of Public Health and Administrative Medicine, n.d.

7. Erwin O. Smigel, *The Wall Street Lawyer: Professional Organization Man?*, New York: The Free Press, 1964, Chap. 4.

8. For related comments see Jules Henry, "The GI Syndrome," *Trans-Action*, 1 (May, 1964), pp. 8-9, 30; and Eliot Freidson, "The Professional Mystique," *ibid.*, pp. 18-20. For a broader analysis, see my "Community Within a Community: The Professions," *American Sociological Review*, 22 (April, 1957), pp. 195-200; and "Encroachment, Charlatanism, and the Emerging Profession: Psychology, Sociology, and Medicine," *American Sociological Review*, 25 (December, 1960), pp. 902-914.

9. O. L. Peterson, *et al.*, "An Analytical Study of North Carolina General Practice," *Journal of Medical Education*, 31 (1956), p. 130.

10. Ely Chinoy, "The Tradition of Opportunity and the Aspirations of Automobile Workers," in Philip Olson, editor, *America as a Mass Society*, New York: The Free Press, 1963, pp. 506, 508, 512 and especially footnote 17; John W. Gardner, *Excellence*, New York: Harper & Row, 1961, p. 110; Melville Dalton, *op. cit.*, pp. 5-6, 128; and his "Economic Incentives and Human Relations," in *Industrial Productivity*, Publication No. 7 of Industrial Relations Research Association, Madison, Wisconsin, 1951, pp. 130-145; as well as Michel Crozier, *The*

Bureaucratic Phenomenon, Chicago: University of Chicago Press, 1964, Ch. 3.

11. For example, see the revealing article in the *Wall Street Journal*, January 24, 1966, "Obsolete Executives," as well as Fred Goldner, "Demotion in Industrial Management," *American Sociological Review*, 30 (October, 1965), pp. 714-724. Consider, too, the perceptive essay by one of our more imaginative social theorists, C. Northcote Parkinson, "Pension Point or the Age of Retirement," in his *Parkinson's Law*, Boston: Houghton Mifflin, 1962, pp. 101-113.

12. James G. March and Herbert A. Simon, *Organizations*, New York: Wiley, 1963, p. 62.

13. For some evidence that they are right, see Dalton, *op. cit.*, Ch. 6, and his "Unofficial Union-Management Relations," *American Sociological Review*, 15 (October, 1950), especially p. 615.

14. Erving Goffman, *The Presentation of Self in Everyday Life*, New York: Doubleday Anchor, 1959, Chap. 2.

15. It is hardly necessary here to cite from the voluminous literature on discrimination of various types. See, however, E. Digby Baltzell, *The Protestant Establishment*, New York: Random House, 1964; Melvin M. Tumin, *Inventory and Appraisal of Research on American Anti-Semitism*, New York: B'nai Brith, 1961; C. Northcote Parkinson should not be overlooked: "The Short List or Principles of Selection," *op. cit.*, pp. 45-48; and George E. Simpson and J. Milton Yinger, *Racial and Cultural Minorities*, 3rd ed., New York: Harper & Row, 1965.

16. John K. Galbraith, *The Affluent Society*, Harmondsworth: Penguin, 1965, pp. 90-91.

17. *Ibid.*, p. 91.

18. See, for example, Ralph Linton, *The Study of Man*, New York: Appleton-Century-Crofts, 1936, pp. 115, 127-129; Talcott Parsons, *The Social System*, Glencoe, Ill.: The Free Press, 1951, pp. 151-200; Leonard Broom and Philip Selznick, *Sociology*, second ed., White Plains: Row, Peterson, 1959, p. 191.

19. Joseph W. Elder found that 44 percent of the Mill Elite and 58 percent of the Brahmins believed that lower caste persons in that status were there because of sins committed in a previous life. "Industrialization in Hindu Society," Ph.D. dissertation (Harvard University, 1959), pp. 411, 415, 439.

20. Richard Hofstadter, *Anti-Intellectualism in American Life*, New York: Knopf, 1963, especially pp. 181 ff.

21. As will be seen, several of these have been adapted from H. M. Blalock, "Occupational Discrimination: Some Theoretical Propositions," *Social Problems*, 9 (Winter, 1962), pp. 240-247.

22. Though numerically less important, it should not be forgotten, on the other hand, that jobs in this environment may be given to *some* tal-

ented and skilled men who would in a tighter market be classified by personnel men as "inept," i.e., "socially unacceptable," or too innovative or deviant, and so on.

23. Space does not permit me to go into the matter, but there are technical and theoretical reasons for considering high demand and low supply separately. Although occupational and other outputs do operate through market processes, I believe that a wide variety of such demands—such as love, emotional support, household and "dirty" types of work—have a high inelasticity, especially at the lower demand levels. At a cautious minimum, there are some obvious sociological factors that limit the *range* within which both supply and demand *can* respond swiftly.

24. See William J. Goode, "A Theory of Role Strain," *American Sociological Review*, 25 (August, 1960), pp. 483-496 [pp. 000-00 in this volume]; and Peter M. Blau, *Exchange and Power in Social Life*, New York: Wiley, 1964, especially Ch. 4.

25. Robert K. Merton, *Social Theory and Social Structure* (revised and enlarged edition), Glencoe, Ill.: The Free Press, 1957, pp. 368-384.

26. See Goldner, *op. cit.*, pp. 714-724.

27. Perhaps the popular stereotype that "Negroes have rhythm" and are "musical" arose in part because it is one of the few areas in which it would be difficult to overlook a great talent. Until recently in the South, whites sometimes visited black churches to listen to their choirs. One result was that a handful of black female singers *did* get the long and expensive education necessary to become concert performers of the standard repertoire. It is also true that especially Southern blacks grew up in a deep experience of polyrhythm and polyphony. See Alan Lomax, *Folk Song Style and Culture*, Washington, D.C.: A.A.A.S., 1968, pp. 54, 92, 95, 119, 163.

28. See especially my "Illegitimacy, Anomie, and Cultural Penetration," *American Sociological Review*, 26 (December, 1961), pp. 910-925; and also "Social Mobility and Revolution," Camelot Conference, Airlee House, Virginia, June 4-6, 1965; and "Family Patterns and Human Rights," *International Social Science Journal*, XVIII (No. 1, 1966), pp. 41-54.

29. This is one reason for the sterility of the search for the "requisites for the continuation of a society." Far too few societies have totally failed at all, and perhaps none has failed because it lacked any of these requisites. Lacking negative cases, it is difficult to test such requisites, and they are therefore to be viewed as a way of defining a society.

30. Nicholas Babchuk and William J. Goode, "Work Incentives in a Self-Determined Group," *American Sociological Review*, 16 (October, 1951), pp. 679-687; and Goode and Fowler, *op. cit.* In the latter case, fortunately for the manager-owner, productivity depended very little on the maintenance of a group structure.

31. Peter M. Blau, *The Dynamics of Bureaucracy*, Chicago: University of Chicago Press, 1955, pp. 44-47, 162-167, 208-213.
32. Alvin Zander, editor, *Performance Appraisals*, Ann Arbor, Mich.: The Foundation for Research on Human Behavior, 1963.
33. Alvin W. Gouldner, *Enter Plato*, New York: Basic Books, 1965, pp. 52 ff.
34. Most of these are noted by Alvin Zander, in "Research on Self-Evaluation, Feedback and Threats to Self-Esteem," in Zander, *op. cit.*, pp. 5-17. See also T. Whisler and S. Harper, editors, *Performance Appraisal: Research and Practice*, New York: Holt, Rinehart, and Winston, 1962; and Arthur R. Cohen, "Situational Structure, Self-Esteem and Threat-Oriented Reactions to Power," in Dorwin Cartwright, editor, *Studies in Social Power*, Ann Arbor, Mich.: Institute for Social Research, 1959.
35. That individuals gain from being in the more successful departments is shown by Diane Crane, "Scientists at Major and Minor Universities," *American Sociological Review*, 30 (1965), pp. 699-714.
36. This is pointed out in my two articles, "Community Within a Community: the Professions," *op. cit.*, and "Encroachment, Charlatanism, and the Emerging Profession: Psychology, Sociology, and Medicine," *op. cit.*; and in more detail in *The Professions in Modern Society*, by William J. Goode, Mary Jean Huntington, and Robert K. Merton, unpub. Mimeo., Russell Sage Foundation, 1956, "Code of Ethics."
37. Fred H. Goldner interprets the varied solutions to this problem as ways of avoiding the "dysfunctions" of demotion, in his "Demotion in Industrial Management," *op. cit.* He also introduces the useful fact that demotion is psychologically easier for some, because the costs of high responsibility are thought to be great: weighed against these costs, demotion can sometimes be palatable.
38. In Talcott Parsons' formulation, each sub-system must go through the "latency phase" of the AGIL sequence from time to time, but other sub-systems (notably the family) may have as a *primary* activity (its "output") the latency function, thus restoring the individual to a healthier state for further effective participation in, say, an "instrumental" system such as the factory. See "An Outline of the Social System," in Talcott Parsons *et al.*, editors, *Theories of Society*, New York: The Free Press, 1961, Vol. 1, pp. 30-79.
39. Crozier, *op. cit.*, pp. 40 ff and 282 ff.
40. See Herbert Passin, *Society and Education in Japan*, New York: Teachers College, Columbia University, 1965, especially Ch. 6; and Ezra F. Vogel, *Japan's New Middle Class: The Salary Man and his Family in a Tokyo Suburb*, Berkeley: University of California Press, 1963.
41. For an examination of some relevant arguments about this matter, see Melvin M. Tumin, "Some Unapplauded Consequences of Social Mo-

bility in a Mass Society," *Social Forces*, 36 (October, 1957), pp. 32-37; and "Some Disfunctions of Institutional Imbalance," *Behavioral Science*, 1 (July, 1956), pp. 218-223; as well as "Rewards and Task Orientations," *American Sociological Review*, 20 (August, 1955), pp. 419-423.

42. Michael Young, in his *The Rise of the Meritocracy, 1872-1933*, London: Pelican, 1963, implies that a pure system by merit could be inaugurated, and the principle of merit really accepted by the lower social strata. The dissidence that develops, in his satire, comes primarily from the proposal to return to placement by inheritance.

43. Wilbert E. Moore, "The Utility of Utopias," *American Sociological Review*, 31 (December, 1966), pp. 765-772.

CHAPTER 6

1. In the summary table 46 in André Normandeau, *Trends and Patterns of Crimes of Robbery*, University of Pennsylvania, Ph.D., 1968, p. 136. Two figures for forcible rape are slightly lower and those for aggravated assault very close to those of homicide. Unfortunately, data from the Task Force victim-offender survey, presented in ch. 5 of the Report, were not available to the author at the time this was written.

2. See, for example, the study by Jacqueline and Murray Straus, "Suicide, Homicide and Social Structure in Ceylon," *Amer. J. of Sociology*, 58 (March 1953), pp. 461-469.

3. See the study reported by the *New York Times* Nov. 3, 1968, which announced that the homicide rate of recent years was close to that of 1931 in New York City. Here again, of course, we are faced with *official* data, and such a report does not reach back to frontier or rural violence, which typically did not appear in any official data.

4. Veli Verkko, *Homicides and Suicides in Finland and Their Dependence on National Character*, Copenhagen, G.E.C. Gads Forlag, pp. 42-54.

5. For some ecological differences, and differences among occupational groups, see the (sometimes confused) summary by Stephen Schafer, *Criminal-Victim Relationships in Violent Crimes*, NIMH report, Washington, D.C.: 1965, pp. 228 ff. See also the summary in Edwin H. Sutherland and Donald R. Cressey, *Principles of Criminology*, 5th ed. New York: Lippincott, 1955, ch. 9.

6. See the summary of studies on this point, and the problems of demonstrating how values are transmitted, in Frank F. Furstenburg, "Transmissions of Attitudes in the Family," Ph.D. dissertation, Columbia University, 1967.

7. Various studies have reported on this point, and though the absolute percentages cannot be treated as valid, in some studies from one-

fourth to an overwhelming majority have committed serious crimes at some point in their lives. See Sutherland and Cressey, *op. cit.*, pp. 39 ff.; James S. Wallerstein and Clement J. Wyle, "Our Law-Abiding Law-Breakers," *Probation*, 5 (March-April, 1947), pp. 107-112; the earlier work of Sutherland; Austin L. Porterfield, "Delinquency and its Outcome in Court and College," *Am. J. Soc.*, 49 (Nov. 1943), pp. 199-208; etc.

8. A brief sketch of "Japanese Family Structure and System of Obligations" can be found in William Caudill, "Japanese-American Personality and Acculturation," *Genetic Psychology Monographs*, 45, 1; February 1952, pp. 29-33. "The main teaching and disciplinary techniques are teasing and ridicule—physical punishment is seldom used" (p. 30). A field study of "Taira: An Okinawan Village" by Thomas and Hatsumi Maretzki corroborates this, adding that threats are much more common than the actual occurrence of spanking or other physical punishment; cf. Beatrice Whiting, ed., *Six Cultures: Studies of Child Rearing*, New York: John Wiley and Sons, 1963, pp. 363-450. See also Reuben Hill and René König, eds., *Families East and West*, Paris: Mouton, 1970, esp. Part I.

9. Hans von Hentig, *The Criminal and His Victim*, New Haven: Yale University, 1948, and "Remarks on the Interaction of Perpetrator and Victim," *J. Am. Inst. Crim. Law and Criminology*, 31 (May-June 1940); B. Mendelsohn, "The Origin of the Doctrine of Victimology," *Excerpta Criminologica*, 3 (May-June 1963).

10. Wolfgang, *op. cit.*, p. 14. See, however, the comparative data from other countries (and decades), in which considerable variation is reported, pp. 217-221.

11. Wolfgang, *op. cit.*, p. 126.

12. *Ibid.*, p. 82.

13. A special irony in the cases of homicide-suicide is in the conclusion that a higher percentage of "persons who commit murder in the first degree inflict death upon themselves as punishment for their crimes than are legally executed by the state." (Wolfgang, *ibid.*, p. 83.)

14. I also suppose that this differential explains some part of the differential in the successful suicide rate as between men and women. Women try more frequently but succeed less frequently.

15. For an extensive analysis of a subsociety of this type, though hardly as violent as many Harlem districts, see Elliot Liebow, *Tally's Corner*, Boston, Little, Brown Co., 1967, especially chs. 5 and 6.

16. The source is the Federal Bureau of Investigation, as cited in Ronald Sullivan, "Violence Like Charity, Begins at Home," *N.Y. Times*, Nov. 4, 1968.

17. Normandeau, *op. cit.*, p. 130.

18. Menachem Amir, *Patterns in Forcible Rape*, Ph.D. dissertation, University of Pennsylvania, 1965.

19. Clifford Kirkpatrick and Eugene Kanin, "Male Sex Aggression on a University Campus," *American Sociological Review*, 22: Feb. 1957, p. 53; and Kanin, "Male Aggression in Dating-Courtship Relations," *American Journal of Sociology*, 63: Sept. 1957, p. 198.
20. Amir, *op. cit.*, p. 490.
21. Sullivan, *op. cit.*, p. 59.
22. See the interesting hypothetical calculations by Frank Zimring, "Is Gun Control Likely to Reduce Violent Killings?" *University of Chicago Law Review*, 35 (Summer 1968), pp. 721-737.

CHAPTER 7

1. Talcott, Parsons, *The Structure of Social Action*, N.Y.: McGraw-Hill, 1937.
2. Implied in the frequent use, in traditional economics, of the "Robinson Crusoe analogy."
3. Parsons, *op. cit.*, p. 655.
4. Richard Thurnwald, *Economics in Primitive Communities*, Oxford University Press, London, 1932; or or S. Viljoen, *The Economics of Primitive Peoples*, King, London, 1936. For a brief but broad history of early economic investigations of primitive communities, v. P. W. Koppers, "Die Ethnologische Wirtschaftsforschung" in *Anthropos 10-11* (1915-6): 611-651, 971-1079. The "stages" of technology are discussed by Leroy Olivier, attacking Karl Bücher (*Industrial Evolution*, Trans. S. M. Wickett, New York, Holt, 1912), *Essai D'Introduction Critique à L'Etude de L'Economie Primitive*, Librairie Orientaliste Paul Guenthner Paris, 1925.
5. This is, however, a major problem of sociological analysis.
6. In *Coral Gardens and Their Magic* (vol. I, pp. 42, 76-6, etc.) Malinowski points out, as he has elsewhere, the importance of the yam in the social life of the Trobrianders. He notes that white traders consider them "irrational" in their insistence on gardening, instead of working for wages and then trading for yams. The economist cannot call this behavior "irrational."
7. Thus, the Tikopia had no money in the ordinary sense, and did not know its value. Presumably this is true of the Murngin, also.
8. Indeed, the "profit motive" is a prime example of means which have been transformed into an *ultimate* end.
9. Firth, *Primitive Polynesian Economy*, p. 7.
10. *Ibid.*
11. *Ibid.*
12. *Ibid.*
13. R. Firth, *Primitive Economics of the New Zealand Maori*, Dutton, N.Y., 1929, p. 17.

14. This does not mean, of course, there was no evolutionary process. It is simply a recognition of the complexity of cultural reconstructions, and a complete denial of any determinate unilinearity in this evolution. With reference to religion proper, see Appendix III, especially the analysis of Andrew Lang and W. Schmidt, who fought this simple evolutionary idea, even though the latter is perhaps impelled by a doctrinaire sentiment. See also the work of Leslie White, *The Science of Culture*, N.Y., Farrar and Straus, 1949, for a strong re-introduction of problems in social evolution.

15. See, for example, K. Bücher, *op. cit.*, pp. 12-14.

16. In a very strict sense, of course, Warner is correct, since he is apparently talking about an independent market system and money economy, and it is true that "other social institutions" regulate economic processes. However, a better understanding of economic theory would indicate that the first is not equated with an economic system, being only one aspect of it, and the latter proposition is true of any society. The lack of orientation toward these problems, however, makes the analysis of such phenomena difficult in the case of the Murngin.

17. Firth, *Primitive Polynesian Economy*, London: Routledge, 1939, pp. 353-354.

18. *Ibid.*, pp. 354-355.

19. The proposition has wider application than Firth suggests here (p. 357). What is known as "vulgar Marxism" makes an analogous error to this hedonistic bias of classical and later orthodox economics, by claiming that this or that phenomenon is "basically economic." Similarly, various brands of psychoanalytic theory have suggested one or another "basic" factor. These can all be reduced to the same structure: (1) A given phenomenon is basically X; (2) But demonstrably other factors are also playing a part in the phenomenon; (3) These factors are also X; (4) X causes everything, because (5) X *is* everything. The last propositions are, of course, never made explicit, since the first is usually a widespread sentiment generally accepted. This is true of the maximization of satisfactions, which turns out to mean that we do whatever we do because we want to do so, proved by the fact that we actually do it: an operationally meaningless, logically closed circle of reasoning.

20. Firth, *Economy*, p. 33.

21. See chs. VII and VIII on the function of the chief as lawmaker with reference to economic enterprise.

22. It must be repeated that at no point is the thesis maintained, that "social action is 'basically' religious." This would be notably inaccurate, and at several stages care has been taken to insist that certain actions were secular—political, economic, technological, etc. It is rather that at the various levels of social action some elements of religious belief and emotion do play a significant part, which must be emphasized in

our age because of the widespread and insistent stress on rational factors.

23. Firth, *The Work of the Gods*, vol. I, p. 91.
24. *Ibid.*
25. Firth, *Work*, vol. I, p. 68. Note also similar and longer formulae, pp. 62-90, with much the same suggestion.
26. *Ibid.*, p. 90.
27. Firth, *Work*, p. 90. See also the more detailed description of the inspection and repair of a canoe, in *Economy*, pp. 117-131.
28. This is interestingly intensified by the attitude which dictates the fast walk as the *tapu* or sacred stride, not the slow and stately walk of our culture. The movement must be hurried, jerky, fast, and efficient, with the weight on the toes and ball of the foot (*Work*, vol. II, p. 230): "The object was to convey the impression to the gods that the person was moving rapidly about their business, yet with due regard for the sacredness of the ground on which he treads."
29. *Ibid.*, p. 319.
30. *Ibid.*, vol. I, p. 62.
31. Somosomo is no longer a sacred house, only its former site. The mats are used for the site, as they are for any other temple. (See *Work*, vol. II, p. 304.) It was built, according to legend, by the Atua i Kafika.
32. The whole scene is given in *Work*, vol. II, p. 307.
33. Firth, *Work*, vol. I, p. 21.
34. That is, enough time to cut, dry, and plait the leaf.
35. Roi: "Taro or breadfruit are sliced, or ripe bananas (green bananas are not used for roi)." (*We the Tikopia*, p. 105.) After the coconut cream and sago flour have been poured over the ingredients, "the dish is then wrapped up and cooked ten hours or so."
36. Firth rightly insists (*Primitive Polynesian Economy*, pp. 168-186, "Ritual in Productive Activity") on a deterrent effect caused by much of ritual, and this negative function has been noted at several points in this study. Asking the aid of the deities is technologically ill conceived, judged by the canons of science, and in terms of the allocation of the resource of time and food (libations) is uneconomically irrational. It is, however, irrational only to the extent that such ceremonies are thought to be means, not ends in themselves. When the ritual is negative in its economic function, it is no less important in other aspects.
37. The food is for both ritual exchanges (secular, for the most part), ritual offerings, and homage to the chief. Bark cloth is produced to "top" the gifts of food, as a mark of prestige, while the mats are necessary for "recarpeting" the temples and replacing the mats of the sacred ancestors.
38. No claim need be made that these particular tasks could not be mostly secular in another society. What could be claimed, however,

is that in any society there will be important economic activities which are directed by the demands of religious beliefs and rituals. This does not imply at all that either "causes" the other.

39. *Primitive Polynesian Economy*, p. 202.

40. This planting is not accompanied by a complex ritual, and the chief goes alone merely because of the small amount of work involved. Cf. *Work of the Gods*, vol. II, p. 333.

41. The extraction is further based on purely secular economic factors, since the ownership of a spring for the washing, and of costly equipment, particularly the large troughs, are also important in the organization of the process. This is one ritual process which may be under the leadership of a commoner, at least in the technical phases.

42. Firth, *Work of the Gods*, vol. II, p. 335.

43. *Ibid.*, p. 337.

44. This whole discussion is taken from the detailed description given by Firth, pp. 332-373.

45. *Ibid.*, p. 344.

46. "Hot" is not a *descriptive*, but a *ritual*, term, since the food when eaten may actually be cold (*ibid.*, p. 344). It is, however, cooked specially for "those within," and is thus not the usual Tikopia cold food, which is merely a morning remnant from the previous afternoon's oven. Some relation may be considered in terms of sex and age divisions, since children in particular symbolize "cold food."

47. *Ibid.*, p. 346.

48. *Ibid.*, p. 349.

49. *Ibid.*, p. 350.

50. *Ibid.*, p. 354.

51. Firth notes (*ibid.*, p. 355) two cases where a very tiny amount was not allowed to be wasted, and maintains (p. 366) that in no case is turmeric thrown away because it did not turn out well in the oven: it is reworked and again baked, thus increasing production because of the sacred character of the product.

52. Firth, *ibid.*, p. 356. The Kafika chief demonstrated his great conscientiousness throughout the Work of the Gods.

53. Firth, *Primitive Polynesian Economy*, p. 213.

54. *Ibid.*, p. 213.

55. Firth says only (*ibid.*, p. 213), "To some extent" is this true. However, the process of receiving and giving as he describes it, coupled with the chief's relatively small consumption, his own and his family's production for their own use, etc., leave little room for doubt that his function as "agent" is rather marked.

56. As would be expected in this rather light-hearted culture, the tabus of mourning are lessened by the chief's kin, who press him to eat, anyway, his acceptance being rationalized as merely an effort to avoid offending his own kin. This is not true of the younger members of the family at that time (*ibid.*, p. 216).

57. *Ibid.*, p. 221.
58. One might, though doubtfully, include *monotanga* from initiations and funerals, since in both cases the sacred ancestors figure.
59. A complete list is given by Firth in *ibid.*, pp. 221-222.
60. Firth, *Work of the Gods*, vol. I, p. 158.
61. *Ibid.*, p. 164.
62. *Ibid.*
63. *Primitive Polynesian Economy*, p. 337.
64. *Ibid.*
65. *Ibid.*, pp. 320-332. Note especially the complex character of this type of exchange, in which the relationship to common and sacred ancestors is emphasized, stressing mostly the kinship ties.
66. The explanation may conceivably lie in the realm of the esthetic, in that the hook must be a special kind, "with the turtleshell barb attached to the shell shank. (The shank is frequently worn separately, as an ornament.)" See *Ibid.*, p. 339.
67. *Ibid.*, p. 342.
68. *Ibid.*, p. 338.
69. As a matter of fact, the question of the bonito hook raises another serious question which Firth attempts to answer (*Economy*, p. 342), as to the cause for such a small production of such valuable objects. The amount of labor put into them is much smaller than their equivalent value in terms of canoes, for example, and comparatively little skill is required. He suggests that there is little response of supply to demand because, mainly, of an indifference which amounts to a philosophy of life. That is, there is little stimulus to such acquisition, since their interests have other channels of expression. He suggests this as a hypothesis, though this study has documented it in several other connections, mostly religious. Their interest is much less in the economic effects of the ritual or the exchange, and much more in the devotion to the gods, the attainment of their favor, and the renewal of social and kinship ties. These latter are further emphasized, and the pattern of exchange leaves no one with what might be called a "profit," thus forcing motivation from the economic aspect of the ceremony.
70. *Ibid.*, p. 344.
71. The lack of equivalence between different series is expressed by Firth's statement that one cannot "express the value of a bonito hook in terms of a quantity of food, since no such exchange is ever made and would be regarded by the Tikopia as fantastic" (*ibid.*, p. 340).
72. This is true, even though commoners may actually own any of them, and may in fact be rather wealthy.
73. This does not imply social mobility, however, since rank is fixed by tradition, legend and religious belief. One can, however, live up to the fullest expectations of one's status, or fail to do so. In this, there can be considerable social emulation.

74. There is, of course, as in any culture, some evasion of these limitations, as in the case of fishing, where an individual may hide a big fish (which should go only to a chief) from the community and eat it with his family (*ibid.*, p. 364).

CHAPTER 8

1. Some interesting points have been raised, which are not immediately relevant, in these polemics. Cf., for example, Malinowski's *Crime and Punishment in Savage Society*, Harcourt, N.Y., 1926, and Wm. Seagle, "Primitive Law and Professor Malinowski," *Am. Anthrop.* 39:280 ff.; as well as A. R. Radcliffe-Brown, "Primitive Law" in the *Enc. Soc. Sci.* Note Malinowski's Introduction to H. Ian Hogbin's *Law and Order in Polynesia*, Christopher's, London, 1934. An interesting treatment is that of K. N. Llewellyn and E. Adamson Hoebel, *The Cheyenne Way*, University of Oklahoma, Norman (Okla.), 1941, pp. 20-65. For more concrete materials, v. Bruno Gutmann, *Das Recht der Dschagga*, Beck, München, 1926; Albert Harrasser, "Die Rechtsverletzung bei den australischen Eingeborenen," Beilagheft zur *Zeitschrift f. Vergleichende Rechtswissenschaft*, Bd. 50 (1936) Stuttgart; "Les derniers rois du Dahomey," by Henri Lefaivre, in *Revue d'Histoire des Colonies* 25 (1937): pp. 25-76; G. Härtter, "Das Gottesgericht bei den Ewe," in *Zeitschrift f. Ethnologie 69* (1937): 62-72; or, among a much less "developed" group, Herbert König's "Das Recht der Polarvölker" in *Anthropos* 22:689-746.

2. It is not certain that the basis of the distinction lies, analytically, in the presence of a writing system.

3. As is done, for example, by Malinowski (*Crime and Custom*), p. 28: ". . . a body of binding obligations, regarded as right by one party and acknowledged as a duty by the other, and kept in force by a specific mechanism of reciprocity [contractualism] and publicity inherent in the structure of their society"; or *The Family Life of the Australian Aborigines*, Hodder, London, 1913, p. 115: "A given social norm or rule is legal if it is enforced by a direct, organized, and definite social sanction." This leaves no analytical distinction between a spanking and an electrocution, though the answer might be made that ultimately there is little, both being concerned with order and social discipline.

4. As is done by Seagle, *op. cit.* This approach is simpler, but on the other hand excludes most societies, where nevertheless there are phenomena *analytically* similar.

5. Hogbin, *op. cit.*, pp. lxv-lxvi, *infra et supra*.

6. In our society. The Murngin have a different attitude, somewhat like ours in a situation of border skirmishes.

7. Cf. Max Weber, *Wirtschaft u. Gesellschaft*, pp. 642-9.

8. It becomes evident that the lawyers and the sociologists may easily bark up different trees. If there is a varying degree of explicitness, as seems obvious, then the sociologist or anthropologist is likely to see the degrees as being *only* degrees, while the legalist will note the differences between the extremes while failing to see the sameness of pattern.

9. Unpub. seminar discussion by Prof. W. E. Moore, Pennsylvania State College, Winter, 1941. I judge that both Llewellyn and Hoebel (E. Adamson Hoebel, *The Political Organization and Law-Ways of the Comanche Indians*, Am. Anthrop. Ass. Mem. No. 54, 1940, p. 47; Llewellyn and Hoebel, *op. cit.*, p. 23) would agree in general to this statement. Both criticize Malinowski in terms somewhat different from Seagle's, and emphasize the fact of authority or force as well as that of (court) conflict. The latter point is also made, as is known, by Vinogradoff (*Outlines of Historical Jurisprudence*, 2 vols., Oxford U., London, 1920-2).

10. Cf. Wilson D. Wallis, *Messiahs: Christian and Pagan*, Badger, Boston, 1918; Curt Nimuendaju, "Die Sagen von der Erschaffung und Vernichtung der Welt als Grundlagen der Religion der Apapoçuva-Guarani," *Zeitschrift f. Ethnologie 46* (1914): 284-403; Weston La-Barre, *The Peyote Cult* (Yale U. Pub. Anthrop.), New Haven, 1938; James Mooney, "The Ghost Dance Religion and Sioux Outbreak of 1890" (*Bur. Am. Ethn. Rep.*), 1892. Cf. Chester I. Barnard, *The Functions of the Executive*, Cambridge, Harvard University Press, 1938, esp. pp. 162-168.

11. Furnishing a good example, under the autocratically harsh Shaka, as is known, many Zulu left the country, forming the Matabele, Nguni, and Shangana. Note that (theoretically) great powers are usually hamstrung by the existence of numbers of officials who carry out the threat of those powers (or who sabotage them). Cf. the Dahomey king in this regard. The group gives the power, but *under conditions*, however implicit.

12. Weber, *op. cit.*, pp. 201-3, 250-7, 753-7.

13. See Ralph Linton's discussion of explicitness as it relates to the Comanche when compared to the highly organized West African cultures, in *The Study of Man*, Appleton-Century, N.Y., Stu. ed., 1936, pp. 227-9. This whole discussion as it deals with Tikopia will not be as complete as would be desired in the light of Firth's *Rank and Religion in Tikopia* (as yet unpublished).

14. For example, the "power behind the throne," the ultimate authority, may be presumed in some cases to be divine, but the bureaucratic structure becomes autonomous. More to home, the Menabe Tanala, the Tallensi, the Nguato, and the Zulu all have as "ultimate authorities" the French and British Governments, and this is true of Daho-

mey as well. The political structures of these tribes seem to operate more smoothly, however, when the ultimate authority stays out of the picture. *Vide* M. Fortes and E. E. Evans-Pritchard, *African Political Systems*, Oxford U., London, 1941, pp. 25-82, 239-71, as also the interesting discussion of recent trends in colonial rule, in L. P. Mair, *Native Policies in Africa*, Routledge, London, 1936. Cf. Weber, *Wirtschaft u. Gesellschaft*, pp. 150 ff.

15. E.g., the Fono of Rarokoka, to be discussed later, in Firth, *Work of the Gods*, vol. II, pp. 189-205.

16. It is difficult to avoid in such analyses the temptation of referring to the immediate past, and describing those patterns as though they existed today. This is particularly true of Dahomey's, whose autonomy was lost only in 1894, and whose inhabitants number many who lived in that former regime. Further, one thinks of changes forced on a group from the outside as being somehow less a part of the "real" society. It is possible to steer a middle ground, of making clear the temporal referent in any given case. For an interesting example of the vividness of Dahomean history to a native, cf. Le Herissé, *op. cit.*, pp. 271-352, "Histoire du Dahomey racontée par un Dahomean."

17. Though the present tense is used, it must be understood that the ordeal is not used now, ". . . except where fear of discovery is slight because of the remoteness of European officials, or the absence of French-speaking inhabitants . . ." (Herskovits, *op. cit.*, vol. II, p. 18, "Knowledge of this judicial magic, and the formulae for the manipulation of it, has been far from forgotten, however, and it is not without significance that in discussing the ordeals informants invariably used the present tense.")

18. Of course, in terms of the purposes and knowledge of a ruler, the choice of the ordeal then becomes a useful judicial tool, though the trial is made *after* his private decision of guilt.

19. Similarly, cf. Malinowski, *Crime* . . . , pp. 85-92, and Hogbin, *op. cit.*, pp. 216-22, though of course the conception of magic is slightly different as it leads to this conclusion.

20. This repeats in vividly concrete form the point mentioned above, that in a highly structured system the top power can be changed without the total pattern being destroyed. The modern fascistic or communist coup d'état is of the same nature.

21. Here, as in the case of the village ordeals, there was ample opportunity for determining the decision by manipulation. Le Herissé notes (p. 75, as Herskovits quotes) that the one who administered the ordeal could easily choke the bird. The administerer received a fee before the ritual.

22. Herskovits, *op. cit.*, vol. II, p. 20.

23. On the analytical level, such limitations always exist, in that neither can completely usurp all man's activity. On the concrete level, except

where the most powerful religious practitioner is also the political leader, conflicts or limitations are always potential between "king" and "high priest."

24. Herskovits, *op. cit.*, vol. II, p. 9.
25. Herskovits, *ibid.*, p. 12.
26. *Ibid.*, p. 14.
27. These were the property of the monarchy.
28. Herskovits, *op. cit.*, vol. I, p. 121.
29. *Ibid.*, p. 122. It should be emphasized, as Herskovits does not here, how signal an occasion this was, when the king allowed others to drink with him.
30. Again, here, Herskovits does not remark on the symbolic significance of the occasion, as indicated by the sprinkling of sacrificial blood on particular objects (akin, of course, to the Ashanti consecration of the stool).
31. There were only twelve which did not make hoes, and these were supervised closely. Cf. Herskovits, *op. cit.*, vol. I, p. 126.
32. Herskovits, *ibid.*, p. 127.
33. This case interestingly documents the worldly importance of religion. Even in this most secular of societies, where the king was ultimately powerful and just possibly somewhat more cynical or skeptical than others, religious powers are being used as means for secular ends (which might be superficially thought to be more easily attained by secular means); and, more important, the secular leader considered it necessary to guard against the power of religious action.
34. "Sacred," but possibly occurring in this world, and thus potentially competitive with the secular.
35. "Customs" is a frequently used term in the literature on Dahomey, referring to both the funeral ceremonies for a king, and the annual ceremonies in the kingly ancestral cult. Herskovits witnessed a one-day ceremonial (*op. cit.*, pp. 57-69) which was much like these. They were once very spectacular, and involved some human sacrifice (exaggerated in report), human beings constituting the most worthy gift for a kingly ceremony. Descriptions occur in Burton and Skertchly, as well as Forbes, though their reports differ as to the number killed. Cf. R. F. Burton, *A Mission to Gelele, King of Dahomey* etc. 2 vols. (III and IV of the Memorial Edition), London, 1893, vol. II, pp. 58 ff.; as well as vol. I, pp. 228 ff.; and J. A. Skertchly, *Dahomey*, London, 1874, pp. 178 ff., and pp. 383 ff.
36. A sacred number.
37. Herskovits, *op. cit.*, vol. I, p. 134.
38. *Ibid.*
39. "The political hierarchy of Dahomey may be thought of in a general way as comprising three ranks. The highest of these, where position was shared with no one, was occupied by the King." (Herskovits, *Da-*

homey, vol. II, p. 22.) Compare his statements with more isolated and less systematic comments on regions nearer the coast, in A. Bartet, "Les rois du Bas-Dahomey, *Soc. D. Geogr. D. Rochefort Bull.* (Rochefort), vol. 30 (1908): 179-216; also Henri Lefaivre, "Les dernier . . . ," *op. cit.* The earlier traveler's reports, of course, emphasized these aspects more than any others.

40. This was one of the most striking elements of the political life of Dahomey, to an outsider, since early reports emphasize the ceremony of throwing dirt on the head, etc. Herskovits points out, and photographs show, how Dahomeans "still prostrate themselves before a superior," *op. cit.*, p. 33.

41. One must be cautious, however, in interpreting this since certainly the larger part of this deep respect was not alone religious in character (i.e., consciously), but a reflection of the extreme power of life and death—even though this secular power had certain bases even further removed, i.e., the religious.

42. Herskovits, *ibid.*, p. 36.

43. *Ibid.*

44. There are, of course, suggestions in Robert S. Rattray, *Religion and Art in Ashanti*, Oxford, Clarendon, 1927, and *Ashanti Law and Constitution*, Oxford, Clarendon, 1929, in that some of the same symbolisms are used in the two cultures, particularly the consecration by blood. Cf. also in this regard, Paul Hazourné, "Le pacte de sang au Dahomey," *Trav. Et. Memoires d'Ethn.* 25 (1937): viii-170.

45. Le Herissé, *op. cit.*, pp. 271-2.

46. Herskovits, *op. cit.*, vol. II, p. 49. The "apartness" of this group is accentuated by the fact that ". . . no prince, and no child of a prince, may become a cult member of any of the gods. He may not even be vowed as a cult member of the royal *Tɔhwiyo*, for the relationship of cult-member to his *Vodun* is that of servant, and no one of royal blood may affiliate himself with a *Vodun* and serve him publicly, for royal blood, even in the living, partakes of godly qualities" (Herskovits and Herskovits, *op. cit.*, p. 30).

47. *Ibid.*

48. *Ibid.*

49. Herskovits claims (*op. cit.*, vol. II, p. 68) that Behanzin's family had been impoverished by the "Great Customs" at Behanzin's death, in accordance with the Dahomean notion of having an incredibly impressive funeral. This ceremony was a commemoration of Behanzin's funeral.

50. Now a chief of one of the quarters in Abomey.

51. Later attention will be given to sex position, though it may be noted here that in spite of the "masculinity" of the society, women, especially elder women, held important positions in the political hierarchy, usually as quasi-official checkers or inspectors of affairs entrusted to various officials.

52. Herskovits, *op. cit.*, vol. II, p. 62; for his description, see pp. 57-69; sources for earlier descriptions of these and the "Great Customs" have been previously noted. These seem to have been ritualized expressions of the wealth, secular power, and sacredness of the king.

53. Animals now; though, as noted, human sacrifices played a part under the monarchy. These were often substituted for by animals.

54. The tragedy of this, in Dahomean terms, ought to be kept in mind. They would therefore lack the proper funeral ceremonies, and would not (probably) ever be a central figure in deification ceremonies.

55. Herskovits calls his movements (*op. cit.*, vol. II, p. 67) "ritually awk-ward," and this may be a proper characterization. However, the awkwardness may be indeed real, since the king (or chief) could not be expected to be capable of priestly grace.

56. *Ibid.*, p. 68.

57. Herskovits mentions (*op. cit.*, vol. II, p. 75) that "even under the present European regime this official exists, though he has no stand-ing with the government." He represents an excellent example of the insight of the monarchy into the pervasiveness of religious activities, and the possibility of utilizing them.

58. Herskovits makes no such qualification, yet the possessors of such an esoteric lore as was under the control of the priests, and the holders of such power in other directions, would certainly reduce in actuality much of this theoretical secular power. This would be further true, since the followers could not be allowed to know much about this control, else the religious control would wane. Actually, there seems to have been no need for any constantly *active* control. Cf. Herskovits, *op. cit.*, vol. II, p. 175.

59. These were the abnormally born.

60. Herskovits, *op. cit.*, vol. II, p. 175.

61. He might also be removed if there were—the other side of the inter-relationship—signs of divine displeasure with the officiant.

62. Though many ceremonies are "secret," i.e., not open to the uninitiate, the Dahomeans do not consider them secret. See Herskovits, *op. cit.*, vol. II, p. 194.

63. This does not mean, however, that the upper class did or does not patronize the diviner: Even the diviner patronizes another diviner, if a crisis arises (Herskovits, *op. cit.*, vol. II, p. 215).

64. *Ibid.*

65. Herskovits, *op. cit.*, vol. I, pp. 118-9. This was only one such tech-nique. Since taxation of livestock took place only once in about three years, variations of this false alarm could be used: floods, general mis-fortunes, etc., there being some difference in what was done to avert the calamities. In each case, however, the supernatural, administered by official religious practitioners, was utilized for political ends, thus emphasizing the wide uses of the religious beliefs. The particular deity involved also varied.

CHAPTER 9

1. On the psychological level, the motivational power of both love and sex is intensified by this curious fact (which I have not seen remarked on elsewhere): Love is the most projective of emotions, as sex is the most projective of drives; only with great difficulty can the attracted person believe that the object of his love or passion does not and will not reciprocate the feeling at all. Thus, the person may carry his action quite far, before accepting a rejection as genuine.

2. I have treated decision analysis extensively in an unpublished paper by that title.

3. Vatsyayana, *The Kama Sutra*, Delhi: Rajkamal, 1948; Ovid, "The Loves," and "Remedies of Love," in *The Art of Love*, Cambridge, Mass.: Harvard University Press, 1939; Andreas Capellanus, *The Art of Courtly Love*, translated by John J. Parry, New York: Columbia University Press, 1941; Paul Tuffrau, editor, *Marie de France: Les Lais de Marie de France*, Paris: L'edition d'art, 1925; see also Julian Harris, *Marie de France*, New York: Institute of French Studies, 1930, esp. Chapter 3. All authors but the first *also* had the goal of writing literature.

4. Ernest R. Mowrer, *Family Disorganization*, Chicago: The University of Chicago Press, 1927, pp. 158-165; Ernest W. Burgess and Harvey J. Locke, *The Family*, New York: American Book, 1953, pp. 436-437; Mabel A. Elliott and Francis E. Merrill, *Social Disorganization*, New York: Harper, 1950, pp. 366-384; Andrew G. Truxal and Francis E. Merrill, *The Family in American Culture*, New York: Prentice-Hall, 1947, pp. 120-124, 507-509; Ernest R. Groves and Gladys Hoagland Groves, *The Contemporary American Family*, New York: Lippincott, 1947, pp. 321-324.

5. William L. Kolb, "Sociologically Established Norms and Democratic Values," *Social Forces*, 26 (May, 1948), pp. 451-456.

6. Hugo G. Beigel, "Romantic Love," *American Sociological Review*, 16 (June, 1951), pp. 326-334.

7. Sigmund Freud, *Group Psychology and the Analysis of the Ego*, London: Hogarth, 1922, p. 72.

8. Willard Waller, *The Family*, New York: Dryden, 1938, pp. 189-192.

9. Talcott Parsons, *Essays in Sociological Theory*, Glencoe, Ill.: Free Press, 1949, pp. 187-189.

10. Robert F. Winch, *Mate Selection*, New York: Harper, 1958.

11. See, e.g., Robert F. Winch, *The Modern Family*, New York: Holt, 1952, Chapter 14.

12. Robert H. Lowie, "Sex and Marriage," in John F. McDermott, editor, *The Sex Problem in Modern Society*, New York: Modern Library, 1931, p. 146.

13. Ralph Linton, *The Study of Man*, New York: Appleton-Century, 1936, p. 175.
14. George Peter Murdock, *Social Structure*, New York: Macmillan, 1949.
15. Max Gluckman, *Custom and Conflict in Africa*, Oxford: Basil Blackwell, 1955, Chapter 3.
16. I hope to deal with the second problem in another paper.
17. Tribal India, of course, is too heterogeneous to place in any one position on such a continuum. The question would have to be answered for each tribe. Obviously it is of less importance here whether China and Japan, in recent decades, have moved "two points over" toward the opposite pole of high approval of love relationships as a basis for marriage than that both systems as classically described viewed love as generally a tragedy; and love was supposed to be irrelevant to marriage, i.e., noninstitutionalized. The continuum permits us to place a system at some position, once we have the descriptive data.
18. See Ludwig Friedländer, *Roman Life and Manners under the Early Empire* (Seventh Edition), translated by A. Magnus, New York: Dutton, 1908, Vol. 1, Chapter 5, "The Position of Women."
19. For a discussion of the relation between behavior patterns and the process of institutionalization, see my *After Divorce*, Glencoe, Ill.: Free Press, 1956, Chapter 15.
20. See Ernest W. Burgess and Paul W. Wallin, *Engagement and Marriage*, New York: Lippincott, 1953, Chapter 7 for the extent to which even the engaged are not blind to the defects of their beloveds. No one has ascertained the degree to which various age and sex groups in our society actually believe in some form of the ideology.

    Similarly, Margaret Mead in *Coming of Age in Samoa*, New York: Modern Library, 1953, rates Manu'an love as shallow, and though these Samoans give much attention to love-making, she asserts that they laughed with incredulous contempt at Romeo and Juliet (pp. 155-156). Though the individual sufferer showed jealousy and anger, the Manu'ans believed that a new love would quickly cure a betrayed lover (pp. 105-108). It is possible that Mead failed to understand the shallowness of love in our own society: Romantic love is, "in our civilization, inextricably bound up with ideas of monogamy, exclusiveness, jealousy, and undeviating fidelity" (p. 105). But these are *ideas* and ideology; *behavior* is rather different.
21. The relation of "courtly love" to social structure is complicated. [1973: However, almost certainly this was literary play-acting, never more than a poetic titillation in the arranged marriages of that time.]
22. Frieda M. Das, *Purdah*, New York: Vanguard, 1932; Kingsley Davis, *The Population of India and Pakistan*, Princeton: Princeton University Press, 1951, p. 112. There was a widespread custom of taking one's bride from a village other than one's own.
23. W. Lloyd Warner, *Black Civilization*, New York: Harper, 1937, pp.

82-84. They may also become "sweethearts" at puberty; see pp. 86-89.

24. See Murdock, *op. cit.*, pp. 53 ff. *et passim* for discussions of double-descent.

25. One adjustment in Australia was for the individuals to leave the tribe for a while, usually eloping, and then to return "reborn" under a different and now appropriate kinship designation. In any event, these marital prescriptions did not prevent love entirely. As Malinowski shows in his early summary of the Australian family systems, although every one of the tribes used the technique of infant betrothal (and close prescription of mate), no tribe was free of elopements, between either the unmarried or the married, and the "motive of sexual love" was always to be found in marriages by elopement. B. Malinowski. *The Family Among the Australian Aborigines*, London: University of London Press, 1913, p. 83.

26. This pattern was apparently achieved in Manus, where on first menstruation the girl was removed from her playmates and kept at "home" —on stilts over a lagoon—under the close supervision of elders. The Manus were prudish, and love occurred rarely or never. Margaret Mead, *Growing Up in New Guinea*, in *From the South Seas*, New York: Morrow, 1939, pp. 163-166, 208.

27. See Das, *op. cit.*

28. For the activities of the *tsu*, see Hsien Chin Hu, *The Common Descent Group in China and Its Functions*, New York: Viking Fund Studies in Anthropology, 10 (1948). For the marriage process, see Marion J. Levy, *The Family Revolution in Modern China*, Cambridge: Harvard University Press, 1949, pp. 87-107. See also Olga Lang, *Chinese Family and Society*, New Haven: Yale University Press, 1946, for comparisons between the old and new systems. In one-half of 62 villages in Ting Hsien Experimental District in Hopei, the largest clan included 50 per cent of the families; in 25 per cent of the villages, the two largest clans held over 90 per cent of the families; I am indebted to Robert M. Marsh who has been carrying out a study of Ching mobility partly under my direction for this reference: Ching-han Li, *Ting Hsien She-hui K'ai-K'uang t'iao-ch'a*, Peiping: Chung-hua p'ing-min Chiao-yu ts'u-chin hui, 1932, p. 54. See also Sidney Gamble, *Ting Hsien: A North China Rural Community*, New York: International Secretariat of the Institute of Pacific Relations, 1954.

29. For Japan, see Shidzué Ishimoto, *Facing Two Ways*, New York: Farrar and Rinehart, 1935, Chapters 6, 8; John F. Embree, *Suye Mura*, Chicago: University of Chicago Press, 1950, Chapters 3, 6.

30. I do not mean, of course, to restrict this pattern to these times and places, but I am more certain of these. For the Puritans, see Edmund S. Morgan, *The Puritan Family*, Boston: Public Library, 1944. For the somewhat different practices in New York, see Charles E. Iron-

ide, *The Family in Colonial New York*, New York: Columbia University Press, 1942. See also: A. Abram, *English Life and Manners in the Later Middle Ages*, New York: Dutton, 1913, Chapters 4, 10; Emily J. Putnam, *The Lady*, New York: Sturgis and Walton, 1910, Chapter 4; James Gairdner, editor, *The Paston Letters, 1422-1509*, 4 vols., London: Arber, 1872-1875; Eileen Power, "The Position of Women," in C. G. Crump and E. F. Jacobs, editors, *The Legacy of the Middle Ages*, Oxford: Clarendon, 1926, pp. 414-416.

31. For those who believe that the young in the United States are totally deluded by love, or believe that love outranks every other consideration, see: Ernest W. Burgess and Paul W. Wallin, *Engagement and Marriage*, New York: Lippincott, 1953, pp. 217-238. Note Karl Robert V. Wikman, *Die Einleitung Der Ehe. Acta Academiae Aboensis (Humaniora)*, 11 (1937), pp. 127 ff. Not only are reputations known because of close association among peers, but songs and poetry are sometimes composed about the girl or boy. Cf., for the Tikopia, Raymond Firth, *We, the Tikopia*, New York: American Book, 1936, pp. 468 ff.; for the Siuai, Douglas L. Oliver, *Solomon Island Society*, Cambridge: Harvard University Press, 1955, pp. 146 ff. The Manu'ans made love in groups of three or four couples; cf. Mead, *Coming of Age in Samoa, op. cit.*, p. 92.

32. Marvin B. Sussman, "Parental Participation in Mate Selection and Its Effect upon Family Continuity," *Social Forces*, 32 (October, 1953), pp. 76-81.

33. Wikman, *op. cit.*

34. Mead, *Coming of Age in Samoa, op. cit.*, pp. 97-108; and Firth, *op. cit.*, pp. 520 ff.

35. Thus Malinowski notes in his "Introduction" to Reo F. Fortune's *The Sorcerers of Dobu*, London: Routledge, 1932, p. xxiii, that the Dobu have similar patterns, the same type of courtship by trial and error, with a gradually tightening union.

36. Gunnar Landtman, *Kiwai Papuans of the Trans-Fly*, London: Macmillan, 1927, pp. 243 ff.; Oliver, *op. cit.*, pp. 153 ff.

37. The pattern apparently existed among the Marquesans as well, but since Linton never published a complete description of this Polynesian society, I omit it here. His fullest analysis, cluttered with secondary interpretations, is in Abram Kardiner, *Psychological Frontiers of Society*, New York: Columbia University Press, 1945. For the Tanala, see Ralph Linton, *The Tanala*, Chicago: Field Museum, 1933, pp. 300-303.

38. Thus, Radcliffe-Brown: "The African does not think of marriage as a union based on romantic love, although beauty as well as character and health are sought in the choice of a wife," in his "Introduction" to A. R. Radcliffe-Brown and W. C. Daryll Ford, editors, *African Systems of Kinship and Marriage*, London: Oxford University Press,

1950, p. 46. For the Nuer, see E. E. Evans-Pritchard, *Kinship and Marriage Among the Nuer*, Oxford: Clarendon, 1951, pp. 49-58. For the Kgatla, see I. Schapera, *Married Life in an African Tribe*, New York: Sheridan, 1941, pp. 55 ff. For the Bavenda, although the report seems incomplete, see Hugh A. Stayt, *The Bavenda*, London: Oxford University Press, 1931, pp. 111 ff., 145 ff., 154.

39. The second correlation is developed from Marion J. Levy, *The Family Revolution in China*, Cambridge, Harvard University Press, 1949, p. 179. Levy's formulation ties "romantic love" to that solidarity, and is of little use because there is only one case, the Western culture complex. As he states it, it is almost so by definition.

40. E.g., Mead, *Coming of Age in Samoa, op. cit.*, pp. 79, 92, 97-109. Cf. also Firth, *op. cit.*, pp. 520 ff.

41. Although one must be cautious about China, this inference seems to be allowable from such comments as the following: "But the old men of China did not succeed in eliminating love from the life of the young women. . . . Poor and middle-class families could not afford to keep men and women in separate quarters, and Chinese also met their cousins. . . . Girls . . . sometimes even served customers in their parents' shops." Olga Lang, *op. cit.*, p. 33. According to Fried, farm girls would work in the fields, and farm girls of ten years and older were sent to the market to sell produce. They were also sent to towns and cities as servants. The peasant or pauper woman was not confined to the home and its immediate environs. Morton H. Fried, *Fabric of Chinese Society*, New York: Praeger, 1953, pp. 59-60. Also, Levy (*op. cit.*, p. 111): "Among peasant girls and among servant girls in gentry households some premarital experience was not uncommon, though certainly frowned upon. The methods of preventing such contact were isolation and chaperonage, both of which, in the 'traditional' picture, were more likely to break down in the two cases named than elsewhere."

42. Fortune, *op. cit.*, p. 30.

43. Personal letter, dated January 9, 1958. However, the Nuer father can still refuse if he believes the demands of the girl's people are unreasonable. In turn, the girl can cajole her parents to demand less.

CHAPTER 10

1. Iceland's rate was 27.9% in 1950 (Meyer F. Nimkoff, "Illegitimacy," in *Encyclopedia Britannica*, 1954.) The Swedish illegitimacy rate has been dropping over the past generation. The highest rates have been found in Stockholm (1841-1860, 43% illegitimate; 1901-1910, 34%; 1921-1925, 28%), but presumably these include many rural mothers.

However, the regions of Gävleborgslän and Jamtlands län have continued to be relatively high (23% and 21% in 1921-1925; 17.6% and 18.5% in 1956). In Steiermark in Austria, the rate was 19% in 1956 (*Stat. J. Oesterreichs*, 1956). Oberbayern in Germany had a rate of 18.5% in 1954 (*Stat. J. Für Bayern*, 1955). I have recently found that certain regions of Portugal (Lisboa, Beja, Evora, and Setubal) have rates of 20%-30%, but I have found no special reports on them.

2. The best surveys of recent changes may be found in *Social Implications of Industrialization and Urbanization South of the Sahara*, Paris, UNESCO, 1956, and Survey of African Marriage and *Survey of African Marriage and Family Life*, edited by Arthur Phillips, London: Oxford University, 1953. Twenty-three per cent of all unmarried women in certain Kxatla groups had borne children, 19% among the Ngwato and 17% among the Kwena (I. Schapera, *Migrant Labour and Tribal Life*, New York: Oxford, 1947, p. 173). An analysis of Bantu attitudes toward illegitimacy may be found in I. Schapera, "Pre-marital Pregnancy and Public Opinion," *Africa*, 6 (January, 1933), esp. pp. 83-89. Krige reported an illegitimacy rate of 59% in three locations in Pretoria (Eileen J. Krige, "Changing Conditions in Marital Relations and Parental Duties Among Urbanized Natives," *Africa*, 9 (No. 1, 1936), p. 4.) Janisch found that some half of the couples in a Johannesburg native township were "merely living together" (Miriam Janisch, "Some Administrative Aspects of Native Marriage Problems in an Urban Area," *Bantu Studies*, 15 (1941), p. 9.) In Capetown, illegitimacy rates of 26%-41% were reported in the period 1939-1944 (Ruth Levin, "Marriage in Langa Native Location," *Communications From the School of African Studies*, Capetown: University of Capetown, 1947, p. 41. The rate was 30% in Capetown in 1958. For Leopoldville, S. Comhaire-Sylvain reports almost half of the couples in certain native wards were living in concubinage, "Food and Leisure Among the African Youth in Leopoldville," *Communications From the School of African Studies*, N.S., No. 25, December 1950, p. 23. Similar processes of "living together" have been described in the urbanizing area of Kampala (A. W. Southall and P. C. W. Gutkind, *Townsmen in the Making, East African Studies No. 9*, Kampala: East African Institute of Social Research, 1956, pp. 72, 74, 79, 174-8.

3. Data courtesy of U.S. National Office of Vital Statistics.

4. There are, of course, numerous monographs on the African societies that furnished the slaves. Because the Indian groups were, for the most part, destroyed before the anthropologists arrived, New World societies are less well known than the African, but an excellent summary of the known South American (including the Circum-Caribbean) societies may be found in *Handbook of South American Indians*, edited by Julian H. Steward, Washington, D.C.: Smithsonian

Institution, Bureau of American Ethnology, Bulletin No. 143, 6 vols., 1946-1950.

5. For details of this process, see William J. Goode, "Illegitimacy in the Caribbean Social Structure," *American Sociological Review*, 25 (February, 1960), pp. 21-30. The best analysis of this process in Jamaica is by Judith Blake, *Family Structure in Jamaica*, Glencoe, Ill.: The Free Press, forthcoming.

6. The most complete description of this pattern, and of its temporal and geographical distribution, is to be found in K. Rob. V. Wikman, *Einleitung Der Ehe*, Abo, *Acta Academiae Aboensis; Humaniora*, 1937. He asserts, however, that the pattern was not found in Iceland.

7. And consequently, the rate of divorce for such marriages would be lower than for "forced" marriages in the United States. See Harold T. Christensen, "Cultural Relativism and Premarital Sex Norms," *American Sociological Review*, 25 (February, 1960), pp. 31-39. See also Sidney H. Croog, "Aspects of the Cultural Background of Premarital Pregnancy in Denmark, *Social Forces*, 39 (December, 1951), pp. 215-219.

8. Mr. John Western has pointed out to me that there may be considerable difference in the assimilation patterns of those who "just landed" in the cities and stayed there and those who deliberately chose to migrate to the city.

9. William J. Goode, *op. cit.*, pp. 27 ff.

10. The dominance of European nations is also weakened by important changes in the political philosophy of Europeans. They no longer accept colonialism as morally right.

11. See the estimates of the proportion of destruction by certain dates, in Sol Tax, *et al.*, *Heritage of Conquest*, Glencoe, Ill.: The Free Press, 1952, p. 264. Most of these groups are among the less acculturated peoples in the New World.

12. Of course, the whites first ruled indirectly in Africa through native chiefs, but this becomes impossible in industrial and urban locations.

13. The Creoles faced similar restrictions also: only four viceroys in Spanish America up to 1813 were American born, and these were sons of Spanish officials; 601 of the 706 bishops and archbishops came from Spain. Moreover, the restrictions had become more severe in the eighteenth century (C. H. Haring, *The Spanish Empire in America*, New York: Oxford University, 1957, p. 209). It can be argued that the first *social* revolution in Latin America was the 1910 Mexican Revolution (Robin A. Humphreys, *The Evolution of Modern Latin America*, New York: Oxford University, 1946, pp. 119-122).

14. Melvin M. Tumin, *Caste in a Peasant Society*, Princeton: Princeton University, 1952.

15. For an analysis of one attempt to solve this problem, see "The Problem of Slave Labor Supply at the Codrington Plantations," by J.

Harry Barnett, *Journal of Negro History*, 37 (April, 1952), pp. 115-141.

16. Frank Tannenbaum, *Slave and Citizen*, New York: Knopf, 1947.
17. Ruth Landes, "Negro Slavery and Female Status," in *Les Afro-Américains, Institut Français d'Afrique Noire* (Dakar), 1952, pp. 265-266.
18. See an examination of these contradictions by George Kubler, "The Quechua in the Colonial World," in *Handbook of South American Indians, op. cit.*, vol. 2, pp. 374-375 *et passim.* Indians in Peru were not even allowed to own horses, though there were many of them: Bernard Mishkin, "The Contemporary Quechua," *ibid.*, p. 427.
19. Mishkin (*ibid.*, p. 448) reports this of the Quechua today The "isolation" of New World villages south of the Rio Grande has been commented on by most observers.
20. It is worth noting that Alexander von Humboldt also commented on the relation between the Indian's anomie and lack of motivation (see Haring, *op. cit.*, pp. 201-202).
21. I am of course aware of the difficulties in interpreting illegitimacy rates in countries where recording procedures are undeveloped: (1) Official urban rates might be higher than rural rates, because recording procedures are more thorough. (2) In some rural areas, those classed as "Indios" may be generally ignored by officials. (3) Where social services are available in the city, as in San Juan, Puerto Rico, some illegitimacies may be recorded there, although the mothers come from rural villages. (4) The disorganization of urban slums may lead to much promiscuity and thus *override* any of the factors presented in my analysis (e.g., Caracas, Venezuela). (5) It is difficult to obtain true "rural-urban" breakdowns, because the political sub-units (provinces, departments, sections) of Latin American nations typically contain both an urban center and a surrounding rural countryside and the data are recorded for the sub-unit as a whole. Nevertheless, all of these except the last (whose effect is unknown) would bias the official rates *against* my hypothesis. Consequently it seems safe to use the data. Many analysts have claimed that consensual unions, and therefore illegitimacy, are more common in rural areas. As we shall see, however, that assertion is correct only for mainland, independent Latin America. (See, for example, Kingsley Davis and Ana Casís, *Urbanization in Latin America*, New York: Milbank Memorial Fund, 1946, pp. 39-40.)

    Included under "illegitimate" are those born of a consensual union, whether or not the offspring are "recognized," as well as those born outside of any continuing marital relationship. These are official rates.
22. Dirección Nacional de Estadística y Censos, Argentina, 1959 (Personal Communication).
23. *Anuario Estadístico de Distrito Federal 1949-53.* Rio de Janeiro, Departmento de Geografia e Estatistica, 1955, p. 46. Also *Demographic*

Yearbook Questionnaire, 1952, Statistical Office of the United Nations, New York.

24. Comité Nacional de Estadísticas Vitales y Sanitaris de Chile, 1959 (Personal Communication).

25. *Anuario Estadístico de la República Oriental del Uruguay*, Año 1943, Volumen I, Montevideo, Imprenta Nacional, 1943, p. 8. The *Boletín de Estadística*, Intendencia Municipal de Montevideo, Dirección de Censo y Estadística, Año 41, 1943, gives figures which yield a rate of 24.4% for Montevideo. I do not know whence the discrepancy.

26. *Anuario Estadístico de la República del Paraguay 1946-47*. Asunción, Imprenta Nacional, 1948, pp. 39-40.

27. *Anuario General de Estadística 1956*. Colombia, Departmento Administrativo Nacional de Estadística, 1957, pp. 33-34.

28. *El Trimestre Estadístico del Ecuador*. Dirección General de Estadística y Censos del Ecuador, 1947, p. 30.

29. *Anuario Estadístico del Peru, 1953*. Lima, Ministerio de Hacienda y Comercio, 1956, pp. 76-77.

30. *Anuario Estadístico de Venezuela, 1954*. Caracas, Ministerio de Fomento, 1957, pp. 82-83, 108-109.

31. *Anuario Estadístico de la República de Nicaragua, Año 1947*. Managua, Publications del Ministerio de Hacienda y Crédito Público, 1953, p. 61.

32. Figures obtained from Dirección General de Estadística y Censos, República de Honduras, C. A., 1959 (Personal Communication).

33. *Anuario Estadístico de Costa Rica, 1957*. San José, Impreso en la Sección de Publicaciones, 1958, p. 25.

34. Dirección General de Estadística, 1959, México (Personal Communication).

35. *Anuario Estadístico 1955*. Volumen 1. San Salvador, Dirección General de Estadística y Censos, 1956, p. 37. Salvador, although in the predicted direction, may be changing: the *Anuario Estadístico* for 1949 yields different figures: San Salvador 72.2% illegitimate, remainder of country 65.1% illegitimate. (*Anuario Estadístico de la República de El Salvador*, Tomo 1, San Salvador, Dirección General de Estadística y Censos, 1953, p. 81.) In 1955, all the urban *areas* had a rate of 57.5, the rural, 56.5).

36. Figures obtained from Dirección General de Estadística y Censos, República de Guatemala, C. A.

37. Excludes Indians in purely Indian territories. Personal communication from Dirección de Estadística y Censos of Panama.

38. The apparent exception, El Salvador, had a rural-urban differential in 1955 of only 1% (42.5%-43.5%). The table compares the extreme of *urban* San Salvador with the rest of the country.

39. Figures supplied by Dirección Nacional de Estadística.

40. Rates calculated from figures furnished by Caribbean Commission, and from U.S. National Office of Vital Statistics.

41. All rates were obtained from the *United Nations Demographic Year Book Questionnaire* for the respective dates, except the figure for Puerto Rico, which was obtained from the Caribbean Commission. It was not possible to obtain recent Cuban data and many smaller political units have been omitted.

Bolivia has been eliminated because any birth is recorded as legitimate if the couple has been living together for two years (personal communication from Dirección Nacional de Estadística). As noted later, in Guatemala many births are classified as illegitimate because no civil ceremony preceded them, though other types of marriage ceremonies may have occurred, so that its real rate is lower than its official rate.

With respect to the independent variable, there is reason to believe that this classification would for the most part be conceded by New World specialists. Several such specialists have already accepted it.

The bases for the classification are these: (1) The maintenance of caste barriers, which remain strong in Guatemala and the Andean Highlands and are weak in Brazil and Mexico. (2) Extent of ethnic hemogeneity. Uruguay and Costa Rica, for example, are very "Spanish" or "European," and in Mexico, Cuba, Chile, and Puerto Rico a thorough-going mixing has occurred, in contrast to Guatemala. (3) The status of political dependency. (4) The existence of national programs for education, literacy, economic development (Puerto Rico, United States, Argentina). (5) The existence of large pockets of geographically and socially isolated populations (Bolivia, Ecuador, Peru). (6) Comparison of comments by New World experts, with respect to how much the natives care about or take part in national political affairs or how long various forms of labor exploitation have continued (e.g., indentured labor was abolished in Jamaica in 1917). Too much weight may have been given to the relatively unintegrated Andean populations of Bolivia, Peru, and Ecuador. If so, they would move to "medium" integration, and their reported illegitimacy rates would "fit" better. For relevant material on the degree to which the populations of these countries are integrated into the national life, see: Harold Osborne, *Bolivia*, London: 1954, Royal Institute of International Affairs, 1954, pp. 93-99; W. Stanley Rycroft, *Indians of the High Andes*, London: Routledge and Kegan, 1952, pp. 211-219, 231-236; Mary Patricia Holleran, *Church and State in Guatemala*, New York: Oxford University Press, 1949, pp. 244-245; Melvin Tumin, *Caste in a Peasant Society*, Princeton: Princeton University Press, 1952; James Preston, *Latin America*, New York: Odyssey, revised edition, 1950, pp. 44, 46, 69, 71, 76, 120, 124-125, 193-195, 212, 213, 221, 316, 352, 531, 619, 644, 662, 708, 710; Olen E. Leonard, *Bolivia*, Washington: Scarecrow, 1952, pp. 90-101; Thomas R. Ford, *Man and Land in Peru*, Gainesville, Florida: University of Florida, 1955, pp. 111-116.

Doubtless, many observers would classify *all* those in D. as "lower integration" units. I have no objection but simply have been unable to obtain sufficient data on them to be certain.

42. Various observers have remarked on the lesser ease, openness, and friendliness of the Andean peasants who work on a *finca* or *hacienda* compared with those who have continued to live on communal lands; Rycroft, *op. cit.*, p. 82; Harry Tschopik, "The Aymara," *Handbook of South American Indians, op. cit.*, vol. 2, p. 501; Osborne, *op. cit.*, pp. 211-12.

43. The relatively highly integrated communities here outnumber the less well integrated, because anthropologists seek out the "unspoiled," the "culturally unified" village.

In the citations which follow I have quoted the pages which are most relevant for the classification presented. To classify a village as *non*integrated appears to be more difficult than to show its integration, possibly because there are many different ways in which a village may *not* be internally integrated. Indices such as these seem relevant: (1) how many of the young adults are attracted to city life and ways, (2) how well the elders still control the young, (3) how important is a "good name in the village," (4) how effectively non-legal, informal relationships may decide local issues, (5) how large a portion of the village participates in ceremonies and how much of village life centers around such ceremonies. Tzintzuntzán: *Empire's Children*, Smithsonian Institution Institute of Social Anthropology, Publ. No. 6, Mexico: Nuevo Mundo, 1948, pp. 1, 2, 11 ff., 23, 33, 247 ff.; Cherán: *Cherán: A Sierra Tarascan Village*, Smithsonian Institution Institute of Social Anthropology, Publ. No. 2, Washington: 1946, pp. 1-2, 12, 176 ff.; *Cruz das Almas*, Smithsonian Institution Institute of Social Anthropology, Publ. No. 12, Washington: 1948, pp. 1-13, 127-143, 197 ff.; Tusik and Quintana Roo: Robert Redfield, *The Folk Culture of Yucatan*, Chicago: University of Chicago, 1941, Chaps. III and VIII; Orange Grove and Sugartown: Edith Clarke, *My Mother Who Fathered Me*, London: Allen and Unwin, 1957, pp. 78-79, 82-84, 90-102, 127; Nyame: Raymond T. Smith, *The Negro Family in British Guiana*, New York: Grove, 1956, pp. 181-182. Saucío: Orlando Fals-Borda, *Peasant Society in the Colombian Andes*, Gainesville, Florida: University of Florida, pp. 37, 204-207, 211; Oliver LaFarge, *Santa Eulalia*, Chicago: University of Chicago, 1947, pp. 21-44; Else Clews Parsons, *Peguche*, Chicago: University of Chicago, 1945, Chap. 1, pp. 54-60; Otóvalo: John Collier and Aníbal Buitrón, *The Awakening Valley*, Chicago: University of Chicago, 1949, pp. 31-32, chap. on "Marriage"; Rocky Roads: Yehudi A. Cohen, "The Social Organization of a Selected Community in Jamaica," *Social and Economic Studies*, 2 (1954), pp. 104-33, and "Four Categories of Interpersonal Relationships in the Family and Community in a Jamaican Village," *Anthropological Quarterly*, 28 (October, 1955), pp. 121-147; John Gillin, *Moche*,

Smithsonian Institution Institute of Social Anthropology, Publ. No. 3, Washington: n.d., pp. 30, 93 ff.; *Tobatí:* Elman R. Service and Helen S. Service, Chicago: University of Chicago, 1954, pp. xix-xxiii, 206-9, Chaps. 9 and 10; *Chichicastenango:* Ruth Bunzel, New York: Augustin, second edition, 1952, pp. 1-14, 25-30, 109-117.

A number of communities have not been classified with respect to their integration, because each might require a separate analysis and debate: Marbial (Remy Bastien, *La Familia Rural Haitiana*, México: Libra, 1951); Mocca (Clarke, *op. cit.*); August Town, Perseverance, Better Hope (Raymond T. Smith, *op. cit.*); Quiroga (Donald D. Brand, *Quiroga*, Smithsonian Institution Institute of Social Anthropology Publ. No. 11, Washington: 1951); Capesterre (Mariam Kreiselman, *The Caribbean Family: A Case Study in Martinique*, Columbia University, unpublished Ph.D. thesis, 1958); Tepoztlán (Oscar Lewis, *Life in a Mexican Village: Tepoztlán Restudied*, Urbana, Ill.: University of Illinois, 1951) and the several areas in Puerto Rico which are described in Julian Steward, *op. cit.* Commonly authors refer to their village as a "community" and treat it generally as a coherent unit, while giving explicit details which would deny any such integration. Considering the island Caribbean studies, I would at present view only Morne-Paysan (M. M. Horowitz, *Morne-Paysan*, unpublished Ph.D. dissertation, Columbia University, 1959), Orange Grove and San José as "relatively integrated" (Eric R. Wolf, "San José: Subcultures of a 'Traditional' Coffee Municipality," in *The People of Puerto Rico*, Julian Steward, *et al.*, Urbana, Ill.: University of Illinois, pp. 171-264.) Quiroga and Tepoztlán may not have high illegitimacy rates because they are now somewhat integrated into the Mexican national social and cultural systems.

CHAPTER 11

1. See Harry Eckstein's perceptive analysis of the conceptual problem in his "Toward the Theoretical Study of Internal War," in Harry Eckstein, ed., *Internal War*, New York: The Free Press, 1964, pp. 12 ff.
2. Note also the possibility, however, of avoiding the problem by moving in the *other* direction, to consider only a few great societies widely apart in space and time, whose disappearance is at least generally conceded. See, e.g., Rushton Coulborn, "Structure and Process in the Rise and Fall of Civilized Societies," *Comparative Studies in Society and History*, 8 (July, 1966), pp. 404-31.
3. Chalmers Johnson, *Revolution and the Social System, Hoover Institution Studies No. 3*, Stanford: Stanford University Press, 1965, p. 27.
4. This remark does not, of course, belittle Lyford P. Edwards's signifi-

cant achievement, published as *The Natural History of Revolution,* Chicago: University of Chicago Press, 1927.

5. Ralf Dahrendorf, *Gesellschaft und Freiheit,* München: R. Piper, 1961, p. 232. (My translation.)

6. For example, see David Willer and George K. Zollschan, "Prolegomenon to a Theory of Revolutions," in *Explorations in Social Change,* eds. George K. Zollschan and Walter Hirsch, Boston: Houghton Mifflin, 1964, p. 127.

7. Thomas P. Thornton, "Terror as a Weapon of Political Agitation," in Eckstein, ed., *Internal War,* pp. 71-99.

8. Andrew C. Janos, "Authority and Violence: The Political Framework of Internal War," in Eckstein, ed., *Internal War,* pp. 130-42.

9. Eckstein, "Introduction," *Internal War,* p. 12 (italics mine). The problem of measuring various aspects and elements in revolution is discussed by Charles Tilly and James Rule, *Measuring Political Upheaval,* Cambridge, Massachusetts: Joint Center for Urban Studies of MIT and Harvard University, 1964 (mimeo).

10. See Lewis A. Coser, *The Functions of Social Conflict,* Glencoe, Illinois: The Free Press, 1956; R. Dahrendorf, *Die Angewandte Aufklärung,* München: R. Piper, 1963, Chapters 4, 5, 8, 9; Arnold S. Feldman, "Violence and Volatility: The Likelihood of Revolution," in Eckstein, ed., *Internal War,* pp. 111-29; William J. Goode, "Norm Commitment and Conformity to Role-Status Obligations," *American Journal of Sociology,* 66 (November, 1960), pp. 246-58; and "A Theory of Role Strain," see pp. 97-120 in this volume.

11. Naturally, I use the term "Lintonian model" because he expressed so persuasively the reigning version of social theory, in his *The Study of Man,* New York: Appleton-Century, 1936. Talcott Parsons has formulated a similar view, and of course both derive directly from Emile Durkheim. Parsons's label for the above hypothesis is "the theorem of institutional integration" (*The Social System,* Glencoe, Illinois: The Free Press, 1951, pp. 36-43).

12. Goode, "A Theory of Role Strain," see pp. 97-120 in this volume. For a concrete analysis of some of these diverse centrifugal forces, see Erik Allardt, "A Theory on Solidarity and Legitimacy Conflicts," in *Cleavages, Ideologies, and Party Systems: Contributions to Comparative Political Sociology,* Helsinki: Trans. of the Westermarck Society, 1964, pp. 78-96.

13. Lucien Pye, "The Roots of Insurgency," in Eckstein, ed., *Internal War,* pp. 159-61.

14. See in this connection the study by Norman M. Bradburn and David Caplovitz, *Reports on Happiness,* Chicago: Aldine Publishing Company, 1965.

15. Feldman (*"Violence and Volatility,"* pp. 115-16) notes that adjustment to social change may lead to still more change.

16. Pusillanimousness and a reluctance to achieve certainty by rereading Hegel prompts me to comment that I believe a detailed examination of his various explications of this point will discover that Hegel's most sophisticated position incorporated both views. Marx's did not, since he looked forward to an eventual utopia after the revolution had worked itself out. Of course, any system *must* be destroyed either by its internal forces or external intrusions from the outside: there are no other possibilities.

17. In any revolution, both leaders and followers change, and so do their programs. Some groups are supporters, but then resist as more radical programs are initiated. Of course, the above mode of exposition does not do injustice to this complex process, and is used only for simplicity. For an especially acute criticism of the simplistic interpretations of the French Revolution, see Alfred Cobban, *The Social Interpretation of the French Revolution*, Cambridge: Cambridge University Press, 1964.

18. Note the efforts of both Roman and Ottoman rulers to eliminate one source of this resentment (while leaving others intact) through the use of eunuchs. See in this connection Keith Hopkins, "Eunuchs in Politics in the Later Roman Empire," *Proceedings of the Cambridge Philological Society*, 189 (1963), pp. 62-80.

19. I have seen no such tabulation but I believe this is a fairly safe conclusion. Of course, in Europe and Latin America, university students have played significant roles in revolutions.

20. Using a different rhetoric and a less stark theoretical outline, Richard Harris's plea makes similar assertions in *Independence and After*, London: Oxford University Press, 1962.

21. James C. Davies, "Toward a Theory of Revolution," *American Sociological Review*, 27 (February, 1962), pp. 5-19. Edwards (*The Natural History of Revolution*, pp. 69-71) comments that in France and Russia, the peasants owned one-third of the agricultural land prior to the Revolution, and had added largely to their holdings during the two generations before that point—but he supposes that the greater the amount, the greater their desire.

22. E.g., the junior or lesser *samurai* in the Meiji Restoration of 1868. As this might apply to Latin America, see George I. Blanksten, "Fidel Castro and Latin America," in *The Revolution in World Politics*, New York: John Wiley & Sons, 1962, pp. 117-18. Blanksten notes by contrast that in Castro's purges, no officer higher than captain was executed.

23. Perhaps the closest approximation is when no goal is explicitly stated, as in mourning for one's kin, or socializing one's children. See, however, the more complex analysis in "The Protection of the Inept," *American Sociological Review*, 32 (February, 1967).

24. G. S. Ghurye, *Caste and Class in India*, Bombay: Popular Book Depot, 1957, Chapter 10.

25. For a persuasive statement of this position, see Emile Durkheim, *Suicide*, translated by John A. Spaulding and George Simpson, Glencoe, Illinois: The Free Press, 1951, pp. 249-52.

26. *The French Bourgeoisie of the 18th Century*, Princeton: Princeton University Press, 1955.

27. For a review of the major relationships between family patterns and upward mobility, see my "Family and Mobility," in Reinhard Bendix and Seymour M. Lipset, eds., *Class, Status, and Power*, New York: The Free Press, 2nd Edition, 1966, pp. 582-601. The various attempts to measure this psychological factor and its links with societal variables may be found in David C. McClelland, *The Achieving Society*, New York: Van Nostrand Company, 1961; see also Bernard C. Rosen, "The Achievement Syndrome and Economic Growth in Brazil," *Social Forces*, 42 (March, 1964), pp. 341-54.

28. For a good summary of the data on China, see Marsh, *op. cit.*; and "Values, Demand, and Social Mobility," *American Sociological Review*, 28 (August, 1953), pp. 565-75. See also the summary of the data on mobility in Bernard Barber, *Social Stratification*, New York: Harcourt, Brace and Company, 1957, pp. 356-87.

29. See Robert M. Marsh, *The Mandarins*, New York: The Free Press, 1961; Chang Chung-li, *The Chinese Gentry: Studies on Their Role in Nineteenth-Century Chinese Society*, University of Washington Publications on Asia, University of Washington Press, 1955; A. Goodwin, ed., *The European Nobility in the Eighteenth Century: Studies of the Nobilities of the Major European States in the Pre-Reform Era*, London: A. and C. Black, 1953; H. J. Habakkuk, *Family Structure and Economic Change in Nineteenth-Century Europe, Journal of Economic History* 15 (1955), pp. 1-12; A. S. Turberville, "Aristocracy and Revolution: The British Peerage, 1789-1832," *History*, 26 (1942), pp. 240-63; P. E. Fahlbeck, "La Noblesse de Suède: Etude Démographique," *Bulletin de l'institut international de statistique*, XII (1900), pp. 169-81; J. H. Hexter, "The Myth of the Middle Class in Tudor England," in Hexter, *Reappraisals in History*, Evanston, 1961; W. E. Minchinton, *The Merchants in England in the Eighteenth Century, Explorations in Entrepreneurial History*, X (1957), pp. 62-71.

30. However, Richard W. Patch insists that Bolivia must be added to these. See "Bolivia: The Restrained Revolution," in *Annals*, 334 (March, 1961), pp. 123-32. This issue of the *Annals* is devoted to the Latin American nationalistic revolutions.

31. "A Latin American Phenomenon: The Middle Class Military Coup," in *Trends in Social Science Research in Latin American Studies*, Institute of International Studies, Berkeley: University of California Press, 1965, pp. 55-99.

32. I first stated this hypothesis in "Illegitimacy, Anomie and Cultural Penetration," *American Sociological Review*, 26 (December, 1961), pp. 910-25.

33. See K. H. Silvert, "Nationalism in Latin America," *Annals,* 334 (March, 1961), pp. 1-9, and his *Reaction and Revolution in Latin America,* New Orleans: Hauser Press, 1961, chapters 1-3; the only empirical data on a comparative basis (comparing Mexico with European countries) are to be found in Gabriel A. Almond and Sidney Verba, *The Civic Culture,* Boston: Little, Brown and Company, 1965.

    See also Gino Germani and K. H. Silvert, "Politics, Social Structure, and Military Intervention in Latin America," *Archives Européenes de Sociologie,* II (1961), pp. 62-81; and Germani, *La Sociología en la America Latina: Problemas y Perspectivas,* Editorial Universitaria de Buenos Aires, 1964; also, his "Classes populaires et démocratie réprésentative en Amerique Latine," *Sociologie du Travail,* 4 (1961), pp. 408-25.

34. For an examination of some of the contradictions in the New World case, see (besides the data in my earlier chapter on illegitimacy): George Kubler, "The Quechua in the Colonial World," in *Handbook of South American Indians,* Julian H. Steward, ed., Washington: Smithsonian Institution, Bureau of American Ethnology Bulletin No. 143, 1946-1950, Vol. 2, pp. 374-75 *et passim.* See also Bernard Mishkin, "The Contemporary Quechua," *ibid.,* pp. 427 ff.

35. S. N. Eisenstadt suggests that a lack of solidarity mechanisms may reverse or slow down a process of modernization, in his "Breakdowns of Modernization," in William J. Goode, *The Dynamics of Modern Society,* New York: Atherton Press, 1966, pp. 435 ff. On the problem of integration and stratification, see the thoughtful analysis by Lloyd Fallers. "Equality, Modernity, and Democracy in the New States," in Clifford Geertz, ed., *Old Societies and New States,* New York: The Free Press, 1963, pp. 158-219. Cf. Celso Furtado, "Development and Stagnation in Latin America," in Irving L. Horowitz, ed., *Masses in Latin America,* New York: Oxford University Press, 1970, pp. 28-64.

36. See however the analysis by Kingsley Davis, "The Role of Class Mobility in Economic Development," *Population Review* (July, 1962), pp. 67 ff.; and S. M. Lipset, "Research Problems in the Comparative Analysis of Mobility and Development," *International Social Science Journal,* 16, No. 1 (1965), pp. 35-48.

CHAPTER 12

1. For an extended analysis of many of the current issues in the field, see the excellent critique by Harold Sheppard, *Managerial Sociology: A Critical Commentary on the Influence of the Mayo School on Industrial Sociology,* Ph.D. Thesis, Wisconsin, 1948; and "The Treatment of Unionism in 'Managerial Sociology,'" *American Sociological Review,* XIV (1949), 310-313; also William J. Goode, "The Pres-

ent Status of Industrial Sociology," Michigan Sociological Society, Detroit, November, 1946 (unpub.); Wilbert E. Moore, "Current Issues in Industrial Sociology," *American Sociological Review*, XII (1947), 651-657, and "Industrial Sociology: Status and Prospects," *ibid.*, XIII (1948), including the subsequent discussion by Robert Dubin, Delbert C. Miller, Paul Meadows, and Alvin W. Gouldner, pp. 382-400; Delbert C. Miller, "The Social Factors of the Work Situation," *ibid.*, XI (1946), 300-314; Walter Firey, "Informal Organization and the Theory of Schism," *ibid.*, XIII (1948), 15-24.

Although a number of studies have emphasized "harmony," one of the most recent may be noted: "Productivity, Supervision, and Employee Morale," Survey Research Center, *Human Relations, Series* 1, Report No. 1, University of Michigan, 1948. Some of the implications of "harmony" in industrial relations have been analyzed shrewdly by Neil Chamberlain, *The Union Challenge to Management Control*, New York: Harper's, 1948.

2. The work of the Mayo group may be mentioned at this point. Even the somewhat more penetrating work by Fox, Scott, and Lombard does not move far from this point of view: Elton Mayo and George F. F. Lombard, "Teamwork and Labor Turnover in the Aircraft Industry of Southern California," *Business Research Studies* No. 32, Harvard University Graduate School of Business Administration, 1944; and John B. Fox and Jerome F. Scott, "Absenteeism: Management's Problem," *Business Research Studies* No. 29, Harvard University Graduate School of Business Administration, 1943.

3. However, it may be suggested that these concepts overlap considerably in their implicit meanings with the Gemeinschaft-Gesellschaft continuum, with the facets of social action categorized under structure-function, and with the division ideal-real. A later published note may help to clarify this overlapping.

4. For one of the better recent analyses on an elementary level, see John W. Bennett and Melvin M. Tumin, *Social Life*, New York: Knopf, 1948, p. 66 ff.

5. Thus resulting in a frequent implicit identification of the "informal" with the less predictable.

6. The best known examples are to be found in the earlier work of the Mayo school.

7. The Committee for Economic Development cites the following figures: of 3,317,000 business units in the country in 1939, some 3,265,000 had fewer than fifty employees. This is about 95 per cent of the total number of firms. See *Meeting the Special Problems of Small Business* (New York: Committee for Economic Development, June, 1947), Ch. I, "The Place of Small Business in Our Economy," pp. 9-21. These figures differ little from those found in the numerous reports of the Smaller War Plants Corporation. See particularly,

John M. Blair, Harrison F. Houghton, Matther Rose, *et al.*, "Economic Concentration and World War II," *Report of the Smaller War Plant Corporation to the Special Committee to Study Problems of American Small Business*, 79th Congress, 2nd Session, Document No. 206, July 14, 1946 (Washington: Government Printing Office, 1946), pp. 4-25. Many of the data cited above are taken from the monographs produced by the Temporary National Economic Committee.

8. Similarities to sweatshops and to the earlier "putting out" phase of the Industrial Revolution are clear.

9. These data will be published in a separate study. They are summarized in: Irving Fowler, *A Small Feeder Plant: Its Structure and Social Relations*, M.A. Thesis, Wayne University, 1949.

10. Although there is no standard work unit in the industry, and each small plant attempts to keep secret its production records, the managers of these small plants claim to know with some accuracy the output of each electroplating shop. The above estimate was made by the technical director of a major plating supply company. An executive of the National Association of Metal Finishers made a similar estimate, concluding that nonunion shops had a higher output than union shops. A semi-automatic plating machine could run approximately 100 racks through a tank in one hour, about 1,600 pieces in one work day. White Company can turn out about 1,400 pieces when there are sufficient orders, without such equipment. White Company's increasing solvency in a highly competitive industry is also of relevance here.

11. As to the cost of the "fringe concessions," see Richard C. Smyth, "Economic Fringe Demands of Unions," *Personnel*, Vol. 24, No. 4 (1948), pp. 243-256.

15. There were five such workers, thus making up from one-third to one-tenth of the total working group.

16. This may be called "antagonistic cooperation." Such cooperation may occur: (a) When individuals cooperate for a group goal, to be achieved only by working together, as for example, army draftees; or (b) When *each* individual knows his personal goal can be attained only in this way, the classical example being that of shipwrecked passengers.

17. Military leaders also utilize these components in the common techniques of making the *group* responsible for the cooperation of *individuals*.

CHAPTER 13

1. These were carried out at Wayne University under the direction of the senior author, Goode. A previous article was William J. Goode and

Irving Fowler, "Incentive Factors in a Low Morale Plant," *American Sociological Review*, 14 (1949), 618-624. Babchuk was one of the participant observers in that study. A further study, carried out by Robert James, concerned identification of selling personnel with management. The present study was originally suggested by Nelson Foote of Cornell University. A related study of aspirational levels among Detroit workers has not been completed beyond the interviewing stage.

2. For a brief analysis of this relationship, reviewing the major studies of the past decade, see Daniel Katz, "Morale and Motivations in Industry," in *Current Trends in Industrial Psychology*, University of Pittsburgh Press, 1949, pp. 145-171. With respect to the first of the Survey Research Center's studies in this area (Prudential Life Insurance Company), he notes, "In fact, some of the attitudes usually regarded as indicative of high morale were negatively related to production" (p. 160).

3. As is clear, the research done on "the human factor" in industry has been centered on these related propositions. A good perspective on this body of practice and theory may be obtained from Georges Friedmann, *Ou va le travail humain?*, Paris: Gallimard, 1950, esp. Part 2, Chap. III, "L'industrie américaine et le facteur humain." The literature of the Mayo group, which has most explicitly dealt with these formulations, is best represented by these studies: Elton Mayo and George F. F. Lombard, "Teamwork and Labor Turnover in the Aircraft Industry of Southern California," *Business Research Studies* No. 32, Harvard University Graduate School of Business Administration, 1944; John B. Fox and Jerome F. Scott, "Absenteeism: Management's Problem," *Business Research Studies* No. 29, Harvard University Graduate School of Business Administration, 1943; and George F. Homans, *The Human Group*, New York: Harcourt Brace, 1950, esp. Chap. 14.

The particular managerial biases of this group need not concern us. They have been analyzed by Goode, Wilbert E. Moore, and others; the most complete analysis being the Ph.D. thesis of Harold Sheppard, *Managerial Sociology* (Wisconsin, 1948). See also his "The Treatment of Unionism in 'Managerial Sociology,'" *American Sociological Review*, 14 (1949), 310-313.

The considerably more sophisticated work of the Survey Research Center covers a substantial body of data, but its findings have not been clearly articulated as yet. Most of the reports have appeared as facets of larger studies or as popular reports to managerial groups.

The possible implications of cooperation, both informal and formal, between management and workers, have been developed by Neil Chamberlain, *The Union Challenge to Managerial Control*, New York: Harper's, 1948.

4. The observations within the department were made by Babchuk over

a period of four months, in shifts that covered the entire working day over a period of weeks. Representative selling seasons, typical to the retail field, were included in this period. All periods of the work day and work week were allotted a proportionate amount of equal time so as to discount any period of the work rhythm situation (which varied on certain days and in certain weeks). A labor representative of the work group was first approached, and he in turn introduced the study to the work group. The consent of management was obtained later, and both work group and management were cooperative during the investigation. Extensive diary notes were recorded in the department itself, and formal and informal interviews were used to corroborate the observational data, the interviews being carried out both at work and at the homes of the sales personnel. Prior sales personnel were also interviewed in order to check the accuracy of the historical materials.

5. Goode and Fowler, *op. cit.* "Low morale" is not here defined in terms of any of the so-called morale "tests," which rely largely upon acceptance or non-acceptance of managerial goals as the differentiating criterion. Although such an instrument can be developed, we are here concerned with gross differences between group feeling-states, degree and number of interpersonal antagonisms, acceptance of the group as an embodiment of personal interests and values, etc. In the Ryme group, furthermore, the members themselves are highly conscious of the change in morale, and are able to verbalize easily the reasons for the change. As noted by Katz (*op. cit.*, p. 160), morale seems to have a number of dimensions.

6. This explanation has not been confined to the U.S. alone. In one form or another, it constitutes the foundation for the major rationalizations of capitalism which were offered by classical economics. In a broader formulation, it was Locke's answer to Hobbes.

7. This was a unilateral decision. For the importance of self-determination, see J. R. French and L. Coch, "Overcoming Resistance to Change," *Human Relations*, 1 (1948), 512-532; Kurt Lewin, "Group Decision and Social Change," in *Readings in Social Psychology*, T. M. Newcomb and E. L. Hartley, eds., New York: Holt, 1947, pp. 330-344; and Alex. Bavelas, "Some Problems of Organizational Change," *Journal of Social Issues*, 4 (1948), 48-52.

8. Note the contrast with the bogey adjustment made by the Hawthorne workers in the Relay Assembly unit, the Bank Wiring unit, and even the piecework Mica Splitting group. For a discussion of the contrast, see the discussion by Harold J. Ruttenberg, in Chap. VI, "Self-Expression and Labor Unions," in *Fatigue of Workers*, Committee on Work in Industry of the National Research Council, New York: Reinhold, 1941, pp. 108-119.

9. Some of the consequences of workers taking over managerial tasks

have been empirically documented in the Survey Research Center studies of a number of insurance agencies (Prudential). See Rensis Likert, *Morale and Agency Management*, Life Insurance Sales Bureau, 1941. See also Alex. Bavelas, "Role Playing and Management Training," *Sociatry*, 1 (1947), 183-191.

10. This area has been investigated in a number of studies. *Cf.*, *e.g.*, Alex. Bavelas and Kurt Lewin, "Training in Democratic Leadership," *Journal of Abnormal and Social Psychology*, 37 (1942), 115-119; and R. Lippit and R. K. White, "An Experimental Study of Leadership and Group Life," in *Readings in Social Psychology*, T. M. Newcomb and E. L. Hartley, eds., New York: Holt, 1947, pp. 315-330.

CHAPTER 14

1. Here, I am using what I consider the major control systems in social action (power, money, prestige, and friendship–civility) without further theoretical elaboration. A forthcoming monograph will analyze their operations. In the present paper, I am not using these terms in any esoteric senses that require conceptual explication.

2. For one version of this view, see William J. Goode, "A Theory of Role Strain," in *American Sociological Review*, 25 (August, 1960), 483-96 [see pp. 97-120 in this volume]. As I understand Homans and Blau, both seem to believe that values and norms are created within such transactions among individuals. In my view, the fact that pre-existing evaluations determine the worth of what is exchanged is crucial to an analysis of exchanges. See George C. Homans, *Social Behavior* (New York: Harcourt, 1961); and Peter M. Blau, *Exchange and Power* (New York: Wiley, 1964).

3. Vernon K. Dibble (in "Occupations and Ideologies," in *Amer. Journal of Sociology*, 67 [September, 1962], 229-41) argues that a high ranking occupation can more easily persuade others that its ideology is acceptable.

4. At a minimum, a substantial percentage of the men in high places came from modest origins, though of course if a society is composed *mainly* of peasants, it is not numerically possible for a high percentage of that stratum to rise to the top. For comparative figures, see Robert M. Marsh, *The Mandarins* (New York: Free Press, 1961), and William J. Goode, "Family and Mobility," in *Class, Status, and Power*, ed. Reinhard Bendix and Seymour M. Lipset (New York: Free Press, 1966), pp. 582-601.

5. There are some very agreeable and beautiful talents . . . of which the exercise for the sake of gain is considered . . . as a sort of public prostitution. . . . The exorbitant rewards of players, opera-singers, opera-dancers, etc. are founded upon those two principles; the rarity

and beauty of the talents and the discredit of employing them in this manner." Adam Smith, *An Inquiry into the Nature and Causes of the Wealth of Nations* (New York: Modern Library, 1937), p. 107.

6. It is likely that Twain was a victim of the usual exaggeration of occupational prestige among practitioners. He was proud of his skill. It is unlikely that pilots were generally ranked among the upper class of the Old South, which included large plantation owners, great merchants or factors, and successful professionals. See Wilbert E. Moore and Robin M. Williams, "Stratification in the Ante-Bellum South," in *American Sociological Review*, 7 (June, 1942), 343-51.

7. Although A. M. Carr-Saunders and P. A. Wilson do not use this concept, their historical inquiry into a wide range of aspiring occupations, *The Professions* (Oxford: Clarendon, 1933), clearly aims at establishing such a sequence. T. A. Caplow presents a sequence of four steps in *The Sociology of Work* (Minneapolis: University of Minnesota, 1954), pp. 139-40.

8. These are presented in Harold Wilensky, "The Professionalization of Everybody?" in *American Journal of Sociology*, 70 (September, 1964), 142-46.

9. Carr-Saunders and Wilson (*op. cit.*, pp. 284-318) summarize them, but also use them throughout their historical descriptions. William J. Goode, Robert K. Merton, and Mary Jean Huntington, in *The Professions in Modern Society* (New York: Russell Sage Foundation, 1956, mineo), Chapter 1, present a tabulation from many sources. Ernest Greenwood, in "The Attributes of a Profession," in *Social Work*, 2 (July, 1957), 44-55, presents such a list. Similar statements will be found in Goode, "Community Within a Community: The Professions," in *American Sociological Review*, 22 (April, 1957), 194-200; and Goode, "Encroachment, Charlatanism, and the Emerging Profession: Psychology, Sociology, and Medicine," in *American Sociological Review*, 25 (December, 1960), 903-4.

10. See Goode, "Encroachment . . . ," pp. 903-4, and Wilensky, *op. cit.*, p. 138.

11. For the reciprocal process by which a monopoly over a valued service supports the standing of an occupation in the prestige market, see Dibble, *op. cit.*, pp. 236-37.

12. Perhaps it should be emphasized that we are referring to the social worker, who has undergone professional training which culminates in the M.S.W. or the doctorate in social work. By contrast, the welfare or case worker in urban departments of welfare is much less likely to have been trained in a formal curriculum, and of course does not fall into this category.

13. I have analyzed this case more extensively in "The Librarian: From Occupation to Profession?" in *The Library Quarterly*, 31 (October, 1961), 306-20.

14. In these analyses, I am largely omitting the manipulations within power markets. I view them as ultimately important, but largely derivative. A professionalizing occupation is more likely to gain power through its success on the prestige and economic markets, rather than the reverse.

15. For the interaction of autonomy, discipline, and knowledge, see William J. Goode, "Encroachment, Charlatanism, and the Emerging Profession . . . ," pp. 910-14, where references are made to various attempts to measure the usefulness of psychotherapy.

16. In these rebuttals we are concerned only with the relation of the occupation to the highest levels of relevant knowledge. A different kind of refutation is that in many instances no medicine is still worse than bad medicine. Therefore, the less trained person should not be allowed to practice independently.

17. Separate from the *amount* of knowledge an occupation needs to learn is its abstractness, as Amitai Etzioni has reminded me, although this problem does not often figure in arguments about professional standing. Even when many concrete facts are missing in a problem, command over an abstract framework may yield productive (if tentative) solutions; at a minimum, it suggests ways of deducing which facts are important, and how to get them.

18. Goode, "The Librarian . . . ,".

19. See the extended analysis of these points in William J. Goode, "The Librarian . . . ," pp. 311 ff., as well as Arthur M. McNally, "The Dynamics of Securing Academic Status," in Robert B. Downs, *The Status of American College and University Librarians*, ACRL Monograph No. 22 (Chicago: American Library Association, 1958), p. 3.

20. See, for example, *The Handbook of Organizations*, ed. James G. March (Chicago: Rand-McNally, 1965).

21. Note, however, the threat of independence in this area. See Harry P. Smith, "Clinical Pathology: Its Creators and Its Practitioners," in *American Journal of Clinical Pathology*, 31 (April, 1959), 283-92, and *Preliminary Report of the Committee on Professional Qualifications for the Practice of Laboratory Medicine*, College of American Pathologists (August, 1959).

22. Thus, very likely most basic medical research is done by biochemists, physiologists, and even physicists, but a far higher proportion of physicians is also engaged in research than were so engaged in 1900 or 1850.

23. For further details, see Goode, "Encroachment, Charlatanism. . . ." See also Alvin Zander, Arthur Cohen, Ezra Statland, and collaborators, "Average Attitudes of One Professional Group Toward Another," in *Professionalization*, ed. H. M. Vollmer and D. L. Mills (Englewood Cliffs, N.J.: Prentice-Hall, 1966), pp. 237 ff.

24. For an analysis of the problems in maintaining autonomy of the *foun-*

dation, see Richard Colvard, "Foundations and Professions: The Organizational Defense of Autonomy," in *Administrative Science Quarterly,* 6 (September, 1961), 167-84.

25. Marjorie Fiske, *Book Selection and Censorship* (Berkeley: U. of California, 1959), pp. 11 ff. and 52-71; and Robert D. Leigh, *The Public Library in the United States* (New York: Columbia U.P., 1950), pp. 120-1.

26. Perhaps all occupations approaching professional status try to control, and assert their claim to autonomy. In a formalized type of society such as ours, both actions may be ignored and the state may impose its own controls. Note the very high stakes involved in transportation. Here, however, the failure is first of all either incompetence or carelessness—*not,* self-interest—and whatever the cause of the failure it is likely that the practitioner himself (railroad engineer, bus driver, airline pilot, steamship captain) will physically suffer when he has an accident. One basic control is thus built into the environment itself.

27. For some of those attitudes, see Richard K. Kerckhoff, "Interest Group Reactions to the Profession of Marriage Counseling," in *Sociology and Sociological Research,* 39 (January-February, 1955), 178-93.

28. See the extended analysis in Talcott Parsons, *The Social System* (New York: Free Press, 1951), Chapter 10.

29. Note that though this is not recent, in various times and places in the past the physician was *not* allowed to examine so thoroughly, especially when the patient was a woman; but so intimate a probing was not thought to be—and, with the knowledge of the time, was not in fact—useful or necessary.

30. For a fuller analysis, see Fred E. Katz, *Autonomy and Organization* (New York: Random House, 1968), esp. Chapters 4-6.

31. See the attempts at measurement of outcome, noted in Goode, "Encroachment, Charlatanism . . . ," p. 912.

32. More extended analysis in Goode, "The Protection of the Inept," in *American Sociological Review,* 32 (February, 1967), 5-19.

33. For example, malpractice suits are much less likely, even when poor medical procedures were followed, if the physician has convinced his patient that he has been solicitous, warm, and so on.

34. As many departmental chairmen in the humanities and social sciences have learned to their sorrow, it is dangerous to fire a man who colleagues agree is incompetent if he has good relations with his students.

35. The best recent analysis of the variables that affect ethical conformity is Jerome S. Carlin, *Lawyer's Ethics* (New York: Russell Sage Foundation), 1966.

36. Analyses of this socialization may be found in Morris Janowitz, *The Professional Soldier* (New York: Free Press, 1960), Chapter 7; *The*

Student-Physician, ed. Robert K. Merton, George G. Reader, and Patricia L. Kendall (Cambridge: Harvard U.P., 1957); and Howard S. Becker, Blanche Geer, *et al.*, *Boys in White* (Chicago: U. of Chicago, 1961).

37. A measure of "occupational community" that embodies both friendship patterns and formal organization is used in a study of lawyers, professors, and engineers in H. Wilensky and J. Ladinsky, "From Religious Community to Occupational Group: Structural Assimilation among Professors, Lawyers, and Engineers," *American Sociological Review*, 32 (August, 1967), 541-61. Professors have a higher index rating than lawyers or engineers, whose training period is shorter.

38. In Wilensky (*op. cit.*, p. 152), professors, lawyers, and engineers were asked whose judgment they thought should count most in the evaluation of their work. Eighty-one per cent of the professors ranked their colleagues foremost, 51 per cent of lawyers, and 18 per cent of engineers.

Index